Portland Community College

Conceptualize, Create, Communicate
Designing Living Spaces with SketchUp

D1571424

Conceptualize, Create, Communicate

Designing Living Spaces with SketchUp

Bonnie Roskes

Annie Elliott

PEARSON

Boston   Columbus   Indianapolis   New York   San Francisco   Upper Saddle River
Amsterdam   Cape Town   Dubai   London   Madrid   Milan   Munich   Paris   Montreal   Toronto
Delhi   Mexico City   São Paulo   Sydney   Hong Kong   Seoul   Singapore   Taipei   Tokyo

Editorial Director: Vernon R. Anthony
Acquisitions Editor: Sara Eilert
Editorial Assistant: Doug Greive
Director of Marketing: David Gesell
Executive Marketing Manager: Harper Coles
Senior Marketing Manager: Alicia Wozniak
Marketing Assistant: Crystal Gonzales
Associate Managing Editor: Alexandrina Benedicto Wolf
Production Project Manager: Alicia Ritchey
Operations Specialist: Deidra Skahill

Art Director: Jayne Conte
Cover Designer: Suzanne Behnke
Cover Art: Surya Murali
Lead Media Project Manager: Karen Bretz
Full-Service Project Management: Jogender Taneja, Aptara®, Inc.
Composition: Aptara®, Inc.
Printer/Binder: Courier/Kendallville
Cover Printer: Lehigh-Phoenix Color/ Hagerstown
Text Font: Bookman

Images credited and acknowledged are borrowed from other sources and are reproduced, with permission, on the appropriate page within this text.

Disclaimer:

This publication is designed to provide tutorial information about SketchUp. Every effort has been made to make this publication complete and as accurate as possible. The reader is expressly cautioned to use any and all precautions necessary, and to take appropriate steps to avoid hazards, when engaging in the activities described herein. Neither the author nor the publisher makes any representations or warranties of any kind, with respect to the materials set forth in this publication, express or implied, including without limitation any warranties of fitness for a particular purpose or merchantability. Nor shall the author or the publisher be liable for any special, consequential, or exemplary damages resulting, in whole or in part, directly or indirectly, from the reader's use of, or reliance upon, this material or subsequent revisions of this material.

Library of Congress Cataloging-in-Publication Data
Roskes, Bonnie.
   Conceptualize, create, communicate : designing living spaces with
SketchUp / Bonnie Roskes, Annie Elliott.—1 [edition].
     pages cm
   ISBN-13: 978-0-13-512580-9
   ISBN-10: 0-13-512580-4
   1. Interior decoration—Computer-aided design—Textbooks. 2. Interior
architecture—Computer-aided design—Textbooks. 3. Three-dimensional imaging—
Textbooks. 4. SketchUp--Textbooks. I. Elliott, Annie. II. Title.
   NK2114.R67 2013
   747.0285'668—dc23
                                      2012019806

10 9 8 7 6 5 4 3 2 1

ISBN 10:   0-13-512580-4
ISBN 13: 978-0-13-512580-9

Brief Contents

CHAPTER 1 Model a Room   1

CHAPTER 2 Furnish a Room   37

CHAPTER 3 Basic Furniture: Straight Lines   67

CHAPTER 4 Advanced Furniture: Curvy Lines   111

CHAPTER 5 Working with 3D Warehouse Models   167

CHAPTER 6 Working with Colors and Materials   205

CHAPTER 7 Working with Digital Images   271

CHAPTER 8 Kitchen Design   321

CHAPTER 9 Presenting Your Designs   355

CHAPTER 10 Labels, Dimensions, and Plans   397

APPENDIX Additional Resources   433

INDEX   437

Contents

CHAPTER 1 Model a Room — 1

1.1 Taking Field Measurements — 1

1.2 Model the Basic Room in SketchUp — 3

1.3 Add the Door — 8

1.4 Add the Windows — 15

1.5 Modify the Windows — 26

1.6 Finishing Touches — 31
    Model It Yourself — 33

Review Questions — 36

CHAPTER 2 Furnish a Room — 37

2.1 Create a Generic Rug — 37

2.2 Add a Sofa and a Coffee Table — 40

2.3 Add a Floor Lamp — 49

2.4 Add an Accent Chair — 54

2.5 Add a Console Table — 57

2.6 Add a Painting — 61
    Model It Yourself — 65

Review Questions — 66

CHAPTER 3 Basic Furniture: Straight Lines — 67

3.1 Simple Rectangular Table — 67
    Model It Yourself — 75

3.2 Rectangular Table with Tapered Legs — 76
    Model It Yourself — 86

3.3 Bookcase — 87
    Model It Yourself — 95

3.4 Cabinet with Doors and Drawers — 96
    Model It Yourself — 108

Review Questions — 109

CHAPTER 4 Advanced Furniture: Curvy Lines — 111

4.1 Basic Circular Table — 111
    Model It Yourself — 116

4.2 Oval Drop-Leaf Table — 117
    Model It Yourself — 128

4.3 Table with Cross Pedestal Base — 129
    Model It Yourself — 142

4.4 Table with Chrome Tubular Base — 143
    Model It Yourself — 151

4.5 Glass Oval Table with Tulip Pedestal   **152**
Model It Yourself   158

4.6 Cushioned Ottoman   **158**
Model It Yourself   164

Review Questions   **165**

CHAPTER 5 Working with 3D Warehouse Models   **167**

5.1 Dining Table, Accent Table, and Coffee Table   **167**
Model It Yourself   181

5.2 Changing a Sofa   **182**
Model It Yourself   187

5.3 Changing a Chaise   **188**
Model It Yourself   190

5.4 Changing a China Cabinet   **192**
Model It Yourself   200

Review Questions   **204**

CHAPTER 6 Working with Colors and Materials   **205**

6.1 Changing Material Color and Size   **205**
Model It Yourself   217

6.2 Material Positioning   **217**
Model It Yourself   225

6.3 Sizing Materials Using Exact Dimensions   **226**
Model It Yourself   234

6.4 Finding and Using Your Own Materials   **235**
Model It Yourself   242

6.5 Creating Your Own Material Collections   **243**
Material Collections: Instructions for PC Users   245
Material Collections: Instructions for Mac Users   249
Model It Yourself   251

6.6 Painting Groups and Components   **252**
Model It Yourself   257

6.7 Painting Textures on Organic Faces   **258**
Model It Yourself   260

6.8 Translucent Materials   **261**
Model It Yourself   267

Review Questions   **269**

CHAPTER 7 Working with Digital Images   **271**

7.1 Decorating with Digital Images   **271**
Model It Yourself   283

7.2 Framed Painting   **284**
Model It Yourself   288

7.3 Objects Created from Irregularly Shaped Images   **289**
Model It Yourself   294

7.4 Using Images to Create 3D Objects   **296**
Painted 3D Object: Wooden Chest   296
Painted 3D Object: Princess Chair   301
Model It Yourself   306

7.5 Tracing Photos to Create 3D Objects   **306**
Model It Yourself   317

Review Questions   **319**

CHAPTER 8 Kitchen Design   **321**

8.1 Dynamic Components   **321**

8.2 Placing Base Cabinets and Appliances   **325**

8.3 Placing Wall Cabinets   **333**

8.4 Adding a Countertop   **340**

8.5 Add a Sink   **346**
Model It Yourself   350

Review Questions   **353**

CHAPTER 9 Presenting Your Designs   **355**

9.1 Using Layers to Hide and Display Objects   **355**
Model It Yourself   363

9.2 Comparing Design Options for the Walls   **364**
Model It Yourself   370

9.3 Comparing Furniture Options   **371**
Model It Yourself   372

9.4 Comparing Room Arrangements   **373**
Model It Yourself   376

9.5 Comparing Materials   **378**
Model It Yourself   386

9.6 Presenting Specific Room Views   **388**
Model It Yourself   393

Review Questions   **396**

CHAPTER 10 Labels, Dimensions, and Plans   **397**

10.1 Labels and Dimensions   **397**
Model It Yourself   409

10.2 Floor Plans   **410**
Model It Yourself   420

10.3 Cabinetry Layouts   **421**
Model It Yourself   429

10.4 Printing   **430**

Review Questions   **432**

APPENDIX Additional Resources   **433**

INDEX   **437**

Preface

When opening a new textbook, it's often tempting to skip the introduction and get straight to the meat of the book. But this preface tells you a few items that you need to know before getting started. Skipping this preface may cause frustration later!

Why SketchUp®?

For interior decorators and designers, SketchUp is a near-perfect software application. Intuitive and easy to learn, SketchUp has a relatively small set of tools compared to other CAD programs. But don't let SketchUp's simple appearance fool you. It's an incredibly powerful application, and this book will show you tools that you might not have expected to be available in a free application.

Created in 2000 as a conceptual 3D modeling program with a low learning curve, SketchUp traditionally has been a program used by architects and engineers. Google acquired SketchUp in 2006 and released a free version, expanding SketchUp's user base to include landscape architects, mechanical designers, film and stage producers, woodworkers, product designers, artists, mathematicians, and, of course, interior designers. (There is a professional version of SketchUp priced at about $500, but you won't need the Pro version for anything in this book.) In 2012, SketchUp was acquired by Trimble, an engineering software company. After the sale, there were no significant changes to the software itself, aside from re-branding.

> **NOTE**
>
> At the time of this writing, the sale of SketchUp to Trimble is official; the deal closed in June 2012. But some of the text and pictures that you see in this book may not reflect exactly what appears on your screen: logos and user interface windows may change slightly, URLs may be different, and so forth. The tools and features of the software itself remain unchanged, so the new ownership of SketchUp should not affect the projects presented in this book.

Once you become proficient in SketchUp, you'll be able to design every element in a room; find furniture and accessories in 3D Warehouse; model furniture from scratch; and accurately represent colors, textures, and materials. SketchUp is easily installed on even the most basic laptops, so you can show your ideas, collaborate, and make instant changes while meeting with colleagues and clients. Because SketchUp is free, you can send your models to clients who can view your designs without needing to know anything about the software itself. (For clients who prefer printouts, documents, or graphics instead of an actual 3D model, SketchUp can produce those as well.)

Getting SketchUp

Everything in this book can be done using the free version of SketchUp. There are a few differences between the free and Pro versions, but none of these differences have anything to do with interior design. The current version, at the time of this writing, is SketchUp 8, and no major changes are anticipated in future versions that would affect the book's contents.

Download SketchUp

Figure 1

If you don't have SketchUp yet, go to http://sketchup.com and click the Download SketchUp button (Figure 1).

This will take you to another web page where you'll see a similar download link, as well as a link where you could download the Pro version (which you can ignore unless you have an extra $500). After clicking the download link, just choose your correct platform (PC or Mac), and the rest of the installation should be automatic.

> **NOTE**
>
> If you're curious about SketchUp Pro and its accompanying LayOut application, you can get an 8-hour, fully functioning trial version. When your 8 hours are up, if you don't purchase this version, SketchUp Pro will simply revert back to the free version.
>
> LayOut is a presentation tool through which you can show SketchUp models in standard views, along with notes, callouts, and dimensions. Changes to the SketchUp model can be automatically incorporated into LayOut.
>
> LayOut is a great tool, and it could be a worthwhile investment for you down the road. But you can do a fine job presenting models with the free version of SketchUp, as you'll see throughout this book!

Three-Button Mouse

It's *possible* to use SketchUp with a laptop's track pad instead of using a mouse; however, using a three-button, scrollwheel mouse like those shown in Figure 2 will make the program exponentially easier to use. A three-button mouse enables you to navigate around your model quickly and effortlessly, and you'll never have to click toolbar buttons for the **Zoom** and **Orbit** tools. (Take it from co-author Annie Elliott, who spent 2 years using SketchUp with a track pad, until Bonnie Roskes convinced her to try a three-button mouse. The mouse changed Annie's entire attitude toward modeling: She couldn't believe how much easier it was.)

The scrollwheel has two functions: You can roll it up and down, and you can click it like a button. Rolling the wheel zooms in and out, making objects

Figure 2

appear larger or smaller. Clicking and holding the wheel while moving the mouse orbits around the view; think of holding an object in your hand and turning your hand to see all sides of the object.

Keep in mind that while using the mouse to zoom and orbit, the location of your cursor on the screen affects what happens to the view. For example, if the cursor is at the bottom of the screen and you scroll down, the view will zoom out while moving down toward the cursor.

If you're a Mac user, the single-button Apple Mouse (formerly known as Mighty Mouse) works well, but the newer Magic Mouse gets less-than-glowing reviews. Keep in mind that any three-button mouse can be used with a Mac; it doesn't need to be an Apple product.

> **NOTE**
>
> If you're a Mac user stuck with a mouse that's not ideal, you can use keyboard shortcuts instead. Pressing and holding the Control and Command keys simultaneously while clicking and holding the left mouse button will activate the **Orbit** tool.

For PC and Mac users: If any of your mouse buttons don't produce the expected function in SketchUp, check your mouse settings. On a PC, you can find these settings under **Control Panel**, and on a Mac, they are found under **System Preferences/Keyboard and Mouse**. The left button should be set to "click," the right button to "right-click," and the wheel button should be "middle click." Your options might appear differently, depending on your mouse drivers, so you may have to experiment with different settings.

User Interface

Before starting to play with the SketchUp tools, take a few minutes to explore a few features of the user interface.

Templates

When you first open SketchUp, you'll see the **Welcome to SketchUp** window. (If you don't see this window, and SketchUp opens immediately, choose **Help/Welcome to SketchUp** from the main menu.) The window shown in Figure 3 is what you'll see if you're using the Pro version; it's slightly different for the Free version. You can explore the various links for tutorials and help, and when you're ready to start, click the **Choose Template** button.

The available templates are established for different types of models: architectural, engineering, product design, and so forth. Different templates also use different units, such as centimeters or feet and inches. Choose any one of the templates and click the **Start using SketchUp** button at the bottom of the window (Figure 4).

The empty file that opens looks like the template swatch that you selected. You may have a blue sky and green ground, you may see a person standing in the middle of the model, or you may just have a white background and nothing else.

Toolbars and Shortcuts

The **Getting Started** toolbar is the horizontal toolbar along the top of the SketchUp window (Figure 5). Most of the tools that you'll use in SketchUp can be found here.

If this looks like a sparse assortment of tools, don't worry because there are many more toolbars available. If you're using a PC, look at the **View/Toolbars** menu to see the toolbars listed, and toggle them on and off if you're curious about what they contain. On a Mac, choose **View/Customize**

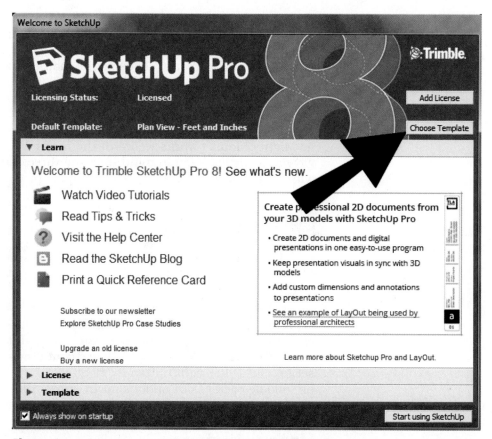

Figure 3

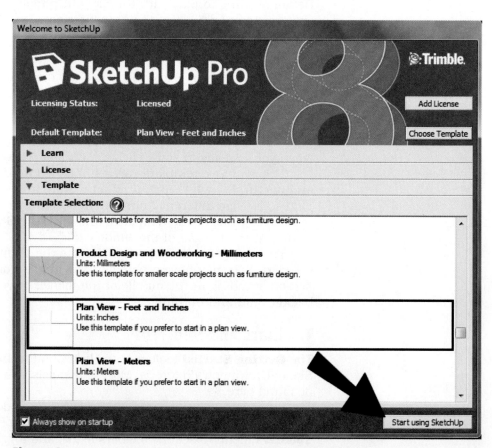

Figure 4

Figure 5

Toolbar. From the large window that appears, you can drag any toolbar onto the main toolbar. You can also drag them off of the main toolbar in the same manner.

Using keyboard shortcuts can be a great time-saver. For example, if you need to draw a line, it's a lot quicker to press the *L* key than to move your mouse over to the **Line** icon. You can look at the SketchUp menus to see what shortcut keys are already defined, such as *L* for **Line**, *R* for **Rectangle**, and so forth (Figure 6).

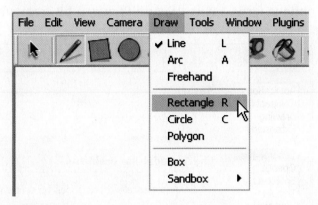

Figure 6

Changing or adding shortcuts can be done on the **Shortcuts** page of the **Preferences**, which is a user interface window that will be described later.

Model Info

The settings on the pages of the **Model Info** window affect the current model only (as opposed to settings that affect all SketchUp models, which are set in the **System Preferences**). To open this window (Figure 7), choose **Window/Model Info** from the main menu.

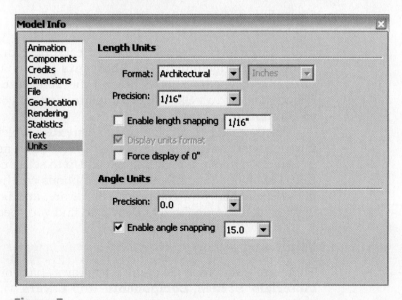

Figure 7

Take a few minutes to look at the options on the various pages. You won't need to change most of these options, and almost everything on this window is self-explanatory. For interior designers, the most important **Model Info** page is **Units**, where you can set whether you're working in architectural (feet and inches) or decimal (choose from inches, millimeters, centimeters, etc.) units. The other pages that will be used in this book are **Dimensions**, **File**, and **Text**.

System Preferences

As with most computer applications, **System Preferences** contain options that affect the application in general. The options that you set here will be used every time that you open a SketchUp file, at least until you change the options. PC users open this window by choosing **Window/Preferences** from the main menu; Mac users choose **SketchUp/Preferences**. The options for PC users (Figure 8) vary a bit from what Mac users will see.

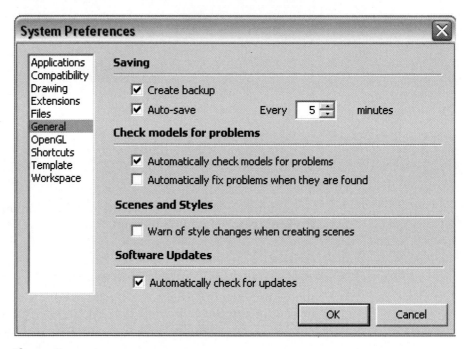

Figure 8

It's worthwhile to take a look at each page on this window, although you won't change much. The **Shortcuts** page enables you to add, remove, or change keyboard shortcuts, and the **Template** page enables you to change the default SketchUp template, just as you could in the **Welcome to SketchUp** window.

Another page to quickly scan is **OpenGL**, which controls how SketchUp interacts with your computer's graphic card. If at any point while working in SketchUp you're not getting SketchUp to select or display objects the way that it should, changing the OpenGL options can help. What each option does depends on your computer's hardware, and because there are only a few options, you can use trial and error to find your perfect settings.

Windows and Docking

There are many more SketchUp windows that you'll be using, such as the **Materials**, **Scenes**, **Components**, and **Layers** windows shown in Figure 9. Any window can be opened by choosing it in the **Window** menu. When several

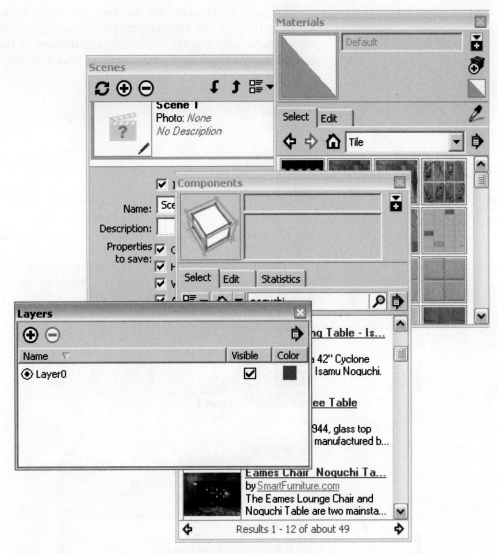

Figure 9

windows are open at once, the screen can get so cluttered that you'll have no room for the model itself.

To save space, you can click on a window's title bar (the bar across the very top of the window, where the name of the window appears). This minimizes each window so that you can still see nothing but its title (Figure 10). To open a minimized window, just click its title bar again.

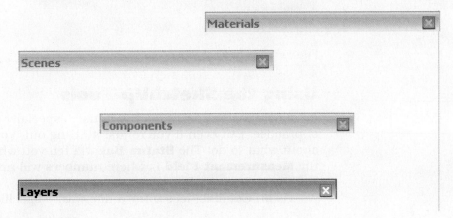

Figure 10

To save even more space, you can *dock* windows (move them to a specific part of the SketchUp window or "glue" them to each other). You can drag a title bar to the left or right edge of the window, or drag a title bar directly above or below another title bar. This way you can stack minimized windows (Figure 11).

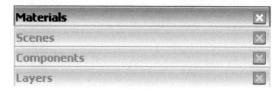

Figure 11

Opening a minimized window while it's stacked will simply move the other windows up or down accordingly (Figure 12).

To take a window out of the stack, simply drag its title bar out of the stack. Of course, you can close any window by clicking the *X* icon in the title bar.

Figure 12

Using the SketchUp Tools

All of SketchUp's tools are easy to use, especially after you've had a bit of practice. But even if you're just starting out, you won't be in the dark about what to do. The **Status Bar** will tell you what steps to take, and the **Measurement Field** is where numbers will appear (if needed), such as length, angle, or radius.

As an example, let's draw a line with a specific length.

1 Click the **Line** tool indicated in Figure 13.

Figure 13

2 Look at the lower left corner of the SketchUp window, where the **Status Bar** tells you "Select start point" (Figure 14).

Figure 14

> **NOTE**
>
> To the left of the **Status Bar** are three icons that won't be used in this book. The Lightbulb icon tells you whether the model has a specific location on earth (known in SketchUp as "geo-located"). This is for models that are integrated with Google Earth. The Person icon indicates whether you've taken credit for the model, which is relevant if you're placing a model in 3D Warehouse. The G icon indicates whether you're logged into your Google account. You need a Google account to upload models into 3D Warehouse.

3 Click anywhere to start the line, and move the cursor in the red (horizontal) direction (Figure 15). Don't click again yet.

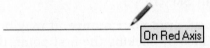

Figure 15

4 Look at the **Status Bar** for instructions on the next step. You have a choice: Either click a point to end the line, or enter a value (Figure 16). To enter a value, in this case, means to set the line's exact length.

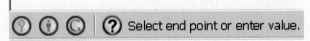

Figure 16

5 While the line is still unfinished and you're moving the cursor in the red direction, look at the **Length** field in the lower right corner (Figure 17). Here you can see the current length of the line. (The units in this field are the ones set on the **Units** page of the **Model Info** window.)

Length 4' 5 15/16"

Figure 17

This is the **Measurement Field**, and its contents and title depend on what tool you're using. For example, if you're creating a rectangle, you can enter two values: width and height. If you're creating a circle, you can enter a radius.

6 You could end the line by clicking a second point, but to set the length of this line, type 12' (the apostrophe is the symbol for feet), and this number appears in the **Length** field (Figure 18). This is an important point: *You never have to click in a measurement field, and if you do click there, your current action will end!* It may feel counterintuitive, but don't click; just type whatever characters you need and they will appear. You'll get used to it!

Length	12'

Figure 18

7 Press Enter, and the line is created with the correct length.

You'll see similar **Status Bar** instructions and measurements for other tools. For example, the **Rectangle** tool will tell you first to click the first corner, then either click the second corner or enter width and height values. **Eraser** instructions will tell you to click edges to erase, or that you can drag the cursor to erase multiple edges at once. The instructions also tell you what the modifier keys Shift and Ctrl/Option will do while erasing.

Each time that you click an unfamiliar tool, make sure to check the **Status Bar**; you'll see just what to do and you may learn features of the tool that you didn't know about. Always look to see what's listed in the **Measurement Field**.

Here are some other important items to keep in mind while creating or editing objects in SketchUp:

- **Don't click and drag your mouse.** It may be instinctive to draw a line or pull out a face by clicking the first point, dragging to the second point, and releasing the mouse button to finish. But SketchUp provides much more flexibility when you get out of the dragging habit. For every tool in which multiple clicks are required, click and release the mouse button, move the mouse to the next point, and click/release again.

- **Undo is your friend.** If you click somewhere that you shouldn't have, or make any sort of error, you can undo your steps, one by one, all the way back to the very start of your model if necessary. On a PC, **Undo** is Ctrl+Z, and it's Cmd+Z on a Mac. If you undo too far, and want to redo a step or two, use Ctrl/Cmd+Y.

- **Bail out with the Esc key.** If in the process of using a tool, you've made a mistake but haven't completed the operation yet, press Esc to start over. For example, if you click to start a line in the wrong place, just press Esc and click the correct spot.

- **Click actual points.** Far too often, SketchUp users click somewhere that's "close enough" when there's an actual point that can be clicked. For example, if you want to move a sofa to the edge of a floor, click somewhere along the back edge of the sofa; don't just click somewhere *near* the back of the sofa. As you'll see throughout this book, SketchUp helpfully tells you when your cursor is on an endpoint, center point, or midpoint; on a face; or on an edge. Take advantage of these indicators because it's a lot better than estimating points by sight!

- **Right-click in blank space to unselect everything.** Many SketchUp operations start by selecting the object on which the tool will perform an action. After the action, the objects usually remain selected. If you leave objects selected and then try to work on other objects, you might end up with strange results! A quick right-click in empty space will unselect everything in the entire model.

- **Don't click in the Measurement Field!** This was stated earlier, but it bears repeating because people do it far too often. You might *want* to click in the spot where the line's length appears, but keep your mouse away! All you have to do is type, and whatever you type will appear.

3D Warehouse

The 3D Warehouse is part of what makes SketchUp such an incredible tool for interior designers. Maintained by SketchUp and hosted by Google, 3D Warehouse is a repository for any kind of model you could possibly imagine. So after you model a room, you can find objects in 3D Warehouse to furnish the room.

Because *anyone* can upload SketchUp models into this repository, amateurs and professional designers have added thousands of models to 3D Warehouse since it was established in 2006. In addition, dozens of furniture and appliance manufacturers have uploaded models of their products, free for all to use.

Sometimes you'll find a 3D Warehouse model that's *almost* what you're looking for, but it's not perfect. This book will teach you how to modify those 3D Warehouse models to meet your exact needs. (Two chapters in this book also show how to model furniture from scratch.)

To get a quick idea about how 3D Warehouse works, open this URL in your Internet browser: http://sketchup.google.com/3dwarehouse

> **NOTE**
>
> If this URL changes in the future, a simple web search for "3D Warehouse" will take you to the correct website.

In the search field, enter a search term for the model in which you are interested (lounge chair, base cabinet, window blinds, Porsche, chainsaw, etc.), and you'll find several models (sometimes hundreds) that match your term. As with a regular Google web search, models are listed in order of popularity. Some models have ratings and reviews, some building models are geo-located (they have a specific location in Google Earth), and some are beautifully created by design professionals, while others are created by SketchUp enthusiasts with varying degrees of quality.

> **NOTE**
>
> Later in this book, we'll see how to access 3D Warehouse from within SketchUp as well, which enables you to import a model directly into the SketchUp file on which you are working.

Because of the ever-increasing number of uploaded 3D Warehouse models, a general search for a term (such as "base cabinet" or "sofa") will result in a huge number of models for you to comb through. There is an Advanced Search tool that you can use to narrow down your search by criteria such as minimum rating, author, or Google Earth location. For most of the models used in this book, you'll be told the author (who uploaded the model), and you can add the author's name to your search. For example, looking for a striped couch by Bonnie Roskes can be found be entering "striped couch roskes" as the search term.

> **NOTE**
>
> Uploading your own models to 3D Warehouse is quite simple; just choose **File/3D Warehouse/Share Model** from SketchUp's main menu, and the uploading steps are self-explanatory. Uploading models requires a Google account, downloading models does not.

About the Authors

Putting this book together required the combination of two distinct skills: a creative and practiced eye for room design, and technical expertise in 3D modeling in SketchUp.

Bonnie Roskes is a SketchUp expert and owner of 3DVinci (http://3dvinci.net), providing manuals, self-guided projects, and tutorials on SketchUp and related applications. Her *Google SketchUp Hands-On* series has been lauded by her loyal reader base as a comprehensive, easy-to-follow book on all things SketchUp. She has also written books for younger audiences: the ModelMetricks series for teaching 3D design for ages 8–12, and GeomeTricks books for teaching 2D/3D geometry to K–12 math students. She also wrote *The Google SketchUp Cookbook* in 2007, published by O'Reilly Press. Bonnie often presents at education conferences, leads software training sessions, and blogs at http://3dvinci.blogspot.com. Trained as a structural engineer, all her years of SketchUp expertise haven't made her much of an interior decorator, as co-author Annie Elliott can attest. In fact, for this book, Bonnie put together a few colorful SketchUp models that made Annie wince, before she made Bonnie change them.

Bonnie met Annie in 2004, when a mutual friend recommended Annie (whose firm is Bossy Color) to help design Bonnie's new kitchen. Annie is an interior decorator and design blogger who worked in some of the nation's top museums before turning to interior design. Quoted frequently in publications from *The Washington Post* to *Real Simple* magazine, Annie is considered an expert on color, residential space planning, and telling people what to do in the nicest way possible. Annie definitely is *not* an expert on software. When Bonnie introduced her to SketchUp, Annie was shocked to discover how intuitive it was. Annie now uses SketchUp for kitchen designs, tile layouts, and, of course, furniture plans. It's the only modeling program that she needs. More information about Annie and her work can be found at http://bossycolor.com.

Both Bonnie and Annie live with their wonderful families in Washington, DC.

About the Cover

The front cover image is a rendered view of a SketchUp model created by designer Surya Murali, whose models also feature prominently in several chapters of this book. A rare case of someone who's both technical *and* creative, Surya is a Kuwait-based electrical engineer who does 3D visualization work as a hobby. Her beautiful room models are well known and admired by those who frequent 3D Warehouse. Her interest in room layouts started in childhood, and her first whole-house project came about while designing a bungalow for her parents in India, which was built almost exactly to her design. Exploring Surya's models is a great way to get an idea of just how powerful SketchUp can be when it's combined with a great sense of style and design.

Download Instructor Resources from the Instructor Resource Center

To access supplementary materials online, instructors need to request an instructor access code. Go to www.pearsonhighered.com/irc to register for an instructor access code. Within 48 hours of registering, you will receive a confirmation e-mail that contains an instructor access code. Once you have received your code, locate your text in the online catalog and click on the Instructor Resources button on the left side of the catalog product page. Select a supplement, and a log-in page will appear. Once you have logged in, you can access instructor material for all Prentice Hall textbooks. If you have any difficulties accessing the site or downloading a supplement, please contact Customer Service at http://247pearsoned. custhelp.com

Acknowledgments

The authors thank the following individuals for their reviews of the manuscript: Milan Krepelka, University of Alberta; JoAnn Wilson, Utah State University; Megan Shaw, Hawkeye Community College; and Sharon Coleman, Middle Tennessee State University.

Conceptualize, Create, Communicate

Designing Living Spaces with SketchUp

1 chapterone
Model a Room

The main focus of this book is using SketchUp to create a 3D model of a room (or series of rooms) and to furnish the room according to your personal designs. And the first task of any design project is to start with the room itself.

In this chapter, you'll learn how to
- Take field measurements and decide what needs to be measured.
- Model the room according to the measured dimensions.
- Add a door.
- Add windows as components.
- Edit the window components.
- Add finishing touches such as baseboards.

At the end of the chapter (and throughout the rest of the book), you'll find a "Model It Yourself" project that will test your knowledge of the concepts presented in the chapter.

1.1 Taking Field Measurements

A typical job for an interior designer is to start with an empty room and figure out what to put in it. And accurate placement of furnishings requires that you start with a geometrically accurate room model. (Of course, if you're working off a set of plans, instead of a physical room, you'll be able to get your measurements much more easily!) So you enter the room, armed with your tape measure; what exactly do you need to measure?

NOTE

Even if you mostly work in Imperial units (feet and inches), it's a lot easier to take measurements in centimeters or millimeters. Because there are no pesky fractions of an inch to deal with, metric units are easy to enter in SketchUp. Once you get your measurements into SketchUp, you can always switch your model units to whatever you want.

Here are some "rules to live by" when taking field measurements of a room:

- Measure each wall in horizontal sections, as shown in Figure 1-1. If a wall contains a window, measure from the left corner of the wall to the left edge of the window moulding, then measure the entire width of the window (including moulding). Finally, measure from the right edge of the moulding to the right corner of the wall. It's also a good idea to measure the overall length of the wall or the floor, just to verify your math.

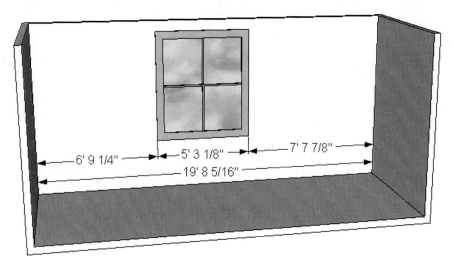

Figure 1-1

> **NOTE**
>
> If your floor has baseboards, the floor measurement will be about 2 inches shorter than the wall measurement (a baseboard projects about 1 inch from the wall).

- Measure each wall in vertical sections, as shown in Figure 1-2. When windows are present, measure from the ceiling to the top of the window moulding. Then measure from the top of the window moulding to the bottom of the moulding (not to the window sill). Finally, measure from the bottom of the moulding to the floor. Again, make sure that these dimensions add up to the overall floor-to-ceiling measurement.

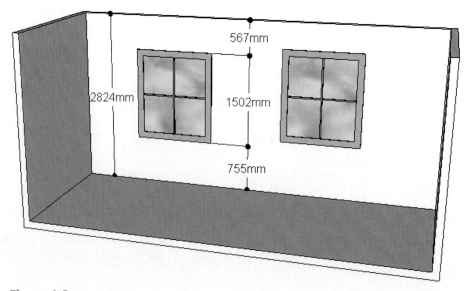

Figure 1-2

- Measure the thickness and depth (how far they protrude from the wall) of all window mouldings.

- Do the same for doors: Measure the total width and height of the door, the distance from the ceiling to the top of the moulding, and the moulding thickness and depth.

- Measure the height and depth of any baseboards and crown mouldings.

Once you're an old hand with SketchUp, you'll be able to take these measurements and plug them into a preliminary SketchUp model on the laptop you've brought to the job site. But until then, you can always jot down measurements on a rough drawing and enter them into SketchUp later.

1.2 Model the Basic Room in SketchUp

We'll now model a simple, rectangular room with a 15′ × 12′ floor (wall-to-wall, not considering the baseboards) and an 8′-6″ high ceiling. Because we're using architectural units, we'll make sure to start with the correct design template.

1 Start SketchUp. You should see the Welcome to SketchUp window shown in Figure 1-3 (this window looks slightly different in the Free version). If SketchUp opens straightaway and you don't see this window, go to the SketchUp main menu and choose **Help/Welcome to SketchUp**. Click the Choose Template button and select Beginning Training Template - Inches (second from last on the templates list). Then click Start using SketchUp at the bottom of the window.

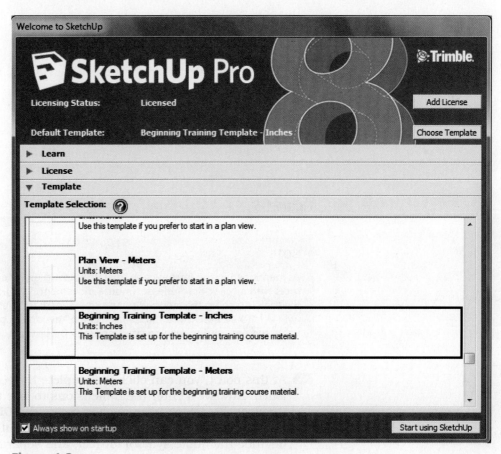

Figure 1-3

Figure 1-4

The file opens in **Top** view, and you should see two axes: red (horizontal) and green (vertical). The point at which these axes meet is called the origin. Unlike some of the other design templates, this one has no extra objects, such as a person, to clutter the display. (In some of the templates, a person is included for scaling purposes, but we don't need any help with that here because we already know our dimensions.)

2 To draw the floor, click the icon for the **Rectangle** tool, which is indicated in Figure 1-4. (You can also press the *R* key.)

> **NOTE**
>
> It's a good idea to familiarize yourself with the keyboard shortcuts for the tools that you use often (*R* for **Rectangle**, *L* for **Line**, etc.). Pressing a key takes less time than clicking an icon or going to the main menu, and less mouse movement is easier on your hands.

3 A rectangle is defined by two corner points. It's good practice to start at the origin, so click at the point where the axes meet, release the mouse button (no dragging the mouse), and then move your cursor so that your rectangle looks approximately as shown in Figure 1-5 (don't click). While you're moving your mouse around, take a look at the **Dimensions** field at the lower corner of the SketchUp window, shown in Figure 1-6. This tells you the width (the larger number) and height (the smaller number) of your rectangle. These dimensions update as you move your mouse.

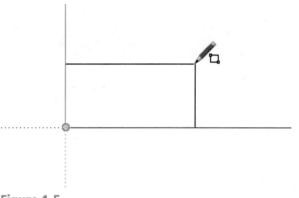

Dimensions | 4' 9 3/8", 2' 2 15/16"

Figure 1-5   Figure 1-6

> **NOTE**
>
> As mentioned in the Introduction, many SketchUp users tend to use drawing and editing tools with a "click-drag-release" mouse movement. While this does work for some of the tools, dragging the mouse is *not* recommended: All SketchUp tools work much better with a "click-release-move mouse-click again" action. So break the mouse-dragging habit and get used to moving your mouse without the button pressed.

4 At this point, you can click to complete the rectangle, or leave it unfinished. Now we'll enter the dimensions to size the rectangle to represent the floor. You don't have to click inside the **Dimensions** field, just start typing and the numbers will appear there automatically. Type 15′,12′ (include the quote symbol for feet, and separate the two dimensions with a comma but no space), shown in Figure 1-7.

Dimensions | 15′,12′

Figure 1-7

5. Press Enter, and the rectangle resizes to the dimensions of the floor. You'll have to zoom out to see the whole rectangle (Figure 1-8). If you have a scroll wheel mouse, just scroll down to zoom out (zooming will be relative to where your cursor is). If you don't have a scroll wheel mouse, then run out and get one, but in the meantime you can use the **Zoom** tool shown in Figure 1-9. Zooming this way is done by dragging the mouse up and down. (The **Zoom Extents** icon is to the right of the **Zoom** icon; you can always click this to place your entire model in the SketchUp window.)

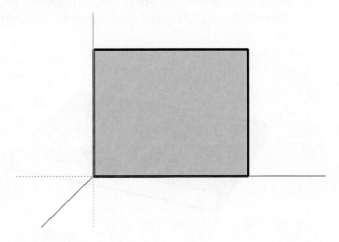

Figure 1-8

Figure 1-9

Figure 1-10

6. Once the floor is drawn, you can break free of thinking in 2D. Orbit the view up, either by holding down the middle mouse button while dragging the mouse up, or use the **Orbit** tool shown in Figure 1-10 (which uses a regular mouse drag). Your view should show a near-flat rectangle like the one in Figure 1-11, with the blue axis representing the vertical direction.

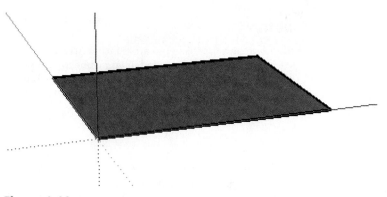

Figure 1-11

Figure 1-12

7 Click the **Push/Pull** icon shown in Figure 1-12, or press P.

8 Click the rectangle, release the mouse button, and move the mouse up so that the box has some height, as shown in Figure 1-13. You can either click again to complete the box, or leave the box unfinished. (Most SketchUp drawing tools work this way: You can enter an exact dimension *before* an operation is finished, or you can complete the operation and enter the dimensions *afterward*.)

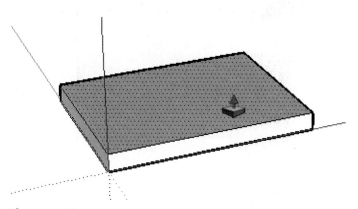

Figure 1-13

9 The room has an 8'-6" ceiling, so type 8'6 (no quote symbols are needed for inches) and press Enter. Your box should look like the one in Figure 1-14.

> **NOTE**
>
> You could also enter this dimension as 8.5' or 102 (the equivalent value in inches). What if your measurements contain fractions, such as 8'-5¾"? Simply enter this measurement as 8'5 3/4 (or as 101.75). See why metric units are so much easier?

10 We need to see inside the room, so to remove the ceiling, right-click on the top of the box and choose **Erase** from the popup menu. You should now have an open box as shown in Figure 1-15.

11 As you can see, SketchUp assigns different default colors to the two sides of any face. With this particular template, front faces are white, and back faces are blue. If you already know what color the walls will be, you might as well include that color as part of the room model. To

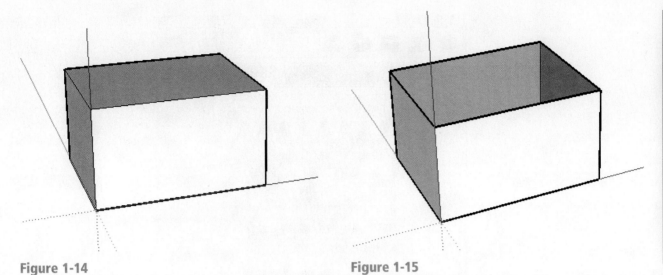

Figure 1-14   Figure 1-15

Figure 1-16

find collections of colors and materials, click the **Paint Bucket** icon shown in Figure 1-16, or press the B key.

If you're using a PC, you'll see the **Materials** window (Figure 1-17). The large color square at the top left corner shows the current color, and the drop-down menu contains collections, such as "Colors," "Translucent," "Metal," and so forth.

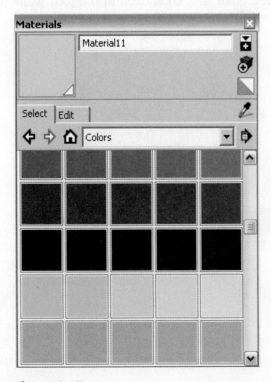

Figure 1-17

If you're on a Mac, you'll see the **Colors** window (Figure 1-18). The top of this window provides several color-picking options (sliders, crayons, etc.), and you can click the Brick icon to see the drop-down menu of color and material collections.

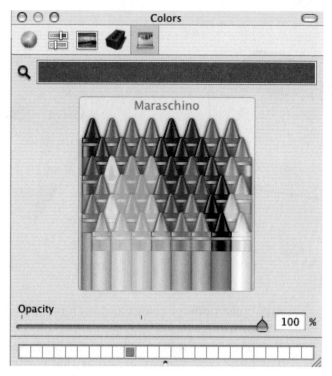

Figure 1-18

12 Pick a color and click each of the four walls (the inside faces). The room shown in Figure 1-19 has yellow walls.

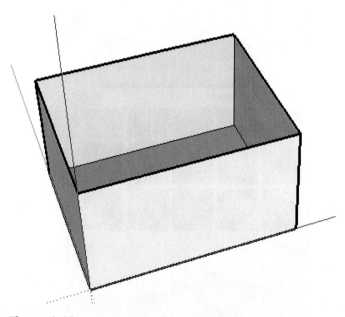

Figure 1-19

1.3 Add the Door

The door to this room is cut from the 15′ wall, as shown in Figure 1-20. It is 7′ high and 4′ wide, including its mouldings. The door is centered in the wall, which means that the left outer edge of the door is 5′-6″ from the left edge of the wall. The door moulding is 4″ thick and 2″ deep.

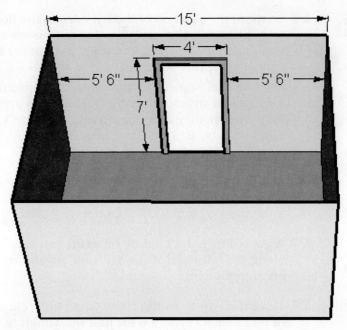

Figure 1-20

1 Orbit around so that you're facing one of the 15′ walls, as shown in Figure 1-21.

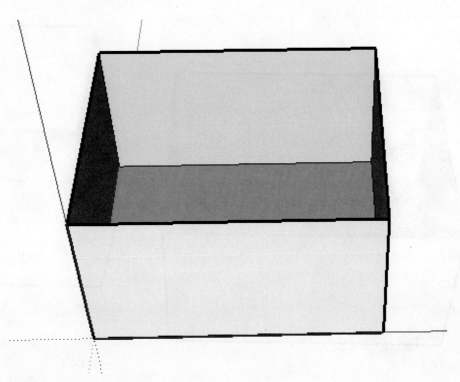

Figure 1-21

2 If you find the display of the colored axes distracting, you can turn them off by choosing **View/Axes** from the main menu. Some people prefer to always keep the axes displayed; it's a matter of personal preference. **View/Axes** is a toggle function, so you can switch them on and off as needed. The rest of the pictures in this chapter will not show the axes.

Figure 1-22

3 To mark the position of the left edge of the door, click the **Tape Measure** icon, shown in Figure 1-22. **Tape Measure** will be used often in this book and can be used for various purposes (including measuring, of course), but this time we'll use it to make a guide line.

A guide line, sometimes also called a construction line, is used to mark locations or measurements. Guides lines are unlike "normal" SketchUp lines in that they are infinite, and they don't interact or interfere with other objects. But they can be selected, moved, and erased like other SketchUp objects.

4 Make sure that there is a plus (+) sign attached to your cursor; otherwise a guide line won't be created. If there is no plus sign, press (don't hold) the Ctrl key (PC) or Option key (Mac).

5 A guide line is created by offsetting an existing edge. Click anywhere along the left edge of the 15' wall, as shown in Figure 1-23 (don't click on an endpoint).

6 Move the cursor to the right, and either click to place the guide line, or don't click. Type 5'6 (or just 66, which is the equivalent distance in inches) and press Enter. This places a dashed guide line at the correct offset distance from the left edge of the wall (Figure 1-24).

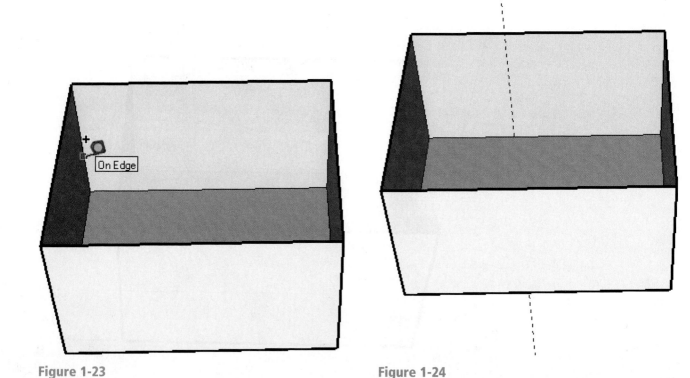

Figure 1-23   Figure 1-24

7 We could create the door with the **Rectangle** tool, but let's use a tool that we haven't tried yet. To create the door, outline one edge at a time, and click the **Line** icon shown in Figure 1-25, or press L.

Figure 1-25

8 Click to start the edge at the intersection of the guide line and the floor, and move the cursor in the direction that you want the line to go: straight up, along the guide line, as shown in Figure 1-26.

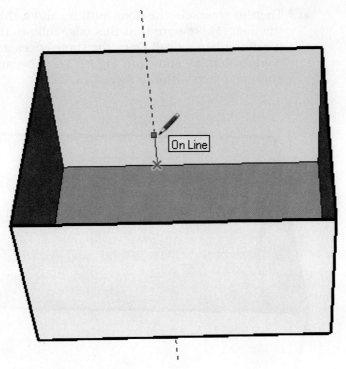

Figure 1-26

9 Type 7′ and press Enter. The vertical line becomes 7′ long.

10 SketchUp is now ready to start the next edge of the door outline. Move the cursor to the right, as shown in Figure 1-27. The preview color of the line should be red, because the line is parallel to the red axis.

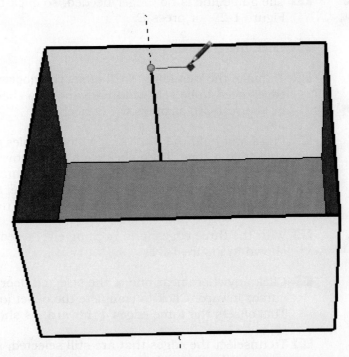

Figure 1-27

11 Enter 4′ to complete this edge.

12 Then to complete the door outline, add a third edge straight down to the floor. Make sure that this edge follows the blue direction; otherwise it will not be vertical! Once the three edges are complete, they turn from bold to thin, as shown in Figure 1-28, because they now completely enclose a face within a face.

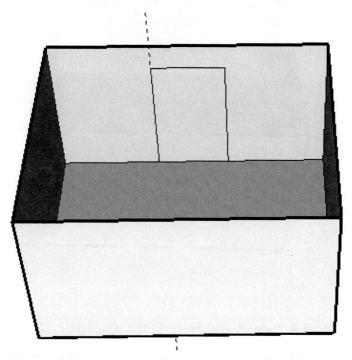

Figure 1-28

Figure 1-29

Figure 1-30

Figure 1-31

13 The guide line is no longer needed, so click the **Eraser** icon shown in Figure 1-29, or press *E*.

14 Click the guide line to erase it.

15 To make the moulding, we'll offset the doorway edges inward. But the edges need to be selected in advance, so click the **Select** icon shown in Figure 1-30, or press the Spacebar.

16 Press and hold the Shift key, which enables you to select multiple objects at a time. Then click each of the three edges of the doorway, which should all become bold and highlighted in blue. (If you inadvertently click the wrong object, such as a face, Shift-Select is a toggle function so you can click the face again to unselect it.)

17 With the three edges (and nothing else) selected, click the **Offset** icon shown in Figure 1-31.

18 Click anywhere near one of the selected door edges, then move the cursor inward. Click to complete the offset (or don't click) and enter 4. This offsets the three edges 4″ inward, as shown in Figure 1-32.

19 To unselect the edges that are still selected, right-click on any blank space in the figure (hereafter, just "blank space").

20 Choose a color and paint the moulding face (dark gray is used in Figure 1-33).

Figure 1-32

Figure 1-33

21 Erase the doorway face, as shown in Figure 1-34. (In addition to using **Erase** from the popup menu, you can also erase a face by first selecting it, then pressing the Delete key.)

Figure 1-34

22 To give the moulding its 2″ depth, activate **Push/Pull**. But before clicking anywhere, press the Ctrl key (PC) or Option key (Mac). Don't keep this key pressed, just tap it once, and you should see a plus sign attached to your cursor. This is a little-used but important modification to **Push/Pull**, which keeps the original faces intact rather than causing them to be erased. Pull the moulding face into the room 2″, as shown in Figure 1-35.

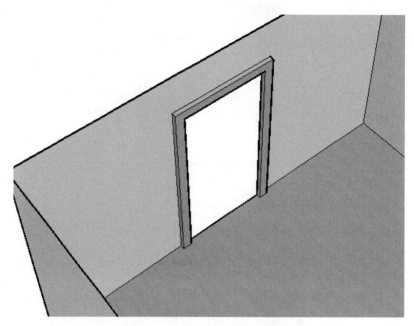

Figure 1-35

23 To see what that Ctrl or Option modifier key just did, orbit around to see the outside of the doorway. There is a moulding face on the outside of the room, as shown in Figure 1-36; without the modifier, that face would not be there. To see this for yourself, you can undo the **Push/Pull** (press Ctrl+Z or Cmd+Z) and try it again without using any modifier keys. Then redo it with the modifier.

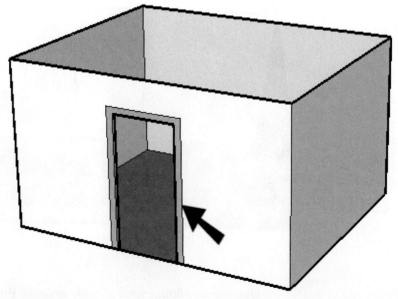

Figure 1-36

1.4 Add the Windows

Creating windows provides the perfect opportunity to get familiar with one of SketchUp's handiest features: components. Whenever you have an object that will repeat and/or have specific alignment properties, it's best to make that object into a component. Among other benefits, using components results in a smaller file size and faster model speed because SketchUp only needs to know what's in the original component—everything else is just a copy.

This room has three identical windows, one in the 12′ wall, as shown in Figure 1-37, and two in the 15′ wall, as shown in Figure 1-38. The bottom of each window is 3′ above the floor and each window is 3′-1″ wide and 4′-2″ high. The window in the 12′ wall is centered horizontally. The windows in the 15′ wall are each located 2′ from the edge of the wall.

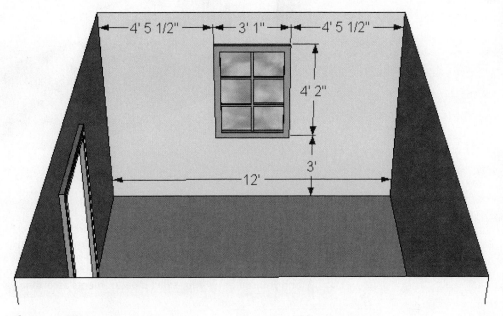

Figure 1-37

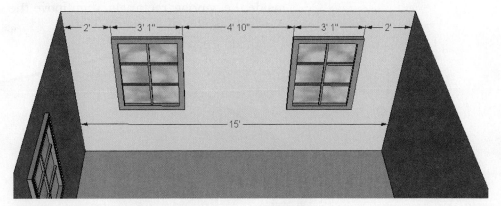

Figure 1-38

The mouldings around the windows are 3″ thick and 2″ deep, and each window has 1″ muntins dividing the pane of glass into six sections.

1 When we drew the rectangle for the door, we created it in its exact spot. That's one way to work, but another way is to create an object first and then move it into place later. This is what we'll do for the first window.

Orbit to view the 12′ wall shown in Figure 1-39 and draw anywhere within this wall a rectangle 4′-2″ (50″) high and 3′-1″ (37″) wide.

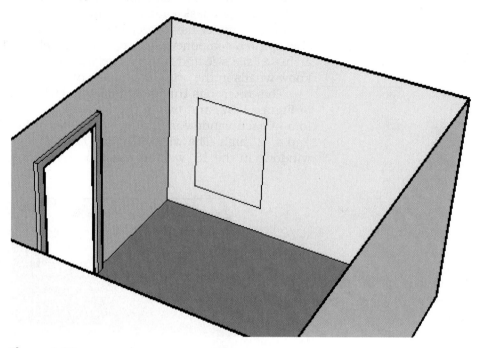

Figure 1-39

NOTE

If you haven't noticed, SketchUp has a quirky way of sizing a rectangle. If you follow this rule, you'll never get your rectangle "reversed": Always orient your rectangle the way you want it to end up, either vertical or horizontal (similar to portrait or landscape orientation when printing). The **Dimensions** field will indicate which length is *longer*, and you can enter your exact measurements accordingly.

2 Because this window will have all of its edges offset for the moulding, you don't need to select edges in advance. Just activate **Offset**, click inside the window rectangle, then move the cursor inward and create a 3″ offset, as shown in Figure 1-40.

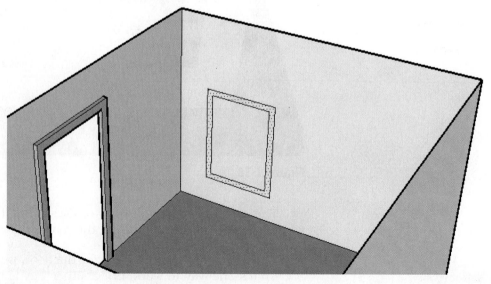

Figure 1-40

3 When painting this moulding face, we want to use the same color we used for the door moulding. Unless you remember the exact color you used, you might have trouble getting an exact match. So go back to the **Materials** or **Colors** window and click the House icon shown in Figure 1-41. (Mac users, you'll need to click the Brick icon first before the House icon will be available.) You will see a list of colors used so far, and you can click the color used for the door moulding (dark gray in this case).

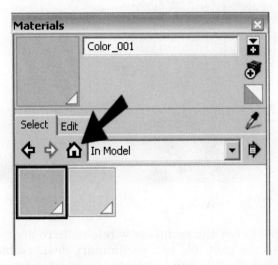

Figure 1-41

4 Paint the window moulding and use **Push/Pull** with the Ctrl or Option key to make it 2″ deep (Figure 1-42).

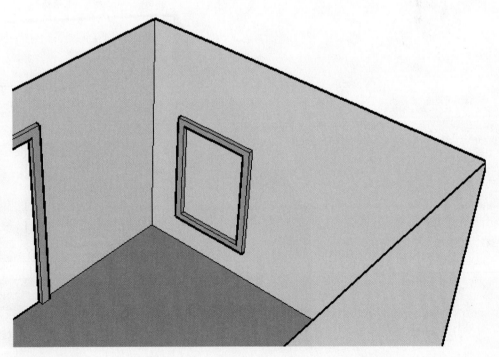

Figure 1-42

5 In the **Materials** or **Colors** window, find the "Translucent" collection and paint the window face to resemble glass. Figure 1-43 shows a translucent material with a sky reflection.

Figure 1-43

This is not the complete window (there are no muntins), but let's assume that this is a preliminary design which doesn't require tons of detail. So this window is good enough, at least for now, and we'll add the muntins later.

6 Because a couple more of these windows are needed in another wall, we'll now make the window into a component. Activate **Select** and drag a selection box from left to right around the entire window, not including any other objects (Figure 1-44).

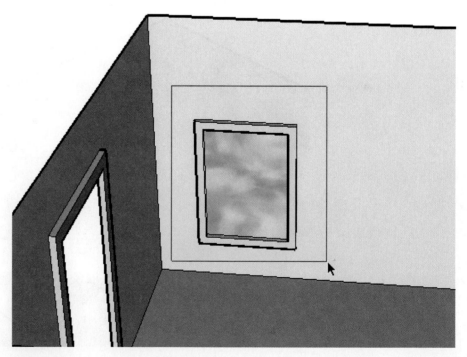

Figure 1-44

7 The entire window and mouldings should now be selected: Its edges are highlighted in blue and its faces are covered by blue dots. Right-click on any selected face or edge (it's always easier to right-click on a face than an edge) and choose **Create Component**.

8 In the **Create Component** window (Figure 1-45), enter a name for the component ("Window" is an obvious choice), and make sure that **Cut opening** is checked so that the window will cut through the wall. Also make sure that **Replace selection with component** is checked. Then click **Create**.

Figure 1-45

9 Once a component is created, it is a single object highlighted in blue, meaning that it is selected. Leave it selected because it will need to be moved into place. But first, to establish where the window will be placed, use **Tape Measure** to create a guide line 3′ above the floor (Figure 1-46).

10 With the window component still selected, click the **Move** icon (Figure 1-47), or press *M*.

11 A move is defined by two points. For the first point, click anywhere along the bottom of the window, against the wall (Figure 1-48).

12 For the second move point, click anywhere on the guide line (Figure 1-49). Now the bottom of the window is 3′ above the floor.

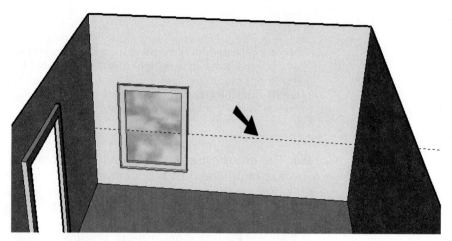

Figure 1-46

Figure 1-47

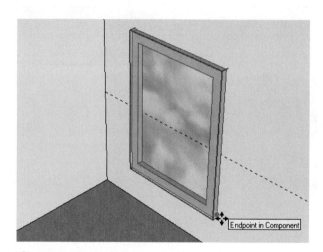

Figure 1-48

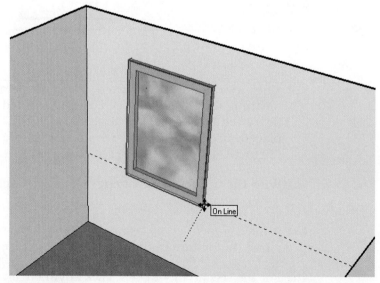

Figure 1-49

13 Remember, this window is supposed to be centered in the wall; the distances from the sides of the window to the wall edges are equal (refer back to Figure 1-37). We could use guide lines again, but it's easier to just center the window. The **Move** tool should still be active, so click the midpoint along the top back edge of the window, as shown in Figure 1-50.

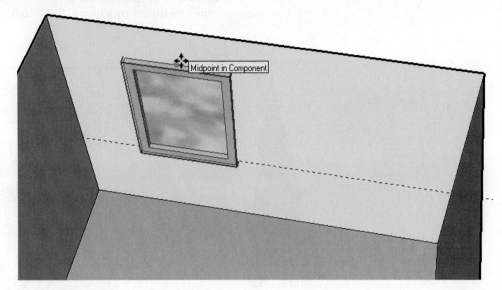

Figure 1-50

14 Move the window directly to the right or left, following the green direction. While the move preview line is green, press and hold the Shift key to lock this direction. Then click the midpoint of the 12′ wall, as shown in Figure 1-51. This centers the window perfectly in the wall.

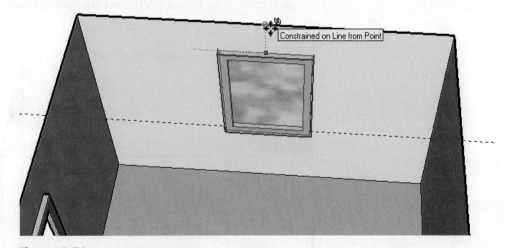

Figure 1-51

NOTE

Another way that you can lock a move direction (without using the Shift key) is by using the arrow keys. To lock the green direction, press (don't hold) the left arrow; pressing the left arrow again toggles off the lock. The right arrow is used for the red direction (mnemonic device: "right" and "red" both start with *R*), and up and down arrows are both used to lock the blue direction. Shift key vs. arrow keys: Again, this is a matter of personal preference.

15 It's always a good idea to check your measurements, so we'll use the **Tape Measure** tool again, this time to measure a distance. Activate **Tape Measure** and make sure that the plus sign is toggled off (use the Ctrl or Option key), because we don't need a guide line this time. Click a point on the left edge of the wall, then move the cursor to the left edge of the window (don't click). The measurement appears as a popup next to the cursor and should be 4′-5½″ (Figure 1-52). This matches the measurement shown in Figure 1-37, which is good news!

Figure 1-52

16 A minor diversion: If you're curious about how translucent materials work, orbit around to a view from outside the room, looking in the window (Figure 1-53). Usually a face can be painted with different colors on the front and back sides, but when you use a translucent material, it automatically gets applied to both sides.

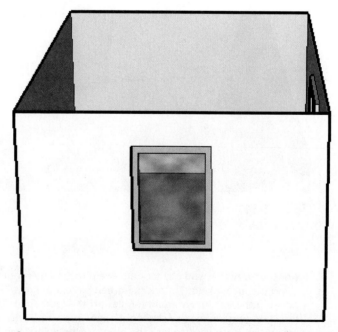

Figure 1-53

17 The 15′ wall that's currently empty needs two more of these windows. We'll start by making one copy, which is done using the **Move** tool. First, select the window, then activate **Move**. Press (don't hold) the Ctrl or Option key, which adds a plus sign to the cursor. For the first move point, click anywhere along the bottom of the wall, below the window (Figure 1-54).

Figure 1-54

18 For the second move point, move the cursor along the bottom of the empty 15′ wall until the window is approximately in the right place (Figure 1-55). As soon as you click to place the copy, the "glass" face will cut the wall (Figure 1-56). Because both move points were along the floor, both windows will be the same height from the floor.

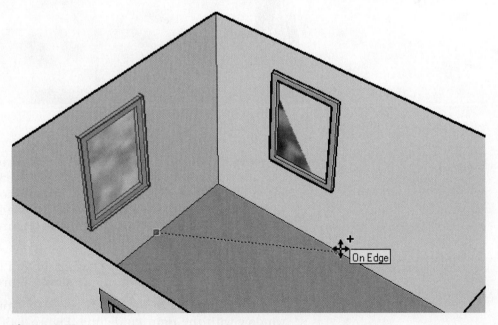

Figure 1-55

Figure 1-56

19 Leaving the copied window selected, draw two guide lines, each 2′ inward from the left and right edges of the 15′ wall (Figure 1-57).

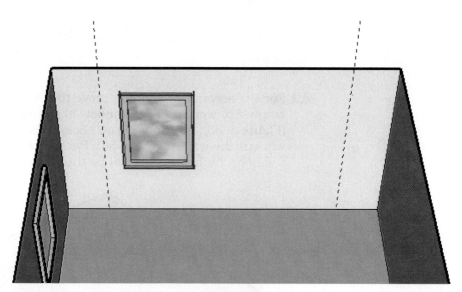

Figure 1-57

20 To move the new window into its correct location, activate **Move** and click any point along the left back vertical edge of the window. Start to move the window in the red direction and hold Shift (or press the right arrow key); click anywhere on the left guide line. This aligns the left side of the window with the guide line (Figure 1-58).

21 Keep **Move** active so that you can copy this window to the other guide line. Press the Ctrl or Option key again and click any point along the right back vertical edge of the window (Figure 1-59).

22 Move out the copy in the red direction, aligning the right edge of the window with the right guide line (Figure 1-60).

23 Erase both guide lines.

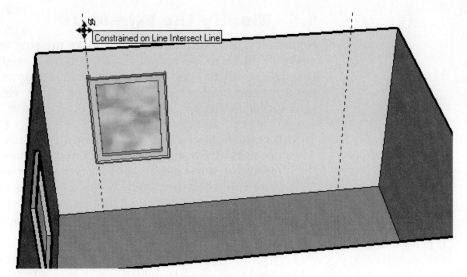

Figure 1-58

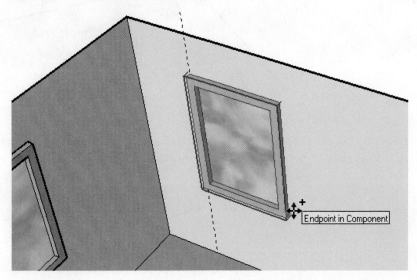

Figure 1-59

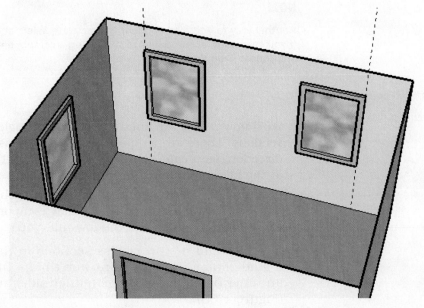

Figure 1-60

1.5 Modify the Windows

Remember, our simplified windows are missing their muntins. It's rather easy to add them, so you might as well do it so that your client won't think that you're cutting corners. Because the windows are all the same component, we can make changes to any one of the windows and the rest will be updated accordingly.

1 To make changes to the windows, right-click on any window and choose **Edit Component**. The edited window appears surrounded by a dotted-line box, and everything else in the model appears faded in the background (Figure 1-61). While a component is open for editing, you can only access what's inside the component; everything else in the model is off-limits until you close the component.

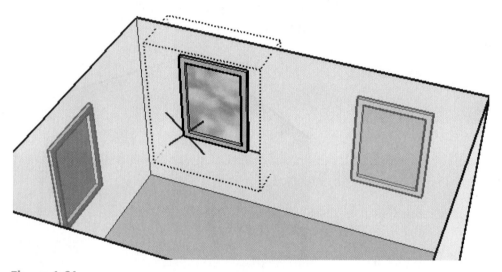

Figure 1-61

> **NOTE**
>
> Another way to edit a component is to activate **Select** and double-click the component. If you ever want a component to stop being a component, you could right-click on it and choose **Explode**.

2 We'll now use guide lines to divide the single pane of glass into six sections. There are supposed to be two glass sections in the horizontal direction, so create a guide line offset from the inner left edge, ending at the midpoint shown in Figure 1-62.

While you're drawing guide lines, you'll probably notice similar guide lines appearing on the other window components; they won't affect what you're doing to the window that you're working on.

3 There should be three glass sections in the vertical direction, so a guide line at the midpoint won't help. Instead, right-click on an inner back vertical edge (either side) and choose **Divide** (Figure 1-63).

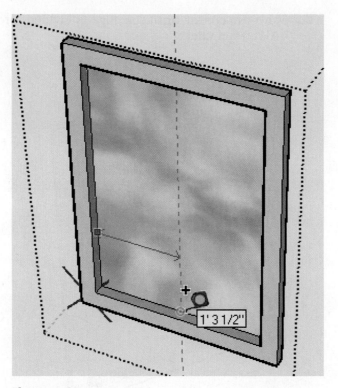

Figure 1-62

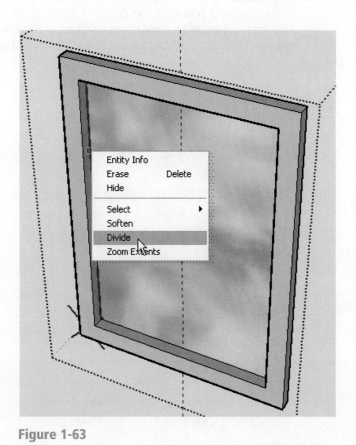

Figure 1-63

4 Move the cursor until the edge is divided into three segments (Figure 1-64), then click.

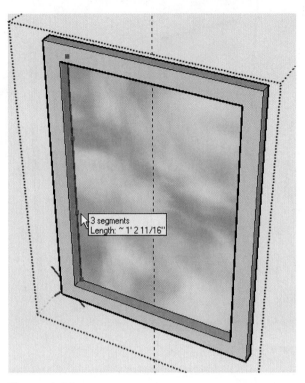

Figure 1-64

5 Now create a guide line offset from the lower inner edge, stopping at the one-third point of the divided vertical edge (Figure 1-65). Because the vertical edge is now composed of three equal edges, you'll see a green endpoint symbol at each one-third point.

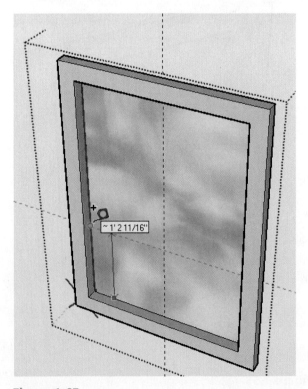

Figure 1-65

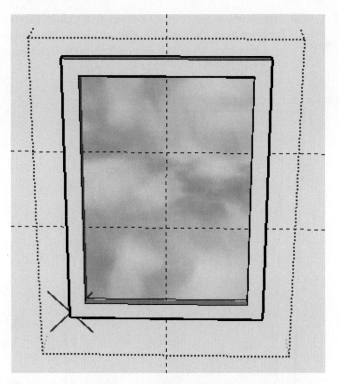

Figure 1-66

6 Add a guide line at the other one-third point (Figure 1-66).

7 To draw the 1″-thick muntins, use **Tape Measure** to offset all three guide lines ½″ in both directions (Figure 1-67). While you're offsetting each guide line, make sure that the offset direction is parallel to the correct axis.

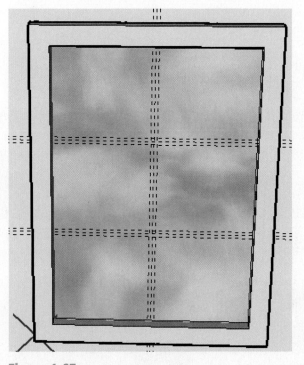

Figure 1-67

8 The narrow spaces between the guide lines define the muntins; the large rectangles define the six glass sections. Use either the **Rectangle** or **Line** tool to trace over the guide lines and define the muntins (Figure 1-68).

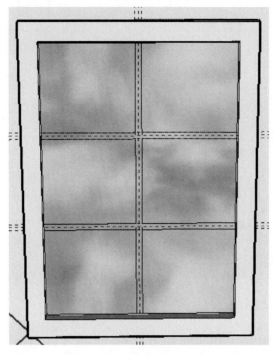

Figure 1-68

9 To erase all of the guide lines at once, choose **Edit/Delete Guides** from the main menu. Then paint the muntin face to match the moulding and pull it out 1″ (Figure 1-69). Don't forget to use the Ctrl or Option key while pulling!

Figure 1-69

10 That's enough to make the window look pretty accurate. To end the editing of this window, right-click in blank space and choose **Close Component**. (You can also close a component by activating **Select** and clicking once anywhere outside of the component.) Figure 1-70 shows what you should have now: three identical windows.

Figure 1-70

1.6 Finishing Touches

The only steps left are to add a simple baseboard and wrap up the whole room as a group.

As with the mouldings we've created so far, a baseboard doesn't need the level of detail that an actual baseboard usually has. Our baseboard will be based on a rectangle 2″ high, protruding 1″ from the walls.

1 We'll use the **Offset** tool again, and this time we'll need to select the edges in advance. Orbit to a view as shown in Figure 1-71 so that you can see the entire floor, and select the five edges that will have baseboards.

2 Offset these edges 1″ inward and paint the baseboard face; then pull up the baseboard face 2″ (Figure 1-72). Again, use the Ctrl or Option key when pulling.

An important step that you should always perform when you have a completed room is to make the room into a group. A group is similar to a component in that it is a single object, and it must be opened to be edited. But since the room itself won't be copied, there is no need to make it into a component (not that a component wouldn't also work). Another benefit of both groups and components is that other objects don't "stick" to them, or otherwise interfere with them. This is important for walls, floors, and windows, which we want to remain stationary and unchanged as we move various furnishings into and around the room.

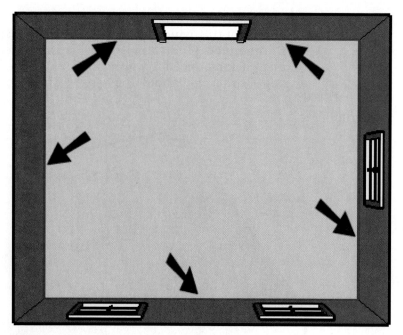

Figure 1-71

Figure 1-72

3 To make the room into a group, first select the entire room: walls, windows, and floors. You can use a selection box for this, or just press Ctrl+A or Cmd+A. Then right-click on any selected face and choose **Make Group**.

4 But wait! There's one change we forgot to make before grouping the room: The floor is supposed to be wood. Don't panic: Editing a group is just like editing a component. Right-click anywhere on the room and choose **Edit Group**. Find a material from the "Wood" collection and paint the floor (Figure 1-73).

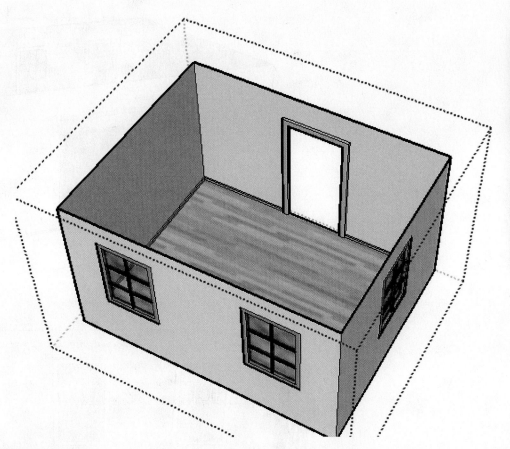

Figure 1-73

5 Close the room group like you closed the window component.

> **NOTE**
>
> Are you wondering how you would make changes to the windows? They are now "nested" components (nested inside the room group). So to edit the windows, you would first have to edit the room group, then edit one of the window components. When finished, you'd have to first close the window component, then close the room group.

6 The room is done and ready to be furnished! To save your work, use **File/Save As** from the main menu. You'll furnish this room in the next chapter.

Model It Yourself

Using the techniques presented in this chapter, model a similar room with the dimensions shown in Figure 1-74.

The longer wall, opposite the large doorway, has three identical windows, each divided into nine panes. The horizontal window spacing is shown in Figure 1-75, and the vertical spacing is shown in Figure 1-76. (The 2'-6" to the bottom of the window is measured from the floor, not from the top of the baseboard.)

There are two windows along the shorter wall, with horizontal spacing as shown in Figure 1-77. The vertical spacing is the same for the windows along the longer wall.

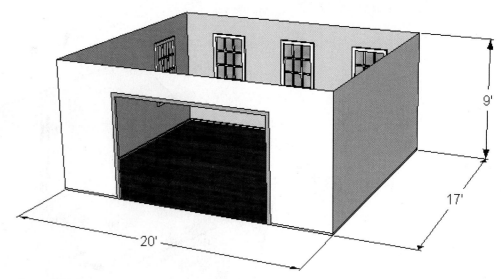

Figure 1-74

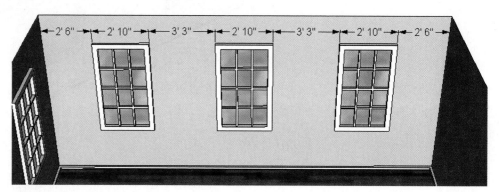

Figure 1-75

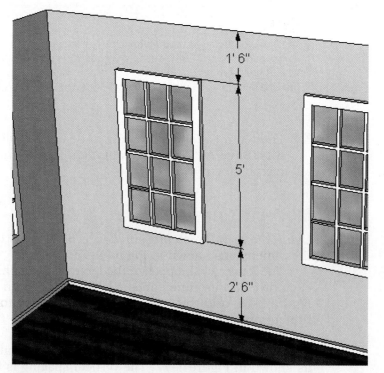

Figure 1-76

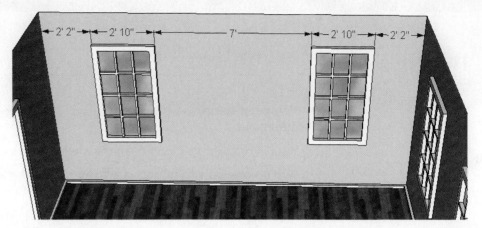

Figure 1-77

The doorway to this room has an 11′ × 7′ opening, with 2″ moulding all around (Figure 1-78). (The 7′ height is measured from the floor, not the top of the baseboard.)

And don't forget the baseboard along the floor, which is 1.5″ × 1.5″ (Figure 1-79).

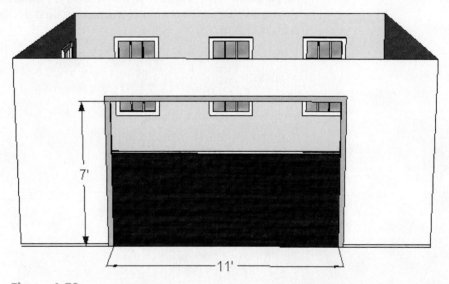

Figure 1-78

Figure 1-79

Review Questions

- You need to draw a line 4'-6¾" long. What are three ways to enter this dimension?

- What are two functions of the **Tape Measure** tool?

- When you want to paint something using the same color used elsewhere in the model, where can you find the list of already-used colors?

- The **Eraser** tool can be used to erase edges. What are two ways to erase a face?

- How do you use the **Offset** tool when you want to offset all edges around a face? Only *some* of the edges around a face?

- Describe two ways that you can lock an axis direction.

- How can you select everything in your model?

- Why would you make a window into a component, but a room into a group? What are some other interior design objects that you might make into components?

- How do you edit a component? How do you end the editing when finished?

2 chaptertwo
Furnish a Room

Now that you've created an empty room, the next task is to figure out what goes in it. This chapter won't help you decide which coffee table looks best with which sofa, but once you make your design decisions, this chapter will show you how to find the objects you want, and how to get these objects into your room. All of the pieces in this chapter come from the 3D Warehouse, which is a repository of models created by SketchUp users. While many 3D Warehouse models are designed properly, many are not. So this chapter will also cover what to do when the model you find needs a little work to make it exactly right.

In this chapter, you'll learn how to do the following:

- Create a generic rug on the floor.
- Find and import a sofa and coffee table.
- Add a floor lamp.
- Add accent chairs.
- Add a console table.
- Add a painting.

NOTE

While the 3D Warehouse probably has models of nearly anything you could want, it doesn't contain every piece of furniture on Earth. So in Chapters 3 and 4, you will learn how to create your own models for furniture and accessories.

2.1 Create a Generic Rug

In this chapter, you'll continue working on the room that you created in Chapter 1. Assuming that you don't want to cover the room's entire floor with wall-to-wall carpet, you'll need a rug. There are ways to create or import a specific rug with a specific design, but in this section, you'll create a generic rug painted with one of SketchUp's default materials.

1 Continue with the room that you created in Chapter 1. As a reminder, just for the sake of orientation, the longer walls (the wall with the door and the wall with two windows) are parallel to the red axis, as shown in Figure 2-1.

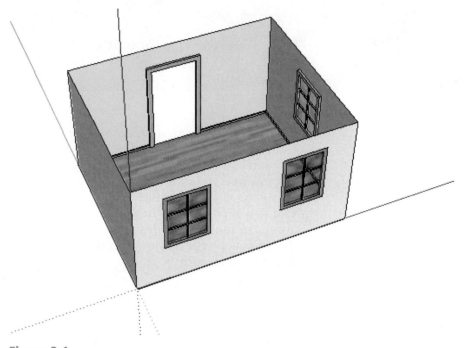

Figure 2-1

2 Assuming that you're still working in the "Beginning Training" template chosen in Chapter 1, you'll see thick profile edges around the outside edges of objects. To make the edge display more uniform, choose **View/Edge Style/Profiles** to turn them off. Now all edges should look uniformly thin.

3 The size of the rug will be 10′ × 6′. Use the **Rectangle** tool to create a correctly sized rectangle, anywhere along the floor. Then use the **Move** tool with direction locking to center the rectangle in the room as shown in Figure 2-2. (Remember to first select the rectangle, then activate the **Move** tool. Click the midpoint of the longer rug edge and move it in the red direction. Lock this direction, and then click the midpoint of the longer wall. Do the same in the green direction.)

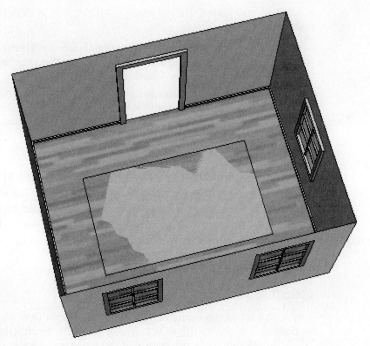

Figure 2-2

4 To paint the rug, choose a material from the "Carpet and Textile" collection (a checkerboard pattern is shown in Figure 2-3). To eliminate any confusion about where the rug is located relative to the floor, use **Push/Pull** to pull up the rug by a very small amount, such as ¼″ (which can be entered as 0.25 or ¼).

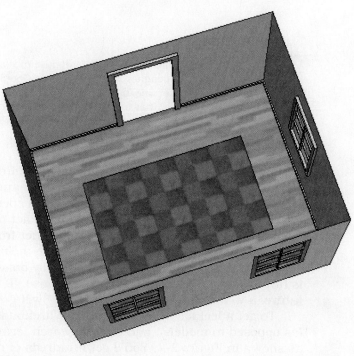

Figure 2-3

5. As a rule of thumb, any piece of furniture should be made into a group or component. As mentioned in Chapter 1, an object that is used only one time can be a group, while objects used repeatedly, such as windows, books, shelves, and so forth, should be components. Because there's only one rug, select it and make it into a group.

2.2 Add a Sofa and a Coffee Table

Now comes the fun part—finding all of the furniture and accessories that you love by searching the 3D Warehouse. This warehouse is basically a repository of models created and submitted by the SketchUp community. Anyone with a Google account can upload his or her models (however, there are file size limitations, as well as restrictions on offensive content), and anyone can download anything because models in the 3D Warehouse are in the public domain.

While most 3D Warehouse models come from individual users, a growing number are uploaded by manufacturers and designers who want their models to be easily found. So if you want a specific IKEA chair or Kitchen Aid appliance, you can probably find its exact model.

You can access the 3D Warehouse either from your Internet browser or from within SketchUp. Both methods have their advantages, but an initial exploration of the warehouse is more easily done from the browser. The URL is http://sketchup.google.com/3dwarehouse. (If this URL changes in the future, a web search for "3D Warehouse" will get you to the right place.)

To get a feel for what's in the 3D Warehouse, do a search for collections (as opposed to models), and enter a search term like "furniture designers," as shown in Figure 2-4. You'll get hundreds of results, many of which come directly from manufacturers.

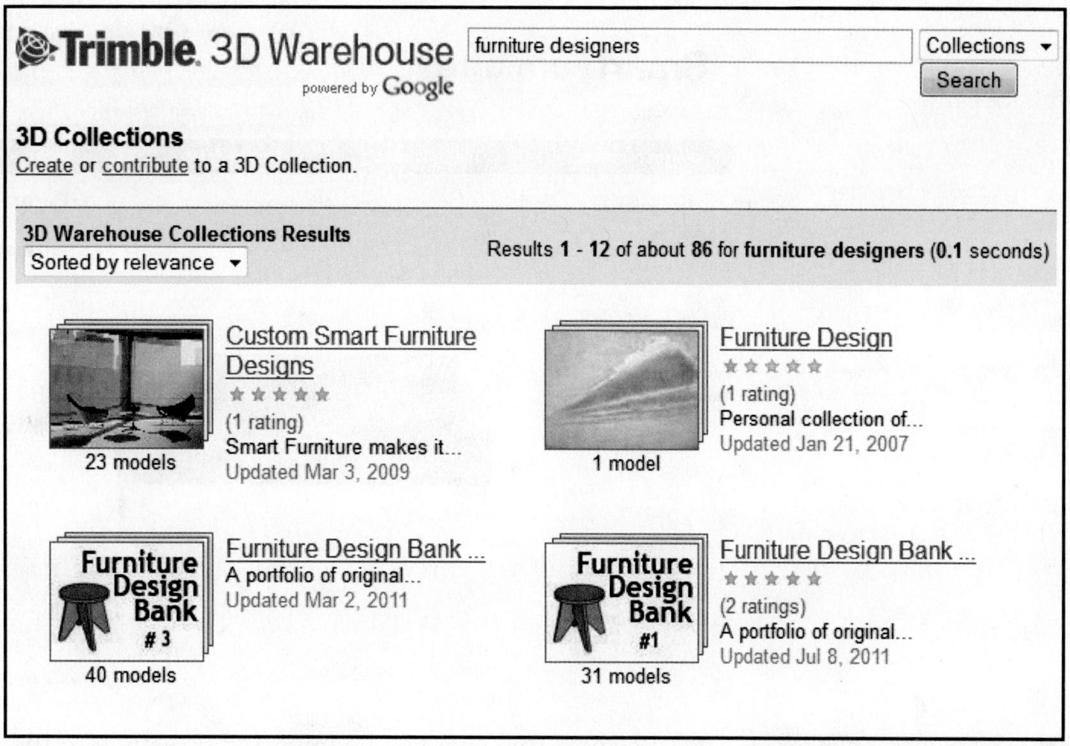

Figure 2-4

If there's a manufacturer that you like, such as Pottery Barn or Ethan Allen, do a search using the company name, either for models or collections. (Not all manufacturers have created 3D Warehouse collections, but you'll probably have some luck with a model search.) Be careful with the models that you get which aren't uploaded by the manufacturer because there's no guarantee that the model will be exactly like what it's supposed to represent. If a particular manufacturer has a limited presence in the 3D Warehouse, or no presence at all, you can try to convince the company's marketing department to hire a modeler (such as yourself?) to help get its pieces more easily into the hands (or computers) of interior designers.

When looking for a sofa, if you do a general model search for "sofa" or "couch," you'll get so many results that it would take you days to sift through them all. So for a common object like this, it's better to start from a known point—a specific sofa. If the exact piece you want doesn't exist (yet) in the 3D Warehouse, you can probably find something similar by another manufacturer. The SketchUp model that you show a client doesn't need to be painstakingly exact; a general idea of a sofa's size, color, and shape is usually sufficient.

NOTE

If you don't have a particular furniture manufacturer in mind, you can narrow down your search by using more specific terms. For example, try "chaise lounge" or "settee." You'll still get dozens of results, but far fewer than if you had used a generic term like "sofa."

The sofa chosen for this room is Paramount Medium by Blu Dot, a manufacturer that has many of its models in the 3D Warehouse, modeled in SketchUp by furniture distributor SmartFurniture. Figure 2-5 shows information on this sofa from the SmartFurniture website.

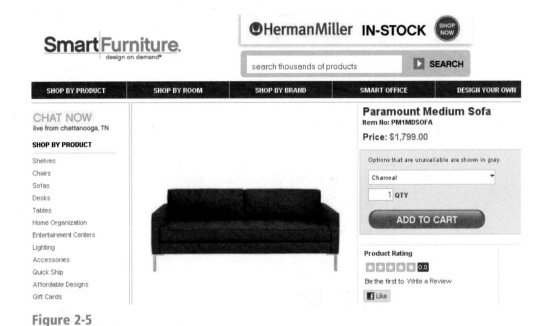

Figure 2-5

Figure 2-6

1 Because this sofa will be imported directly into the room model, we'll search the 3D Warehouse from within SketchUp. Click the **Get Models** icon shown in Figure 2-6.

2 In the search field, enter "blu dot paramount" (Figure 2-7). This results in the model shown in Figure 2-8 (the only relevant result, at least at the time of this writing).

Figure 2-7

Figure 2-8

3 If you know that this is the exact model you need, and you don't need to see any more information or details, you could click on the Download Model link to bring the sofa directly into the room. But instead, we'll check out the sofa in more detail before downloading. Click on either the thumbnail (the small picture of the model) itself, or click on the model's name. This opens the model's details page, shown in Figure 2-9. On this page, you can see the model's ratings, read reviews (which shouldn't always be taken too seriously), and see links for similar models and collections. To turn the model around, you can click the 3D View button and drag the mouse to the left and the right.

Figure 2-9

> **NOTE**
>
> One disadvantage of accessing the 3D Warehouse from within SketchUp is that you can't find out the file size of the model. Importing too many large models will cause your overall model to perform slowly, so it's best to bring in models of the smallest possible file size. However, you can see a model's file size if you search the 3D Warehouse from your web browser; file size information will appear when you click the Download Model button on the model's details page.

4 To import the sofa, click the large Download Model button below the sofa's image. You'll see a prompt asking you whether you want to bring it directly into the model; click Yes or OK. (The alternative is to save the model as its own file on your hard drive.) In the room model, the sofa is now attached to your cursor, as shown in Figure 2-10.

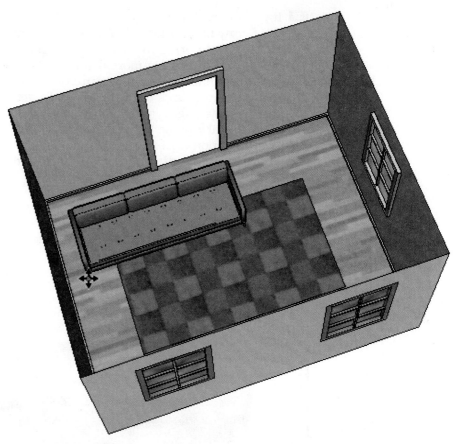

Figure 2-10

Figure 2-11

5 Click anywhere on the floor to place the sofa. It is imported as a component and is highlighted because it is selected (leave it selected for now). When you import a model into another model in this manner, SketchUp assumes that you'll want to adjust the imported object's location and/or orientation, so the **Move** tool becomes active (Figure 2-11).

6 An imported model can be both moved and rotated while the **Move** tool is active. We want to place this sofa along the long wall that has the two windows, so it needs to be turned around and moved. Keep the sofa selected, and move your cursor over the top of the sofa. When you hover over one of the red plus (+) signs, the protractor appears (Figure 2-12), which means that you'll be rotating the object. (These plus signs are called rotation handles.)

7 Click when the protractor appears, then move your mouse to rotate the sofa 180 degrees (keep an eye on the **Angle** field at the lower right corner; the rotation angle that appears may read 0, 90, 270, or 180, depending on which rotation handle you clicked). Click again to complete the rotation. Then orbit around to face the wall with the windows, and move the sofa as shown in Figure 2-13.

When moving the sofa into place, you'll probably need to move it using a few iterations, while also adjusting your view. For each move, it's best to click both move points on the floor (not on the sofa itself) so

Figure 2-12

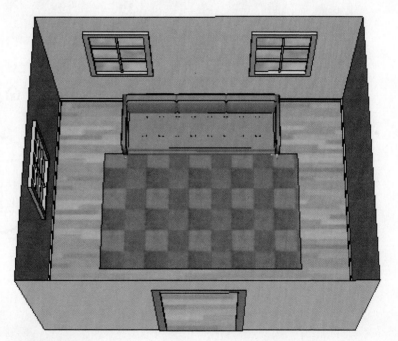

Figure 2-13

that you'll make sure not to change the sofa's height (it's easy to inadvertently move things up or down). Remember to use the Shift-lock or arrow keys to lock an axis direction. If you're a perfectionist, you can center the sofa along the wall. And if you lose your entire model view while orbiting around, use **Camera/Zoom Extents** to get back to an overall view of the room. When the sofa is in place, right-click anywhere in blank space to unselect it.

From the website that features this sofa, it's clear that this model comes in some other colors, but what if your client wants (or already has) an orange sofa? You could hunt around the 3D Warehouse for an exact model of an orange sofa, but an easier solution is to change the color of the sofa that you just imported.

8 First, we have to figure out which material in the model is the one that needs to be changed. This is called sampling a material. PC users: Open the "In Model" collection of the **Materials** window, and click the Eyedropper icon shown in Figure 2-14, then click anywhere on the sofa material (the upholstery, not the legs). Mac users: Sorry, you have no such Eyedropper icon. Instead, make sure that the **Paint** tool is active, open the "Colors in Model" collection, press and hold the Cmd key, and click anywhere on the upholstery. (PC users have a similar option: The Eyedropper icon appears when **Paint** is active and the Alt key is pressed.) On either computer, the gray material of the sofa is highlighted and made active, as shown in Figure 2-15.

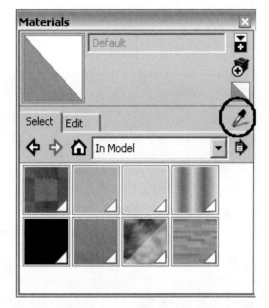

Figure 2-14

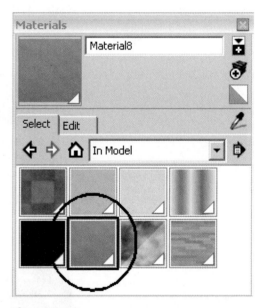

Figure 2-15

NOTE

This model only has a few materials in use, so it's rather obvious which belongs to the sofa; there's not much need to sample its color. But for a model with dozens of objects and materials, sampling can be quite handy.

9 To change the gray to orange (or whatever color strikes your fancy), double-click on the color swatch. On a PC, this opens the **Edit** tab of the **Materials** window, where you can change the color via the color wheel or color sliders, such as the HLS (hue, luminance, saturation) sliders shown in Figure 2-16. On the Mac, the **Colors** window changes

to the **Edit Material** window. At the top of this window, choose one of the color pickers, such as the color wheel shown in Figure 2-17, and set the new color. In either operating system, the sofa color updates in real time.

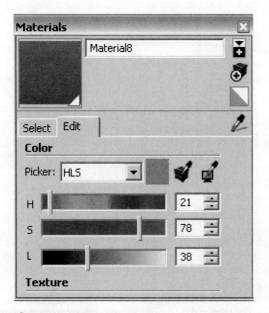

Figure 2-16

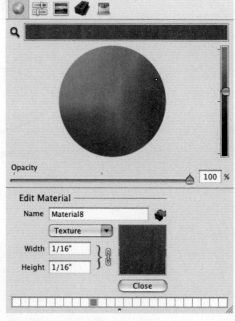

Figure 2-17

10 When the sofa has the color you want, go back to the **Select** tab (PC) or click the **Close** button at the bottom of the **Edit Material** window (Mac).

11 Now we'll add a specific coffee table. We've seen two ways to access the 3D Warehouse: from a web browser and via the **Get Models** tool. A third way to find models is by searching directly in the **Components** window. Open this window by choosing **Window/Components** from the main menu. Enter "noguchi table" in the search field at the top of the window, and choose one of the models presented in the list. The model by the user known as Martin is shown in Figure 2-18, but you can use a different one, including the one by Bonnie Roskes, which you may have to scroll down to find.

12 If you wanted to see the details page for this table, you could click the model's title. This acts like the **Get Models** tool. You would see a larger view of the model and have the option of downloading the model directly into your SketchUp file, or you could download it as its own file. But if you're sure that this is the model you want, and you don't need to see any more details, just click the model thumbnail. The model becomes attached to your cursor; click somewhere in the middle of the rug to place it (Figure 2-19). There's no need to turn it around.

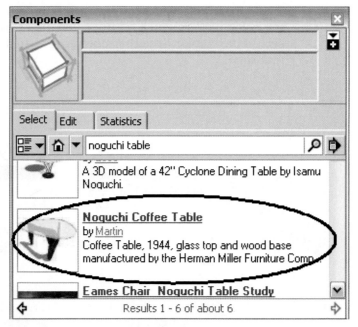

Figure 2-18

NOTE

Even though this table has an asymmetrical shape, you could still center it with respect to the rug (if that's important to you, because your client would probably never notice). Here's how to do this: While the model is still attached to your cursor, hover (don't click) on the midpoint of any rug edge, then hover over the midpoint of an adjacent rug edge. You would then move the cursor toward the center of the rug, and click when you see dotted red and green lines appear from both midpoints.

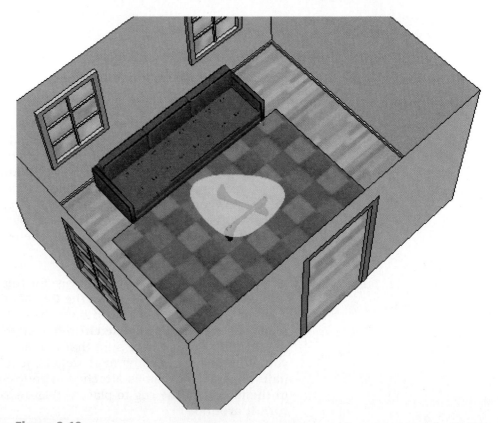

Figure 2-19

Note that the glass tabletop shown in Figure 2-19 has no visible edges. This is because Martin, the modeler, hid the glass edges before uploading the model. This was done by using the **Eraser** tool on the edges while pressing the Shift key, which we'll see in Chapter 4.

2.3 Add a Floor Lamp

In the 3D Warehouse, you'll find a lot of amazing models that will save you hours of work. But because it is a public exchange with no acceptance requirements, you'll also find models with problems, including the wrong size, wrong color, wrong alignment properties, extra objects, and so forth. The rest of this chapter will show you what you can do to fix some of the problems that you'll encounter while still making use of the models that you find. The problem that we'll run into with the lamp is that it has the wrong insertion point.

We'll also learn how to narrow down a 3D Warehouse search to get exactly what you want.

1 First, it would be helpful to remove from view one wall of the room to make it easier to look directly inside and see the furniture. Remember, the room is a group, so open it for editing.

2 We'll remove the wall that contains the door, so orbit to the view shown in Figure 2-20. Activate **Select** and drag a left-to-right selection window that encompasses the entire wall and door; no other objects should be completely inside this selection window.

3 Erasing this wall would certainly get rid of it, but then it and the door would have to be re-created later. Let's *hide* the wall instead so that

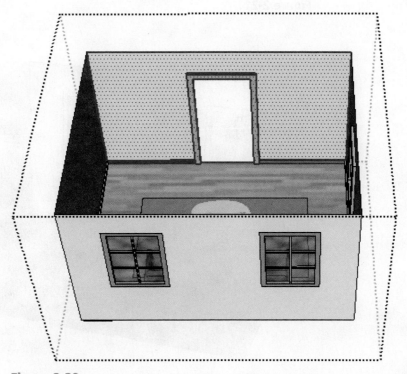

Figure 2-20

it can easily be brought back. Right-click on any selected edge or face (it's always easier to right-click on a face) and choose **Hide**. Now the room should contain only three walls (Figure 2-21).

4 Close the group and orbit to see inside the room (Figure 2-22).

5 Now we can look for the specific lamp with the specific problem that we need to resolve. Click the **Get Models** icon. Entering "lamp" in the

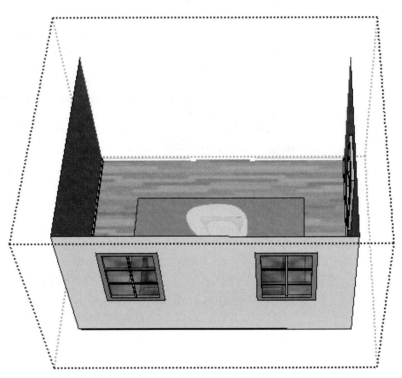

Figure 2-21

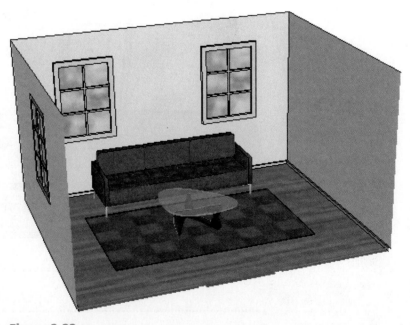

Figure 2-22

search field won't be very useful, so click the Advanced Search link shown in Figure 2-23.

Figure 2-23

6 Clicking the Advanced Search link opens a large and rather cumbersome window with numerous search filters that you can apply. For example, you can search for models with a minimum rating, models within a certain geographical area, or models with low complexity. In this case, we want to find a model that was uploaded by a specific author. Enter "floor lamp" for the title and "roskes" for the author, as shown in Figure 2-24. Then press Enter, or click **Search 3D Warehouse**.

Trimble 3D Warehouse
powered by Google

Advanced 3D Warehouse Search

Find results	Find items with all of these words in the title	floor lamp
	Find items with any of these words in the description	
	Find items with all of these tags	
	e.g.,"tea house" building	

Item type Find items that are ○ collections
Find items that are ● models with this complexity any ▼ [?]
find models with this file type any ▼
☐ Show only models that are in the "3D Buildings" layer of Google Earth
☐ Show only downloadable models
☐ Show only dynamic models

Rating Find items with this star rating or better any ▼

Author Find items by this author roskes
e.g., "AIA Colorado South"

Date Find items created in this time frame any time ▼

Figure 2-24

7 The search produces the single floor lamp model uploaded by Bonnie Roskes. But before importing it, look at the syntax in the search field shown in Figure 2-25, which specifies the title and the author. If you didn't want to bother with that large **Advanced Search** window, you could have entered this syntax directly and achieved the same results.

Figure 2-25

> **NOTE**
>
> You wouldn't actually have to enter that long string, including the quotation marks and colons. To specify the author, you could enter "floor lamp author:roskes," or even just "floor lamp roskes." It's a good idea to play with the Advanced Search features to see what the search syntax looks like, after which you won't need to bother with that huge window again.

8 Import this lamp into your room model. Move your cursor into some blank space (but don't click to place it yet). You'll notice that you're dragging the lamp not by the bottom of its base, as you would expect, but by the top of its base (Figure 2-26). This means that the original

Figure 2-26

floor lamp model was set up so that the top of the base meets the model origin, which is not very logical, but it is an error that you'll encounter quite often in the 3D Warehouse.

9 Knowing that the lamp's location can be adjusted later, click to place the lamp just to the right of the sofa. Obviously, the lamp's base comes through the floor (Figure 2-27).

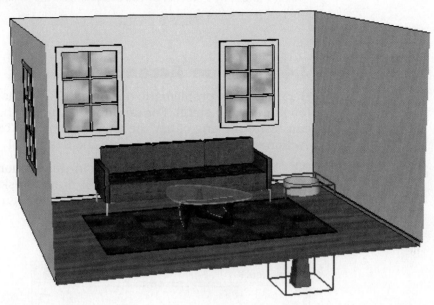

Figure 2-27

10 The **Move** tool is already active, so click any point on the bottom of the base, move up and lock in the blue direction (or press the up or down arrow), and click anywhere on the floor. The "Constrained on Line Intersect Plane" popup should appear (Figure 2-28).

11 Adjust the location of the lamp along the floor if necessary, and we're done with the lamp.

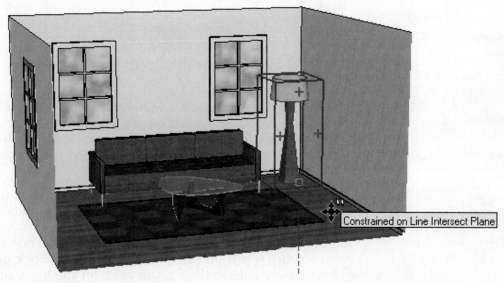

Figure 2-28

> **NOTE**
>
> Models with problems can, of course, be fixed permanently so that you won't have to make changes when using them in the future. Here's a good rule of thumb: If the model is a one-time download, make a quick fix after importing it and move on. But if the model is an object that you'll use over and over, download it to your hard drive (rather than importing it into another model), open the model in SketchUp and fix the problem, and save the file. Then you would use the **File/Import** tool to bring this model into future models, or you could upload the repaired model to your own 3D Warehouse account.

2.4   Add an Accent Chair

Here's another problematic downloading situation: a model that is either too large or too small. For an imported model that is the wrong size, you can resize it using either the **Scale** tool or the **Tape Measure** tool. This section will show you how to use the **Scale** tool.

1 To find the specific chair used in this section, open the **Components** window and enter "striped chair author:roskes" in the search field. You should get just one result, as shown in Figure 2-29. (Entering "striped chair roskes" would also work.)

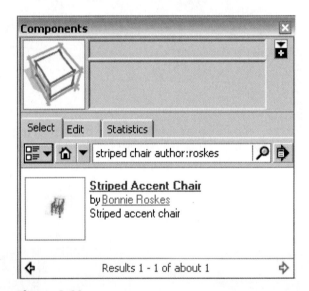

Figure 2-29

2 Bring in this chair and move the cursor into blank space as shown in Figure 2-30 (don't click yet). There are two apparent issues with this model: The insertion point is quite far from the chair itself, so it would be difficult to place the chair directly on the floor. Also, the chair is enormous.

3 Click to place the chair in blank space, then use the rotation handles to turn it so that it has the orientation shown in Figure 2-31. Move the chair into the room by clicking a point on the bottom of any chair leg (you'll have to zoom in to pick one of these points), and click again on the floor or rug. (If you click on the rug, the chair will be ¼" higher than if you click on the floor, not that anyone would ever notice.)

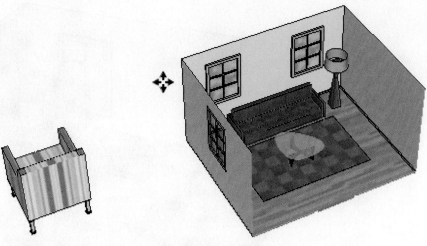

Figure 2-30

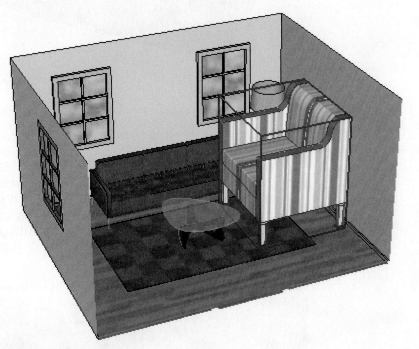

Figure 2-31

4 While the chair is still selected, choose **Tools/Scale** from the main menu. A set of green cubes appears all around the chair; these are called drag handles. Different types of handles do different things, depending on whether the handle is at a corner, in the middle of a face, or in the middle of any edge. We want to resize the entire chair while maintaining its proportions, so hover over one of the corner handles along the top, as shown in Figure 2-32. The "Uniform Scale" popup indicates that the chair will be resized equally in all directions; it will not be made taller, shorter, wider, and so forth.

NOTE

There is no icon for the **Scale** tool in the default toolbar that you see across the top of the SketchUp window. But you can display a more complete set of tools, which includes **Scale** and many others. PC users: Choose **View/Toolbars/Large Tool Set**. Mac users: Choose **View/Tool Palettes/Large Tool Set**.

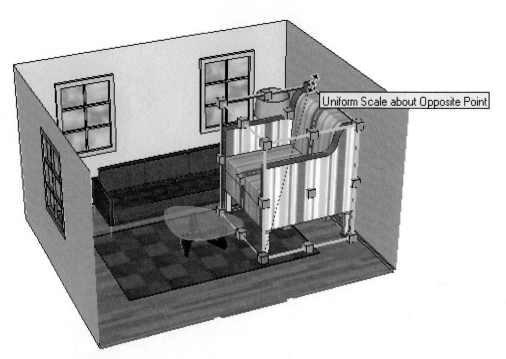

Figure 2-32

5 Click the corner drag handle and move the mouse to shrink the chair (don't click just yet). While the chair's size is changing, look at the **Scale** field in the lower right corner of the SketchUp window; it tells you the ratio between the new size and the original size. You could enter an exact value (0.45 would be a good scale ratio), or just stop when the chair looks about right. Click again to complete the resizing. You'll probably need to move the chair into place again once it's smaller (Figure 2-33).

Figure 2-33

6   To copy the chair to the other side of the coffee table, use the **Move** tool with the Ctrl/Option key, moving the copy in the red direction. Then use a rotation handle to turn the new chair around 180 degrees (Figure 2-34).

Figure 2-34

NOTE

These chairs look great, but they probably don't go so well with the rug, depending on the carpet material that you picked. A material's color can also be changed in a manner that is similar to the way that the sofa's color was changed. This will be shown in Chapter 6, along with other ways that you can manipulate materials and textures.

2.5   Add a Console Table

Now we'll look at another problematic model: a console table that is too small. This time, we'll resize it using the **Tape Measure** tool. We saw in Chapter 1 how this tool can be used for measuring and for creating guide lines. Resizing is the third purpose for this versatile tool.

1   The console table will be placed along the wall, next to the door, but that wall is currently hidden. Let's bring that wall back and hide another one. First, open the room group for editing and choose **Edit/Unhide/All**. The wall with the door reappears (Figure 2-35).

2   While the room group is still open for editing, select the wall with the two windows, plus the windows themselves, and hide them. Then close the room group (Figure 2-36).

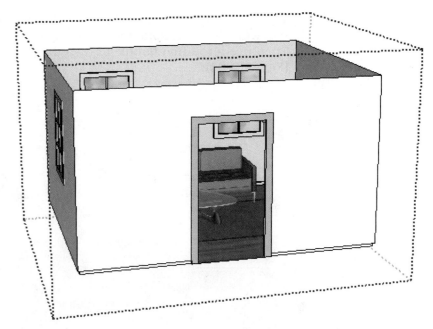

Figure 2-35

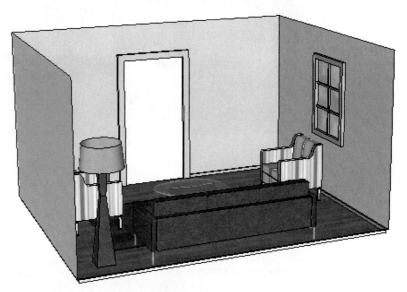

Figure 2-36

3 From the 3D Warehouse, find the console table model by Bonnie Roskes (the size of this table would make it better suited for a dollhouse). Place it to the right of the door (Figure 2-37).

4 What's going to slightly complicate the resizing of this model is that the vase and the phone on the table are themselves components. (A component within another component is called a nested component.) To verify this, open the table component for editing, right-click on the vase or phone, and choose **Entity Info**. This opens the small **Entity Info** window, which informs you that what you've selected is a component. Keeping this window open, select the phone, which is also listed in **Entity Info** as a component.

But here's the problem: The various components act differently in this table model. When the table model was created, the vase was imported from the 3D Warehouse (and scaled down to have the same incorrect size as the table itself). The phone, however, was created from scratch

Figure 2-37

on top of the table and made into a component (i.e., it was not imported from outside the model). The **Entity Info** window doesn't differentiate between imported components and those created from scratch, so there's really no way to know what you're going to get ahead of time. This difference will be evident once the table is resized.

5 With the table model still open for editing, activate the **Tape Measure** tool. The height of this table is supposed to be 30″, so we'll measure this distance and then set the correct value. First, if you see the plus sign next to the cursor, press the Ctrl or Option key to toggle it off. (Remember, the plus sign indicates that a guide line will be created, which we don't need.) Click a point at the bottom of one leg, then hover over the point at the top of the table, directly above the first point. The distance listed next to your cursor, as well as in the **Length** field, is about 10½″ (Figure 2-38).

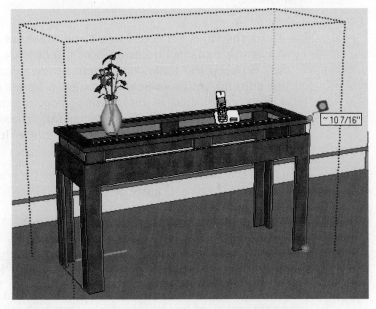

Figure 2-38

6. Click this top point, then type 30 and press Enter. You'll get a message asking whether you want to resize the component; click Yes. The table is now the correct size, as is the phone, which was created as part of the table model. But the imported vase component remains its same small size (Figure 2-39). (If the table model contained a group, the group would resize like the phone did.)

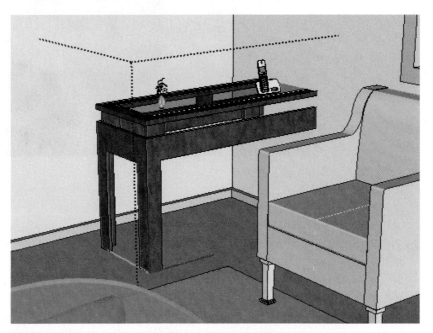

Figure 2-39

NOTE

When we resized the chair component, it wasn't open for editing, so why does the table need to be open? Because unlike the **Scale** tool, which works on only the selected objects, **Tape Measure** resizes *everything* that's accessible in the model. If the table component were closed, and you set the table height to 30″, the *entire room* would become three times larger. By using **Tape Measure** within the confines of the component when no other parts of the model can be touched, the resizing only affects the component.

7. To fix the vase, we could use **Tape Measure**, but that requires an exact value and who knows how tall or wide this vase is supposed to be? So keep the table component open, select the vase (don't open it for editing), and use **Scale** to make it larger (Figure 2-40). If maintaining proportion is important to you, remember that the table itself became approximately three times larger (from about 10″ to 30″). So you can watch for the number 3 to appear in the **Scale** field, or just type 3 and press Enter.

8. Close the table component and adjust its position if necessary; the table is complete (Figure 2-41).

NOTE

Another common problem with 3D Warehouse models is that they sometimes contain extra objects. For example, you can download a model of a car that also happens to have a person standing next to it. Or you can download a console table like the one used here, and you'll want to erase the phone or vase that's included on top of it. This problem is easy to fix: Open the component for editing, erase what you don't want, and close the component.

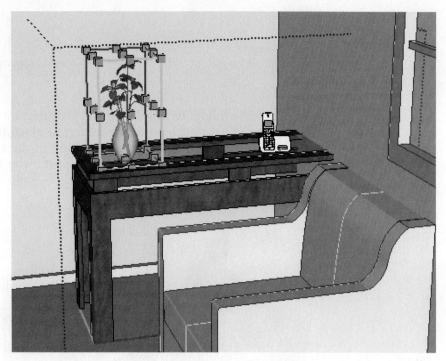

Figure 2-40

Figure 2-41

2.6 Add a Painting

In addition to issues such as proper size and insertion point, models such as paintings, wall hangings, wall clocks, and windows can have the additional characteristic of *alignment*. Recall that when you copied the window component from wall to wall in Chapter 1, the window aligned with any wall. But most SketchUp users who upload models to the 3D Warehouse that can be aligned don't perform the minor steps needed to set the proper alignment. So this section will show you what to do when you download a model that has not been aligned.

1 Find the model Orange Abstract Painting by Bonnie Roskes, and bring it into your model without clicking to place it. Move the cursor to try various locations for the painting. It does not align correctly with walls, and also has an insertion point away from the painting itself (Figure 2-42).

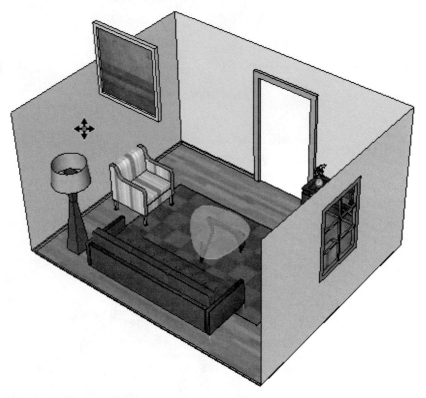

Figure 2-42

2 We'll need to do some work on this model, so click to place it in blank space. (Once the model is repaired, we'll erase this "hovering" model and bring in the correct one.) There are two issues to address: insertion point and alignment. First, we'll take care of the insertion point.

3 Right-click on the painting and choose **Change Axes**. The model's current axes are displayed (Figure 2-43), and they match the origin location in the painting's original file.

4 When working with alignment, it is crucial to understand the following: *The face in the model that you want to align with other faces must lie in the red-green plane.* Right now, the painting is vertical, parallel to the red-blue plane. So when we change the painting's origin and axes, we'll also be defining its alignment plane. Changing axes is done with three clicks: defining the origin, the red direction, and the green direction. For the first click, place the new origin at the lower left back corner of the frame (Figure 2-44) because this is the point by which you will want to drag the model onto a wall.

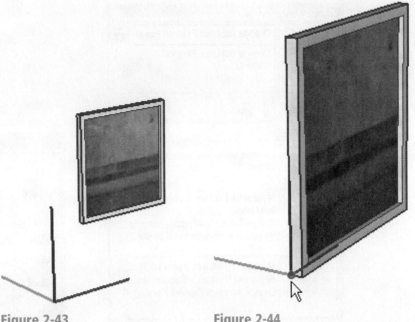

Figure 2-43   Figure 2-44

5 For the second point, we'll stick with the current red direction, along the bottom of the painting. Move the cursor directly to the right, and click when you see the dotted red axis line (Figure 2-45).

6 The third point defines the painting's green axis, which should go along the back of the painting. Move the cursor directly above the new origin, in what's actually the model's blue direction (Figure 2-46), and click. Now this becomes the green direction of the painting.

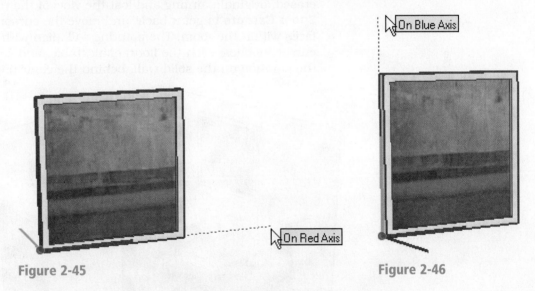

Figure 2-45   Figure 2-46

7 This painting is no longer needed, so keep it selected and press the Delete key. Don't worry, it's still stored in the model.

8 Now we'll set the painting's alignment properties. Open the **Components** window and click the House icon. As in the **Materials** or **Colors** window, this shows a list of all of the components currently in the model (Figure 2-47).

9 Highlight the painting model (click it even if it's already highlighted), then open the **Edit** tab. Next to **Glue to**, choose the **Any** option (Figure 2-48).

Figure 2-47

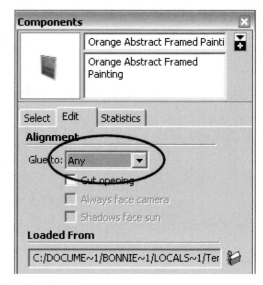

Figure 2-48

10 Move the cursor into the model, and the new and improved painting is attached to it, ready to be glued to a wall. If you had zoomed in on the erased, original painting and lost the view of the room, choose **Camera/ Zoom Extents** to get it back, and move the cursor along the various faces within the room. The painting will align with whichever wall your cursor touches, even the floor, chair, table, and so forth. Click to place the painting on the solid wall, behind the chair (Figure 2-49).

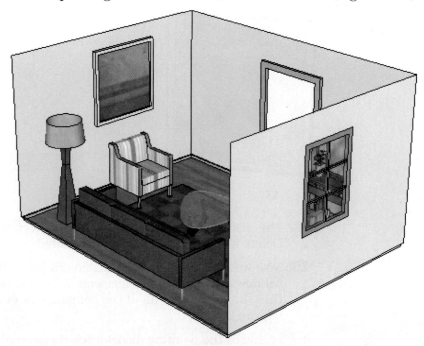

Figure 2-49

11 This room is now completely furnished, unless you want to dig around the 3D Warehouse for accessories, plants, and so forth. But we'll cover one last item in this chapter: a quick look at how the model can be displayed differently. From the main menu, choose **View/Edge Style/Edges** to toggle off the edge display. This results in a slightly more realistic look (Figure 2-50).

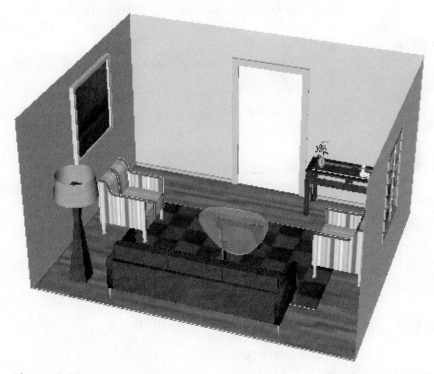

Figure 2-50

12 Use **File/Save As** to save your work.

Model It Yourself

Use the **Eraser** tool to erase everything from this room (except the room itself), and design a different room, one that has a different use, using models from the 3D Warehouse. For example, design a bedroom, utility room, or den. Don't forget to add accessories such as paintings, lights, and clocks.

Review Questions

- Describe the two ways that you can search the 3D Warehouse from within SketchUp.

- If you want to find a dining chair model created by someone named Jill Smith, what search terms could you use?

- Where can you find a list of all components currently used in your model?

- Once you import a model from the 3D Warehouse into a room, the **Move** tool becomes active. What are the two things that you can do to an imported model while **Move** is active?

- How do you find the material of an object in your model?

- How do you change a material's color?

- How can you temporarily remove a wall from a room that's within a group?

- If you import a model that's too large or too small, the **Scale** or **Tape Measure** tool can be used to correct the model's size. What is the difference between these two tools when used for resizing?

- When using the **Tape Measure** tool to resize a group or component, why must the group or component be opened for editing before **Tape Measure** is used?

- What are the two steps that you must take to make a model, such as a painting, align with a wall?

- What are some other types of objects that would need to have their alignment properties defined?

3 chapterthree

Basic Furniture: Straight Lines

As you saw in Chapter 2, the 3D Warehouse has models of just about any piece of furniture or accessory that you could ever want. But if you have a client with a very specific object in mind, which has not yet been created and uploaded to the 3D Warehouse, you may have to create the object on your own. (Of course, once you model something that is not yet available in the 3D Warehouse, you could do your fellow designers a service by uploading your model using the **Share Model** tool.)

The pieces discussed in this chapter are straightforward, common objects based on linear shapes (squares and rectangles). For each object, we'll locate its design specs from its online store, create a correctly scaled model in SketchUp, and save the model file so that it can be imported into a room.

NOTE

There are still a few products out there whose details can't be found on the Internet, such as your great-grandfather's rolltop desk. To model such an object, you'd simply have to take out your tape measure and produce your own specs.

Each piece of furniture in this chapter introduces a new design tool or technique, which you should be able to apply to any straight-line object that you might want to model. Then, in Chapter 4, you'll build upon these concepts and add some curves to your furniture models.

In this chapter, you'll learn how to model the following:
* Simple rectangular table
* Table with tapered legs
* Bookcase
* Buffet with drawers and glass doors

3.1 Simple Rectangular Table

In this section, we'll start with the easiest type of table, composed of only vertical and horizontal lines. But even the most basic model presents an opportunity to take advantage of SketchUp groups or components. This is the type of model that you could certainly find in the 3D Warehouse, but it's important to understand how to create it yourself. As we saw in Chapter 2, not all models that you find in the 3D Warehouse are perfect!

The table we'll model is Parsons Counter by Room and Board. This counter-height table (Figure 3-1) comes in a few sizes and options; the one we'll model is 60″ × 30″ × 35″ high, with a frosted glass top.

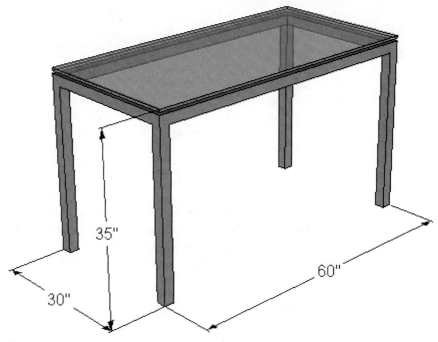

Figure 3-1

These are the details that we need for our model:

- The natural steel base is 60″ × 30″ × 34″ high.
- The steel pieces that form the base are 2″ wide.
- The overall table height is 35″.
- The frosted glass top is 60″ × 30″ × ½″ thick.

1 Open a new SketchUp file, using the same template used in the previous chapters, or any template whose base unit is inches.

2 We'll start with the steel base, then add the top later. It's easiest to start at the top of the base rather than the bottom, so draw a 60″ × 30″ rectangle, and then pull the rectangle up 2″, which is the thickness of the steel pieces. (Remember, as long as the base unit of your file is inches, you don't have to include the double-quote symbol for inches.) This thin box will become the top of the steel base (Figure 3-2).

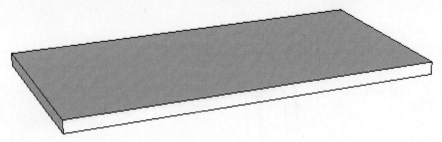

Figure 3-2

3 Orbit to see the underside of the box, and use the **Offset** tool on the bottom face, specifying an offset distance of 2″ inward (Figure 3-3).

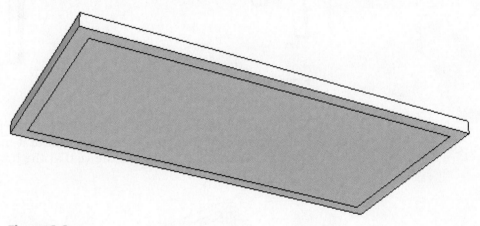

Figure 3-3

4 To outline the top of one table leg, draw a rectangle between the box corner and the offset rectangle corner (Figure 3-4).

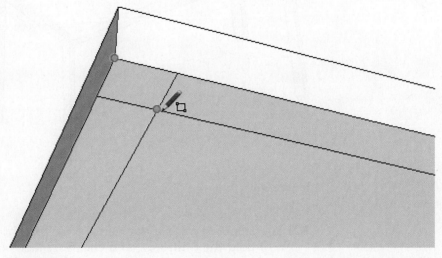

Figure 3-4

5 Repeat this rectangle (which is actually a square) for the remaining three corners, and use **Push/Pull** to pull each leg down. How far down does each leg go? The top of the base was already 2″ high, so we need 32″ more to achieve the overall base height of 34″. Here's a useful **Push/Pull** feature: Pull down one leg 32″, then simply *double-click* the other squares to pull those legs down by the same amount (Figure 3-5).

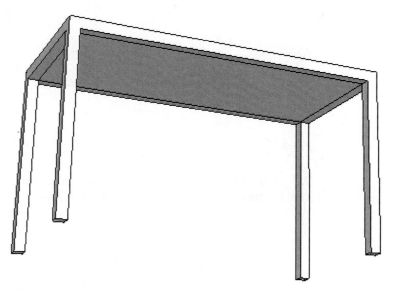

Figure 3-5

6 To complete the base, use **Push/Pull** on the offset rectangle on the underside of the top, pushing it up until it meets the top of the base (or just enter 2″). This creates the void at the top of the base (Figure 3-6).

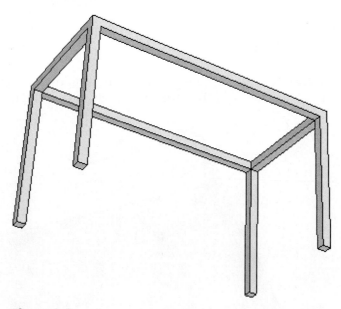

Figure 3-6

7 The steel base has a dark gray color. So choose a similar color, press and hold the Shift key, and click any face of the base. This paints all faces at once.

> **NOTE**
>
> Painting multiple faces can be done by pressing either the Shift key or the Ctrl key (PC)/ Option key (Mac). Here's the difference: Pressing Shift will paint all faces in the entire model that have the same color or material as the face you click, even if the face just has the default color. Pressing Ctrl/Option will paint all same-colored faces that are *contiguous* to the face that you clicked. Put simply, if you have several steel bases in your model, pressing Shift would paint all of them. Pressing Ctrl/Option would just paint the base that you clicked.

8 For models with more than one part, the best design practice is to keep the parts separated so that one part won't affect the others. (This is why, in Chapter 1, we made the room into a group, so that furniture and other accessories wouldn't "stick" to the walls and floor.) This table has two parts: base and top. So before continuing with the top, we'll make the entire base into a group: Select the whole thing, right-click on any selected face, and choose **Make Group**. The entire base is surrounded by a bounding box (Figure 3-7).

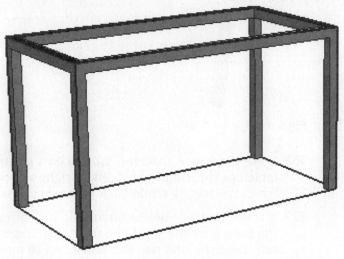

Figure 3-7

9 Now we can create the tabletop, which is ½"-thick frosted glass. Draw a rectangle that traces the top of the base, and pull this rectangle up ½" (Figure 3-8).

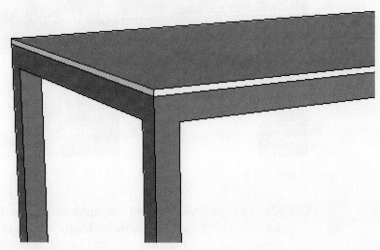

Figure 3-8

10 Find a gray, translucent material and paint the glass top (Figure 3-9). Again, use the Shift key to paint the entire top. This won't affect the base for two reasons: The base is "protected" within a group and, even if it weren't a group, the faces of the base already have a different color.

Figure 3-9

11 Make the entire glass top into its own group. (To select the entire tabletop, you could use a left-to-right selection window that surrounds the entire top, or triple-click any face of the tabletop.)

12 The overall table height should be 35″, but right now it's 34.5″ (34″ of the base plus the ½″ of the tabletop). To get the correct overall height, select the top and use the **Move** tool to move it up ½″ (Figure 3-10). Remember to move in the blue direction.

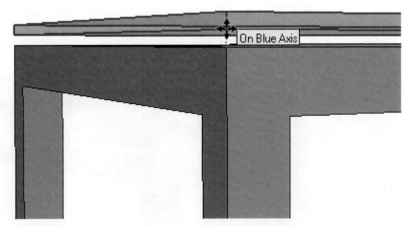

Figure 3-10

13 Always check your work! To make sure that the overall height is correct, activate the **Tape Measure** tool, and toggle off the plus (+) sign. Click a corner point at the bottom, and hover over the corner directly above, at the top. You should see 2′-11″, which is the same as 35″ (Figure 3-11).

Figure 3-11

14 The table is done, but it's important to optimize your model so that it will be easier to import later. If your model axes aren't displayed, turn them on by choosing **View/Axes** from the main menu. Unless you started modeling the base exactly at the origin, the table won't be located along any axis. Because we started at the top and worked our way down, the table legs are actually "below ground" (Figure 3-12).

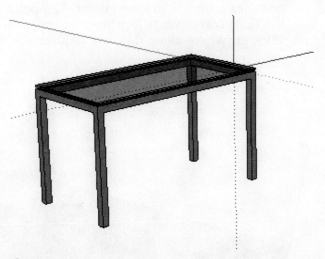

Figure 3-12

15 Select the entire table and activate the **Move** tool. Click a bottom, outside corner of one of the legs, and move the table by this point to the origin (Figure 3-13).

16 *Now* the table is done. Use **File/Save As** to save the model.

17 Now that we have a piece of furniture modeled, how do we get it into another model? To see how it's done, open a new SketchUp file and create a room (one floor, two walls), like the one you created in Chapter 1. Then choose **File/Import** from the main menu. Make sure that you are searching for SketchUp files as opposed to graphic files (Figure 3-14). Find the table model that you saved, and import it.

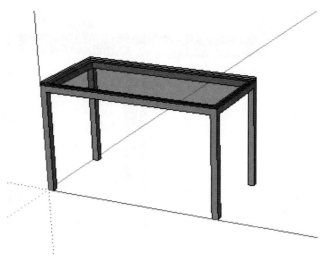

Figure 3-13

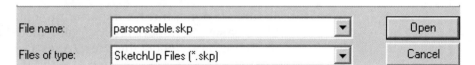

Figure 3-14

18 Just like when you import models from the 3D Warehouse, the table becomes attached to your cursor. The point at which you're holding the table corresponds to where the origin is in the table's own file. Click anywhere along the floor to place the table (Figure 3-15).

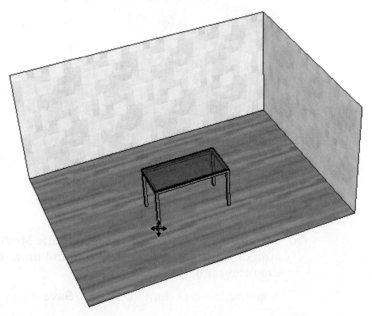

Figure 3-15

Just like when you import a model from the 3D Warehouse, this table is imported as a component. If you were to edit or explode the table, you would see that it consists of the two groups that you created: top and base.

Model It Yourself

Using the skills that you learned from the Parsons Table, create either of the following models:

Trig Desk by CB2 (shown in Figure 3-16 without its keyboard tray): Width = 40″, Depth = 26″, Height = 29¾″. Estimate the width of the steel base pieces at 1.5″.

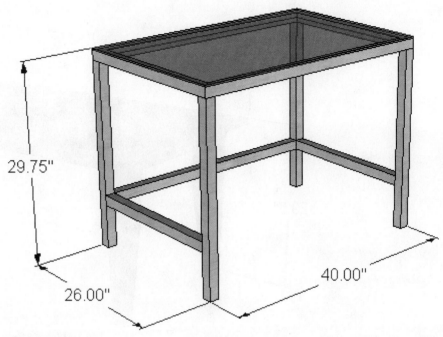

29.75″

26.00″

40.00″

Figure 3-16

Or model the Tavola Glass Table from Design Within Reach (Figure 3-17): Width = 71″, Depth = 31.5″, Height = 29.5″. Note the eight spacers separating the tabletop from the frame; assume that the glass top is ½″ thick and the space between the top and base is 1″. Use 1.5″ for the width of the steel pieces.

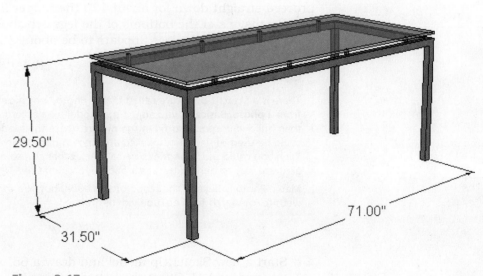

29.50″

31.50″

71.00″

Figure 3-17

3.2 Rectangular Table with Tapered Legs

Our next table has a feature that is seen in many contemporary furnishings: tapered legs. If we use the right modeling techniques, and take advantage of components, this kind of table can be designed quickly and efficiently.

The table shown in Figure 3-18 is the Basque Honey Dining Table from Crate and Barrel. This table is 65″ wide × 38″ deep × 29.5″ high; all other measurements will have to be estimated.

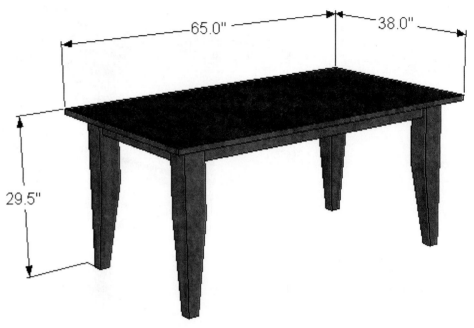

Figure 3-18

When you know the name of the piece you're modeling, it's not really necessary to get yourself and your tape measure to a specific store; estimated measurements usually work just fine. After all, furniture models provide an overall look to the layout of the room; your clients probably aren't going to zoom in and go over each table leg with a fine-toothed comb. We'll go with a 1″ depth for the tabletop, and because of the chunky look of the legs, we'll assume that they are 4″ square at the top. It looks as if the legs proceed straight down for about 12″, then taper inward. We'll assume that the dimensions of the bottoms of the legs are about 2″. The table overhang beyond the top of the legs appears to be about 3″.

> **NOTE**
>
> There is a SketchUp feature called Match Photo, which can be used to build a 3D model from a photo. Basically, you adjust the model axes according to points on the photo, then build your model to fill in the picture. Once the model is complete, the **Scale** tool could be used to size the model to any known dimensions (e.g., table height or width). Then you could use **Tape Measure** to check other measurements. It's not the most accurate way to design, but it's a good approximation.
>
> Match Photo is beyond the scope of this book, but you can read about it on SketchUp's website, or search for YouTube videos on it.

1 Start a new SketchUp model and draw a 65″ × 38″ rectangle, and pull it up (or down) 1″. Offset the bottom of this box 3″ inward (Figure 3-19).

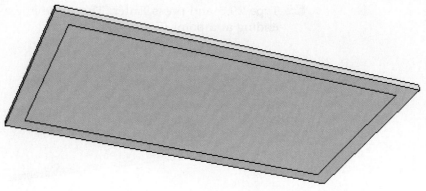

Figure 3-19

2 From one corner of the offset rectangle, draw a 4″ square (Figure 3-20).

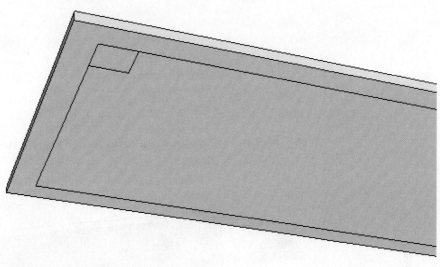

Figure 3-20

3 We know the overall table height is 29.5″, so we could use a little math when pulling down the table leg. But an easier alternative is to mark the bottom of the table with a guide line. We previously created guide lines that were parallel to existing edges; this time we'll mark a specific *point*. Activate the **Tape Measure** tool, make sure that the plus sign is there, and click any corner point at the top of the table. Move the cursor straight down in the blue direction (Figure 3-21), but don't click.

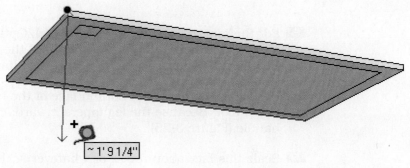

~ 1′ 9 1/4″

Figure 3-21

4 Type 29.5 and press Enter. The guide line extends to the correct length, ending at a point (Figure 3-22).

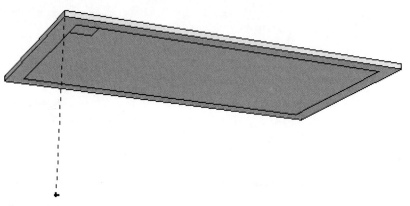

Figure 3-22

> **NOTE**
>
> You also could have clicked to complete the vertical guide line, then entered 29.5 to resize it.

5 Pull the table leg down about 12″ for the non-tapered portion of the leg (Figure 3-23).

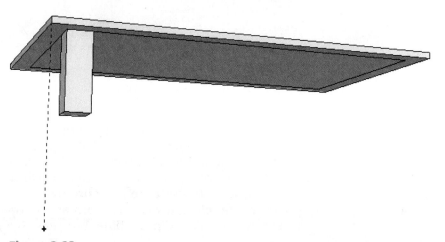

Figure 3-23

6 For the tapered portion, press the Ctrl/Option key to add the plus sign to the **Push/Pull** cursor, then pull the leg down again. To end the **Push/Pull**, click the bottom of the guide line (Figure 3-24).

7 For tapering: Select the bottom face of the table leg and activate the **Scale** tool. Because the leg tapers inward, click the inner corner drag handle (Figure 3-25).

8 Scale this face about 50%, or whatever scale value looks right to you (Figure 3-26).

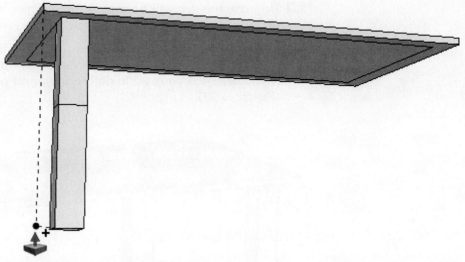

Figure 3-24

Uniform Scale about Opposite Point

Figure 3-25

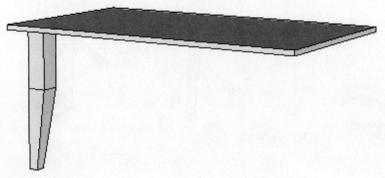

Figure 3-26

NOTE

What if you wanted to taper the leg uniformly from all four sides? You would use the same corner drag handle, but you would keep the Ctrl/Option key pressed, which enables scaling from the center.

9 Because this leg will be copied three times, select it (make sure that you do not select any part of the tabletop) and make it into a component.

10 Make a copy of this leg component in the direction of the long side of the table. Make sure that you stick to the red direction (or green, if you oriented your table differently), and place the copy anywhere (Figure 3-27).

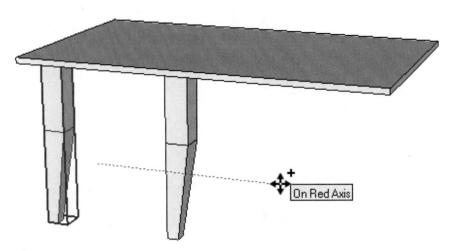

Figure 3-27

11 Now we'll look at another use for the **Scale** tool: mirroring. With the copied leg selected, activate **Scale** again. Click the drag handle shown in Figure 3-28, which will scale the leg in the direction of the long side of the table.

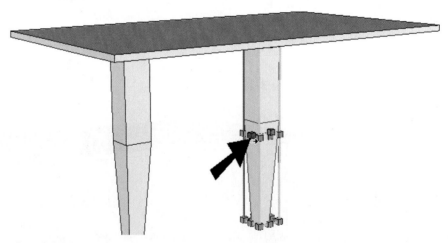

Figure 3-28

Red Scale -1.00

Figure 3-29

12 Move this handle into the leg itself, and keep going in the same direction until the leg turns inside-out. Stop when the **Scale** value is −1 (Figure 3-29), or type −1 and press Enter.

13 With the mirrored leg still selected, switch to the **Move** tool. Click the top, outer corner of the leg, and move the leg by this point to meet the corner of the offset rectangle on the underside of the table (Figure 3-30). Now the outward taper is consistent at both corners.

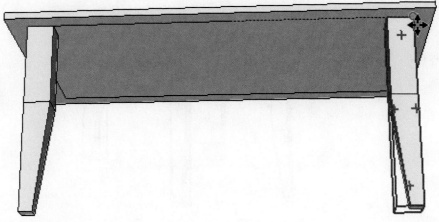

Figure 3-30

14 Now select both legs and copy them in the green direction (or red, if your table is oriented the other way). Place them anywhere in blank space (Figure 3-31).

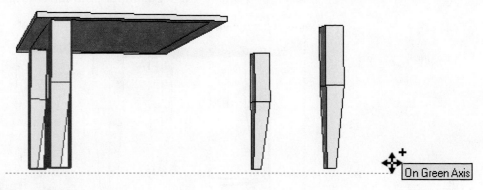

On Green Axis

Figure 3-31

15 With the two copied legs selected, activate **Scale** again. The drag handle to click this time is indicated in Figure 3-32.

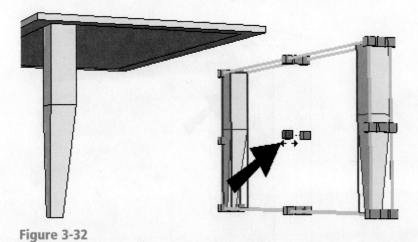

Figure 3-32

16 Scale the legs inside-out as before (using a scale value of −1), then move them into place (Figure 3-33).

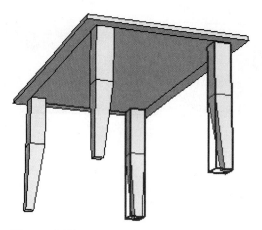

Figure 3-33

We're not quite done. In the photo of the table, we can see aprons that span between the legs, just under the tabletop. Because each table leg is a mirrored component, these aprons are quite easy to model (not that they would be so difficult to model on their own).

17 Open one of the leg components for editing (Figure 3-34).

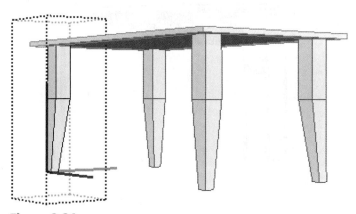

Figure 3-34

18 Draw a rectangle like the one shown in Figure 3-35. An estimated size could be 3″ × ½″.

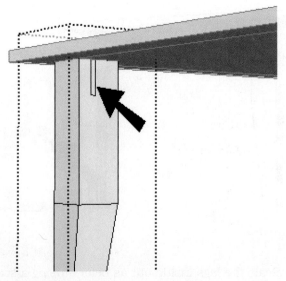

Figure 3-35

19 Use **Push/Pull** on this rectangle, and start to pull out the apron. Of course, because the leg's mirrored copy is on the other side of the table, the same apron extends from that side (Figure 3-36).

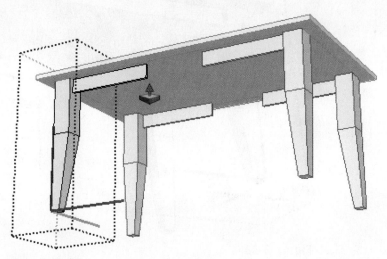

Figure 3-36

20 Where do we stop pulling? Even though we're working inside the component, we can still access objects outside the component. Click a midpoint of one of the tabletop edges so that both halves of the apron meet exactly in the middle (Figure 3-37).

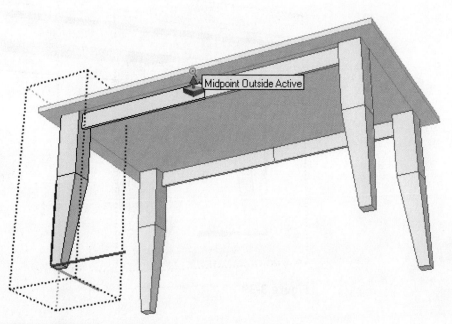

Figure 3-37

21 This is perfect except for the little edges that now appear in the middle of the apron. To hide these edges (there are three of them: front, bottom, and back), right-click on each edge and choose **Hide** (Figure 3-38). Don't erase the edges because this would erase the faces of the apron!

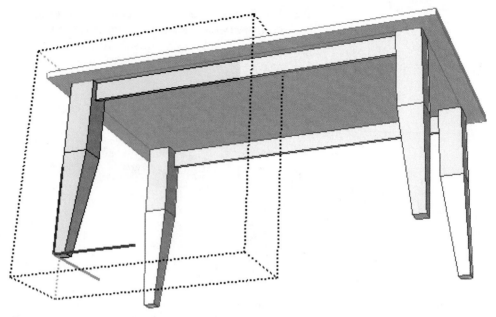

Figure 3-38

22 While the component is still open, we might as well also hide the edges between the tapered and non-tapered parts of the leg (Figure 3-39). You can use the **Hide** option, or activate the **Eraser** and press Shift while clicking each edge.

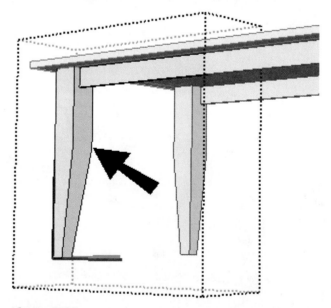

Figure 3-39

NOTE

As we've seen, edges can be hidden. Another edge display option is softening. The difference is that after the edges are hidden, you can still see the sharp corner where the edge was. When an edge is softened, any sharp corners are smoothed over, as we'll see in Chapter 4.

Hiding edges can be done with the **Hide** option, or while pressing Shift while erasing. Pressing the Ctrl/Option key while erasing will soften the edges.

23 The only thing left to do is extend the aprons in the other direction, then close the component (Figure 3-40).

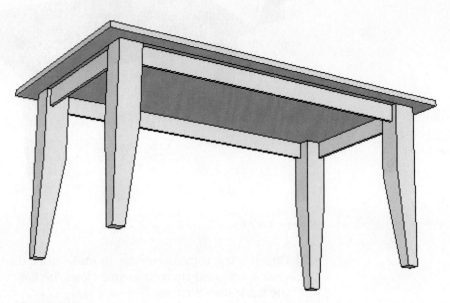

Figure 3-40

24 Paint the table with a dark wood material, and move it to meet the origin. Figure 3-41 shows the origin at the corner of a table leg.

Figure 3-41

25 When placing a table in a room, however, it's best to drag in the table by its outermost corner, which corresponds to the tabletop. So the origin should be directly below a corner of the tabletop. Move the table 3″ in both the red and green directions (remember, 3″ was the original offset on the table underside) so that the blue axis meets the tabletop (Figure 3-42).

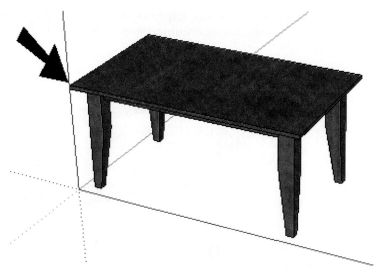

Figure 3-42

26 Check a few measurements to make sure that everything is OK, admire your work, and then save and close the file. You can also try importing the table into a room.

> **NOTE**
>
> The two table models that we've created so far both have legs based on a square cross section. At this point, you might be wondering how to model a turned leg, like the ones shown in Figure 3-43. This and other round objects, as well as extruded objects like mouldings, require the **Follow Me** tool, which is described in Chapter 4.

Figure 3-43

Model It Yourself

Using the skills you learned from the Basque Table, create a model of the Shaker-style table shown in Figure 3-44. This model is similar to the previous one, but the taper starts just below the apron, the legs have a small offset from the tabletop, and the taper at the bottom is more dramatic.

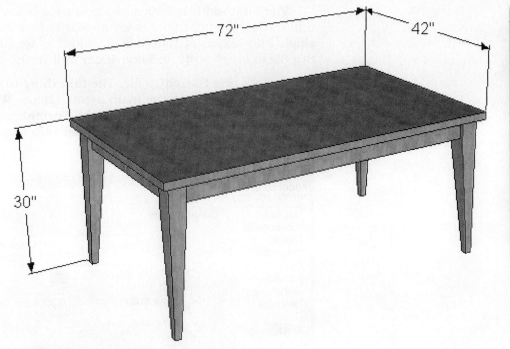

72"
42"
30"

Figure 3-44

3.3 Bookcase

The next piece we'll model is a simple and straightforward bookcase. Modeling pieces that have identical shelves can be simplified by creating multiple copies, which is another great feature of the **Move** tool.

This three-part bookcase, shown in Figure 3-45, is one configuration of Ikea's Billy Bookcase System. We'll model using metric units because they're so much easier to use than imperial units.

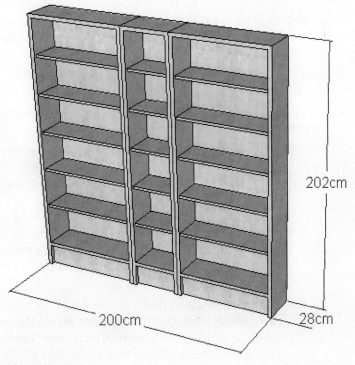

202cm
200cm
28cm

Figure 3-45

The total width is 200cm, so how wide is each of the three bookcase units? The two outer bookcases appear to be identical, and Ikea carries a single Billy bookcase that is 80cm wide. So we can assume that there are two 80cm outer units and one 40cm unit in the middle.

1 Open a new SketchUp file. The first thing to do is to set the correct model units. From the main menu, choose **Window / Model Info**. Open the **Units** page, and set the **Format** to **Decimal Centimeters** (Figure 3-46), then close the **Model Info** window.

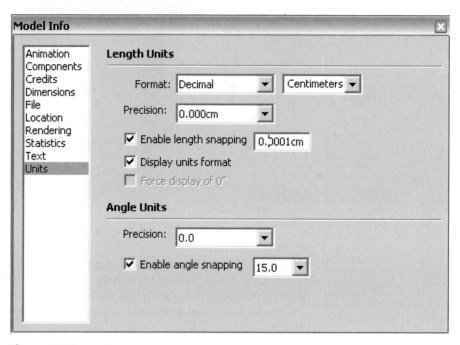

Figure 3-46

2 For the first outer bookcase, draw a flat rectangle 80cm wide and 28cm high. (Remember, centimeters are the base unit, so you can just enter 80,28 without appending any units.) Paint the rectangle with a light wood material, then pull the rectangle up 202cm (Figure 3-47).

> **NOTE**
>
> Remember, even if the base units of this file were different (e.g., inches or millimeters), you could still enter values in centimeters. You would just need to enter 80cm, 28cm instead of just numbers.

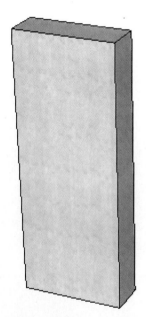

Figure 3-47

3 Use **Offset** on the front of the box to make a 2cm inner border. Then, to make space for the bookcase base, select the lower edge of the offset rectangle and use the **Move** tool to move this edge up by a few centimeters (Figure 3-48).

4 Use **Push/Pull** to push in the offset face. To avoid erasing the back face, make sure that you do not go all the way back or else you'll push through a hole. (Although, if you were modeling an open shelving unit, you *would* push all the way through.) Using a push distance of 26cm will keep a 2cm backing (Figure 3-49).

Figure 3-48

Figure 3-49

5 The photo of the bookcase shows five shelves and six spaces. It appears that each space has the same height (although these shelves are probably adjustable). Instead of calculating what each shelf height should be, we can simply divide one of the vertical edges into six segments. Right-click on one of the back, inner vertical edges, and choose **Divide**. Move the cursor until you get six segments (Figure 3-50), then click.

6 To create the first shelf, activate the **Rectangle** tool. For the first corner point, find and click the first endpoint from the top (Figure 3-51), which is one-sixth of the way down from the top.

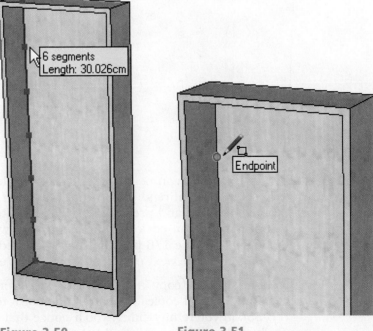

Figure 3-50

Figure 3-51

7 Click the opposite rectangle corner on the other side, creating a narrow box about 2cm high (Figure 3-52). The rectangle should be above, not below, the endpoint where you started.

Figure 3-52

8 Pull this rectangle forward 25cm, or just use your eye and stop just before the shelf reaches the front of the bookcase (Figure 3-53).

Figure 3-53

9 Now this shelf can be copied. First, use a left-to-right selection window to select the entire shelf, but not any other part of the bookcase. Then activate **Move** and press the Ctrl/Option key to copy the shelf. For the first move point, click the same endpoint where you started drawing the shelf: at the 1/6 point of the divided edge. For the second move point, click the next endpoint down (Figure 3-54).

10 Right after the copy is made, type 4x and press Enter. This creates four equally spaced copies instead of one, for a total of five shelves (Figure 3-55). (If you're nitpicking, you'll notice that the six spaces don't actually all have the same exact height because the shelves themselves aren't

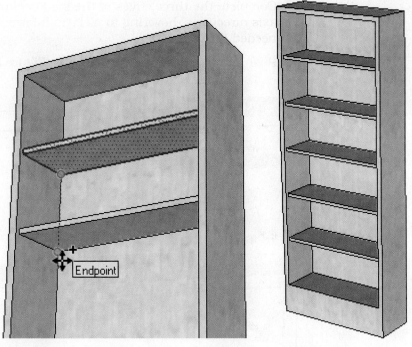

Figure 3-54   **Figure 3-55**

centered on those segment endpoints. But such a tiny difference falls squarely within the category of "nobody will notice.")

11 Now we can work on the base of the bookcase, a minor but easy detail. Activate **Line**, hover over the corner point indicated in Figure 3-56, and move the cursor straight down. Click when you reach the bottom edge.

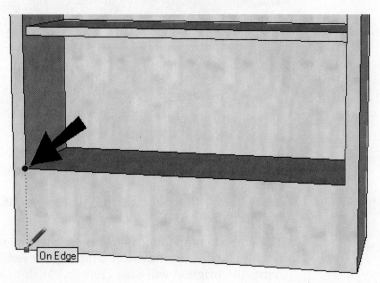

Figure 3-56

12 Complete the three edges of the base rectangle by drawing along the axis directions, hovering to pick up information from other points when needed (Figure 3-57).

13 Push this rectangle slightly inward (Figure 3-58).

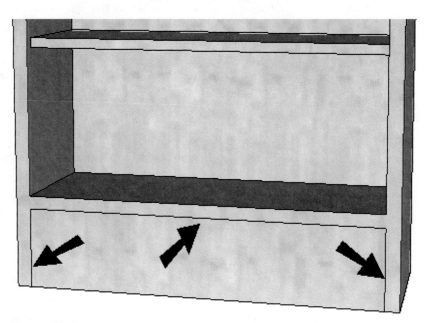

Figure 3-57

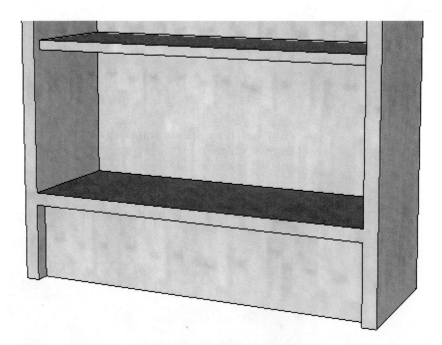

Figure 3-58

14 Make the entire bookcase into a component, and make one adjacent copy (Figure 3-59).

15 The copied component is to become the middle bookcase unit, which is half as wide as the outer units. However, if you change this component, the original will also change. So right-click on the copied bookcase and choose **Make Unique** (Figure 3-60).

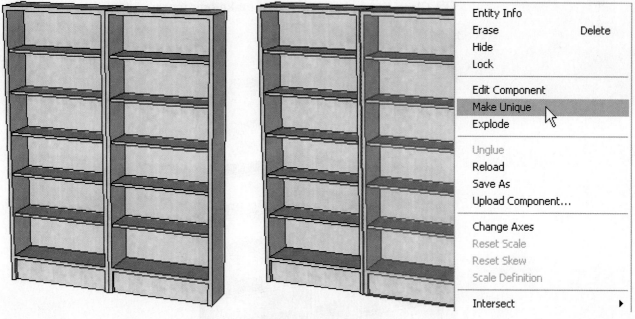

Entity Info	
Erase	Delete
Hide	
Lock	
Edit Component	
Make Unique	
Explode	
Unglue	
Reload	
Save As	
Upload Component...	
Change Axes	
Reset Scale	
Reset Skew	
Scale Definition	
Intersect	▶

Figure 3-59

Figure 3-60

16 Now, any changes to this component will not affect any other component. Open this component for editing, and use a left-to-right window to select the entire vertical board on the right side (do not include anything else). Then use the **Move** tool to move this board 40cm to the left (Figure 3-61).

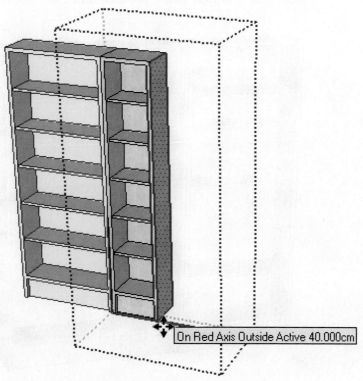

On Red Axis Outside Active 40.000cm

Figure 3-61

17 Close the component, then make one more copy of the wider unit (Figure 3-62).

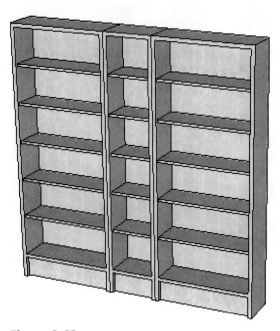

Figure 3-62

18 Make sure that the overall width is 200cm, move the entire object so that one of the lower back corners meets the origin, and save the file. Done!

If you wanted a more random look, you could edit each bookcase component and move shelves up or down, or take shelves out altogether (Figure 3-63). Of course, if you want the two outer bookcases to be different from one another, you'd have to make one of them unique.

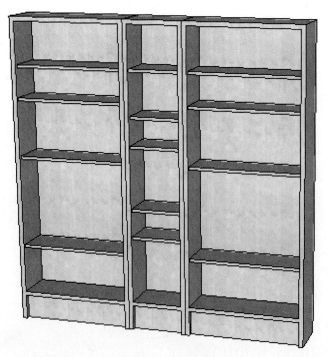

Figure 3-63

If you don't like the look of empty shelves in a room, you could look for books, vases, and other knickknacks in the 3D Warehouse and populate your bookcase (Figure 3-64). A word of caution: Loading up a model with tiny details can cause your file size to mushroom, making your model perform slowly when changing your view. So look for simple models, and use copied components whenever possible.

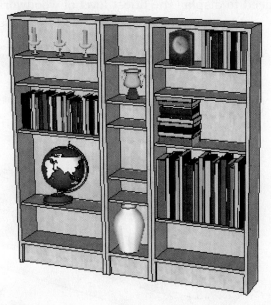

Figure 3-64

Model It Yourself

Using the skills you learned from the Billy Bookcase, create a model of a similar set of bookcases with extension height units (Figure 3-65). The center bookcase of the set is the same six-shelf unit that we modeled before, the bookcase on the left has one additional shelf, and on the right there are three fewer shelves.

Figure 3-65

3.4 Cabinet with Doors and Drawers

The last piece in this chapter will combine most of the concepts used so far in the previous models and will introduce you to a few new techniques.

We'll model Pottery Barn's Tucker Buffet (Figure 3-66). Its overall dimensions are 66.5″ wide, 16.5″ deep, and 35″ high. The actual piece has more decorative detailing than we'll be modeling, but furniture models don't need to display the finest level of woodworking detail.

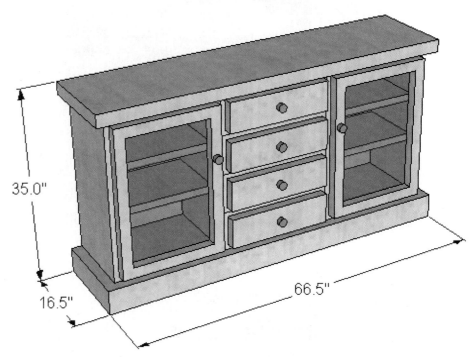

Figure 3-66

1 In a new SketchUp file using Architectural units (feet and inches), create a 66.5″ × 16.5″ × 35″-high box (Figure 3-67). Keep the default colors for now.

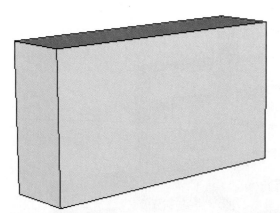

Figure 3-67

2 To model the top and base, use the **Push/Pull** tool with the Ctrl/Option key. Pull slightly down from the top of the box, then press Ctrl/Option again and pull up from the bottom (Figure 3-68). This results in both the top and bottom faces of the box being reversed; the back color is now showing on both faces. But painting will be done later, so leave the colors as they are.

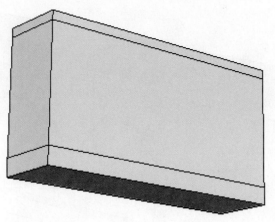

Figure 3-68

3 This time use **Push/Pull** without the Ctrl/Option key, and push in the side face just a bit. With **Push/Pull** still active, double-click both the front face and the other side face to push them in by the same amount (Figure 3-69).

4 Zoom in on the corner indicated in Figure 3-70. There's a small, extra edge that resulted from the **Push/Pull** of the front face. Use the **Eraser** to get rid of this edge, plus the other small edge on this face and the two others on the underside of the top.

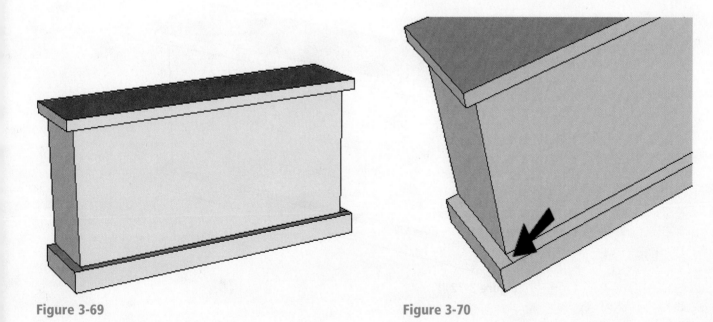

Figure 3-69   Figure 3-70

5 From the buffet photo and specs, we know that the piece is equally divided into three parts: glass doors and shelves on either side, and drawers in the middle. So right-click on the lower front edge of the main section (not the edge of the base), choose **Divide**, and break the edge into three segments. Then use **Line** to draw vertical dividing lines at the one-third points (Figure 3-71).

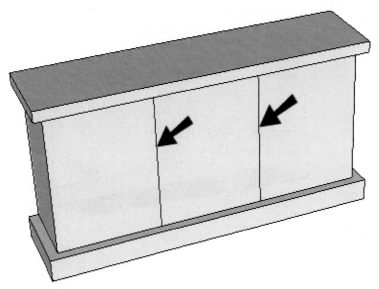

Figure 3-71

6 To model the drawers, use **Line** to divide the middle section horizontally between the midpoints. Then draw two more lines between the new midpoints. This creates the spaces for the four drawers (Figure 3-72).

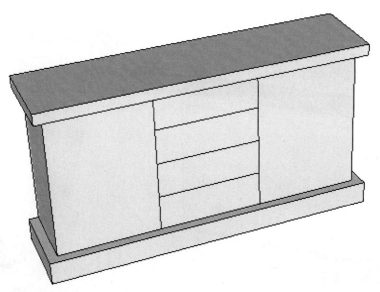

Figure 3-72

7 Use **Offset** to create an inner rectangle in one of the drawer faces. Just like with **Push/Pull**, double-clicking will repeat the last distance that you used. So keep **Offset** active and double-click inside the other three drawer faces (Figure 3-73).

8 Use **Push/Pull** to pull out one drawer just a bit, then double-click the other three drawer faces to pull them out the same amount (Figure 3-74).

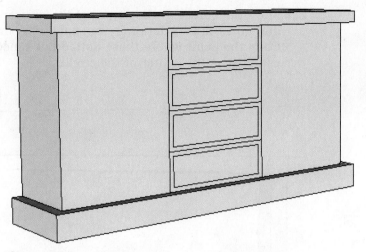

Figure 3-73

Figure 3-74

Figure 3-75

9 The drawer handles appear to be small, round knobs, but we'll simplify them as cylinders. Activate the **Circle** tool, indicated in Figure 3-75.

10 In order to ensure that the handle is perfectly centered within the drawer, we need to first place a couple of points in SketchUp's memory buffer. First, hover (don't click) over the midpoint shown in Figure 3-76, then hover over the midpoint shown in Figure 3-77.

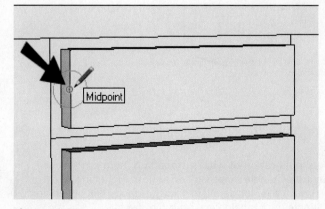

Figure 3-76

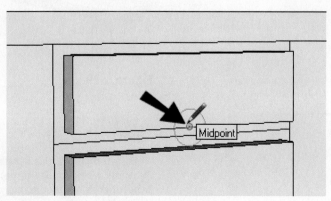

Figure 3-77

11 Move the cursor to the center of the drawer until you see dotted red and green lines extending from each midpoint that you hovered on. Click the point where these dotted lines meet (Figure 3-78), which establishes the center of the circle.

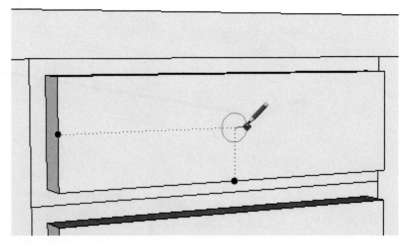

Figure 3-78

12 Click again to complete the circle, making it a reasonable size for a drawer handle. Paint the circle a solid brass or silver color, and pull it out slightly to complete the handle (Figure 3-79).

Figure 3-79

NOTE

As stated above, this handle is a simplification of what's probably a more ergonomic handle with complex curves. The actual handle shape isn't difficult to model in SketchUp, but there's no need to complicate such a minor detail; in theory, nobody will be looking closely at each drawer handle. Simple details help keep your file size low.

13 The handle will be repeated several times, so select the entire handle and make it into a component. Each drawer needs its own handle, so make one copy down to the second drawer. For the two move points, be sure to click similar points on each drawer, such as the points indicated in Figure 3-80.

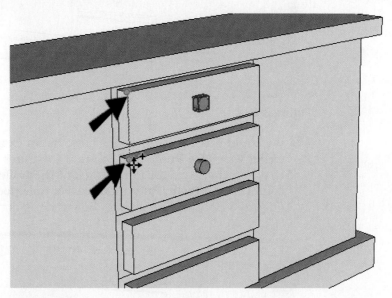

Figure 3-80

14 Type 3x and press Enter to create three copies of the handle (Figure 3-81).

Figure 3-81

15 Now we can start on the shelves on the two outer sections. Use **Offset** to create an inner frame on one face, then double-click the other face to create an identical frame (Figure 3-82).

Figure 3-82

16 We could push the inner face back by an exact amount, but here's an easier way: Use **Push/Pull** to push the inner face all the way back, clicking when you get to the back of the buffet (Figure 3-83). After you complete the **Push/Pull** and create a hole, look at the **Distance** field (Figure 3-84), which tells you how exactly far you just pushed that face.

Figure 3-83

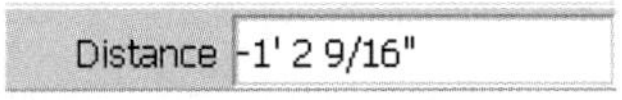

Distance -1' 2 9/16"

Figure 3-84

17 To change the push distance so that a bit of the back face remains intact, simply type a slightly smaller number than what appears in the **Distance** field. For example, if 1'-2⁹⁄₁₆″ is your through-distance, type 13 (13″ equals 1'-1″) and press Enter. This reduces the push distance and brings back the back of the buffet (Figure 3-85).

Figure 3-85

18 With **Push/Pull** still active, double-click the same face on the other side to push it in by the same amount (Figure 3-86).

Figure 3-86

19 In the empty spaces on either side of the drawers, erase the horizontal edges along the inner walls.

20 Now we can create the shelves to fill these empty spaces. Draw a thin rectangle along the back face, and either draw a second thin rectangle or make a copy of the first one (Figure 3-87).

Figure 3-87

21 Select both thin rectangles and copy them to the other side of the back wall. Again, for the two move points, click similar points on both sides (Figure 3-88).

22 Pull each shelf forward by the same amount, stopping just before the front of the buffet (Figure 3-89).

23 All that's missing now are the glass doors. But first, so that the doors won't "stick" to the buffet, select everything that you've made so far and make it into a group.

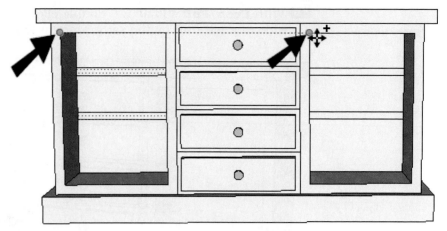

Figure 3-88

Figure 3-89

24 Then choose a wood material and click anywhere on the group (don't open the group for editing). Every face that wasn't already painted (in other words, everything but the drawer handles) gets the new material (Figure 3-90).

Figure 3-90

25 On the left section with shelves, draw a rectangle on the front representing the outer border of the glass door (Figure 3-91). This rectangle should be slightly offset inside the outer border of this section, but you can't use the **Offset** tool on any face that's locked away inside a group. So just estimate the rectangle's location by sight.

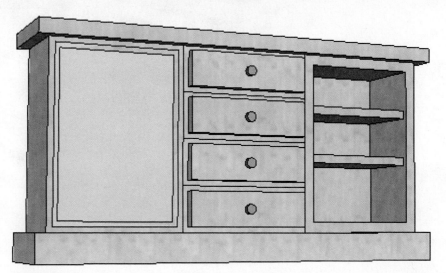

Figure 3-91

26 Now use **Offset** on the rectangle that you just created to make the inner rectangle that will become the glass (Figure 3-92).

Figure 3-92

27 Paint the inner face with glass, and paint the frame face with the same wood that you used for the rest of the buffet. Then pull the frame out to the same depth as the drawers (Figure 3-93).

28 We're almost done! Each glass door needs a handle, and we already have a handle for each drawer. To copy this handle, first open the buffet group for editing, and select any handle (Figure 3-94). From the main menu, choose **Edit / Copy**. (You can also use the standard keyboard shortcut for copying: Ctrl+C on a PC, Cmd+A on a Mac.)

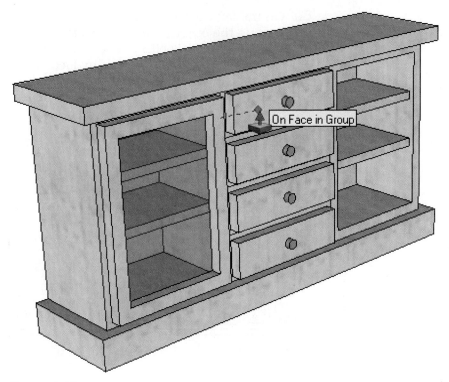

Figure 3-93

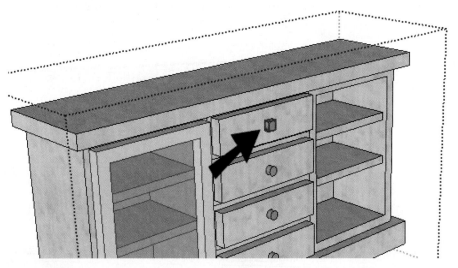

Figure 3-94

29 Close the buffet group, then paste the handle using **Edit / Paste**, or Ctrl/Cmd+V. Place the handle on the frame of the glass door (Figure 3-95).

30 Because the door is to be repeated on the other side, it should be made into a component. Activate **Select** and *triple-click* on any face of the door, which selects the whole door and nothing else. Make sure that the door's handle is also selected, then make the entire door into a component.

Figure 3-95

31 Copy the door to the other side, again using similar move points (Figure 3-96).

Figure 3-96

32 The handle of the copied door is on the wrong side. We already saw how to use the **Scale** tool to turn objects inside-out, but if we do that here, we'll move the door out of its location, and it will be difficult to put it back correctly. So instead, right-click on the copied door and choose **Flip Along / Component's Red**, which is another way of mirroring an object (Figure 3-97).

33 That's it! Move the model so that the back corner meets the origin, and save the file.

Figure 3-97

Model It Yourself

Using the skills that you learned from the Tucker Buffet, create a model of Crate and Barrel's Kavari Media-Storage Console (Figure 3-98, 57″ wide × 21″ deep × 36″ high). The exact spacing isn't crucial; just make sure that there are two glass doors and one set of three drawers, spaced approximately equally. Inside the glass doors are three shelves.

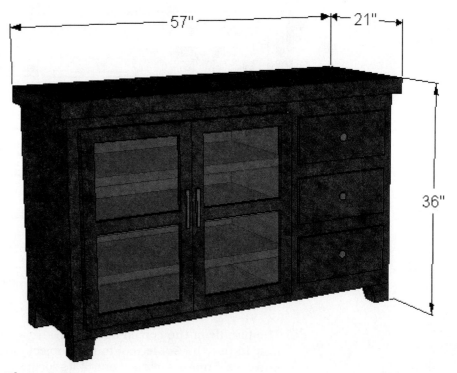

Figure 3-98

Review Questions

- How do you paint multiple faces at one time?

- When modeling a piece comprised of separate parts, it's always good practice to separate the various pieces into groups and components. What are the advantages of separating a piece into groups and components? When should a component be used rather than a group?

- Why is it important to locate a model correctly with respect to the model origin?

- How do you import a model that you created into another model?

- How can the **Tape Measure** tool be used to create a guide point, as opposed to a guide line?

- How can you use the **Scale** tool to make a mirrored copy?

- Describe two ways to hide edges.

- Where can you change the units of your model?

- How can you use the **Move** tool to make multiple copies?

- Which two SketchUp tools enable you to use them repeatedly with the same specified distance by double-clicking?

- Other than using the **Scale** tool to turn an object inside-out, what's another way to flip an object over?

4 chapterfour
Advanced Furniture: Curvy Lines

Now that you're an expert in creating objects with straight edges, we'll throw some curves into the mix. This chapter focuses on round things: circular tables, rotated copies, and rounded corners. As with the previous chapter, each object in this chapter introduces a new design tool or technique.

In this chapter, you'll learn how to model the following:
- Basic circular table on a cylindrical pedestal
- Oval drop-leaf table
- Table with a cross pedestal
- Table with a tubular base
- Glass oval table with a tulip pedestal
- Cushioned ottoman

4.1 Basic Circular Table

We'll start this chapter off with an easy table that comprises a circular top and base. All we'll need are three easy tools: **Circle**, **Push/Pull**, and **Scale**.

The table we'll model is the Orion Walnut Round Table by Crate and Barrel (Figure 4-1). The only dimensions we know are the 48″ diameter tabletop and the 30″ height. As usual, the rest we'll model by sight.

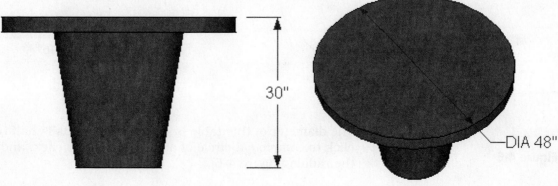

30″   DIA 48″

Figure 4-1

Figure 4-2

Sides 24

Figure 4-3

1 We'll start with the tabletop and work our way down to the base. In a new, blank SketchUp file, activate the **Circle** tool, indicated in Figure 4-2. We used this tool briefly in the previous chapter, but now we'll look at circles more closely.

2 Before clicking anywhere, look at the **Sides** field, where the default number of circle sides should be listed as 24 (Figure 4-3). Are you wondering why a circle has sides? SketchUp circles are really segmented polygons that look and act like circles. Unless you're using SketchUp for a highly sophisticated geometric model, this approximation of a circle works just fine. You could change this number if you wanted, just by typing a new number and pressing Enter, but leave 24 for this circle.

> **NOTE**
>
> Keep in mind that a 24-sided circle comprises 24 edges, no matter how large or small the circle's radius. Compare this to a rectangle, which has only four sides; round objects have a much higher object count than straight-line objects. A high number of objects can make your model perform slowly, so if you have a complex model with lots of curvy things, keeping the number of sides low can keep things running smoothly. For example, a doorknob can be approximated as a hexagon (six sides), and nobody will notice that it's not perfectly round.
>
> The complexity of round objects also makes a good case for using components. Consider a sphere-shaped drawer handle, which could have hundreds of faces and edges. Making just one handle into a component and copying it will keep many *more* hundreds of objects out of your model.

3 Click anywhere to place the center of the circle, and move the mouse (don't click yet) in either the red or green direction as shown in Figure 4-4. (It's good practice to always use standard axis directions when creating just about anything.) While you're moving the mouse, the circle's radius updates in the **Sides** field (Figure 4-5).

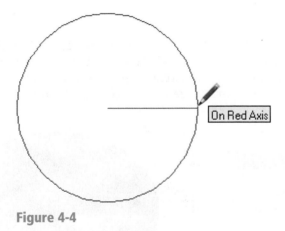

On Red Axis

Figure 4-4

Radius 3' 4 11/16"

Figure 4-5

Radius 24

Figure 4-6

4 The diameter of this table is 48″ and its radius is half that. So either click to complete a circle of any size, or don't click, and enter 24″ for the radius (Figure 4-6).

5 Use **Push/Pull** to make the tabletop 3″ thick (Figure 4-7).

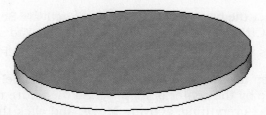

Figure 4-7

6 Now for the base: Orbit to see the underside of the base, and activate **Circle** again. We want the center of this circle to coincide with the center of the tabletop. But if you move your cursor around the tabletop, you probably won't be able to find its center. So hover your cursor over any point along the underside's edge (Figure 4-8) to remind SketchUp that this circle is there. Then move back to the center and click when you see the "Center" popup (Figure 4-9).

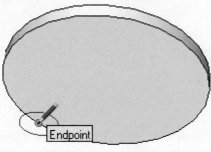

Figure 4-8

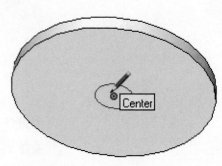

Figure 4-9

NOTE

SketchUp sometimes needs a gentle reminder about existing objects because it only keeps the last few points you've created in its short-term memory buffer. Hovering over a point bumps that point's object up to the top of the buffer. This isn't to be confused with SketchUp's **Undo / Redo** memory; you can use Ctrl+Z/Cmd+Z as many times as you need, going all the way back to the start of the model.

7 Click again to make a circle approximately as shown in Figure 4-10.

8 The tabletop takes up 3″ of the 30″ overall table height, so pull the base down 27″ (Figure 4-11).

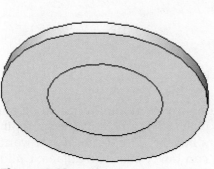

Figure 4-10

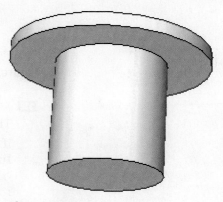

Figure 4-11

9 Select the bottom face of the base, activate **Scale**, and press and hold the Ctrl or Option key, which enables you to scale relative to the center. Drag one of the corner handles inward to slope the base (Figure 4-12).

10 When inserting this table into another model, we want to move this table by the center of its base. So the entire model has to be moved. Select everything, activate **Move**, and click the center of the bottom of the base as shown in Figure 4-13 (remember, you'll probably have to hover over an edge point before you can pick up the center).

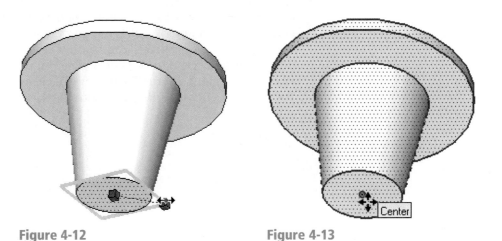

Figure 4-12   Figure 4-13

11 Then find the origin (use **View / Axes** if you need to display the axes) and click to move the table to the origin. (Figure 4-14).

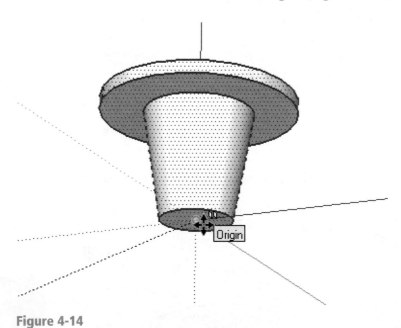

Figure 4-14

12 Find a dark wood material and paint the entire table (Figure 4-15). Then save the file.

If you create a room in another SketchUp file, you can use **File / Import** to place this table into the room; it will be dragged by the center of its base (Figure 4-16). If you want the table centered in the room, you can hover over two adjacent midpoints of floor edges (Figure 4-17 and Figure 4-18), then find the room's exact center (Figure 4-19).

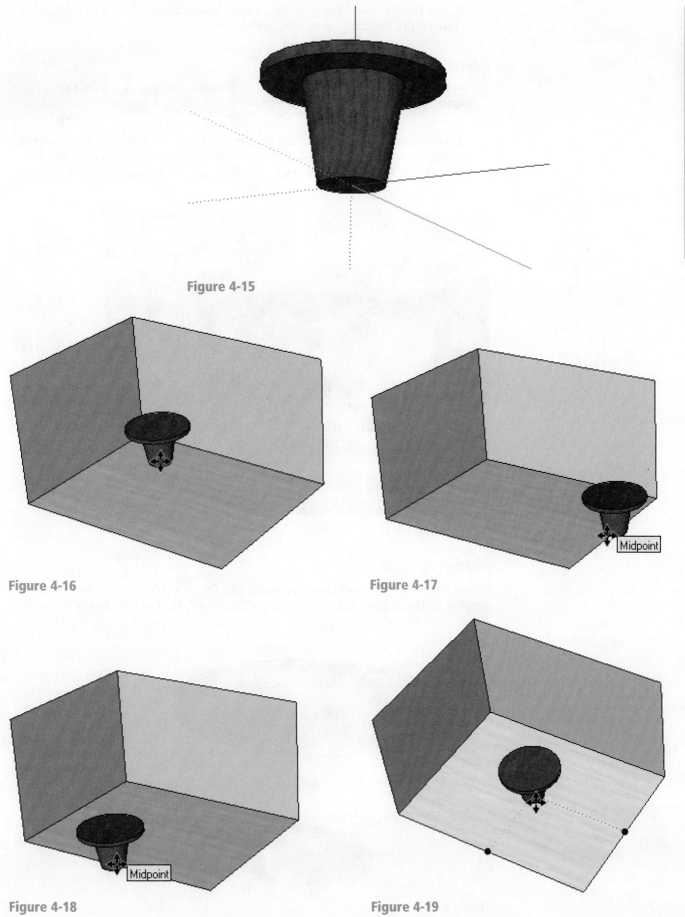

Figure 4-15

Figure 4-16

Figure 4-17

Figure 4-18

Figure 4-19

If you have a hard time finding those midpoints, it helps to orbit so that you're looking up at the underside of the floor.

You can also bring in a chair and make three copies of it, each facing toward the table (Figure 4-20). But later in this chapter, we'll see how to use the **Rotate** tool to make rotated copies, which makes it easy to place chairs around a circular table.

Figure 4-20

Model It Yourself

Using the skills that you learned from the Orion table, create the round version of the Billsta table from Ikea (Figure 4-21). The top has a diameter

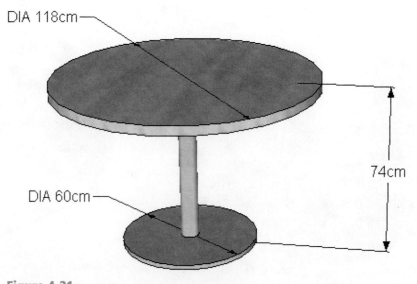

DIA 118cm

74cm

DIA 60cm

Figure 4-21

of 118cm and a table height of 74cm. Instead of starting with the top and working down toward the base, start with the base (estimating its radius to be 30cm) and work up to the top. The first circle that you draw should be the bottom of the base; if you place the center of that circle right at the origin, you won't have to move the entire model later.

4.2 Oval Drop-Leaf Table

There are oval tables that are true ovals (curved all the way around), and there are "oval" tables that are really rectangles with round ends added to opposite edges. For this example, we'll model the latter: the Hans J. Wegner Drop-Leaf Dining Table (Figure 4-22), which, at the time of this writing, can be seen on the Room and Board website, among other places. The rectangular part of the table is 54″ wide × 35″ deep × 28″ high. The two 19″ half-round leaves can be added to extend the table's width to 92″ (54″ + 19″ + 19″). Another feature to note about this table is that its rectangular legs taper down slightly and are splayed; they proceed from top to bottom at a slight outward angle. The important tool that will be introduced in this example is **Arc**.

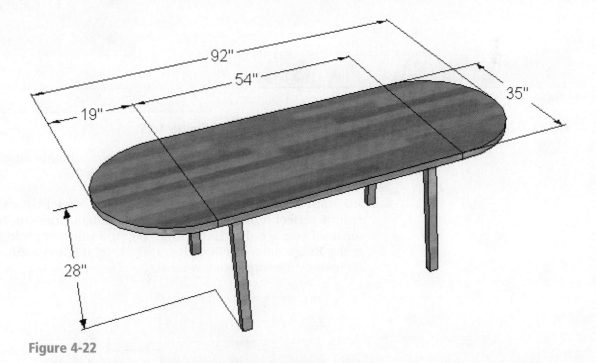

Figure 4-22

> **NOTE**
>
> If you're curious about creating a true oval, that'll come later in this chapter.

1. In a new file, draw a rectangle 54″ wide and 35″ deep (Figure 4-23). The 54″ side should be parallel to the red axis. It doesn't matter where you place the rectangle because when the model is complete, we'll move it to the right place.

2. For the first half-round extension, activate the **Arc** tool indicated in Figure 4-24. An arc is created with three clicks; the first two clicks define the arc's start and end points. So click Points 1 and 2 indicated

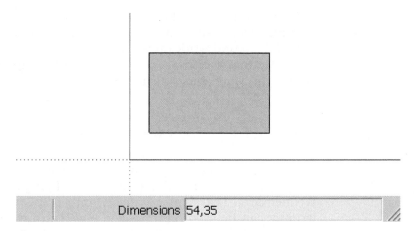

Dimensions 54,35

Figure 4-23

Top

Figure 4-24

Length 2' 11"

Figure 4-25

in Figure 4-25; the length between these two points should match the depth of the rectangle: 2′-11″, which equals 35″.

3 The third click defines the bulge of the arc. SketchUp enables you to draw a perfect half-circle, but there is a slight problem. Move your cursor until you see the "Half Circle" popup but don't click; instead, look at the **Bulge** field. The length is only 17½″ (Figure 4-26), but these extensions are supposed to be 19″.

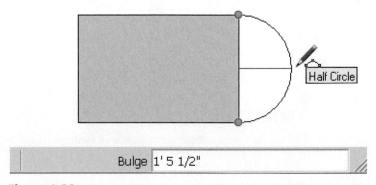

Half Circle

Bulge 1' 5 1/2"

Figure 4-26

4 It's important to stick to the model's dimensions, so we'll assume that the arc isn't a true half-circle. Type 19 and press Enter, which results in an arc that's *slightly* larger than a half-circle (Figure 4-27); but, again, it's one of those details that nobody will ever notice. (Of course, if the difference were more substantial and noticeable, say 6″, we wouldn't ignore it!)

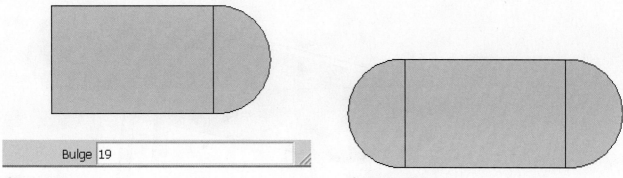

Figure 4-27

Figure 4-28

5 Draw the same 19″ arc on the other side of the rectangle (Figure 4-28).

6 Pull up each face of the tabletop 1½″, using the Ctrl/Option key to ensure that you don't lose any faces on the bottom. You can use the double-click method to pull up faces by the same amount, or just click an already-pulled face to match its height (Figure 4-29.). If you see any face on the top or bottom that has the wrong color, you can right-click on it and choose **Reverse Faces**. (Or you can leave the faces alone; they will all be painted later.)

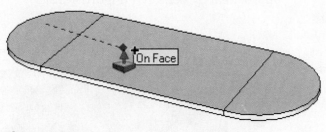

Figure 4-29

7 To mark the tops of the table legs, use **Offset** to make a smaller rectangle on the underside of the tabletop 4″ from the outer edges, then make another rectangle 2″ further inward (Figure 4-30).

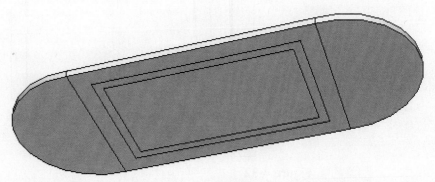

Figure 4-30

8 Draw squares in the four corners between the two offset rectangles, and pull each one down 26½″ to keep the overall table height of 28″ (Figure 4-31).

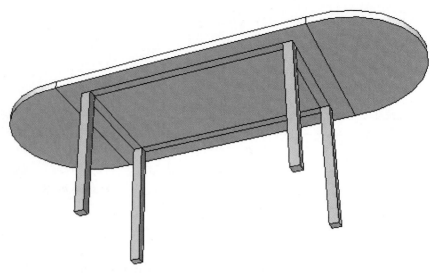

Figure 4-31

9 Erase the extra offset lines.

10 This table has an apron that runs along both long sides of the table. Draw a 2″ × ½″ rectangle at the inside top of one leg, making it approximately centered (Figure 4-32).

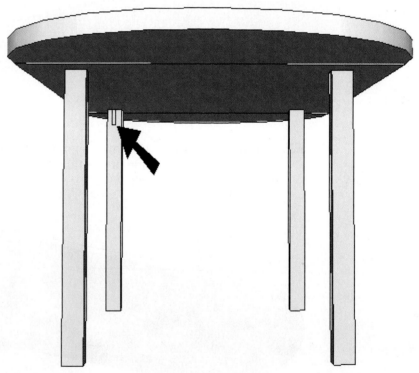

Figure 4-32

11 Select this small rectangle and use the **Move** tool with the Ctrl/Option key to copy it to the other leg. For the two move points, click two similar points on the two legs, such as Points 1 and 2 in Figure 4-33, making sure to keep the move in the green direction.

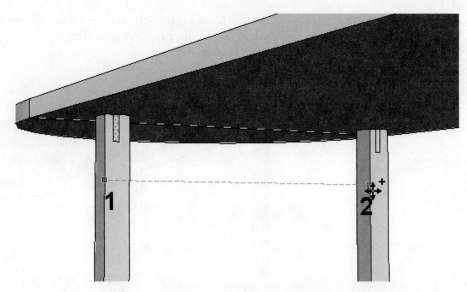

Figure 4-33

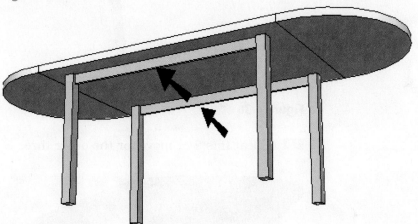

Figure 4-34

12 Pull out both small rectangles to meet the legs on the other end of the table to form the long sides of the apron (Figure 4-34).

13 Now we can work on splaying the legs. Start by selecting the bottom face of any leg (Figure 4-35).

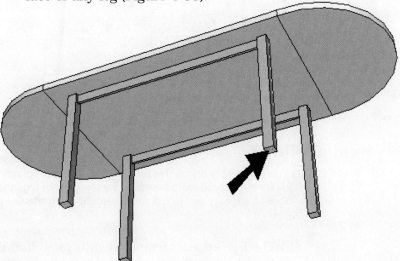

Figure 4-35

14 With that small face selected, activate **Move** and start to move the face outward in the green direction (Figure 4-36); then enter 2.5 to set the move distance.

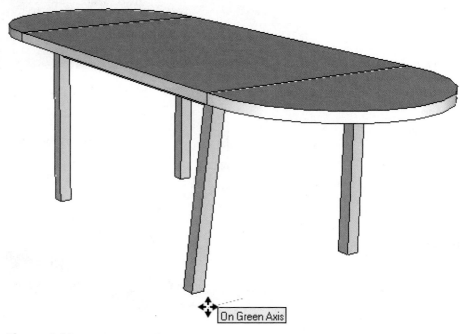

On Green Axis

Figure 4-36

15 Repeat this 2½″ move for the other three legs (Figure 4-37).

Figure 4-37

> **NOTE**
>
> You'll probably encounter tables whose legs are splayed in both the red and green directions. So you would perform two moves per leg: one outward in the green direction, then again outward in the red direction, using the same move distance.

16 The legs appear to taper slightly as well, but only in the green direction. So select one leg bottom again and activate **Scale**. Start scaling in the green direction (Figure 4-38), keeping the Ctrl/Option key pressed in

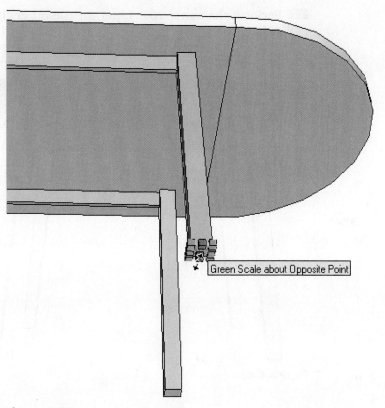

Figure 4-38

order to scale toward the center. We want to use a scale value of 0.75, but there's a problem: While the Ctrl/Option key is pressed, you can't enter a number for the scale value. The solution: Click to complete the scale using any scale value (Figure 4-39), then immediately afterward, enter 0.75 and press Enter.

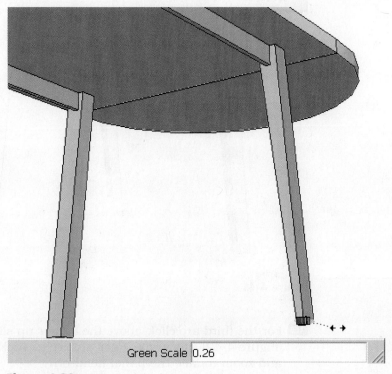

Figure 4-39

17 Perform the same 75% taper for the other three legs (Figure 4-40).

Figure 4-40

18 Now we can complete the apron along the width of the table. These panels appear to be deeper than the longer ones, and they are also arched. To start the first panel, activate **Arc** and click the first two points in the green direction between the table legs a few inches below the rectangular panels (Figure 4-41).

Figure 4-41

19 For the third arc click, move the cursor up slightly in the blue direction (Figure 4-42). If you can't get the arc to stick to the blue direction, orbit and zoom to face the panel head-on.

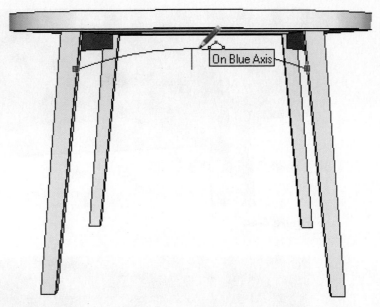

Figure 4-42

20 Complete the front face of the panel by adding the line between the tops of the legs (Figure 4-43).

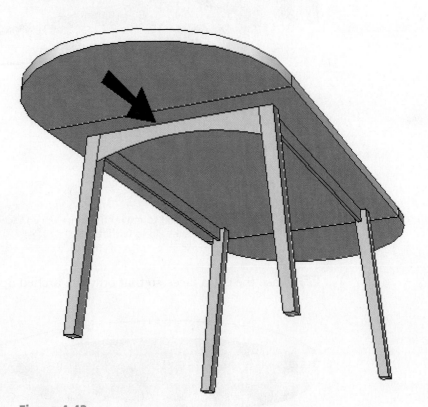

Figure 4-43

21 Assume that this panel is 1″ thick and that it is centered at the tops of the legs. Use **Push/Pull** to push the face ½″ inward (Figure 4-44); then press the Ctrl/Option key and do another push 1″ further inward (Figure 4-45). This leaves ½″ along the leg on the other side.

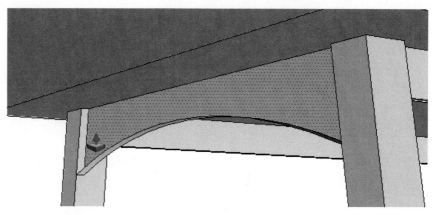

Figure 4-44

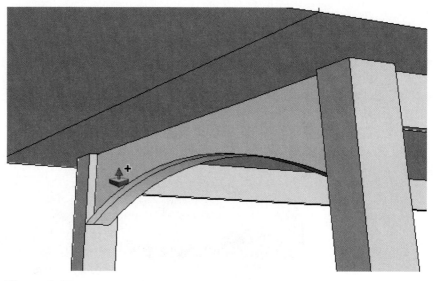

Figure 4-45

NOTE

You can't use the **Move** tool to move the entire apron face ½″ into the leg because you'll bring the other faces along with it.

▨▨ Erase the extra faces so that only the arched apron remains (Figure 4-46).

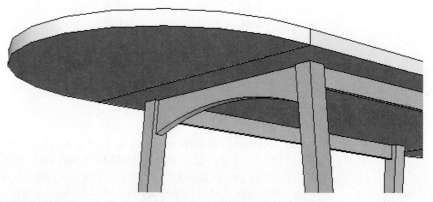

Figure 4-46

23 Then select the entire arched panel (you can carefully use a left-to-right selection window or just press Shift and click its front, bottom, and back faces) and copy it to the other side of the table. As before, use two similar move points on the table legs, sticking to the red direction (Figure 4-47).

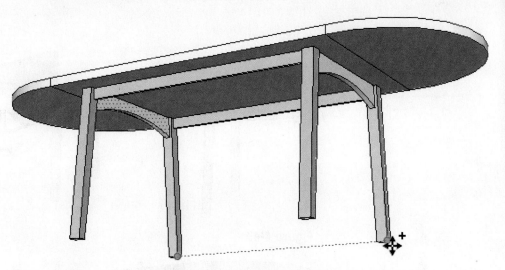

Figure 4-47

24 For the final touch, paint the entire table with a light wood material, or use a solid light brown color. If you use the Shift key to paint all faces at once, and you have both front and back faces showing on your model, you'll have to click twice: first to paint all front faces, and again to paint all back faces. Then move the table so that a corner of one leg meets the origin (Figure 4-48).

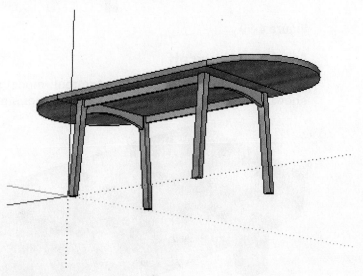

Figure 4-48

> **NOTE**
>
> You might find it more logical to place this table centered above the origin. But because the table will probably be moved anyway when placed into a model, its exact origin location isn't overly important.

A quick aside: This is a drop-leaf table; what if you need to show your client what the table looks like when the leaves are folded down? The easiest way to do this is to make a group or component from one of the round leaves, and keep it selected while activating **Move**. This way you can easily rotate the leaf 90 degrees (Figure 4-49) and then move it into place (Figure 4-50).

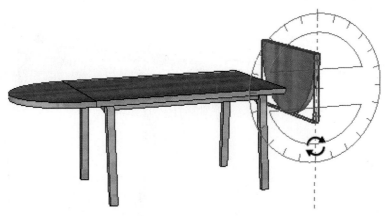

Figure 4-49

Figure 4-50

Model It Yourself

With your new expertise in the **Arc** tool, model a pool table like the one shown in Figure 4-51. The overall dimensions are 8′ wide, 4′ deep, and

Figure 4-51

30″ high. The corners of the table itself are rounded, so use **Arc** to fill in small round corners (Figure 4-52), and then trim away the sharp ends. (Don't worry about the size and uniformity of the round corners; in the next section, we'll see how to make them identical.) The **Offset** tool is needed to make the cutout for the playing field part of the table. Don't leave out the arches between both table legs (Figure 4-53).

Figure 4-52

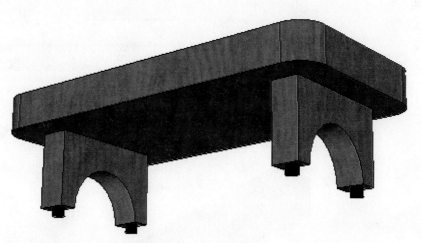

Figure 4-53

4.3 Table with Cross Pedestal Base

Ikea's Billsta table comes in several shapes and configurations; the smaller ones are supported by a simple, cylindrical pedestal with four evenly spaced feet. The table we'll model in this section is shown in Figure 4-54. The rectangular tabletop is 70cm × 60cm, and the table height is 74cm.

We'll start this model with the feet, using the **Rotate** tool to make rotated copies of one foot. The tabletop has rounded corners, so we'll see how to create identical arcs in each corner. The tabletop will be created separately, then placed on its base.

1. In a new file, create a 30cm × 6cm rectangle (Figure 4-55), which will be used to create one of the four feet of the pedestal base. You can switch your model units to decimal centimeters, or just type "cm" after each unit.

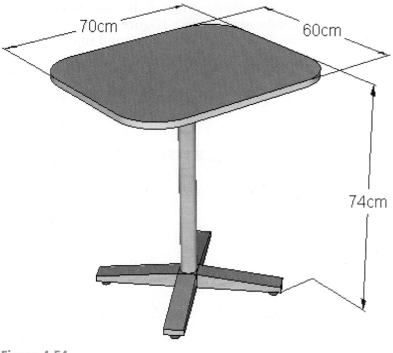

Figure 4-54

Dimensions	30cm,6cm

Figure 4-55

2 Paint the rectangle using a silver color or metallic material, and pull it up 5cm. Then use the **Move** tool on one of the top edges to move it down slightly (Figure 4-56).

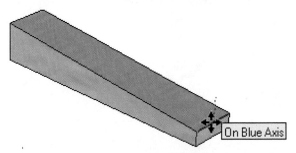

Figure 4-56

3 On the underside of the foot, below the shallower end, draw a small circle for the rubber stopper. Paint the circle dark gray, and pull it down 2cm (Figure 4-57).

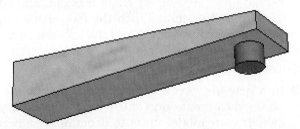

Figure 4-57

Figure 4-58

4 This is the entire foot; three rotated copies of it are needed. Select the entire item, and activate the **Rotate** tool indicated in Figure 4-58.

5 The protractor is now attached to your cursor, and it will align to any face that you move over. If you place the protractor on the sloped top face of the foot, the rotated copies will be slightly off because this face isn't flat. So move the protractor into blank space, where its color will be blue because it is perpendicular to the blue axis (Figure 4-59).

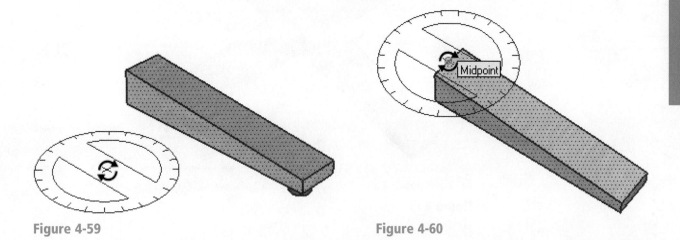

Figure 4-59   **Figure 4-60**

6 Press and hold the Shift key to lock the protractor into this blue orientation, but don't click yet. Keeping Shift pressed, move the blue protractor to the top midpoint of the higher edge of the foot (Figure 4-60). Click this point to place the protractor, then let go of the Shift key.

7 The next two clicks set the angle of rotation. Press the Ctrl/Option key to make a copy, pull the cursor away from the protractor in any direction, and click anywhere. Then move the cursor to pull out the rotated copy, and click again when you see 90 in the **Angle** field (Figure 4-61). (You can also type 90 and press Enter after, or instead of, clicking that last point.)

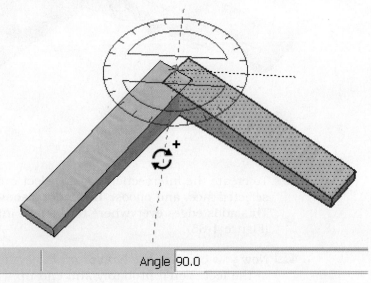

Angle 90.0

Figure 4-61

8 After that first 90-degree copy is made, type 3x and press Enter. This creates three copies instead of one, for a total of four legs (Figure 4-62).

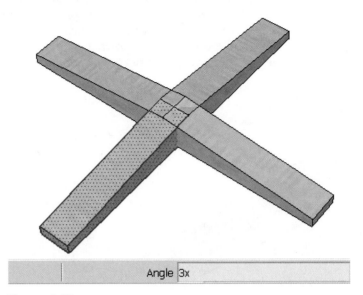

Figure 4-62

The area where the four legs meet is a bit messy, with lots of little extra edges that should be removed (Figure 4-63). But these edges can't be erased yet or you'll end up erasing entire faces. First, some intersection edges are needed.

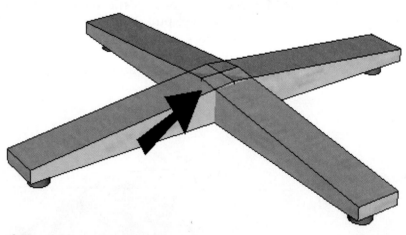

Figure 4-63

9 To create the intersection edges, select everything, right-click on any selected face, and choose **Intersect Faces / With Model** (Figure 4-64). This adds edges everywhere that a face intersects with another face (Figure 4-65).

10 Now you can use the **Eraser** on those little extra edges at the center of the feet. You'll probably still end up with a few erased faces (Figure 4-66), but these can easily be replaced by tracing edges

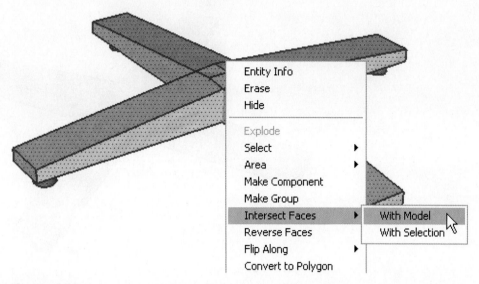

Entity Info	
Erase	
Hide	
Explode	
Select	▶
Area	▶
Make Component	
Make Group	
Intersect Faces	▶ With Model
Reverse Faces	With Selection
Flip Along	▶
Convert to Polygon	

Figure 4-64

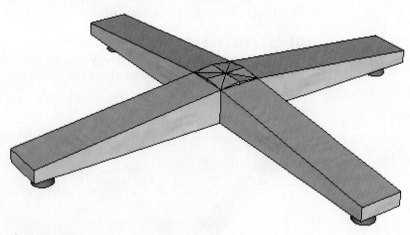

Figure 4-65

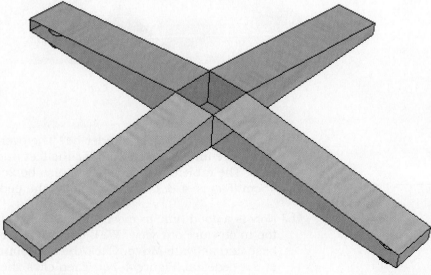

Figure 4-66

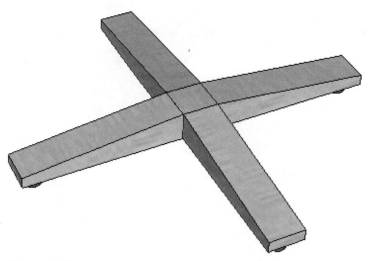

Figure 4-67

with the **Line** tool (Figure 4-67). The center of the feet should consist of one flat square at the top.

11 To create the circle for the cylindrical pedestal, activate **Circle** and hover over midpoints so that you can find the exact center. Then make the circle slightly smaller than the center square (Figure 4-68).

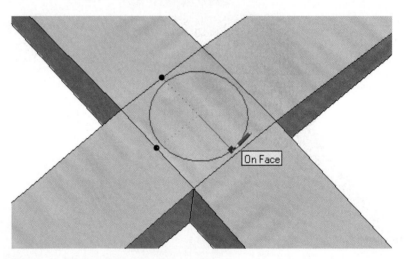

Figure 4-68

12 How high should this cylinder be? The overall table height is 74cm, and we've already used 5cm for the feet and another 2cm for the stoppers. The tabletop thickness will also be 2cm. So pull up the circle 65cm (Figure 4-69). This completes the pedestal base.

13 Now is a good time to move the base into place, while there is no tabletop to obscure our view. We'll use two moves for this: Select the entire base and activate **Move**. Click the first point at the center of the top of the pedestal (Figure 4-70). Then click the origin as the destination

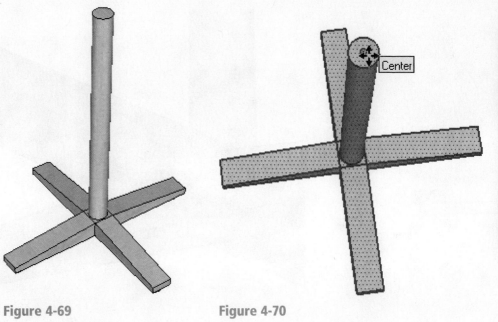

Figure 4-69　　　　　　Figure 4-70

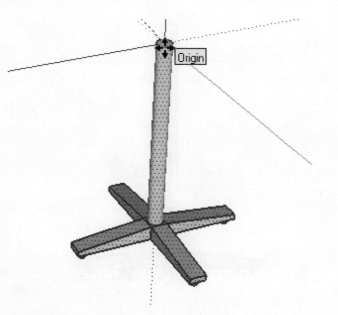

Figure 4-71

(Figure 4-71). Remember, you might have to hover over a circle endpoint to remind SketchUp where its center is.

14 Next, we'll move the table straight up so that the stoppers will meet the floor. Keep **Move** active, and click any point at the bottom of a stopper (Figure 4-72). Then press the Up or Down arrow to lock the move to the blue direction, and click the origin (Figure 4-73). This brings the stoppers up to the level of the ground plane (i.e., the floor) while still keeping the base centered at the origin. Now the table will be inserted into future models perfectly centered. Keep the base selected because there is still one more step.

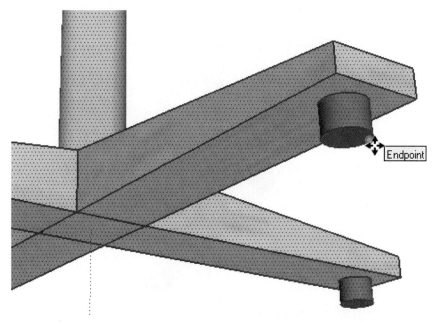

Figure 4-72

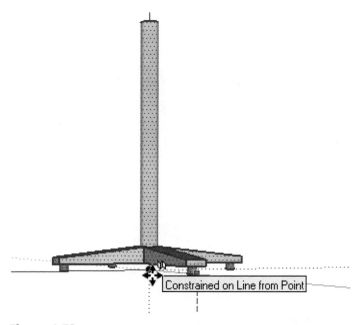

Figure 4-73

15 If you look at the picture of the completed model (go back to Figure 4-54), you'll see that the base is rotated 45 degrees with respect to the tabletop. So with the entire base still selected, activate **Rotate** and place the protractor at the center of the top of the pedestal. Click anywhere to start the rotation, then click again when the rotation angle is 45 (Figure 4-74).

It's a good rule of thumb when creating a table, or anything with multiple distinct parts like a table base and top, to enclose a completed part as a group before continuing on to the next part. It's not crucial in this case because the top will be created separately (the base will have no effect on the top itself). But it's a good idea to get into the grouping habit.

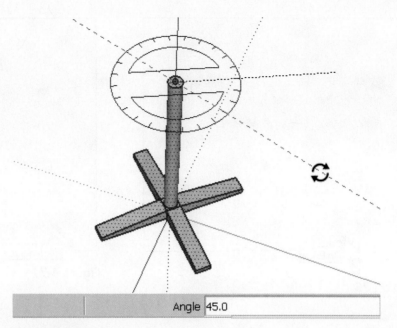

Angle 45.0

Figure 4-74

16 Now we can start on the tabletop. It's easiest to create it flat on the ground, then move it into place later. So create a 70cm × 60cm rectangle in blank space, and paint it a light brown color (Figure 4-75).

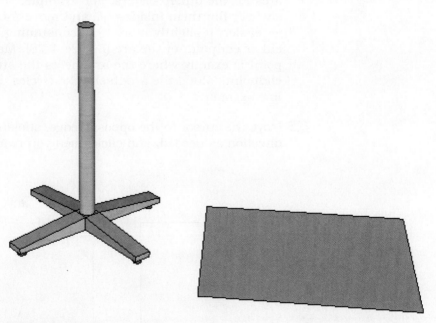

Figure 4-75

17 We now need some arcs for the rounded corners. This is easiest to do when looking straight down at the table, so choose **Camera / Standard Views / Top** from the main menu. Then activate **Arc** and click two points in one corner, such as Points 1 and 2 in Figure 4-76, so that the preview line between the points is magenta. This means that the arc start and end points are located the same distance from the corner.

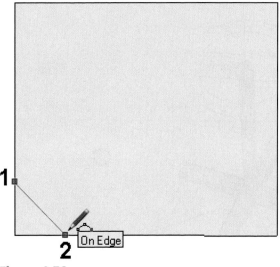

Figure 4-76

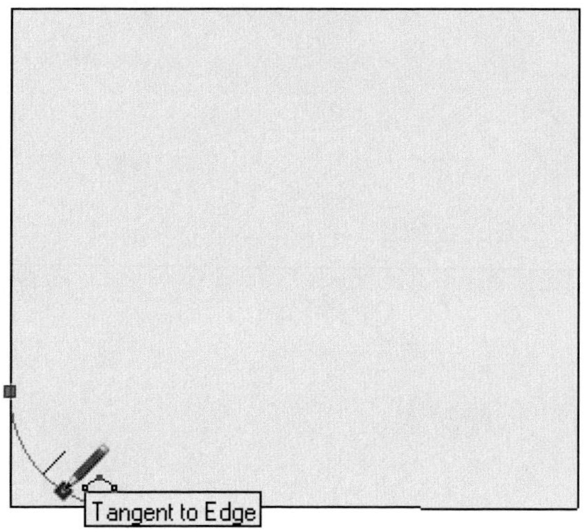

Figure 4-77

18 To set the arc's bulge, move the cursor so that you see the "Tangent to Edge" popup (Figure 4-77), then click. When an arc is tangent to an edge, the transition from the straight line to the arc is perfectly smooth; there are no sharp corners.

19 Keep the **Arc** tool active. There are a few ways to create identical arcs for the other corners. For example, you could make copies, scale or flip them inside-out, and move them into place. But here's an easier, if slightly more time-consuming, way: First, hover over either endpoint of the arc (Figure 4-78). Make sure that this endpoint is exactly where the arc meets the straight edge; there are also endpoints along the arc itself (like circles, arcs are made of short line segments).

20 Move the cursor to the opposite edge, sticking to either the red or green direction as needed, and click when you reach the edge (Figure 4-79).

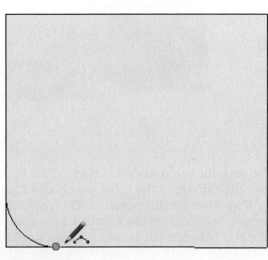

Figure 4-78

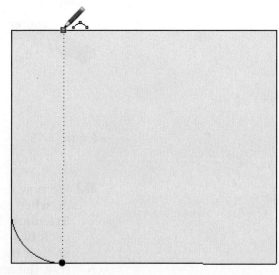

Figure 4-79

21 With that first arc point set, click the point on the other edge so that the preview line is magenta, and create another tangent arc (Figure 4-80).

22 Use the same method, hovering over endpoints and moving in the red or green direction, to complete the other two arcs (Figure 4-81).

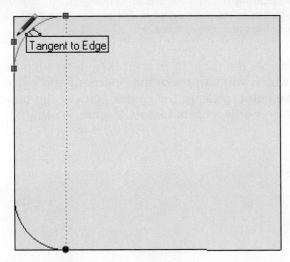

Figure 4-80

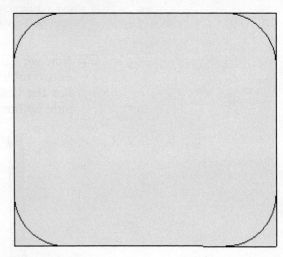

Figure 4-81

23 Use the **Eraser** to trim away the sharp edges, and pull up the tabletop 2cm. Within the thickness of the tabletop, you can see the small edges where each arc begins and ends (Figure 4-82). To smooth these edges (hide them while smoothing the transition between adjacent faces), activate the **Eraser**, press and hold the Ctrl/Option key, and click each of these small edges (Figure 4-83).

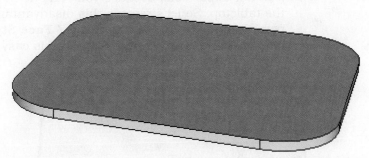

Figure 4-82

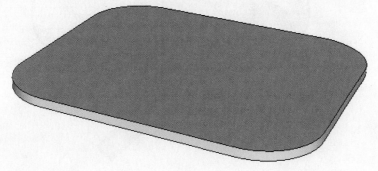

Figure 4-83

24 Now we can assemble the table (it *is* from Ikea, after all!). Select the entire tabletop (which you can make into a group) and activate **Move**. For the first move point, pick up the center point of the table's underside by hovering over adjacent midpoints (Figure 4-84).

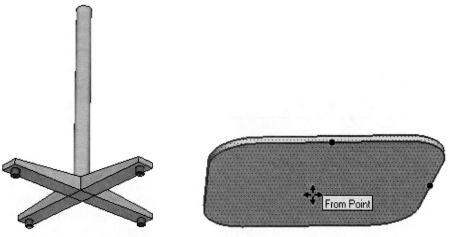

Figure 4-84

25 Placing this center point at the top of the pedestal can be a little tricky (but not impossible) because you can't actually see the pedestal under the tabletop. So let's remove this disadvantage by making all faces temporarily translucent: Choose **View / Face Style / X-ray** from the main menu. Now the center of the pedestal is easy to find (Figure 4-85).

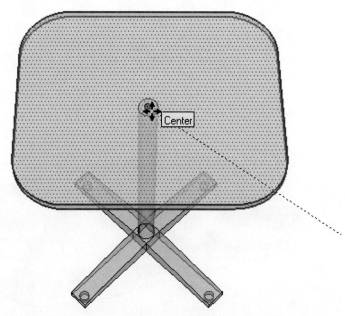

Figure 4-85

26 Toggle **X-ray** view off by choosing it again from the menu. That's it; the table is complete (Figure 4-86).

One last thing: We need some chairs. Instead of importing a chair, making copies, and positioning each chair individually, we can use the **Rotate** tool to make rotated copies of a single chair. (This table is meant for two chairs, but we'll crowd the table with four just to practice using the tool.)

27 Start by importing a single chair like the one in Figure 4-87 and position it next to the table. Keep the chair selected.

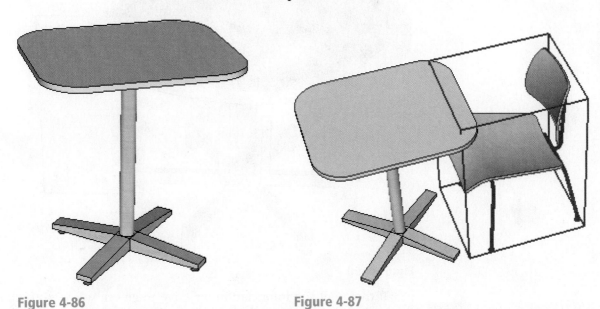

Figure 4-86   Figure 4-87

28 Activate the **Rotate** tool, and use midpoints on the tabletop to find the center of the table. (You could also make things easier by just clicking the origin). Make one 90-degree rotated copy (Figure 4-88), then enter 3x for a total of four chairs (Figure 4-89).

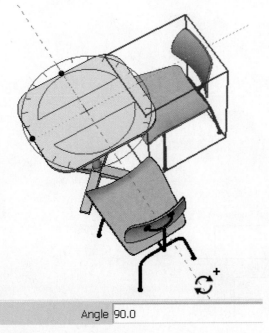

Angle 90.0

Figure 4-88   Figure 4-89

Model It Yourself

The Montego Round Dining Table from Room and Board (Figure 4-90) has a pedestal base with six evenly spaced feet. The tabletop diameter is 48″ and the table height is 30″.

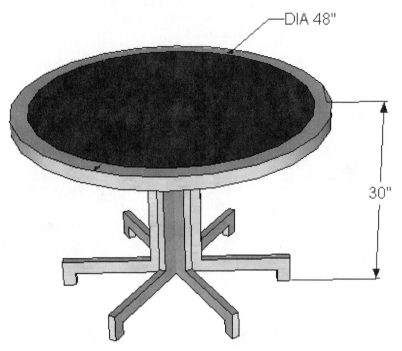

Figure 4-90

If that's all the information we have to go on, we need to do some dimension estimating and planning (unless of course you can find this exact table and measure it). It helps to make a schematic drawing of one of the pedestal sections, such as the rough estimate shown in Figure 4-91.

So that you won't have to rotate the piece later to be vertical, start drawing it in **Front** view (**Camera / Standard Views / Front**).

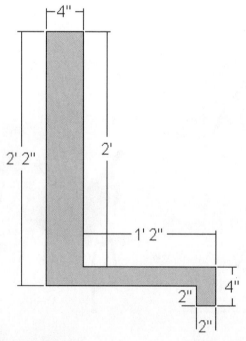

Figure 4-91

Once you get the 3D model of one of these leg pieces, use the **Rotate** tool to copy it. The protractor should be at the midpoint shown in Figure 4-92. Because six legs are needed, what will you use for the rotation angle and number of copies?

Remember to make a group from the base so that the circular tabletop will be a snap to complete.

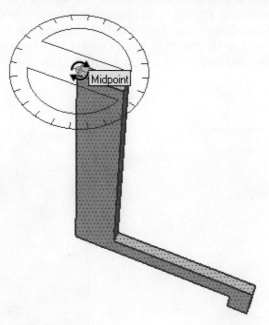

Figure 4-92

4.4 Table with Chrome Tubular Base

Only a quirky client would require you to model the 1950s era table shown in Figure 4-93, but this table is perfect for demonstrating the useful (and fun) **Follow Me** tool. The four cylindrical pieces of the pedestal base can't

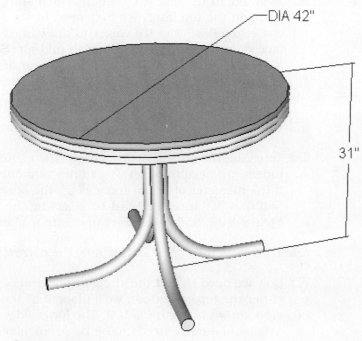

Figure 4-93

be replicated with just a circle and **Push/Pull**; you have to make a circle follow a curving path. The same **Follow Me** tool is also needed to model the interesting grooved edge of the tabletop.

Here's all we know about this table: Its diameter is 42″ and its height is 31″.

When you don't know many specifics, take out a pencil and calculator and make a quick sketch. Half of the table's cross section would look something like Figure 4-94, based on the 21″ radius of the tabletop (half of the 42″ diameter) and the fact that the bottom ends of the base appear to extend nearly to the edge of the tabletop. The assumed 2″ diameter for the base's curved cylinders might be high, but it's an easy number to use.

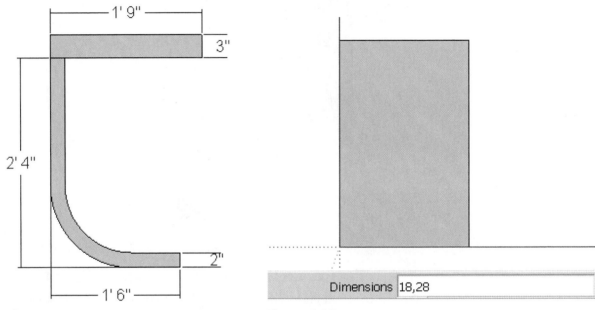

Figure 4-94   Figure 4-95

1. Just like in the last few sections, we'll start with the pedestal base and add the top later. We first need to lay out the curved path for the circle to follow, and it's easier to draw lines and arcs on an existing face rather than drawing them in mid-air. So switch to **Front** view (**Camera / Standard Views / Front**) and draw a 1′-6″ × 2′-4″ rectangle (in other words, 18″ × 28″) starting at the origin so that we won't have to move the table later (Figure 4-95).

2. Make a tangent arc similar to the one shown in Figure 4-96.

3. To create the path that runs down the center of one of the curved cylinders, we need to offset these lines and curves inward. How much? If the diameter of the cylinder is 2″, the offset to the cylinder center is half that distance: 1″. Start by selecting the three edges indicated in Figure 4-97, and use **Offset** to create a 1″ inward path (Figure 4-98).

4. Trim away the edges, leaving only the narrow strip shown in Figure 4-99.

5. Now we need to add the circle at one end of the cylinder. It could go at either the top or bottom; we'll place it at the bottom. First, orbit to the view shown in Figure 4-100. The lower edge of the path follows the red axis, so the circle needs to be *perpendicular* to the red axis; its preview color must be red. Activate **Circle**, and move the cursor around

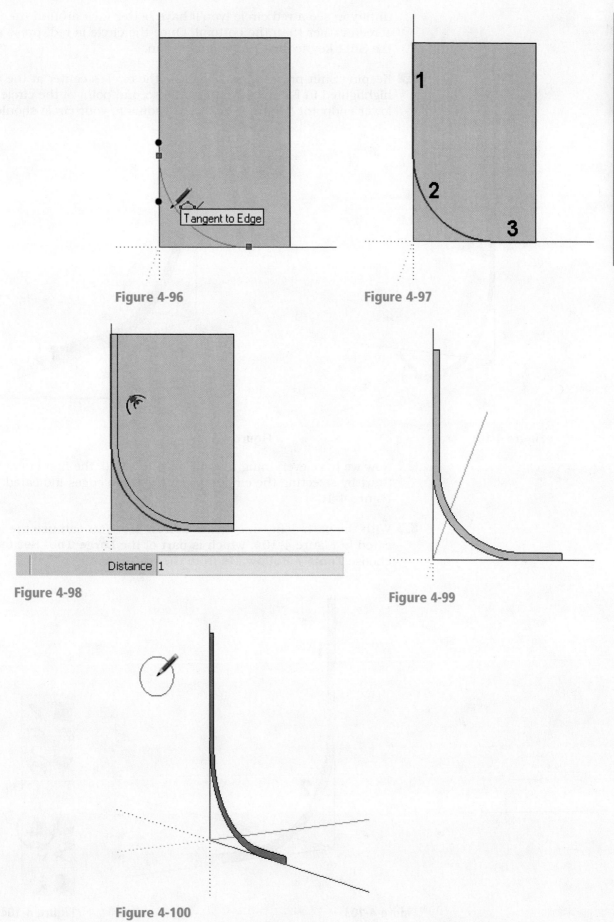

Figure 4-96

Figure 4-97

Figure 4-98

Distance 1

Figure 4-99

Figure 4-100

until you see a red circle (you'll have better luck around the top of the screen rather than the bottom). Once the circle is red, press and hold the Shift key to lock in the orientation.

6   Keeping Shift pressed, click to place the circle's center at the endpoint highlighted in Figure 4-101. For the second point of the circle, click the lower endpoint (Figure 4-102). The radius of your circle should be 1″.

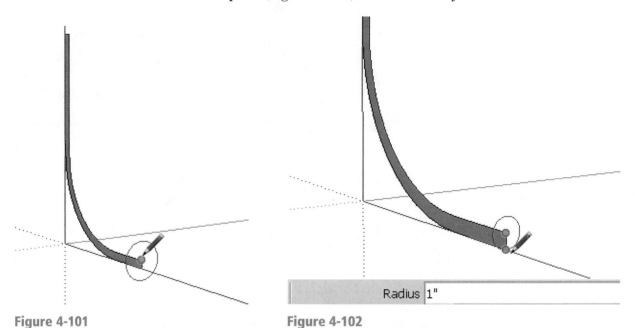

Figure 4-101   **Figure 4-102**

7   Now we have everything that we need to create the first curved cylinder. Start by selecting the circle's path: the three edges indicated in Figure 4-103.

8   With the path defined, activate **Follow Me**. You can use the icon indicated in Figure 4-104, which is part of the **Large Tool Set** toolbar, or choose **Tools / Follow Me** from the main menu.

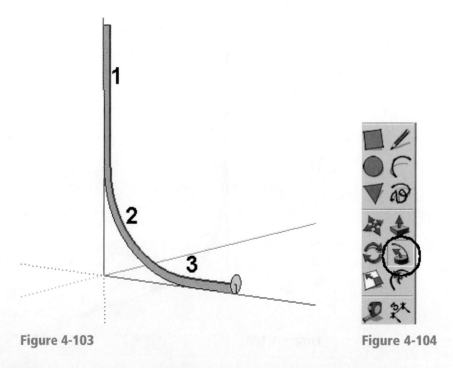

Figure 4-103   **Figure 4-104**

9 All that's left is to click the face of the small circle at the bottom of the base. (**Follow Me** works only on a single, flat face.) The circle proceeds along the path that you defined to create the curved cylinder (Figure 4-105).

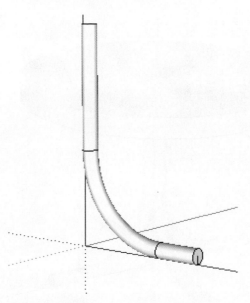

Figure 4-105

10 To create the other three pieces of the pedestal base, select the entire cylinder and use the **Rotate** tool to make three 90-degree copies (Figure 4-106). Use the origin to place the protractor.

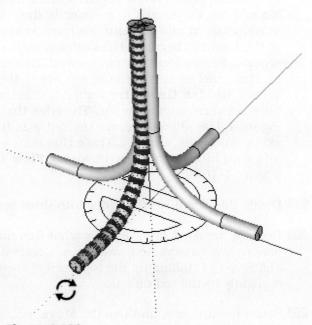

Figure 4-106

Each leg has sets of small edges between the straight and curved parts of the cylinders. These edges could be softened with the **Eraser** as we did before, but there are so many small edges to click that softening them would take some time. But don't worry; as the last step in creating this model, we'll soften all of the edges at once.

11 Make the base into a group, then create the circular tabletop, whose radius is 21″ and thickness is 3″ (Figure 4-107). When creating the circle for the tabletop, be sure to click the second point in either the red or green direction.

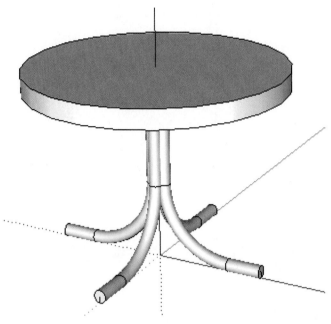

Figure 4-107

12 Creating the grooved surface around the tabletop is a little trickier. We need to create a few 2D (flat) faces that can be used for **Follow Me** and, as we've seen, it's easier to draw faces onto existing faces rather than in mid-air. But it's hard to know where to draw any face at the moment because the tabletop appears smooth all the way around. Remember that circles and, therefore, round faces are segmented, and we can actually see where these segments are. Choose **View / Hidden Geometry** from the main menu to see the dashed lines between each segment. The edge that we need is indicated in Figure 4-108, directly above the red axis (the edge above the green axis would work as well). Trace this edge with the **Line** tool, then toggle off hidden edges by choosing **View / Hidden Geometry** again (Figure 4-109).

13 Divide this small, vertical edge into three segments (Figure 4-110).

14 Because we don't know exactly what this tabletop edge surface looks like, we'll approximate it with arcs. Create a small arc as shown in Figure 4-111, taking up the top third of the vertical edge and extending it slightly in the red direction.

15 Select the arc face, and use the **Move** tool to make two more copies to fill the rest of the vertical edge (Figure 4-112).

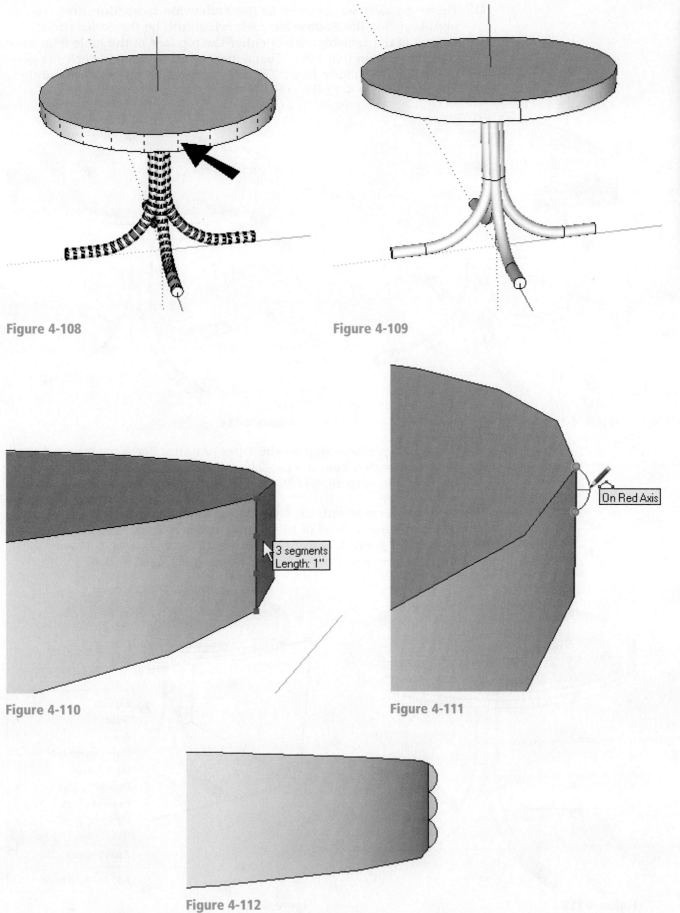

Figure 4-108

Figure 4-109

Figure 4-110

3 segments
Length: 1"

Figure 4-111

On Red Axis

Figure 4-112

16 These arc faces will be used as the **Follow Me** faces. But, first, we need to define the **Follow Me** path, which will be the entire circumference of the tabletop. Select either the top face of the table (Figure 4-113) or its circular edge, then activate **Follow Me** and click the first of the three small arc faces. The arc face goes all the way around the tabletop (Figure 4-114).

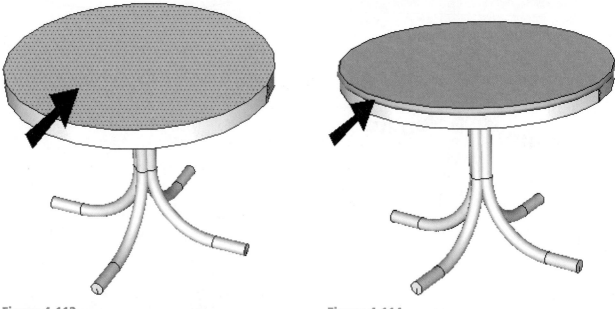

Figure 4-113   Figure 4-114

17 Repeat the previous step for the other two arcs. For some buggy reason, the faces created from the two lower arcs have vertical edges separating the segments (Figure 4-115).

18 Using the **Eraser** with the Ctrl/Option key to soften the edges would be maddening with all of those small edges to click, so we'll take care of them all at once. Select the entire table model, right-click on any selected face, and choose **Soften / Smooth Edges** (Figure 4-116).

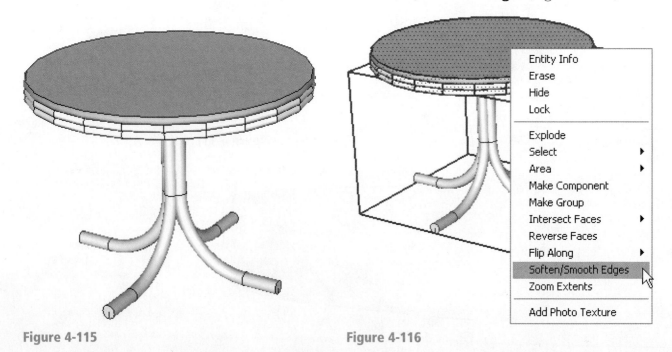

Figure 4-115   Figure 4-116

19 This opens the **Soften Edges** window, which has a slider and two checkboxes. (The checkboxes aren't important for this example.) Adjust the slider so that only the edges that you want to see are displayed (Figure 4-117).

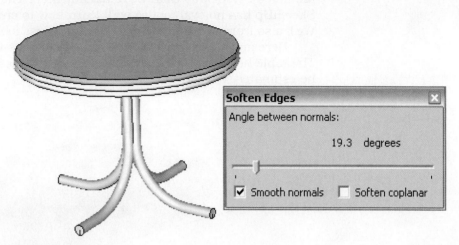

Figure 4-117

20 Close the **Soften Edges** window. The table is complete.

Model It Yourself

A great model to create using **Follow Me** is a fireplace mantel. Create a model like the one shown in Figure 4-118, and draw a small vertical face off the back onto which you can draw a **Follow Me** face.

Use arcs, lines, or whatever strikes your fancy to create the face that will be the cross section of the mantel, then use **Follow Me** to complete the gorgeous mantel (Figure 4-119). When defining your **Follow Me** path, keep in mind that the mantel shouldn't continue along the back of the fireplace!

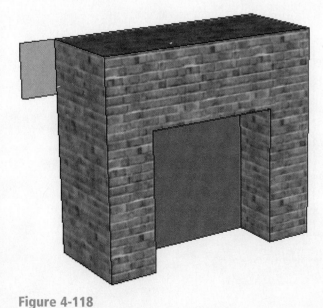

Figure 4-118

Figure 4-119

4.5 Glass Oval Table with Tulip Pedestal

This chapter contains a lot of table examples; here's the last one! It's the Satellite Oval Glass Top Table by Nuevo Living, which has a spun aluminum, tulip-like pedestal base (Figure 4-120). The base will be created using **Follow Me** in a different way than we've already seen. The tabletop is an oval, but SketchUp has no oval tool so we'll learn how to create an oval from a circle. We'll also learn how to hide edges so that glass looks more like glass.

Here are the known dimensions: The oval is 63″ wide and 40″ deep. The table height is 29.5″ and the glass is ½″ thick. As usual, the rest will be estimated.

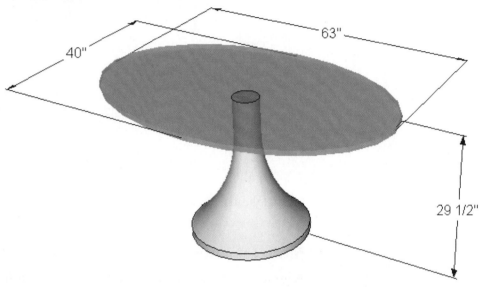

Figure 4-120

1. As a reasonable guess, we'll assume that the bottom of the base has a diameter of 24″ (radius = 12″). The base height is ½″ less than the total table height of 29″. Start again in **Front** view, and create a 12″ × 29″ rectangle. Again, stick to the origin so that the table won't need to be moved later (Figure 4-121). The base shape will be cut from this rectangle.

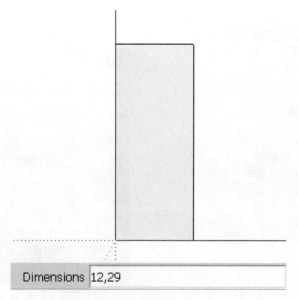

Dimensions 12,29

Figure 4-121

2 Within this rectangle, we'll draw half of the base's cross section. We'll draw the top of the pedestal as a straight vertical line; it actually curves slightly, but we're going to modify it a bit. Draw a vertical line as shown in Figure 4-122, then add a tangent arc that extends to the bottom of the rectangle (Figure 4-123).

3 Trim away everything but the half-cross section (Figure 4-124).

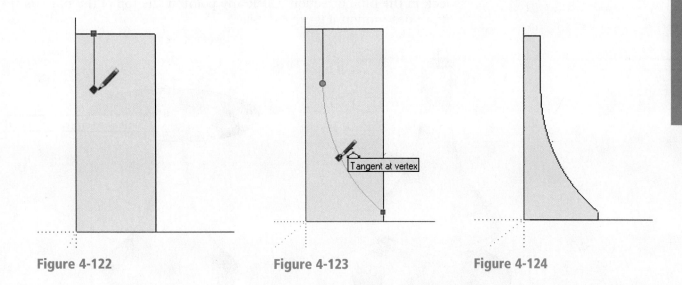

Figure 4-122　　　　**Figure 4-123**　　　　**Figure 4-124**

4 This face needs to be spun around a circle, so a circle must be created for the **Follow Me** path. This circle must lie flat (perpendicular to the blue axis) and be centered at the origin. (It's always good practice to keep a **Follow Me** circle away from the object itself; otherwise you might lose some faces that you would later have to recreate.) Activate **Circle** and hover over the origin (Figure 4-125), then move the cursor straight down in the blue direction and click to place the center (Figure 4-126). You can make the circle any size (Figure 4-127).

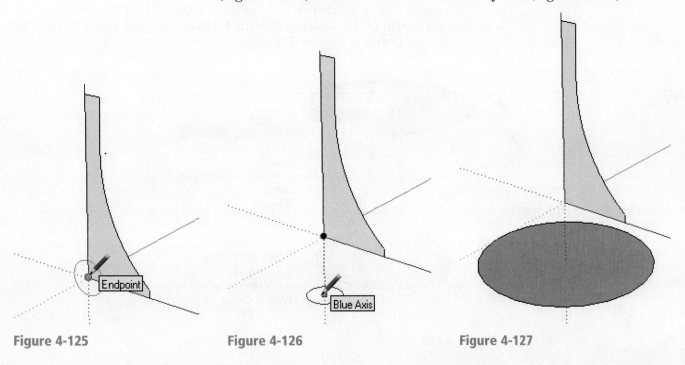

Figure 4-125　　　　**Figure 4-126**　　　　**Figure 4-127**

5 Select the circle or its edge as the path, activate **Follow Me**, and then click the cross-section face to complete the base (Figure 4-128).

6 Make the base (do not include the circle below it) into a group.

7 Because we already have a circle, we might as well use it for the tabletop; we'll adjust its diameter later. Select the circle that you created as the **Follow Me** path and move it up, using the Up or Down arrow to lock in the blue direction. Click any point at the top of the base as the move destination (Figure 4-129).

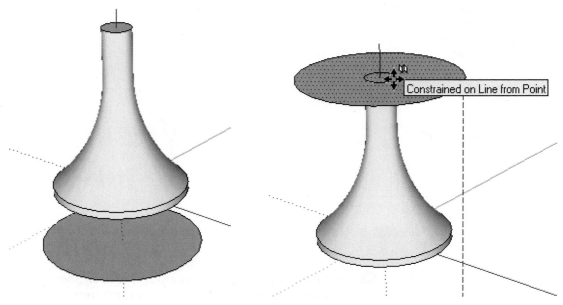

Figure 4-128   Figure 4-129

8 There are a few ways to change this circle to obtain the correct size. Here's the easiest method: Right-click on the circle's edge and choose **Entity Info** (Figure 4-130). The **Entity Info** window lists a few features of this circle, including some features that you can change. One of these features is **Radius**; change what's there to 31.5″, which is half the 63″ width of the tabletop (Figure 4-131). Once you press Enter, the tabletop will resize (Figure 4-132).

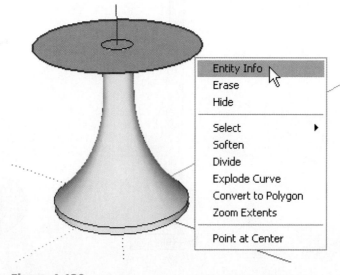

Figure 4-130

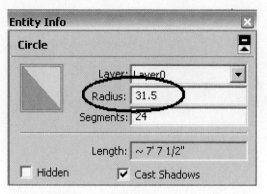

Figure 4-131

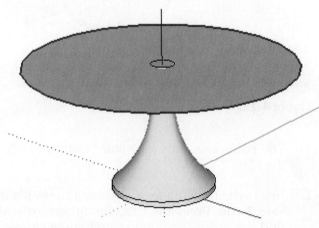

Figure 4-132

The depth of the tabletop is 40″. There are a few ways that we could squash this circle into an oval to achieve the 40″ width; we'll mark its depth point with a guide point. We've already used the **Tape Measure** tool to create guide lines, and when you click a point instead of an edge, you get a guide *point*.

9 Activate **Tape Measure**, make sure that the plus (+) sign appears on your cursor, and click the center of the tabletop (Figure 4-133). Move the cursor in the green direction (it doesn't matter whether you click or not) and enter 20, which is half of the 40″ depth (Figure 4-134).

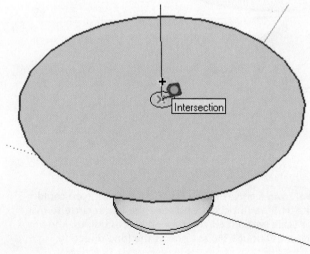

Figure 4-133

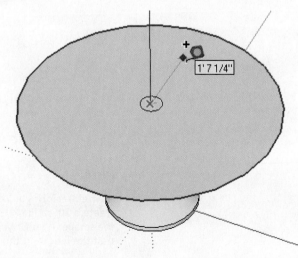

Figure 4-134

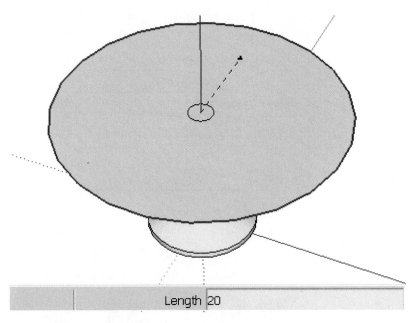

Length 20

Figure 4-135

The guide line ends at a point exactly 20″ from the table center (Figure 4-135).

10 Select the tabletop face or edge (unless it's already selected) and activate **Scale**. Press the Ctrl/Option key to scale about the center, and find the green-direction scale handle closest to the guide point. Drag this handle to meet the guide point (Figure 4-136). Then erase the guide line and point.

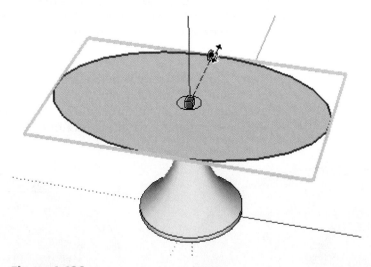

Figure 4-136

NOTE

How else might you create an oval from a circle? Instead of a guide point, you could create a 20″-radius circle inside the 31.5″-radius circle, and scale the larger circle to meet the smaller one. Or you could use **Scale** without using other objects as guides, knowing that the length in the short direction is about 63% as large as the long direction.

---

11 Paint the tabletop with a translucent glass material, and pull it up ½″ (Figure 4-137).

Figure 4-137

12 Remember the Noguchi table model that we used in Chapter 2? That model had no visible edges around the glass top. This is easy to do: Either use the **Eraser** with the Shift key to hide these tabletop edges, or right-click on each edge and choose **Hide**. The result is a more glass-like look (Figure 4-138).

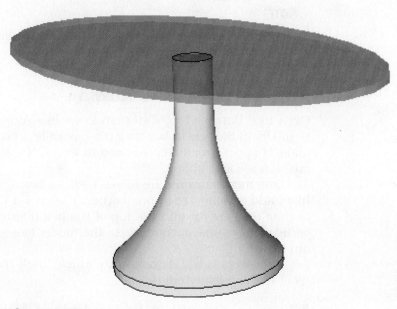

Figure 4-138

Placing chairs around an oval table is pretty straightforward. You can use **Rotate** to arrange chairs in a circle, then move some chairs to the right and some to the left. This particular table has room for six chairs (Figure 4-139).

Figure 4-139

Figure 4-140

Model It Yourself

Use the **Follow Me** circle method to model a lamp with a shade and round base (Figure 4-140). You might have to try a few cross sections before you get the result that you want, and you can include both tangent and non-tangent arcs. The shade can be created by scaling the top of a cylinder.

> **NOTE**
>
> In Chapter 7, we'll learn how to create a model of a round object (a lathed table leg) based on a digital photograph.

4.6 Cushioned Ottoman

Crate and Barrel's Troy Ottoman looks like something that would be easy to model in SketchUp because it's basically a box (Figure 4-141). But to make it appear realistic, we need to round the sharp edges to give the cushion a softer shape.

One method would be to start with a box 28″ wide × 21″ deep × 18″ high, add a small arc in one corner (Figure 4-142), and use **Follow Me** to drag that arc around the top of the box (Figure 4-143). This leaves the vertical edges sharp, though, so the model looks more like a chest than an ottoman.

This section will demonstrate a neat trick that you can use to round *all* of the necessary edges.

1 Create a 28″ × 21″ × 18″-high box and draw identical arcs in the top corners (Figure 4-144). Use **Push/Pull** to pull the round corners down to the bottom of the box, removing the sharp edges (Figure 4-145).

> **NOTE**
>
> Of course, you could have created this box like you created the round-cornered tabletop: rounding the sharp rectangle corners *before* pulling up.

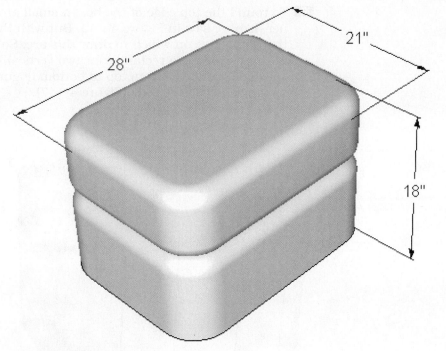

28"

21"

18"

Figure 4-141

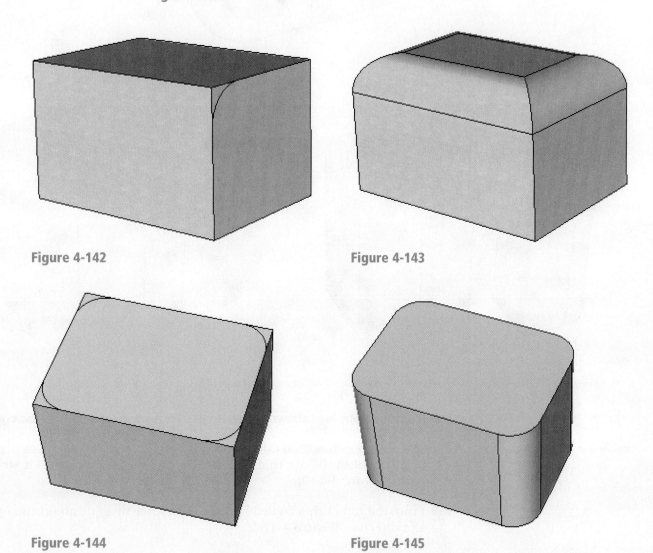

Figure 4-142

Figure 4-143

Figure 4-144

Figure 4-145

2 To round the top edge of the box, a small arc is needed in the corner, like we saw in Figure 4-142. But with the vertical edges rounded, there's no face on which to draw this arc. So we'll make our own face. Start by drawing a rectangle (or two vertical lines) on one of the vertical sides of the box from top to bottom (Figure 4-146). Then push this rectangle inward slightly (Figure 4-147).

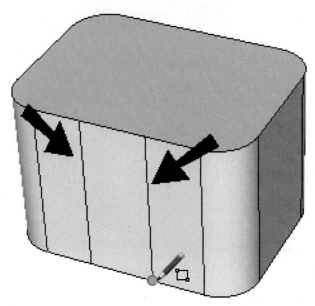

Figure 4-146

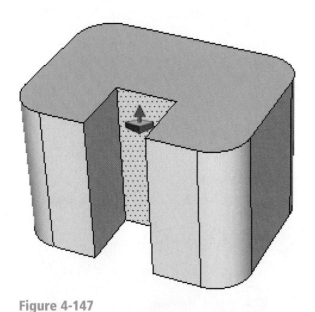

Figure 4-147

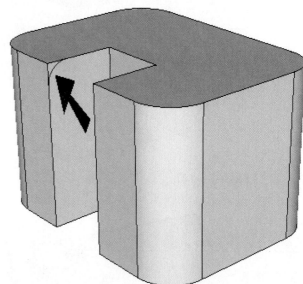

Figure 4-148

3 On the cutout face shown in Figure 4-148, draw a small arc in the corner.

4 This ottoman has a cushion on top of a base, so two more arcs are needed. Select the arc that you just drew and make a copy of it straight down (Figure 4-149).

5 From the top of this copied arc, draw another tangent arc in the opposite direction (Figure 4-150).

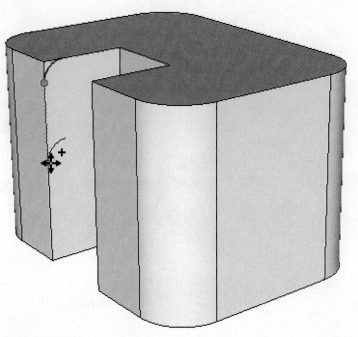

Figure 4-149

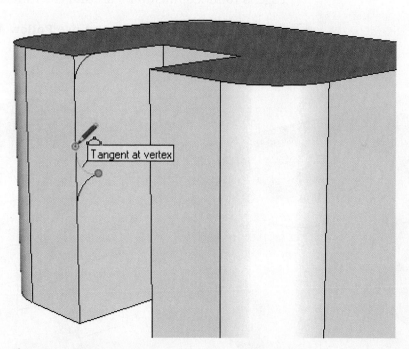

Figure 4-150

6 These arcs are ready for **Follow Me**, but first the **Follow Me** path must be defined. This is easiest to do on the bottom of the ottoman. We could select each individual edge one by one, but there's a faster way. Activate **Select** and *double-click* on the bottom face, which selects both the face and its surrounding edges (Figure 4-151). Then press and hold Shift and click to unselect the face itself, plus the three cut-out edges indicated in Figure 4-152). The remaining selected edges define the path that we need to use.

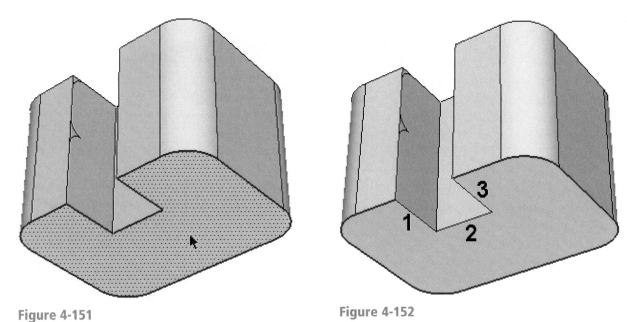

Figure 4-151

Figure 4-152

7 Activate **Follow Me** and click the arc face at the top; now the entire top edge is rounded, including around the rounded corners (Figure 4-153).

8 Select the same path again and use **Follow Me** on the arc face in the middle of the ottoman (Figure 4-154).

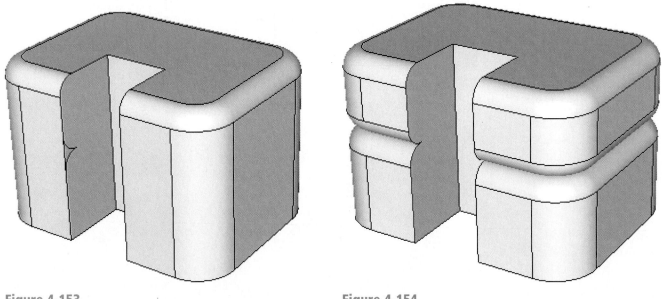

Figure 4-153

Figure 4-154

9 To fix the cutout, just use **Push/Pull** on the face indicated in Figure 4-155, pulling it all the way closed (Figure 4-156).

10 Select everything and use the **Soften Edges** window to smooth the entire ottoman (Figure 4-157). The **Soften coplanar** option will remove any edges left over by the **Push/Pull** action.

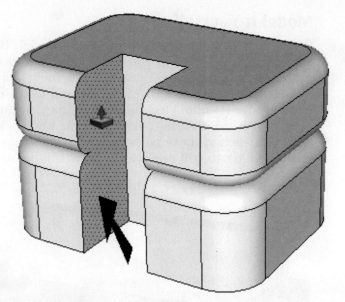

Figure 4-155

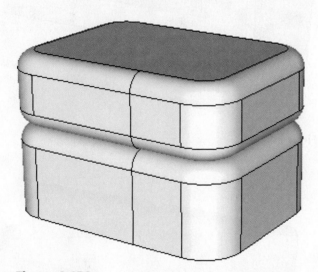

Figure 4-156

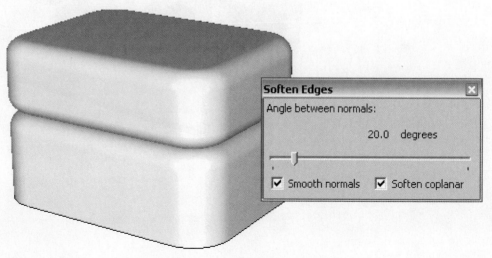

Figure 4-157

Model It Yourself

From the 3D Warehouse, download the model "Boxy Loveseat" by Bonnie Roskes (Figure 4-158). If you had to model your own basic sofa, you would probably start with something like this model, created with straight lines and right angles. But it's rather ugly and looks awfully uncomfortable. So use the edge-rounding technique from the Troy ottoman to round the various parts of this model: arms, seat cushions, and back pillows (Figure 4-159). Note that each of these parts is a separate component, which means that you only have to edit one and its copy will be updated as well.

Figure 4-158

Figure 4-159

- Circles and arcs are not true circles and arcs in SketchUp; they comprise short, linear segments. What is the advantage of using arcs and circles with a high number of segments? A low number?

- If you need to find the center of a circle or arc, and SketchUp can't find the center, what should you do?

- How can you scale an object from the center while specifying an exact scale ratio?

- When using the **Rotate** tool, how do you lock the protractor to a specific orientation? What other tool allows you to lock the orientation on an object before you begin to create it?

- How can you use the **Rotate** tool to create rotated copies?

- How can you use the **Arc** tool to create a rounded corner that starts and ends at the same distance from the corner?

- What is the difference between hiding and smoothing edges?

- The **Follow Me** tool was used in two different ways in this chapter. Describe how this tool can be used to "drive" a flat face along a path, and how it can be used to create round objects.

5 chapterfive
Working with 3D Warehouse Models

In Chapter 2, we imported models from the 3D Warehouse, and in Chapters 3 and 4, we demonstrated how to create your own models when you can't find exactly what you want in the 3D Warehouse. This chapter combines concepts from preceding chapters, showing how to *make changes* to a 3D Warehouse model to create exactly the object you need.

> In this chapter, you'll learn how to do the following:
> - Create three different versions of the same table.
> - Lengthen or shorten a sofa.
> - Change a chaise into a sofa.
> - Modify a china cabinet.

5.1 Dining Table, Accent Table, and Coffee Table

Say you're looking for a specific dining table, and you find a "close enough" model in the 3D Warehouse. But perhaps the overall size of the model is wrong, or parts of it are too large or too small. This section will show you the three main aspects that you need to check when you download a 3D Warehouse model (**location, size**, and **composition**) and familiarize you with SketchUp's **Outliner**.

1. Using your Internet browser (don't use the **Get Models** tool), open the 3D Warehouse and download the model Round Table with Baluster Pedestal by Bonnie Roskes.

2. For any 3D Warehouse model you find, the first thing to check is whether it is **located** correctly, so display the axes (choose **View / Axes** from the main menu). Here we have two problems: The table is located far from the origin, and the tabletop is at the level of the origin (Figure 5-1). So if you were to use **Get Models** to import this table into another model, you'd be dragging it by its top, not by its base, and the table would be far from your cursor.

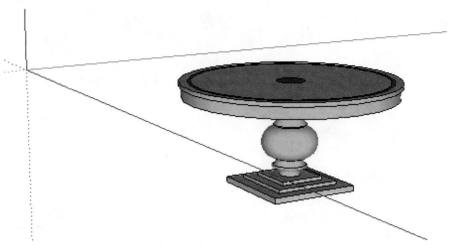

Figure 5-1

3 The table should be moved so that the center of the bottom of the base sits at the origin. You could find the center of the bottom square by hovering over midpoints, but for a slightly quicker way, activate **Line** and draw a diagonal line between opposite corners (Figure 5-2).

4 Select the entire table, including the diagonal line, and use **Move** to place the midpoint of this diagonal line at the origin (Figure 5-3). It's easiest to do this in two steps: First, move the table straight up in the blue direction above the level of the origin; then, move it again by the same midpoint so that this point meets the origin.

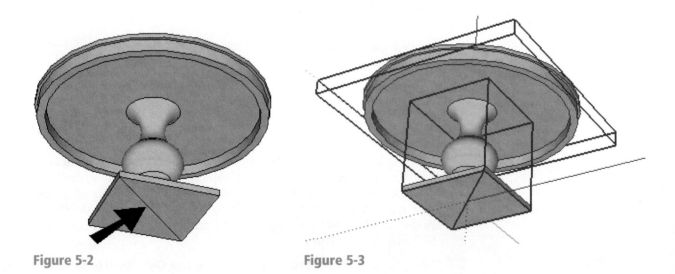

Figure 5-2   Figure 5-3

5 The diagonal line is no longer needed, so erase it.

6 The second item to check on a 3D Warehouse model is its **size**. We want to know this table's height, so activate **Tape Measure**. Click anywhere along the top edge of the table, then press the Up or Down arrow to lock the measurement to the blue direction. Hover (don't click) over any point at the bottom of the base, and the approximate measurement of 2′-6″ will appear next to your cursor (Figure 5-4) and in the **Length** field. This is a good height for a dining table, so we don't need to resize the entire model.

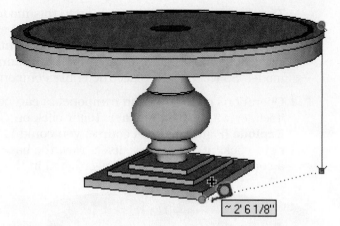

Figure 5-4

> **NOTE**
>
> In previous chapters, we've already used arrow keys, as well as the Shift key, to lock directions. As a rule, the arrow keys are easier to use because they don't require you to keep the Shift key pressed, leaving your hands (and the mouse) free to zoom and orbit to find the exact points that you need. Remember, **Right = Red**, **Left = Green**, **Up or Down = Blue**.

The third item to check on a 3D Warehouse model is its **composition** (whether it is made up of groups or components, or whether all or some of the model is a collection of ungrouped faces and edges). Well-crafted models make use of groups and components, although you'll find many 3D Warehouse models that do not. SketchUp's **Outliner** provides the best way to see how a model is made.

7 Choose **Window / Outliner** from the main menu. Under the model name, two components are listed, which is always a good sign. When a model is divided into groups and/or components, it becomes much easier to make changes to specific parts of a model. To match a component's name to objects in the model, just highlight the component's name in the **Outliner**, which is the same as selecting it. For example, highlight Component#2 in the **Outliner**, and the tabletop is selected (Figure 5-5). If you were to do the same for Component#4, you'd see that the entire base had been selected.

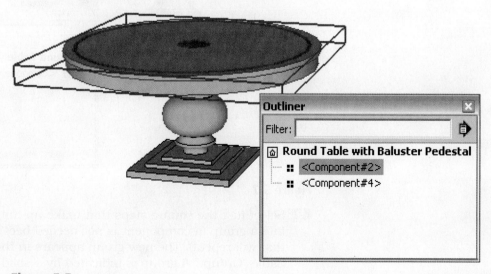

Figure 5-5

The changes that we'll be making to this model will be easier once the pedestal base is divided into two parts: the baluster itself and the square base at the bottom. We could edit Component#4 and make two nested components inside it, but that would add unnecessary complexity to this model. So we'll just replace the entire component with two groups.

8 Operations on groups and components can be performed on the model itself, or within the **Outliner**. Right-click on Component#4 and choose **Explode** (Figure 5-6). Of course, you could have done the same thing by right-clicking on the base itself. Now the base is selected but is no longer a component, and it is no longer listed in the **Outliner** (Figure 5-7).

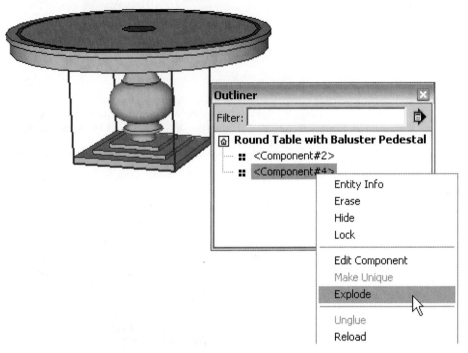

Figure 5-6

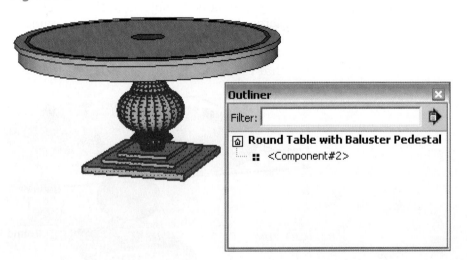

Figure 5-7

9 Select just the square steps that make up the base and make the base into a group (a component is not needed because this is not an object that will repeat). The new group appears in the **Outliner** with the generic name "Group." A group is indicated by a solid black square icon, as opposed to the four-square icon that identifies a component (Figure 5-8).

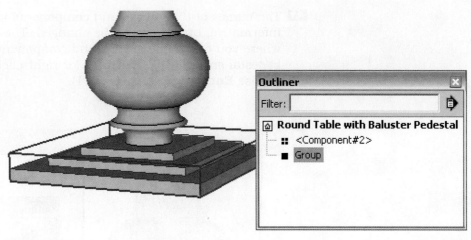

Figure 5-8

10 Make another group from the objects that form the baluster pedestal (Figure 5-9).

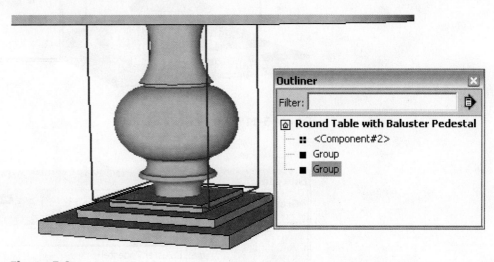

Figure 5-9

> **NOTE**
>
> If you had kept the entire base as a component (if you had not exploded it), and edited it to create the two groups within, you would see the nested format in the **Outliner** shown in Figure 5-10.
>
> The **Outliner** also has drag-and-drop capability, so you can easily drag objects into and out of groups and components for easy nesting and un-nesting.

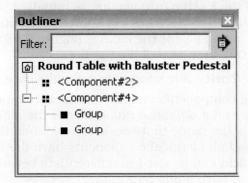

Figure 5-10

11 The names of the groups and components in the **Outliner** aren't very informative, but these can be changed. The **Entity Info** window is where you can name groups and components, so right-click on the pedestal group in the **Outliner** (or right-click on the group itself) and choose **Entity Info** (Figure 5-11).

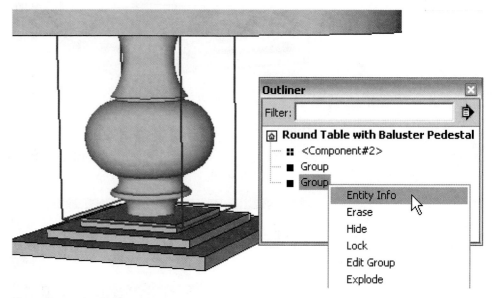

Figure 5-11

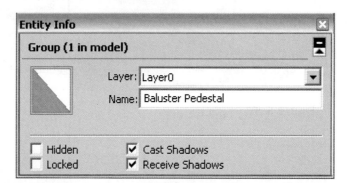

Figure 5-12

12 Groups aren't assigned names when they are created, so the **Name** field of the **Entity Info** window is initially blank. In this field, enter "Baluster Pedestal," then click anywhere outside this field (don't press Enter) to implement the change (Figure 5-12). The new name appears in the **Outliner** as well (Figure 5-13).

13 Use the **Entity Info** window to name the base group as well (Figure 5-14).

Naming components is a little trickier, because a component has both a *name* and a *definition name*. Here's the difference: The **Definition Name** is the name that was assigned when the component was created, and all identical components have the same definition name. The **Name** field can be used to differentiate between identical components; each can have a different name.

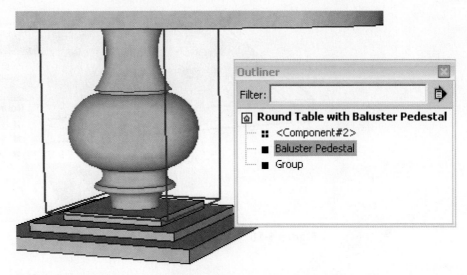

Figure 5-13

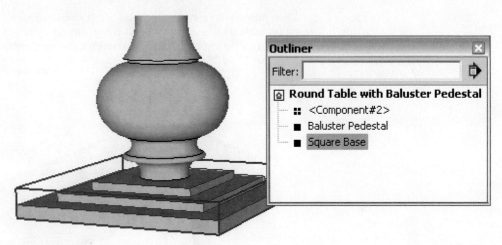

Figure 5-14

14 For this table, there is only one tabletop component, so there's no need to change the name, but use **Entity Info** to change the **Definition Name** (Figure 5-15). This new name appears in the **Outliner**, surrounded by angle brackets (Figure 5-16).

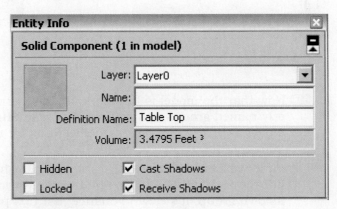

Figure 5-15

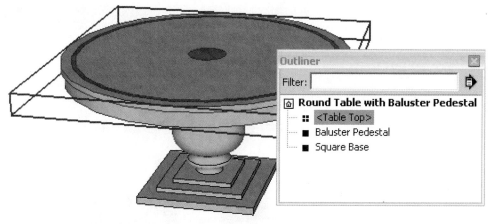

Figure 5-16

> **NOTE**
>
> When might you want to assign different names to identical components? Take the dining table shown in Figure 5-17, which has two identical Table Leg components ("Table Leg" being the definition name). Each leg component has a different name, "Left Side" and "Right Side."

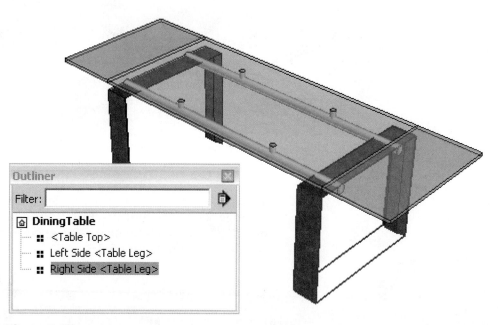

Figure 5-17

15 Now that the model is located and sized correctly, and comprises properly named groups and components, use **File / Save As** to save this model as a new file. This model will now be used to create the three different tables.

First, we'll create the dining table. The height and diameter are fine, but the pedestal is a bit too bulbous and wide. Because the pedestal is its own group, it's easy to change just this part of the model without affecting the tabletop and square base.

16 Select the pedestal group and activate the **Scale** tool. The green drag handles appear around just this group. The various handles along the edges and at the corners all perform different scaling tasks, but we want to shrink this pedestal uniformly inward without affecting its height. So move your cursor to the handle shown in Figure 5-18, which scales in the red direction, and press and hold the Ctrl/Option key so that the scaling will be toward the center.

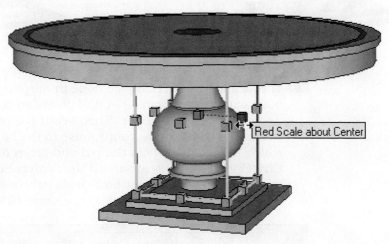

Figure 5-18

17 Move the cursor inward to shrink the pedestal in the red direction to any size (Figure 5-19). After this scaling is complete, enter 0.7 (Figure 5-20) to shrink the pedestal 70% in the red direction.

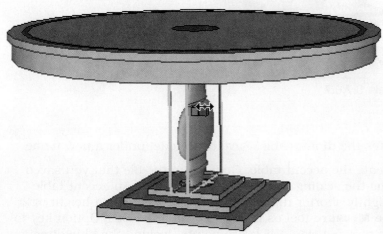

Figure 5-19

Red Scale	0.7

Figure 5-20

18 Now do the same in the green direction (Figure 5-21), entering the same 0.7 value. The pedestal should look less wide, having been reduced uniformly in both the red and green directions (Figure 5-22).

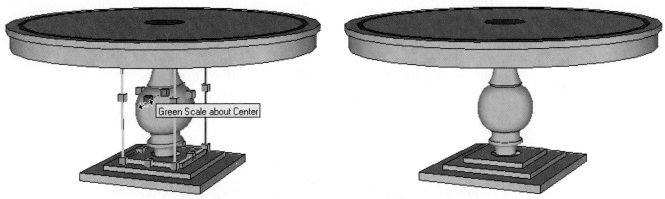

Figure 5-21

Figure 5-22

19 This scaling can actually be done in one step instead of two. **Undo** both scaling operations (red and green) so that the pedestal is back to its former, bulbous shape. Then select the pedestal again and activate **Scale**. This time, move your mouse to the handle shown in Figure 5-23, which scales about *both* the red and green directions. Again, use the Ctrl/Option key to scale about the center. Shrink the pedestal by clicking anywhere, then enter both scale values separated by a comma: 0.7, 0.7 (Figure 5-24). The result is the same 70% narrower pedestal.

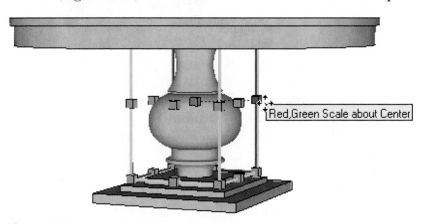

Figure 5-23

Red,Green Scale	0.7,0.7

Figure 5-24

20 This completes the dining table. Save this model under a new name.

21 Next we'll create the accent table. Go back to the file that you saved before making the scaling changes to the pedestal. An accent table should be slightly shorter than a dining table; we'll use a height of 26″. Use the **Tape Measure** tool as before, pressing the Ctrl/Option key to toggle off the plus (+) sign. Click two points, locking the blue direction, to measure the current height, and enter 26 so that the entire table is a bit smaller.

22 This accent table should have a much smaller top, so we'll use a diameter of 20″. Use the **Circle** tool to create a circle whose center point meets the center of the tabletop, extending the circle in either the red or green direction. Enter a radius (half of the diameter) of 10″. Because the tabletop itself is a component, the circle drawn on top of it is a separate object, so you'll see that familiar shimmering effect (Figure 5-25).

Figure 5-25

23 Select the tabletop component, activate **Scale**, and use the red-scale drag handle shown in Figure 5-26 while pressing the Ctrl/Option key. Scale the tabletop inward until you reach the outermost corner point of the circle that you drew in the previous step (Figure 5-27). You'll have to zoom in on the circle to click the correct point.

Figure 5-26

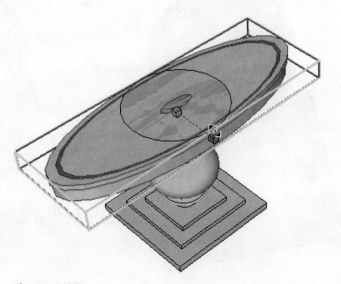

Figure 5-27

24 Do the same scaling in the green direction (Figure 5-28).

Figure 5-28

25 The circle on the top is no longer needed, so activate **Select**, double-click on the circle to select both its face and edges, and press the Delete key.

26 The base at the bottom of the table should be 10″ square. So draw a 10″ × 10″ square on the bottom of the base (Figure 5-29), and use midpoint inferences, in both red and green directions, to move the square to the exact center of the base (Figure 5-30).

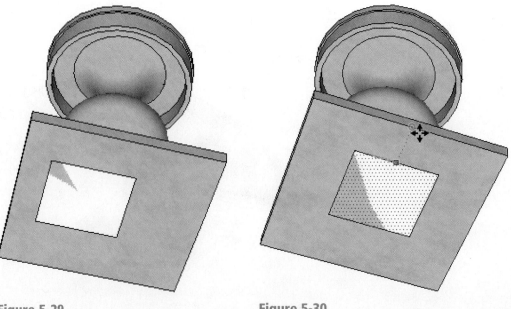

Figure 5-29   **Figure 5-30**

27 Just as you scaled the tabletop, use **Scale** in both the red and green directions to adjust the base to meet the edges of the square (Figure 5-31). Then erase the square.

28 The pedestal is now too large for this delicate accent table, so scale it down as well (Figure 5-32).

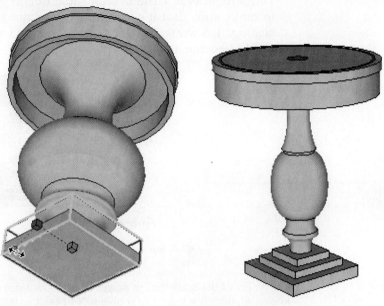

Figure 5-31   Figure 5-32

29 Save this file as the "accent table" model, and once again go back to the original table model that you saved. Now we'll create the coffee table.

The height of this coffee table will be 18″. We could use the **Tape Measure** to set the table height, but there's another way: We can use the **Scale** tool. We've seen that **Scale** works with relative scale values (for example, 0.7 means 70% as large), but **Scale** can also work with exact measurements. You just need to add a unit to the number (such as m or mm).

30 Select the entire table, activate **Scale**, and click the top center handle shown in Figure 5-33, which scales in the blue direction. Move this

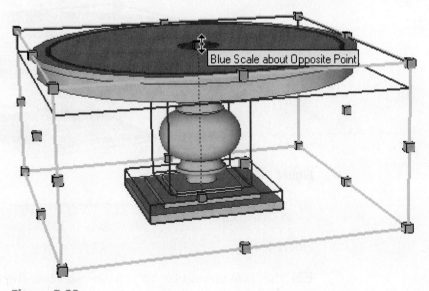

Blue Scale about Opposite Point

Figure 5-33

handle anywhere, up or down, then enter 1.5′ (don't forget the apostrophe symbol), as shown in Figure 5-34. This "squashes" the table so that its total height is 18″, or 1.5 feet (Figure 5-35). The **Tape Measure** tool would have resized the entire table uniformly, but scaling in just the blue direction keeps all red and green dimensions the same. In other words, the tabletop diameter remains the same, but it is thinner. You should check the overall table height with the **Tape Measure** tool to make sure that it's 18″. (If you had not used the foot symbol when scaling, 1.5 would be the assumed scale value, and the table height would become 1.5 times *higher*.)

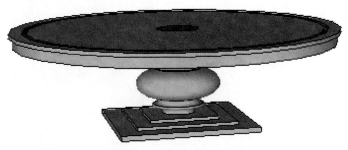

Blue Scale 1.5′

Figure 5-34

Figure 5-35

> **NOTE**
>
> The ability of the **Scale** tool to accept exact measurements is a very nice and little-known feature, but there is a problem: You can't enter a measurement in inches. The symbol for inches is quotation marks, which requires the use of the Shift key, and the Shift key can't be "read" by the **Scale** field. The apostrophe symbol for feet doesn't require Shift, so this symbol can be used, as can units such as m, cm, or mm.

31 The tabletop should have a 36″ diameter, which is equivalent to 3′. Exact measurements in two directions can also be entered when scaling: Select the tabletop component, activate **Scale**, and shrink the tabletop to any size, using the red/green handle shown in Figure 5-36 with the Ctrl/Option key. Then enter 3′,3′ (Figure 5-37) to set the new tabletop size in the red and green directions (Figure 5-38). Again, check your work by using the **Tape Measure** to measure the diameter.

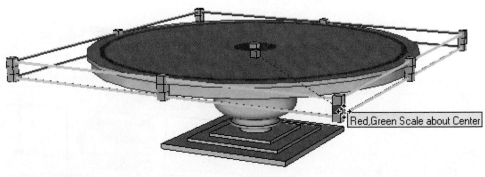

Red,Green Scale about Center

Figure 5-36

Red,Green Scale 3′,3′

Figure 5-37

32 The base should be 16″ square, so scale the base the same way, entering 1.33′ for both the red- and green-scale values (Figure 5-39).

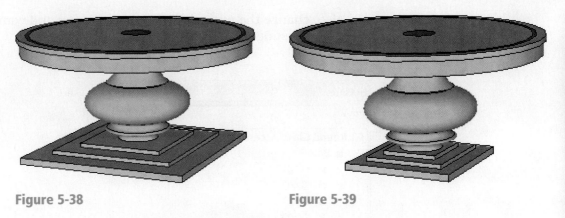

Figure 5-38

Figure 5-39

33 Finally, scale the pedestal to an attractive proportion (Figure 5-40).

Figure 5-40

Model It Yourself

Download the model Round Glass Accent Table with Shelf by Bonnie Roskes (Figure 5-41). A little investigating will tell you that the table's size and location need to be fixed. Make the table 26″ high, keeping all other objects the same relative size, and move it to the correct spot relative to the origin (Figure 5-42).

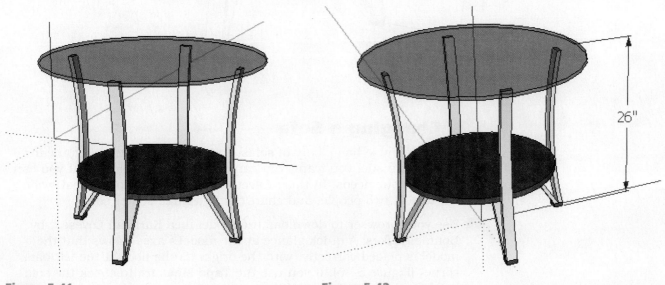

Figure 5-41

Figure 5-42

Also, change the names of the table's groups and components so that it's easy to distinguish among them (Figure 5-43).

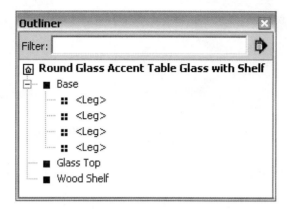

Figure 5-43

Finally, create another version of this table: a coffee table 18″ high, with the tabletop 32″ in diameter and the shelf 24″ in diameter (Figure 5-44). You'll also need to adjust the table's base to accommodate the new shelf location.

Figure 5-44

5.2 Changing a Sofa

The 3D Warehouse has plenty of sofas, so it's a safe bet that if you can't find the exact model you want, you can find something close that you can modify to fit your needs. In this project, you'll start with a loveseat, wide enough to seat two people, and change it to a three-seater sofa.

1 Use your browser to download the model Ikea Karlstad Loveseat by Bonnie Roskes. A quick glance at the model's axes shows that the model is placed correctly, with the origin on the floor at the left back corner (Figure 5-45). If you use the **Tape Measure** to check the sofa's height or length, you'll find that it's sized correctly.

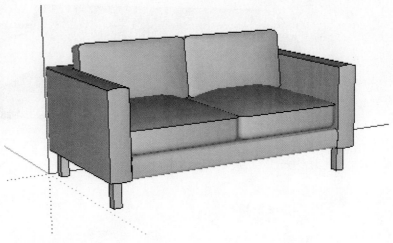

Figure 5-45

2 Open the **Outliner** for this model to see how it's set up (Figure 5-46). There are four identical cushions: two seat cushions and two back cushions. The "arm & back" components are symmetrical copies, and each contains two leg components nested within. The group is the sofa's base.

3 To make room for the third set of seat and back cushions, we'll move one of the arms. So that the sofa will remain in the same spot relative to the origin, the left side of the sofa should stay where it is. So we'll move the arm on the right. Start by selecting this "arm & back" component (Figure 5-47).

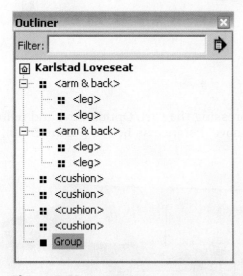

Figure 5-46

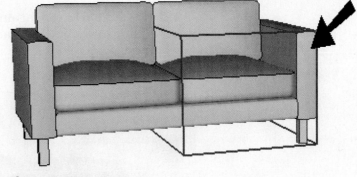

Figure 5-47

4 Activate the **Move** tool. The two move points must define the width of one cushion, so start by clicking anywhere on the left edge of one of the cushions, such as Point 1 in Figure 5-48. Press the right arrow key to lock the red direction, then click any point along the right edge of the same cushion (Point 2).

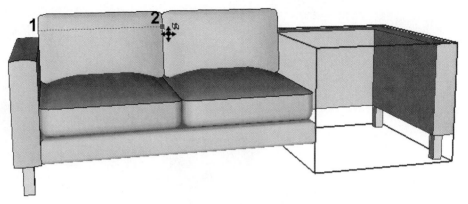

Figure 5-48

5 Now we can fill this new space with cushions. Select the back and seat cushions to the left of the empty space (Figure 5-49).

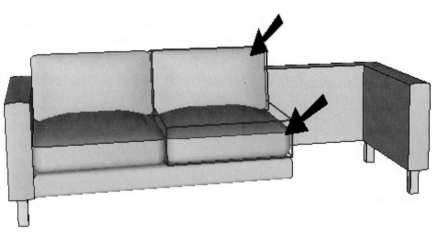

Figure 5-49

6 Use the **Move** tool again, pressing the Ctrl/Option key, and using the right arrow and the same move distance as before (Figure 5-50).

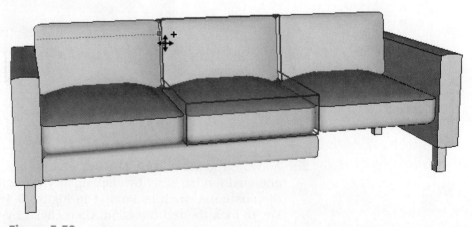

Figure 5-50

7 These new cushions are hovering in the air, so the base below the cushions needs to be extended to the right. Open the base for editing (remember that this object is a group, according to the **Outliner**). Only the right side of the base needs to move, but when you select this face, the entire base is selected (Figure 5-51).

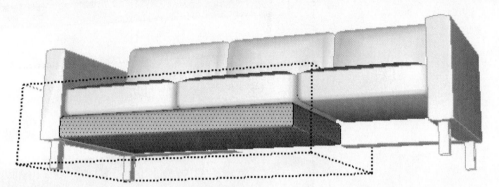

Figure 5-51

8 The base obviously comprises separate faces, so why can't individual faces be selected? Because all of its edges have been *softened*, which is what happens when you use the **Eraser** on an edge while pressing the Ctrl/Option key. To see these softened edges and the individual faces of the base, choose **View / Hidden Geometry** from the main menu.

9 Now you can select all of the faces on the right side of the base. Because there are so many long, narrow faces here, the best way to select the entire right side is to use a left-to-right selection window like the one shown in Figure 5-52.

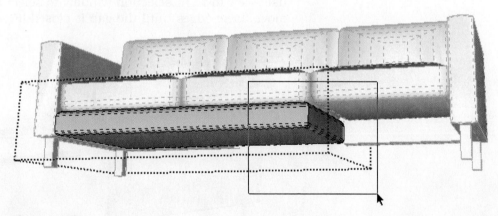

Figure 5-52

10 With the entire right side of the base selected, use the **Move** tool to extend the base until it meets the right arm (Figure 5-53).

11 Close the base group, and leave the softened edges displayed.

12 Orbit around to see the back of the sofa. There's a gap between the two "arm & back" components (Figure 5-54). If this sofa is placed against a wall, you would never see this gap, but it would be noticeable if you relocated the sofa.

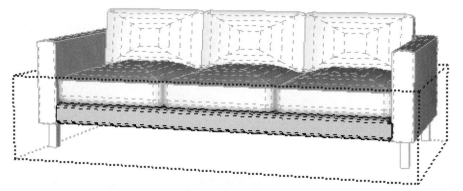

Figure 5-53

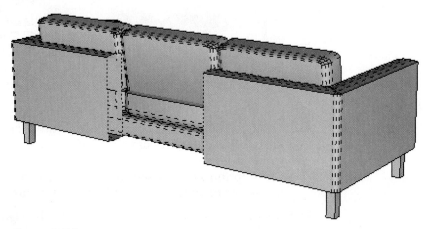

Figure 5-54

13 Closing the gap is easy: Open either "arm & back" component for editing, use a left-to-right selection window to select all edges of the gap, and move these edges until the gap is closed (Figure 5-55).

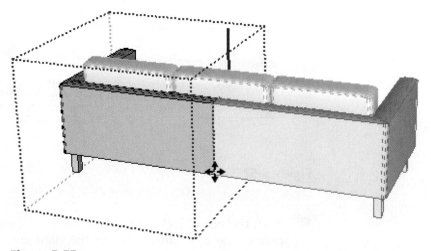

Figure 5-55

14 Close the component, and choose **View / Hidden Geometry** again to toggle off the display of softened edges (Figure 5-56). Make sure that the sofa looks correct from the front, too (Figure 5-57).

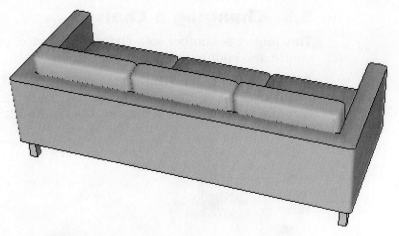

Figure 5-56

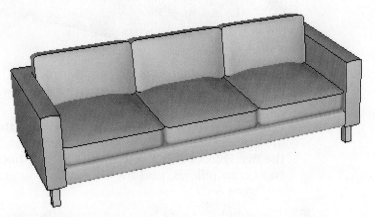

Figure 5-57

Model It Yourself

Download the model Ikea Ektorp Three-Seat Sofa by Bonnie Roskes (Figure 5-58). This model comprises seven groups: six for the cushions and one for the base and arms.

Remove the center cushions and make this sofa into a two-cushion loveseat (Figure 5-59). Remember, you'll have to display hidden and softened edges in order to make the base narrower.

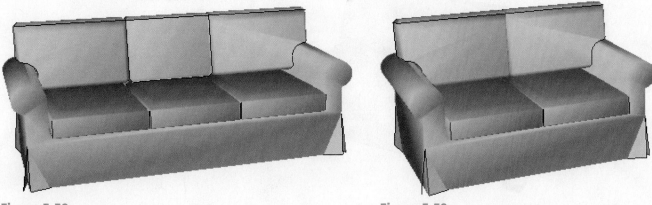

Figure 5-58

Figure 5-59

5.3 Changing a Chaise

This project is another sofa-changing exercise, in which you'll start with a chaise and end up with a standard sofa.

1 Download the model Crate and Barrel Axis Chaise by Bonnie Roskes (Figure 5-60). The goal is to remove the chaise section on the right side and replace it with what appears on the left side.

Figure 5-60

2 As always, check the **Outliner** to see how this model is made. All parts are either components or groups. On the right side of the model, erase the five objects that make up the chaise: back cushion, chaise cushion, two throw pillows, and the chaise base (a group). What's left is shown in Figure 5-61.

3 The remaining sofa base is a group, but because it will be copied to the right side, it should be made into a component. You can right-click on the group name in the **Outliner** and choose **Make Component** (Figure 5-62), or right-click on the base on the model itself and choose the same option.

Figure 5-61

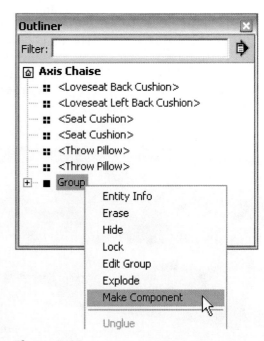

Figure 5-62

4 Select the entire left side of the couch (everything except the seat and back cushions that will be in the center of the sofa), and make a copy of these objects in the green direction (Figure 5-63).

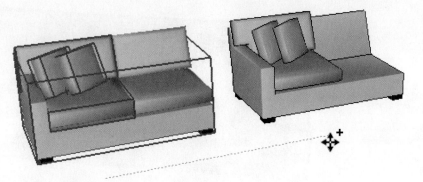

Figure 5-63

5 With all of the copied objects still selected, use the **Scale** tool to flip them inside-out (Figure 5-64).

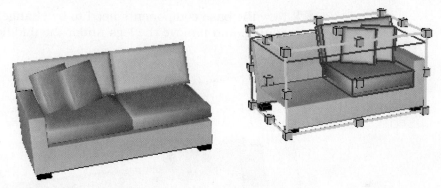

Figure 5-64

6 Before moving these objects into place, display the hidden geometry. In addition to helping select the specific faces, hidden edges can make it easier to find exact move points.

7 Activate **Move**, and for the first move point, click anywhere along the front left corner of the seat cushion (Figure 5-65).

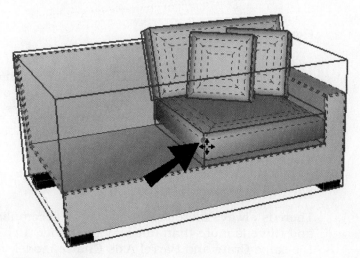

Figure 5-65

8 Press the left arrow to move in the green direction and move the cushion to meet the cushion to its left (Figure 5-66).

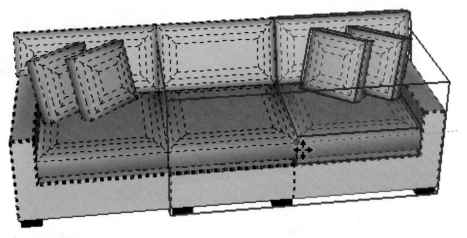

Figure 5-66

9 Now the base components need to be changed. Open either one for editing, and remove the legs under the middle of the sofa (Figure 5-67).

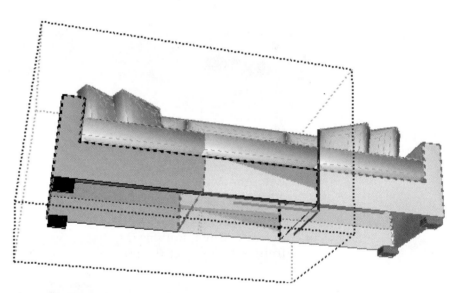

Figure 5-67

10 Orbit to face the back, and adjust the width of the base (Figure 5-68). Because the two base components initially overlap, you'll have to use a left-to-right selection window to select edges that are not visible.

11 When finished, make sure that the sofa looks good from the front as well (Figure 5-69).

Model It Yourself

There is always more than one way to accomplish a task in SketchUp, and there is more than one way to change a chaise to a sofa. Download the same Crate and Barrel Axis Chaise model, but this time, don't remove the entire chaise section. Instead, remove just the chaise cushion

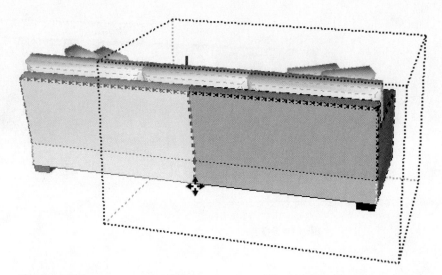

Figure 5-68

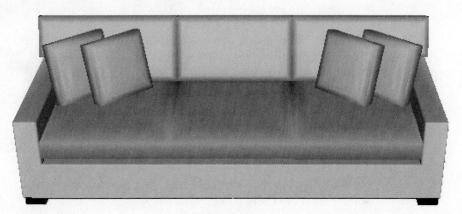

Figure 5-69

Figure 5-70

(Figure 5-70), and shorten the chaise base (Figure 5-71). This also requires some adjustment of the arm on the right side. You'll also have to make a copy of a seat cushion, adjust the width of the back cushion on the right, nudge the throw pillows a bit to the right, remove legs, and overlap the bases (Figure 5-72).

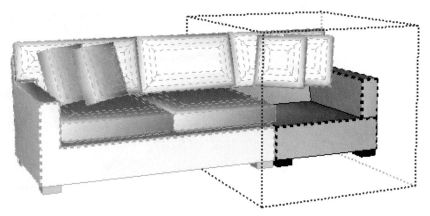

Figure 5-71

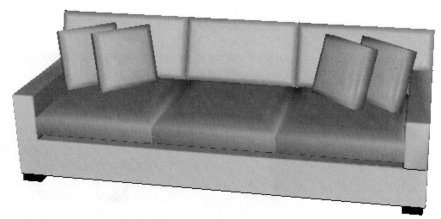

Figure 5-72

5.4 Changing a China Cabinet

There is a staggering number of cabinets, wall units, sideboards, and breakfronts in the 3D Warehouse. But Murphy's Law dictates that the exact piece that you need won't be available. Pieces like these are not always so easy to create from scratch, so it's useful to know how to modify a piece that's already been modeled. In this project, we'll change a wide, four-door china cabinet into a two-door cabinet. To accomplish this, we'll use the extremely useful (and often underused) **Section Plane** tool. This section is challenging, but stick with the steps: Once you learn how to "slice" models with section planes, you'll be able to apply the technique to all sorts of models.

1 Download the model China Cabinet by Bonnie Roskes (Figure 5-73). If you check the **Outliner** for this model, or just start selecting various objects, you'll see that there are no groups or components. There are also some minor design issues, including the fact that door handles are not placed symmetrically.

This cabinet is to be changed into a piece half as wide. It must be symmetrical, and we want to keep the same supports at the bottom. So we'll keep only the column at the far right side, erasing everything else; then we'll make a symmetrical copy of that column.

Figure 5-73

The **Section Plane** tool will be used to "slice" through the cabinet, so that everything but the far-right column can be easily erased. But we first need to establish where to place the section plane. Because the slice should occur halfway between the two right drawers or doors, the section plane should be placed at the midpoint of the line indicated in Figure 5-74.

Figure 5-74

Figure 5-75

2 Activate the **Section Plane** tool, either using the **Large Tool Set** icon shown in Figure 5-75, or by choosing **Tools / Section Plane** from the main menu.

3 Before clicking anywhere, move the mouse over various faces of the model. The preview of the section plane aligns to whatever face it touches. Move to the right side of the cabinet (Figure 5-76) and click to place the section plane. The right side of the cabinet is now gone from view (don't worry, it hasn't been erased), and you can see into the cabinet (Figure 5-77).

Figure 5-76

Figure 5-77

> **NOTE**
>
> The **Section Plane** tool wasn't specifically created for peering inside furniture; it's a handy way to look inside a room or building. Imagine that you are designing a multi-story house; a section plane can help you visualize what's in a specific story by slicing away the view of everything above that story. It's also a good tool for creating plan and elevation views, as we'll see in Chapter 10. But as with many of SketchUp's tools, this one has more uses than the software designers envisioned!

4 This section plane isn't where we want it, and it's not always easy to move a section plane to an exact spot. So we'll copy the section plane, placing the copy in the correct spot. A section plane can be selected, moved, copied, or even rotated like any other SketchUp object, so start by selecting it. It should turn blue, like any other selected object would (Figure 5-78).

Figure 5-78

5 Activate **Move** and press the Ctrl/Option key. For the first move point, click anywhere on the section plane itself. This means clicking the section plane near its edges, away from points on the cabinet itself. Click when you see the "On Section" popup (Figure 5-79).

Figure 5-79

6 For the second move point, click the midpoint of the line between the two doors on the right side (Figure 5-80).

Now there are two section planes. Because SketchUp doesn't know which one should be cutting the cabinet, *neither* is active and the cabinet is not cut (Figure 5-81).

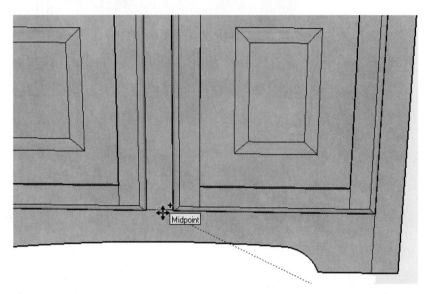

Figure 5-80

Figure 5-81

NOTE

There is another way to place a section plane at this midpoint, without the need for copying. You would activate **Section Plane** and move the cursor to the right-side face, but instead of clicking to create the section plane, you would hover over this face while keeping the Shift key pressed. This locks the section plane's orientation. With Shift pressed, you would then click the midpoint of that short line.

7 Right-click on the copied section plane (the one on the left) and choose **Create Group from Slice** (Figure 5-82). This creates a series of edges all around the cabinet where its faces meet the section plane. (Imagine the section plane as a cutting blade slicing down through the cabinet; these edges show where the slice occurs.) These edges are all part of a group, which is indicated in Figure 5-83.

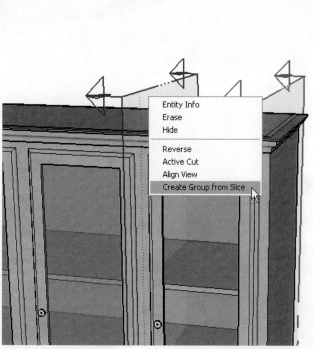

Figure 5-82

Figure 5-83

8 The section planes are no longer needed, so use the **Eraser** to erase them both. Now the group of edges is easier to see (Figure 5-84).

9 The edges created from the section plane aren't useful to us inside a group, so right-click on any of these edges (be careful to click an edge and not on a face of the cabinet), and choose **Explode**. The edges go from thick to thin, showing that the edges are now part of the cabinet itself, and you have successfully divided the cabinet faces (Figure 5-85).

10 Now comes the fun part: erasing all faces and edges to the left of the slice lines. You could use the **Eraser** and start clicking to erase objects one by one (Figure 5-86), or you could use right-to-left selection windows to erase chunks of objects at one time. When finished, you should be left with one column of the cabinet plus its support (Figure 5-87).

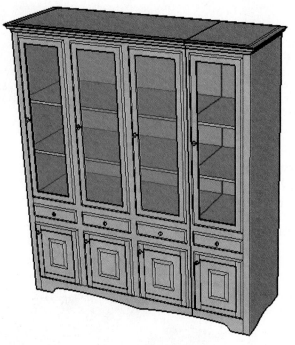

Figure 5-84

Figure 5-85

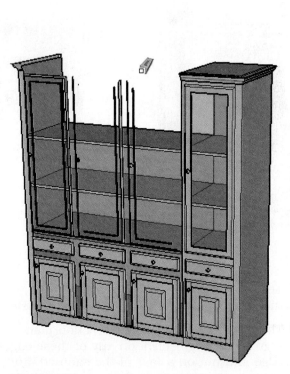

Figure 5-86

Figure 5-87

11 Make a component from this section of the cabinet, copy the component, and use **Scale** to turn the copy inside-out (Figure 5-88). Move the copy into place, and the cabinet is complete, except that the edges of both components are visible. This results in what looks like a slice going vertically through the center of the piece (Figure 5-89).

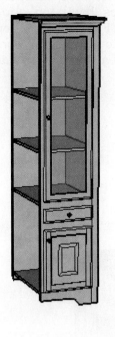

Figure 5-88   **Figure 5-89**

12 The solution is to hide these inside edges. Open either component for
editing. The other half of the cabinet is still visible, although faded
(Figure 5-90), so finding the edges to soften is difficult. To hide the other
half, choose **View / Component Edit / Hide Similar Components**.
Now only the edited component is visible (Figure 5-91).

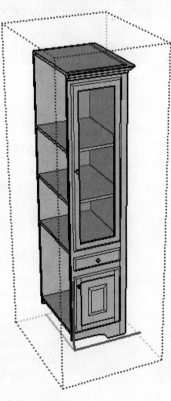

Figure 5-90   **Figure 5-91**

13 Use the **Eraser** with the Shift key pressed to hide the inside edges of the shelves, back, top, and front of the cabinet, such as the edges indicated in Figure 5-92. There are a lot of small edges along the top, so zoom in to get them. When finished, close the component and the cabinet appears to be one smooth piece (Figure 5-93).

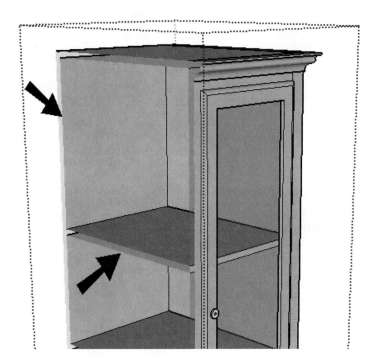

Figure 5-92

Figure 5-93

> **NOTE**
>
> Of course, you also could have hidden these edges *before* making the half-cabinet into a component!

Model It Yourself

Another way to modify a china cabinet is to make it into a breakfront. Start by downloading the same China Cabinet model, and create a section plane that will enable you to slice off the top, above the drawers (Figure 5-94).

After removing the top of the cabinet, you'll be left with a credenza or sideboard. Make sure that you add the face for the top of this piece, and save the entire object as a group or component (Figure 5-95).

For the hutch that will sit atop the sideboard, draw a rectangle on the top, set back from the front. Then offset the back and sides slightly inward (Figure 5-96).

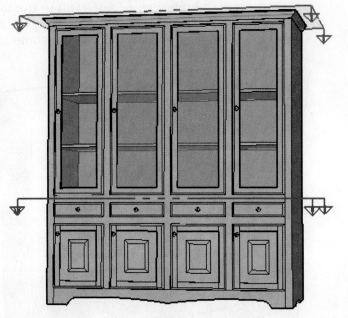

Figure 5-94

Figure 5-95

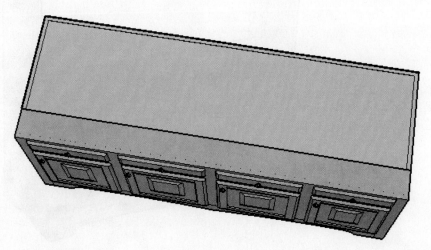

Figure 5-96

Chapter 5 | Working with 3D Warehouse Models **201**

Pull up the hutch (Figure 5-97), fill in the top (Figure 5-98), and finally add some shelves and even moulding along the top (use the **Follow Me** tool for this). The final piece should look something like Figure 5-99.

Figure 5-97

Figure 5-98

Figure 5-99

- After downloading a model from the 3D Warehouse, what are the three items that you should check immediately, before making any changes?

- For a component, what is the difference between its name and definition name?

- How would you use the **Scale** tool to shrink an object in both the red and green directions, without using the tool more than once?

- How can you use the **Scale** tool to set an object's exact length or height? What do you do when the dimension that you want to use is in inches? And how does this differ from using the **Tape Measure** tool for resizing?

- How can hidden edges help you make changes to objects with softened edges?

- How can the **Section Plane** tool be used to remove part of a model?

- How can you adjust your model display so that while editing a group or component, nothing else is visible?

Working with Colors and Materials

So far we've used colors and materials from SketchUp's default material collections. But simple clicking and painting is just a fraction of what you can do with colors and materials in SketchUp. This chapter opens up a world of painting possibilities.

You'll learn how to do the following:
- Change material color and size.
- Position materials.
- Size materials using exact dimensions.
- Find and use your own materials.
- Create your own material collections.
- Paint groups and components.
- Paint organic (irregular) faces.
- Use translucent materials.

NOTE

Among other tasks, this chapter covers what you can do with digital images that tile to form a seamless pattern. You can also paint with digital images that are used individually (not tiled). This will be covered in Chapter 7.

6.1 Changing Material Color and Size

If you've been thinking that the materials in SketchUp's collections are pretty meager, you're right. But you can change these materials to create new ones.

The handling of colors and materials is the only area in which SketchUp has significant differences between the PC and Mac versions. Because PC users represent the clear majority of SketchUp users (even among interior designers), the steps throughout this chapter will show PC screen captures. When different screen captures and instructions are required for Mac users, they will be provided as well.

1 We'll start with a solid color. Back in Chapter 2, we changed the color of a sofa; now we'll take a solid color and change it to a color with a specific numerical color value. Create a rectangle of any size, and using the paint bucket, paint it any solid color (Figure 6-1).

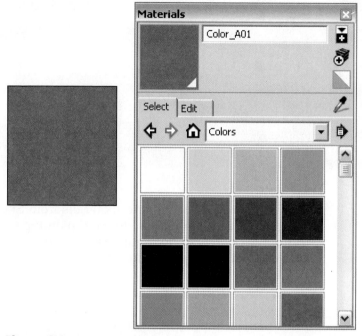

Figure 6-1

> **NOTE**
>
> Looking straight down on this rectangle gives you the most accurate color representation, although you might find that different monitors display colors differently. When you look at a face from an isometric (tilted) view, you've probably noticed that it can appear darker or lighter than its actual base color.

2 PC users: You can't edit a color in one of SketchUp's folders; you can only edit the "In Model" collection. Mac users: You *can* edit any color or material in any folder, but you should be careful *not* to do this; only edit the contents of the "Colors in Model" collection. On the **Materials** (PC) or **Colors** (Mac) window, click the House icon to see the one color used so far (Figure 6-2). (Mac users: You need to click the Brick icon first in order to get the House icon to appear. Also, you'll see two swatches in the "Colors in Model" collection, one for the color you used, the other gray/white divided swatch for the default face color.)

3 Double-click the color swatch to edit it. On a PC, the **Edit** tab opens, which provides a few ways to specify a new color (the color wheel is shown in Figure 6-3).

On a Mac, the **Colors** window changes to **Edit Material**, where the original color is shown on the lower half of the window, and the choices of new colors are shown on the top half. To get the color wheel to appear, click the wheel icon at the top of the window, as indicated in Figure 6-4.

Choosing a new color by sight is one option, but what if you or your client has a specific paint color in mind? All colors can be specified

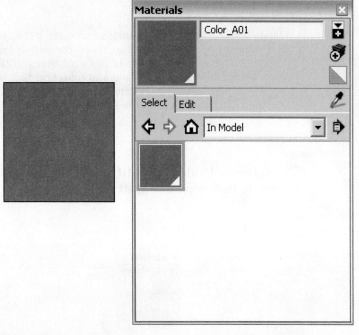

Figure 6-2

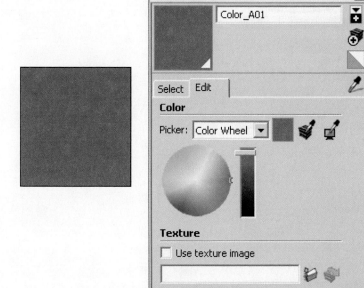

Figure 6-3

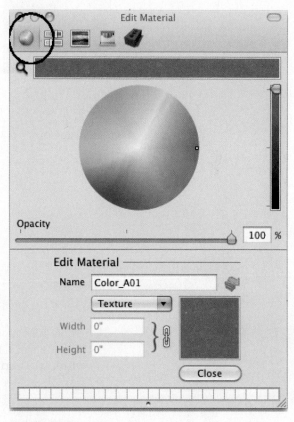

Figure 6-4

by numerical values (most commonly RGB for red, green, blue), and you can find these numbers for pretty much any color from any paint brand. Let's paint this wall with Basil Green from the Benjamin Moore Color Preview line. The RGB values for this color are 93.6, 143.75, 50.08.

4 PC users: Under the **Edit** tab of the **Materials** window, switch to RGB where indicated in Figure 6-5.

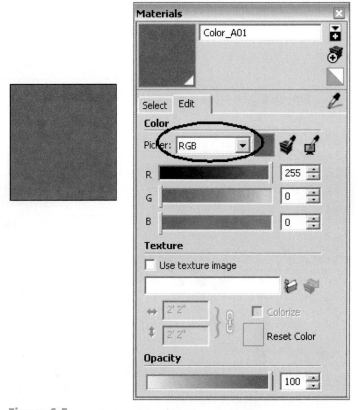

Figure 6-5

Mac users: Click the **Sliders** icon at the top of the **Edit Material** window, then choose **RGB sliders** (Figure 6-6).

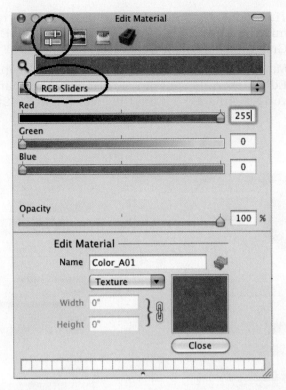

Figure 6-6

5. Enter the RGB values in their fields (93.6, 143.75, 50.08), and the color updates, both in the **Materials/Edit Materials** window, and on the painted rectangle itself (Figure 6-7).

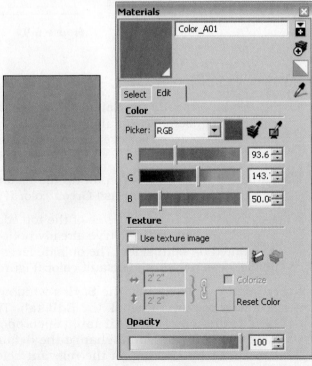

Figure 6-7

Chapter 6 | Working with Colors and Materials **209**

6 The names that SketchUp assigns to solid colors aren't usually very informative (such as Color_A01). PC users: Enter the new name, Basil Green, at the top of the **Materials** window (Figure 6-8).

Mac users: Enter the new name, Basil Green, at the bottom of the **Edit Materials** window, then make sure that you click **Close** when you are finished editing the color (Figure 6-9).

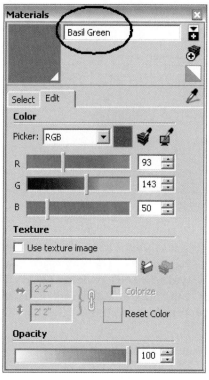

Figure 6-8

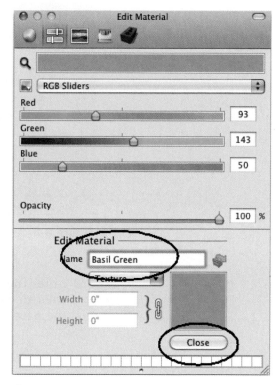

Figure 6-9

7 PC users: Return to the **Select** tab to see the updated "In Model" colors. Mac users: You're already back in the "Colors in Model" collection. Hover your cursor over the green swatch, and its name appears as a popup (Figure 6-10).

8 Use the **Push/Pull** tool to pull up the rectangle into a box. Its walls and top have the same Basil Green color (Figure 6-11).

9 Use the **Eraser** to remove one of the top edges. This is a good place to point out something you've already noticed: Faces in SketchUp can be painted on both sides. The outside faces are Basil Green, and the inside faces remain the default color (Figure 6-12).

10 As a quick aside, open the **Styles** window (**Window/Styles** in the main menu) and click the **Edit** tab. Then click the second icon at the top of the **Edit** tab, which opens the **Face** settings. Here is where you could change the default colors for front and back faces by clicking on the relevant color box (Figure 6-13). But there's no need to change these right now (unless you want to try it out).

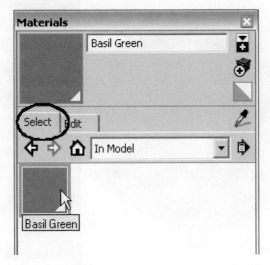

Figure 6-10

Figure 6-11

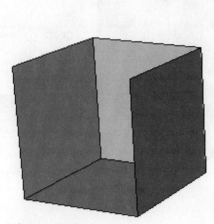

Figure 6-12

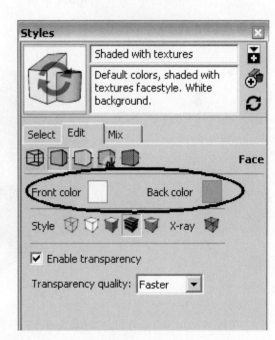

Figure 6-13

NOTE

SketchUp usually gets it right with front and back faces, but not always. If you ever create something that gets the default back color when it's supposed to be a front face, just right-click on the offending face and choose **Reverse Faces**.

---

11 Now we'll change the appearance of materials. Erase the edges of another wall to get a better view of the floor, and paint the floor with Stone_Masonry_Multi, which you can find in the "Stone" collection (Figure 6-14).

12 Paint the walls with Brick_Antique from the "Brick and Cladding" collection (Figure 6-15).

Now your "In Model" or "Colors in Model" collection should contain three swatches: Basil Green, stone, and brick. (Mac users will also

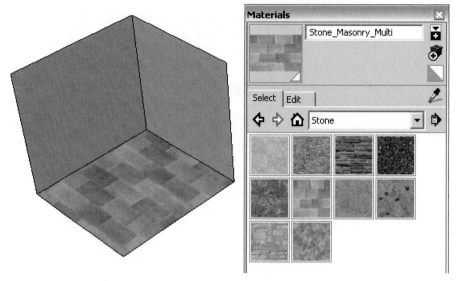

Figure 6-14

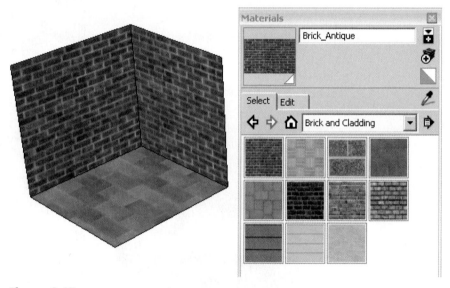

Figure 6-15

see the default swatch.) On a PC, the small triangle in the lower right corner of a swatch indicates that the material is in use Figure 6-16. If you change a face's color, its previous color will still appear in the "In Model" collection, but without that little triangle.

NOTE

SketchUp has a problem just letting go: You can replace a material and the original material will still appear in your **Materials** or **Colors** window. Similarly, you can erase a component, but you'll still see it in the **Components** window. This is intentional: SketchUp wants you covered in case you later want to get something back that you had removed. (Imagine that you scoured the 3D Warehouse for the perfect chair, then changed your mind and replaced the chair with another one, then decided you wanted the first chair after all. If it wasn't still lurking in the **Components** window you'd have to do your search from scratch!) But carrying around extra baggage in the form of unused materials, components, and so forth can slow down your model's performance. When your computer is moving slowly, try this: Open the **Model Info** window to the **Statistics** page, and click **Purge Unused**.

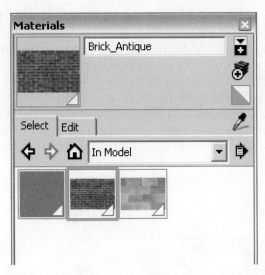

Figure 6-16

13 First, we'll change the stone floor. Double-click its material swatch, and under the **Edit** tab or in the **Edit Material** window, choose a new color. A light blue on the color wheel is shown in Figure 6-17, but you can use any of the slider methods as well. On a PC, there is a checkbox called **Colorize**; keeping this box empty makes the overall stone color uniform, otherwise you'll get some speckles of color.

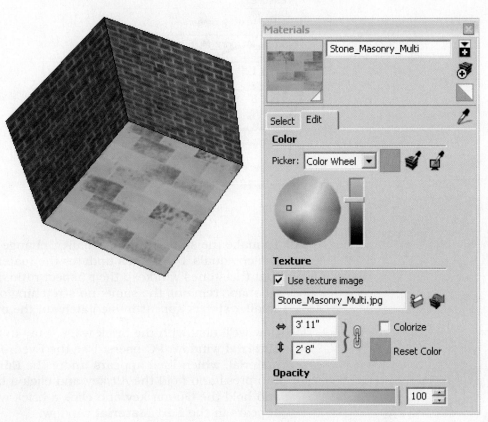

Figure 6-17

The size of the stones also can be changed. The current size is listed as 3'-11" wide × 2'-8" high (Figure 6-18); your measurements will reflect your model units. This doesn't mean that the stones themselves are that huge. This stone material (and all other materials) are based on digital images that tile seamlessly to fill a face. You can see the stone image's file name on the editing window: Stone_Masonry_Multi. jpg. The width and height listed here are the dimensions of one of these images. In other words, you could draw a 3'-11" × 2'-8" rectangle right on the floor, which would enclose one of the repeating stone images.

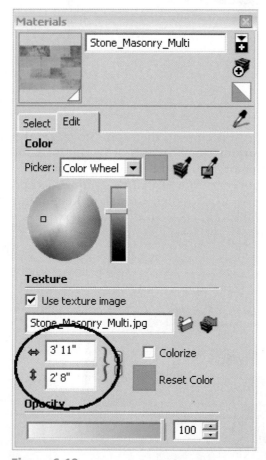

Figure 6-18

14 To make the stones appear smaller, change the 3'-11" width to 20" (which equals 1'-8"). This updates the material height as well so that the stones will keep their aspect ratio. In other words, the overall shape remains the same; no stretching or squashing occurs. The smaller stones appear immediately on the model (Figure 6-19).

15 Now we'll deal with the brick walls. Stay in the **Edit** tab on the **Edit Material** window. PC users: Use the Eyedropper to sample the brick material, which then appears under the **Edit** tab (Figure 6-20). Or you can press and hold the Alt key and click a brick wall. Mac users: Press and hold the Option key and click a brick wall, and that material appears in the **Edit Material** window.

Figure 6-19

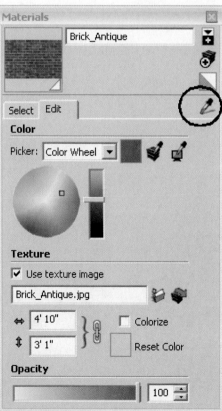

Figure 6-20

16 Change the base color to make the bricks lighter, and change the width of one brick image to 8'. And to make the bricks taller, click the Locked Chain icon indicated in Figure 6-21, which breaks the aspect ratio (width and height are no longer connected). Then enter a height of 12', which stretches the bricks vertically so that they appear almost square.

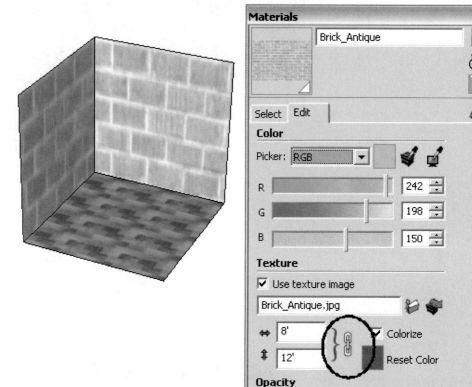

Figure 6-21

> **NOTE**
>
> Your "In Model" collection now shows the edited materials, although they exist just for this model. If you open a new file, you won't have access to these materials. Later in this chapter, we'll learn how to save materials in collections that you can access for any SketchUp model.

17 Just to confirm that the outside faces haven't changed, orbit to see the back of one of the walls. It is still Basil Green (Figure 6-22).

> **NOTE**
>
> As you've seen, you can use different materials and colors on both sides of a face, as long as the materials are opaque. When you paint with a translucent material, however, that material can be applied to both sides of the face, depending on what you paint and when. This will be shown at the end of this chapter.

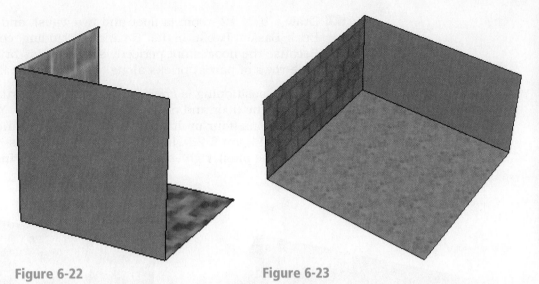

Figure 6-22   Figure 6-23

Model It Yourself

Using what you know about editing materials and colors, draw a similar room and paint one wall a solid color. Paint the other wall using Concrete_Block_8x8_Gray from the "Asphalt and Concrete" collection, and paint the floor with Tile_Travertine_2inch from the "Tile" collection (Figure 6-23).

Just for fun, let's make this room a bit crazy as shown in Figure 6-24, with large, light blue tiles on the floor, elongated yellow concrete blocks on one wall, and Duron's Brilliant Orange on the solid wall (RGB = 255, 159, 17).

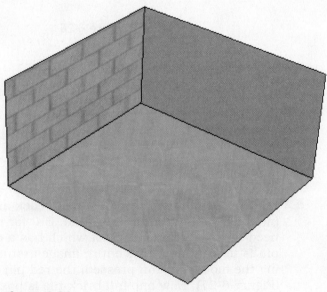

Figure 6-24

6.2   Material Positioning

The material adjustments that we made in the previous section are great for general, by sight material changes. This section takes material modification a bit further, using texture positioning to place your material exactly where you want it go and to get the sizing more precise.

1 Draw a 9′ × 12′ room (a floor and two walls), and paint the floor using Brick_Basket_Two from the "Brick and Cladding" collection (Figure 6-25). Because the floor is not perfectly sized for this brick pattern, you'll have rows of partial bricks along the edge of the floor.

2 Texture positioning is great for getting rid of partial materials. Right-click on the floor and choose **Texture/Position**. You should see a set of fixed pins (four multicolored pushpins surrounding one of the tiling images) (Figure 6-26). If you see four yellow pins instead (these are called free pins), right-click and choose **Fixed Pins**.

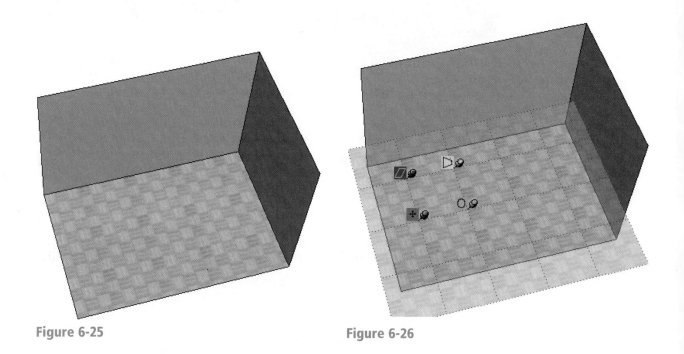

Figure 6-25   Figure 6-26

> **NOTE**
>
> Fixed pins are used to make changes to tiling materials, which is what we're doing in this chapter. Free pins are generally used to position non-tiling images to fit a face in a model, which we will do in Chapter 7.

3 While in positioning mode, you can click anywhere on the material (not on a pin) and drag it around. But for more exact placement, we need to use the pins, each of which has a different function. The red pin is used to move the entire image around, so click and drag (keeping the mouse button pressed) the red pin to a corner of the floor (Figure 6-27). Now one full brick tile is positioned squarely in this corner.

4 The green pin has two uses: sizing and rotating. We'll only be resizing for now. Drag the green pin straight along its floor edge so that the brick tiles expand (dragging it diagonally will rotate the material, which we'll do in the next section). Stop when the other edge (the edge where the blue pin sits) is exactly six bricks wide (Figure 6-28).

5 The blue pin is used for non-uniform scaling, or resizing in only one direction. Drag the blue pin straight along its edge, toward the red

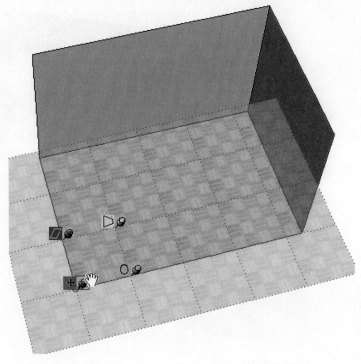

Figure 6-27

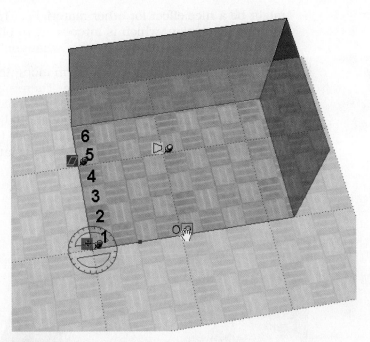

Figure 6-28

pin, until 10 complete bricks fill this edge (Figure 6-29), as though the tiles are being pulled in from beyond the wall. The bricks are no longer square; they've become distorted by having been squashed into rectangles.

Moving the blue pin anywhere other than along its edge will result in diagonal bricks, which would look a little strange (although diagonal

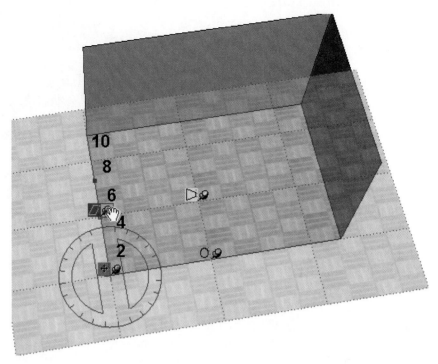

Figure 6-29

might be a nice effect for other materials). The yellow pin is used for diagonal distortion, which is interesting to play with (try it!), but it's not the most useful feature for most of what you'll be doing with materials.

6 The bricks should now look uniform along three of the edges, so right-click on the floor and choose **Done**. There's one edge that still has partial bricks (Figure 6-30). You've got two choices for fixing this: You can either go back into positioning mode and adjust the green and blue pins, or just move a wall to match the floor (you won't get this option in real life, but it's nice to be able to do what you want in SketchUp!).

Figure 6-30

7 Use **Push/Pull** to slide the wall so that there are 10 complete bricks along both edges (Figure 6-31).

8 Now we'll use the pins a little differently on the walls. First, make a window: Draw a rectangle of any size and erase its face (right-click on the face and choose **Erase**). Then paint the wall with Stone_Masonry_Multi (Figure 6-32).

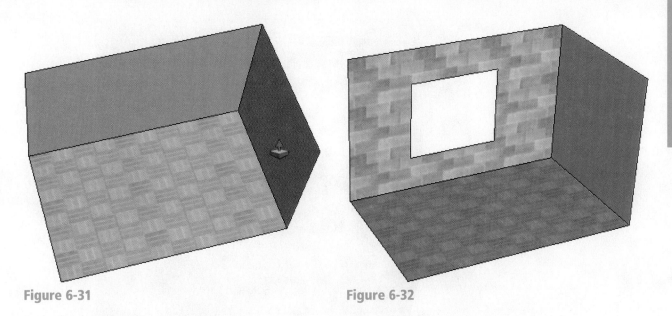

Figure 6-31   Figure 6-32

9 Right-click on the wall and choose **Texture/Position**, and drag the red pin to the lower left corner of the wall (Figure 6-33).

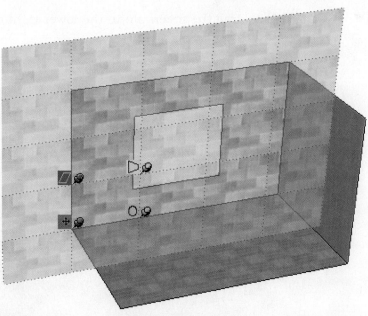

Figure 6-33

10 Now the goal is to have five stones along the width of the wall, and we already saw how to drag the green pin to make this happen. But for a more exact positioning, we can pick up the green pin and place it in a new spot on the material image. To do this, move your cursor over the green pin and click once (don't drag). This lifts the pin off of the wall, leaving it attached to the cursor. Click again to drop the pin at the lower right edge of the fifth stone (Figure 6-34). Zooming in closely will help you get the pin in exactly the right spot. The sharp end of the pin, not its green handle, is what you want to place. If you don't like where the pin ends up, just lift and drop it again.

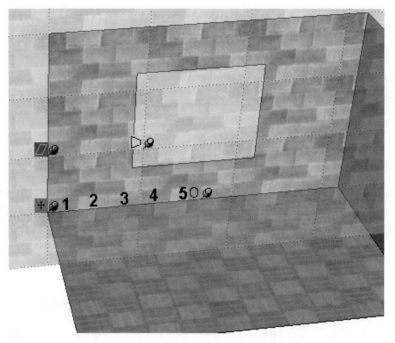

Figure 6-34

11 Now drag the green pin to the lower right corner of the wall (Figure 6-35).

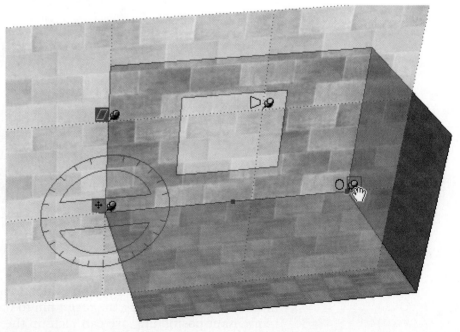

Figure 6-35

12 These are huge stones; we want only three rows going up the wall. So lift the blue pin and place it at the top left edge of the third stone (Figure 6-36), and drag the blue pin to the top of the wall (Figure 6-37).

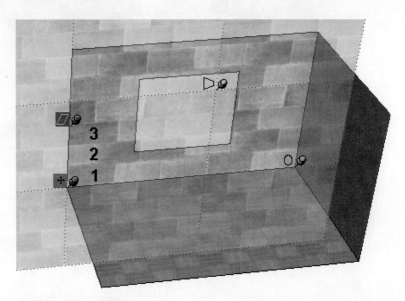

Figure 6-36

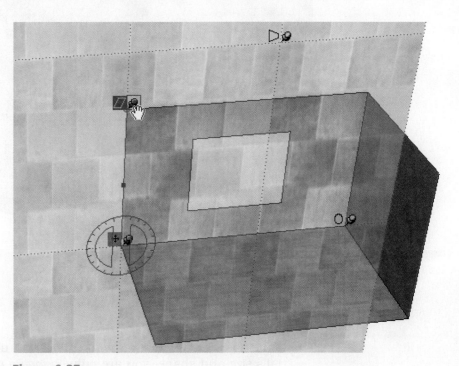

Figure 6-37

13 Right-click on the stone material and choose **Done**. The window can now be resized to occupy the space of two side-by-side stones. (True, you'll probably never get to actually move a window, but a similar situation could arise for, say, a painting.) This time, use the **Move** tool and drag the window edges left, right, up, or down (Figure 6-38.) until the window is the correct size (Figure 6-39).

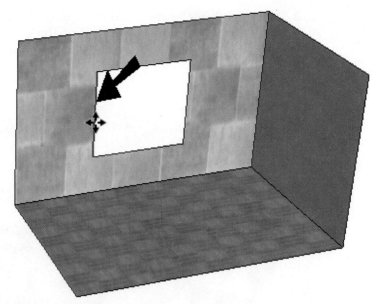

Figure 6-38

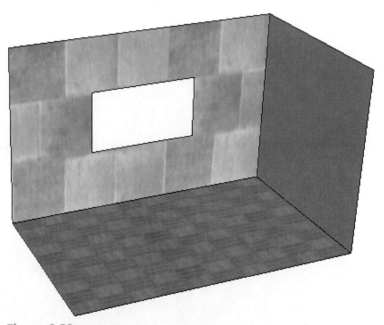

Figure 6-39

14 Remember this important point: When you use pins to change a material's size and shape, you are *only changing the face that you're editing*; you're not changing the original material. Look at the "In Model" stone and brick materials; their swatches are unchanged (Figure 6-40). Use the stone swatch to paint the blank wall; you will see that the stones retain their original sizes (Figure 6-41).

15 If you want both stone walls to have the larger stone size, use the Eyedropper or the Alt key (PC)/Option key (Mac) to sample the material, and then click the wall that you want to get that material (Figure 6-42).

Figure 6-40

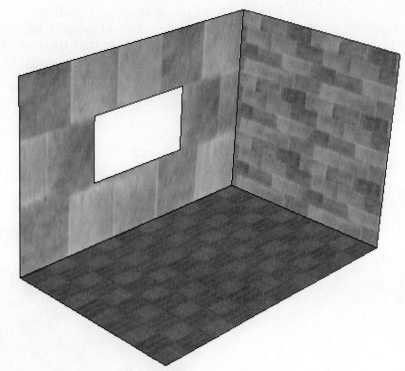

Figure 6-41

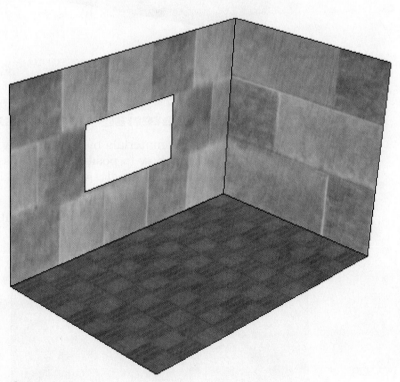

Figure 6-42

Model It Yourself

Draw a room with a rug on the floor (just draw a rectangle within a rectangle). You can leave out the windows. Paint the floor with Wood Parquet from the "Wood" collection, and paint the rug with Carpet_Pattern_Squares_Multi from the "Carpet and Textiles" collection. Use texture positioning so that there are no partial parquet squares along the floor edges, and position the rug material so that there are no partial squares (Figure 6-43). For the rug, you'll have to lift and drop the red pin to get the squares to start in the corner.

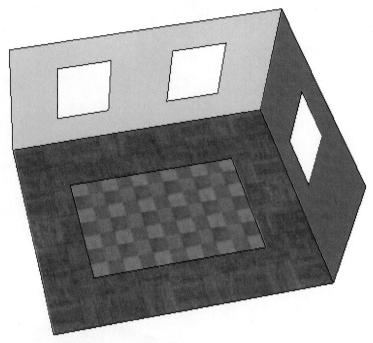

Figure 6-43

6.3 Sizing Materials Using Exact Dimensions

Until now, we've sized materials by sight and by using exact points. In this section, you will learn how to position materials when you know actual numbers: either the actual angles or the actual sizes of the materials themselves.

1 Draw a rectangle for a floor, and paint it with Wood_Floor_Light from the "Wood" collection (Figure 6-44).

Figure 6-44

2 Get the positioning pins for this material, and drag the green pin along an angle, to rotate the wood planks. The cursor snaps to, or stops at, a few standard angles, like 30 and 45 degrees, but it's hard to tell exactly what the angles are, because the angle dimensions are not identified. Also, when you keep the cursor along the dashed, curved line, the size of the material stays the same (Figure 6-45). But you can move the cursor in or out to change the size. Click anywhere to complete the positioning because we're going to undo it later.

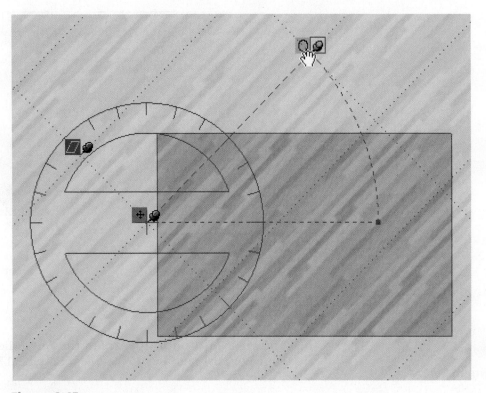

Figure 6-45

3 Right-click on the floor and choose **Reset** to return the material to its original size and orientation (Figure 6-46). Then exit positioning mode.

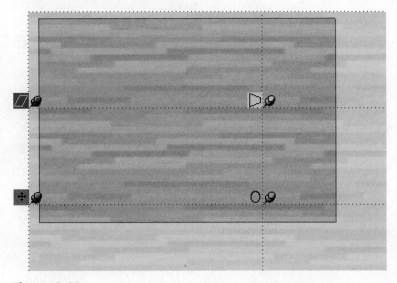

Figure 6-46

4 What if we want the floor planks to lie at an unconventional 17-degree angle? The best way to get this exact rotation is to mark the angle before going back to positioning mode. Activate the **Protractor** (**Tools/ Protractor** in the main menu); this tool creates an angled guide line. This line is created with three clicks: the first at the corner of the floor (Point 1 in Figure 6-47), then anywhere along the lower floor edge (Point 2), and then move your mouse up and click (or don't click) around Point 3.

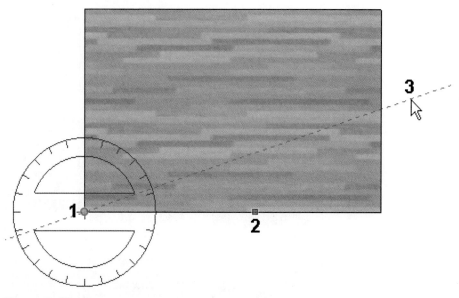

Figure 6-47

Angle 17

Figure 6-48

5 The angle of the line appears in the **Angle** field, but you can't get your cursor to stop at 17 degrees. So type 17 (Figure 6-48.) and press Enter.

6 With the angle now marked by the dashed guide line, go back into positioning mode. Drag the red pin to the corner of the floor that meets the guide line (Figure 6-49).

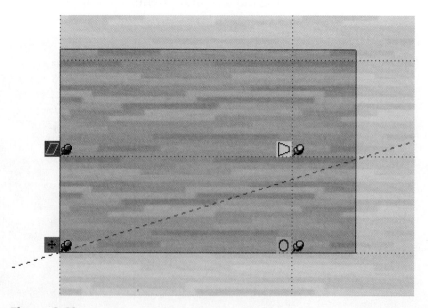

Figure 6-49

7 Then drag the green pin until it meets the guide line, staying on the dashed curve so that the material keeps its size (Figure 6-50).

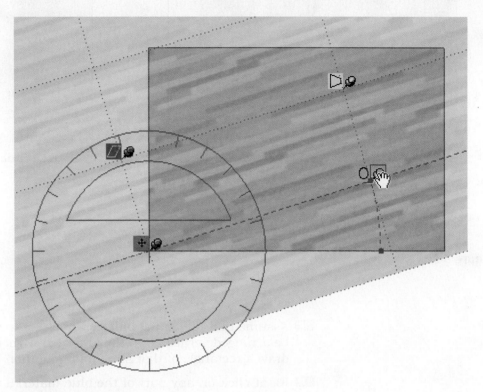

Figure 6-50

8 So that's it: Exit positioning mode, erase the guide line, and here's the floor (Figure 6-51).

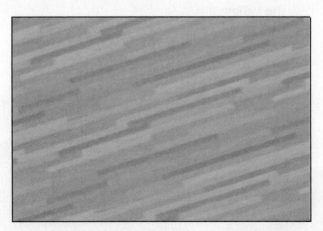

Figure 6-51

9 The next example will involve tiles of known dimensions. We'll model what could be a kitchen backsplash, but it's just going to be a rectangle lying on the floor. In blank space, draw a rectangle 4′ wide × 3′ high, and use **Offset** to create another rectangle offset 6″ inside (Figure 6-52).

10 Paint the two faces with Tile_Ceramic_Multi and Tile_Limestone_Multi from the "Tile" collection. Figure 6-53 shows the ceramic tile in a light blue just to make the model more interesting.

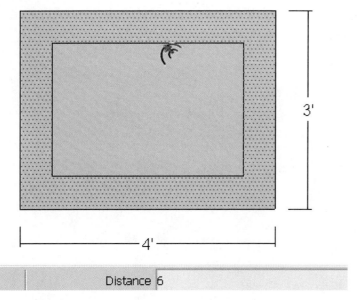

Figure 6-53

Distance 6

Figure 6-52

11 Assume that the actual blue ceramic tiles measure 2″ × 6″, and are to be arranged vertically. In the lower left corner of the outer rectangle, draw a rectangle of that size and orientation (Figure 6-54).

12 Right-click on any part of the blue material that *is not* inside this small rectangle to enter positioning mode. Because this material needs to be scaled non-uniformly (stretched vertically), we need to use three pins: red, green, and blue. Arrange them as shown in Figure 6-55: red at the lower left corner of a tile, green at the lower right corner, and blue at the upper left corner. As usual, just ignore the yellow pin.

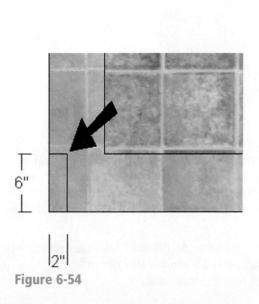

Figure 6-54

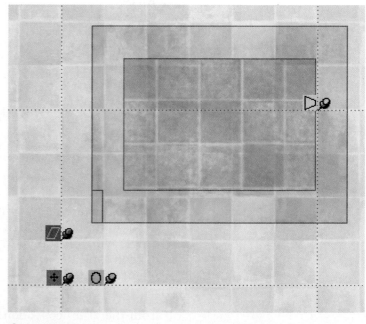

Figure 6-55

13 Drag the red pin to the corner of the 2″ × 6″ rectangle, then drag the green and blue pins to their corners. You should now have 6 tiles in the vertical direction and 24 tiles in the horizontal direction. It's tough to get this positioning exact because the smaller rectangle is so small; a tiny error here becomes larger when repeated (Figure 6-56).

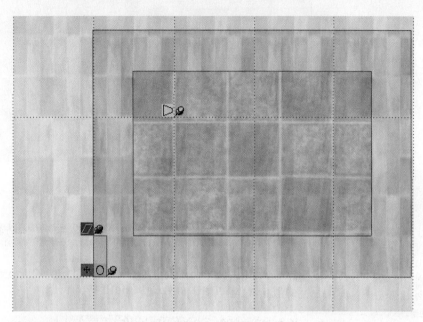

Figure 6-56

14 Because tiling in real life has to be pretty exact, you can tweak the blue and green pins until your vertical tiles are perfect. Then exit positioning mode. The only thing left to do with this face is to erase the extra edges of that small rectangle (Figure 6-57).

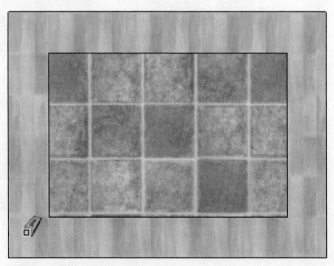

Figure 6-57

15 The limestone tiles in the center are 6″ × 6″, and are to be oriented at a 45-degree angle. But to avoid repeating the inexactness of the vertical tiles, we'll start with a larger area, representing four tiles arranged two by two. The size of this square, then, should be 12″ × 12″; draw this square somewhere in the middle (Figure 6-58).

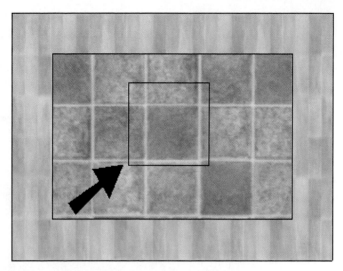

Figure 6-58

16 This square now needs to be rotated. Start by selecting it, then activate the **Rotate** tool. Then click in three places as shown in Figure 6-59: first, somewhere in the middle of the square (Point 1); then directly to the right (or anywhere, actually [Point 2]); and then a third time when you see 45 in the **Angle** field (Point 3).

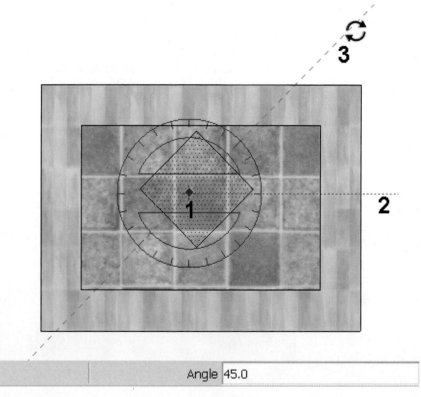

Figure 6-59

17 Right-click on this material anywhere that is not inside the diamond to start positioning. This time, the blue pin is not needed; just place the red and green pins two tiles apart (Figure 6-60).

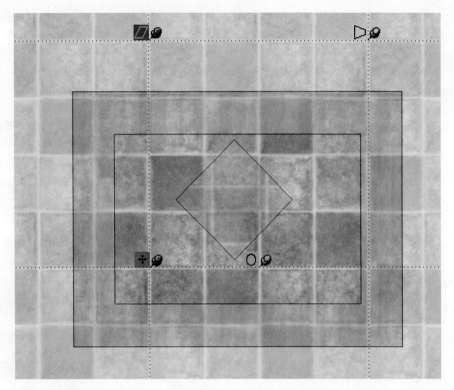

Figure 6-60

18 Drag the red pin and then the green pin to adjacent corners of the diamond (Figure 6-61).

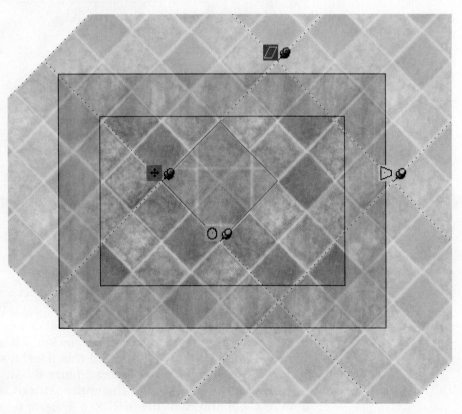

Figure 6-61

19 Exit positioning mode, and the material looks good everywhere except inside the square itself (Figure 6-62). Simply erase the square. Then you could position the texture again to make sure that it's centered (Figure 6-63).

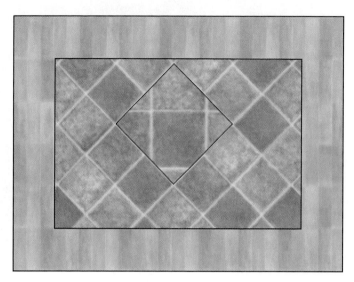

Figure 6-62

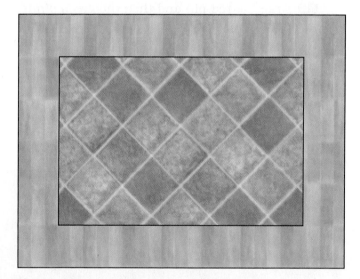

Figure 6-63

Model It Yourself

Using what you know about texture positioning, rotating, and scaling, draw a floor and paint it with Tile_Checker_BW from the "Tile" collection. Because you'll be drawing lines on this floor, it's a good idea to change the tile's base color to be a bit lighter (Figure 6-64).

Change the tiles so that the entire pattern is at a 30-degree angle (Figure 6-65) and each tile is 2′ × 1′ (Figure 6-66). Remember to use a sample area that's sized to fit several tiles, not just one.

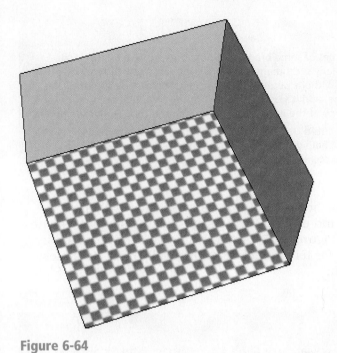

Figure 6-64

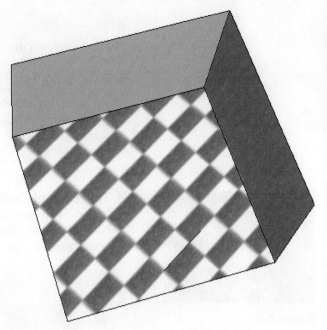

Figure 6-65

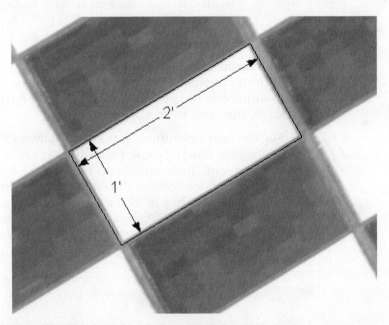

Figure 6-66

6.4 Finding and Using Your Own Materials

Even though you can change the color, size, and orientation of the default SketchUp materials, your available material selections are still limited. But *any* image can be used as a material in a model, whether it's a photo that you take yourself or something that you find online. This section will teach you how to build your own material libraries, or in SketchUp terminology, material *collections*.

Figure 6-67

1 This example will show how to find and use a specific wallpaper based on a swatch found online. The paisley swatch used here is one that tiles seamlessly (Figure 6-67). You can find your own swatch by searching image sites for terms such as "tiling wallpaper," "seamless textures," and so forth.

NOTE

One good resource for seamless swatches is Citrus Moon Patterns (http://citrusmoon. typepad.com/patterns). If you're on Facebook, search for "SketchUp Textures" to find some pages where you can download all types of seamless swatches. You can also use your own digital photo of wallpaper, as long as the swatch in your photo tiles seamlessly. More information about seamless tiling can be found at the end of this section.

When using this sort of image as a texture, you should know the dimensions of the repeating pattern; most manufacturers will list pattern dimensions on their product pages. For this example, we'll assume that the paisley pattern repeats horizontally every 3′ (rather large, but easy to see).

2 For the best resolution, you should always find the version of the image that has the most pixels (the image that appears largest on your screen). To download an image from the web, simply right-click on it and choose one of the options for saving the image. Just remember where you save it! The most common image file formats for web images are JPG, BMP, and PNG, which all work well in SketchUp. If you download a GIF image, you'll need to convert it to another format; for some reason, SketchUp can't import a GIF image.

NOTE

Many images, particularly those on manufacturer's websites, are copyright protected. Some can't be downloaded at all, and others are protected by disclaimers found on the website. You can generally use a screen capture to save an image for personal use, but be aware of the legal limitations once you start using images commercially! When in doubt, contact the website owner for permission to use images.

3 Draw a room with a floor and two walls. To set the width of the repeating pattern, draw a 3′ line anywhere on one of the walls (Figure 6-68).

4 On the main menu, choose **File/Import**. On the window that opens (Figure 6-69), make sure that you search for graphics files rather than SketchUp models. Then browse to where you saved the swatch, choose **Use as texture**, and import the image.

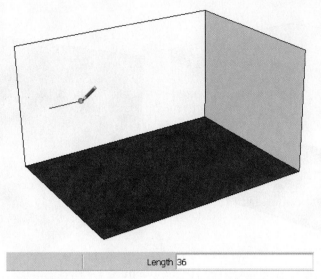

| Length | 36 |

Figure 6-68

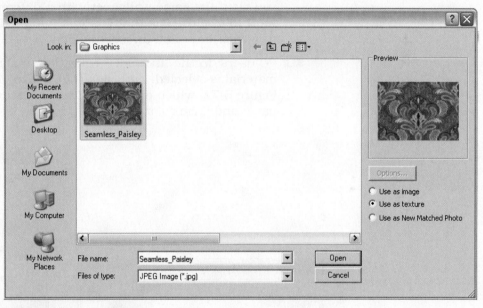

Figure 6-69

5 The swatch image is now attached to your cursor. Click the two endpoints of the small line (Figure 6-70), which sizes the swatch perfectly to its actual width.

6 The image tiles to fill the wall. Erase the small line (Figure 6-71).

NOTE

You can actually set the image width or height without the use of a dummy line. When placing an image as a texture, its width or height (depending on where your cursor is) appears at the bottom of the SketchUp window, and you can enter the desired value. This will be demonstrated in the next chapter.

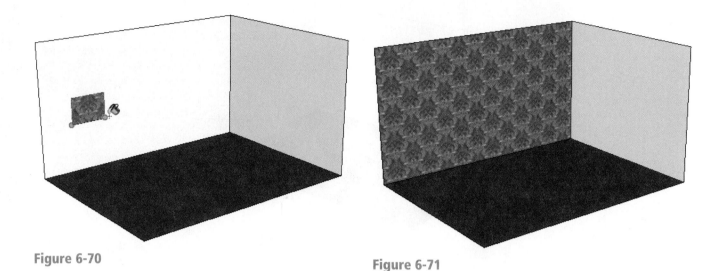

Figure 6-70

Figure 6-71

7 Look at your "In Model" materials; the wallpaper is now listed. Perhaps you want the same wallpaper with a different base color, but don't want to lose the one that you just imported. The solution is to create a new color based on an existing one.

8 PC users: In the "In Model" collection, make sure that the wallpaper material is selected, and click the **Create Material** icon indicated in Figure 6-72, which opens the **Create Material** window. Assign a new name and base color (Figure 6-73), then click OK.

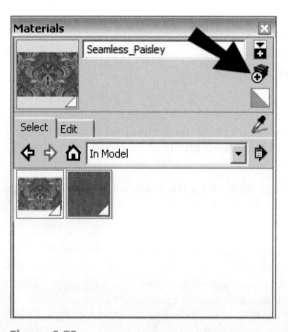

Figure 6-72

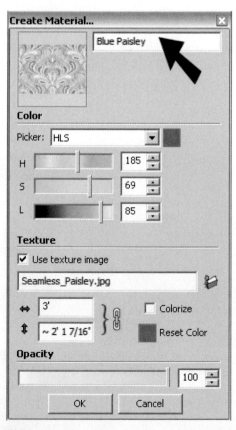

Figure 6-73

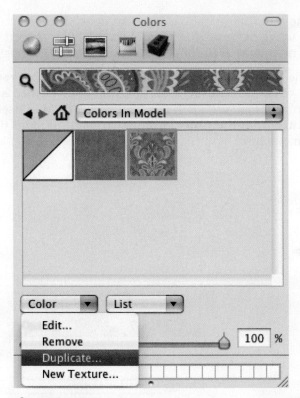

Figure 6-74

Figure 6-75

Mac users: In the "Colors in Model" collection, make sure that the wallpaper material is selected, and choose **Duplicate** from the **Color** drop-down menu (Figure 6-74). Enter a new material name (Figure 6-75) and the copied swatch now appears in the "Colors in Model" collection. Edit this copy so that it has a different base color, then click **Close** to return to "Colors in Model."

Now both swatches appear in your "In Model" collection (Figure 6-76).

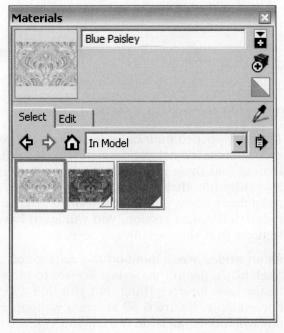

Figure 6-76

9 You can also create a new material based on an image without importing it or copying an existing material. Find and download any striped wallpaper swatch, again noting (or assuming) the actual pattern dimensions.

10 PC users: Click the **Create Material** icon again, and on the **Create Material** window, click the **Browse icon** and find your striped swatch. Set its size, assign a name, and click OK (Figure 6-77). Mac users: Choose **New Texture** from the **Color** drop-down menu (Figure 6-78), and follow the same steps.

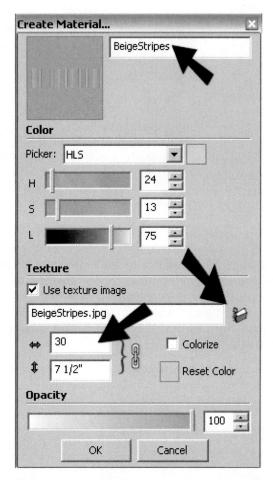

Figure 6-77

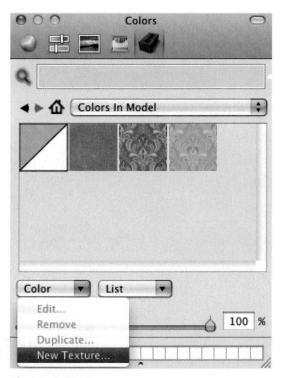

Figure 6-78

This new striped material now appears in your "In Model" collection even though it's not yet used in the model (Figure 6-79). It's important to note that these materials exist *only* in this file. If you start a new SketchUp file, these materials will no longer appear in your "In Model" collection (unless you import a model that's painted using these materials). In the next section, you will learn how to save materials in collections that you can always access.

As an aside, here's more on the concept of "seamlessness": All of SketchUp's default materials are set to tile seamlessly, but that won't be the case for everything that you find online or photograph yourself. For example, Figure 6-80 shows a wallpaper swatch that looks nice, but when used as is on a wall, you can see the seams between each image (Figure 6-81).

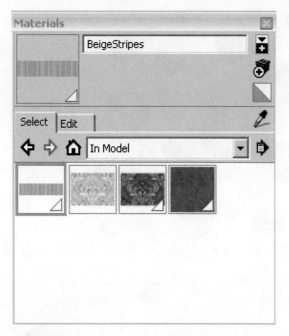

Figure 6-79

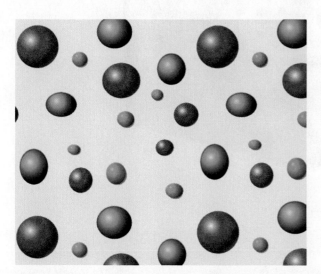

Figure 6-80

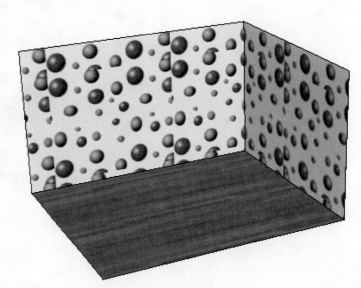

Figure 6-81

The solution is to trim the image so that the right edge meets the left edge, and the top edge meets the bottom edge. You can't do this in SketchUp; you'll need a graphics editor such as Photoshop. All graphics editors have a cropping tool that can be used for this; more sophisticated applications can help you figure out where to trim for perfect tiling. When this material is made to be seamless (Figure 6-82), it looks a lot better on the wall (shown in a larger scale in Figure 6-83).

When using a search engine such as Google Images or Yahoo! Image Search to find material images, adding the term "seamless" can filter

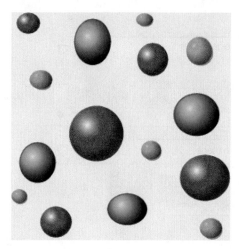

Figure 6-82

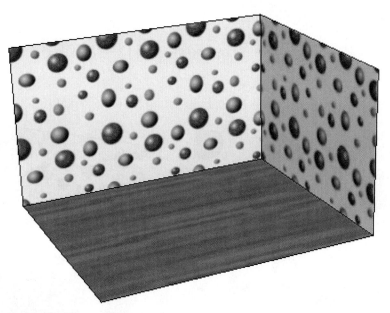

Figure 6-83

the results to produce more useable images. For example, entering "bricks" will result in thousands of pictures that show brick houses, sidewalks, and so forth. A term like "seamless brick material" will work much better. You can also try "tiling brick textures" and other similar search terms.

Model It Yourself

Find and download a flooring material that you like; Figure 6-84 shows a tiling wood swatch from Public Domain Images (http://www.public-domain-image.com). Knowing or assuming the size of the repeating pattern, place them on the floor at their correct size (Figure 6-85). Then copy that material to make another one of a different color (Figure 6-86).

Figure 6-84

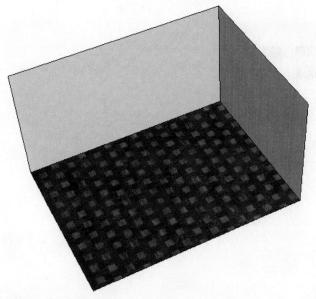

Figure 6-85

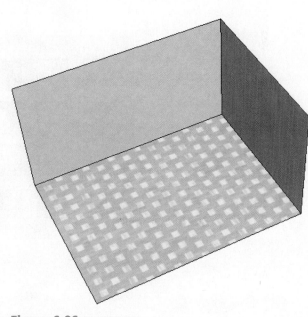

Figure 6-86

6.5 Creating Your Own Material Collections

Perhaps you've found and created materials out of dozens of images, and because you have hundreds of clients, you want to be able to access these materials anytime you use SketchUp. This section covers how to assemble materials into new collections.

1 We already know how to find material swatches online, so rather than repeat the search-and-import/create material process, we'll start with a SketchUp file that already has a set of materials. Search the 3D Warehouse for "corian" and choose one of the countertop swatch models. This example uses 03 Corian Naturals as shown in Figure 6-87.

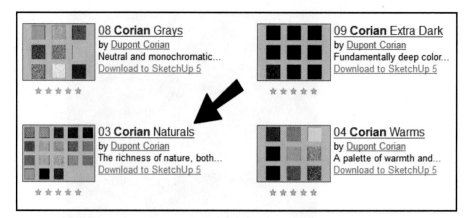

Figure 6-87

2. You can import this model into a blank SketchUp model, or just open it on its own. The model consists of simple squares, each painted with a different material (Figure 6-88).

Figure 6-88

> **NOTE**
>
> To help out designers and to encourage them to use their products, there are a growing number of 3D Warehouse models being uploaded by manufacturers of tile, carpet, paint, and so forth. For example, search for "sherwin williams" to see their paint swatches, or "tessera" to see glass tiles. You'll also find swatch models uploaded by helpful individuals who are happy to share. For example, search for "silestone." The company itself doesn't have models (at least not at the time of this writing), but a few models can be found that contain Silestone countertops or swatches.

3. Open the "In Model" collection to view all of the material swatches. Each swatch is listed by the name given by its manufacturer, such as Pepper Ivory, as shown in Figure 6-89.

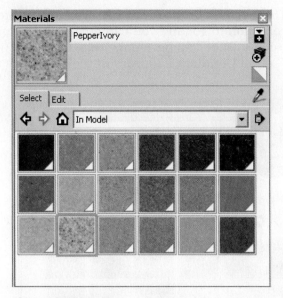

Figure 6-89

Because the process for setting up a collection is quite different for the Mac and the PC, this is the one spot in this book that requires separate instructions. PC users: Read on. Mac users: Please skip to the section on page 249.

Material Collections: Instructions for PC Users

1 These materials can't be categorized to fit into any of SketchUp's existing collections; they need their own collection. So click on the **Details** arrow indicated in Figure 6-90 and choose **Save collection as**.

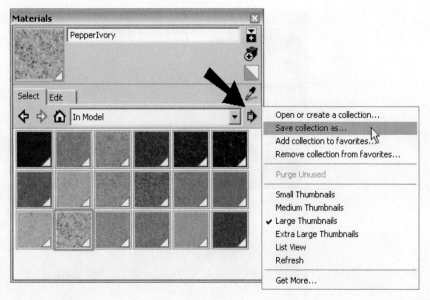

Figure 6-90

2 This opens a browser in which you can locate where you want this new collection to go, and you can create and name a new folder for this collection. Once you have done this, the name of your new folder (such as "Corian Counters") appears in the **Materials** window (Figure 6-91).

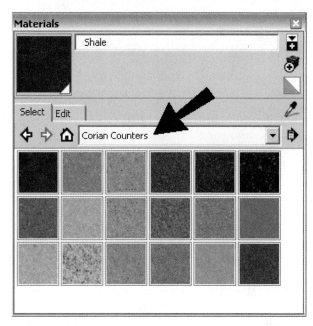

Figure 6-91

3 Now the collection has been saved to your hard drive, and you can access it in future files by clicking on the **Details** arrow and choosing **Open or create a collection**. But if you want the collection to appear in the drop-down menu of collections that already include "Roofing," "Translucent," and so forth, the collection must be added as a favorite. Click the **Details** arrow again and choose **Add collection to favorites** (Figure 6-92).

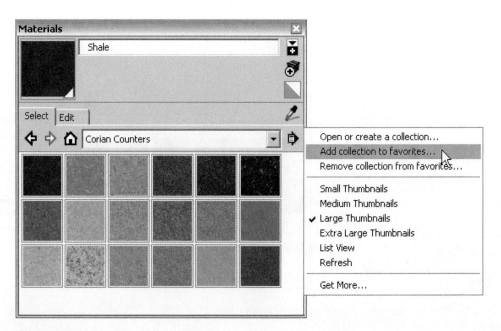

Figure 6-92

4 Close the SketchUp file, and find and open another Corian model from the 3D Warehouse. Figure 6-93 shows 08 Corian Grays. These materials are to be added to the collection that you just created.

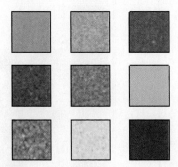

Figure 6-93

5 Open the **Materials** window to the "Corian" collection that you created, then click the icon indicated in Figure 6-94, which opens the secondary selection pane.

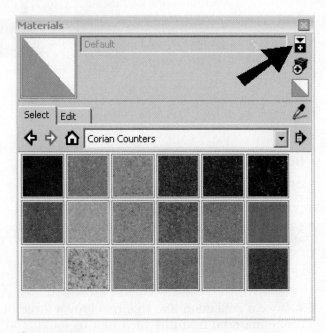

Figure 6-94

6 Open the lower pane to the "In Model" collection, which lists all of the current model's Corian materials (Figure 6-95).

7 To add the new materials to the "Corian" collection, simply drag the swatches, one by one, from the "In Model" collection to the "Corian" collection (Figure 6-96).

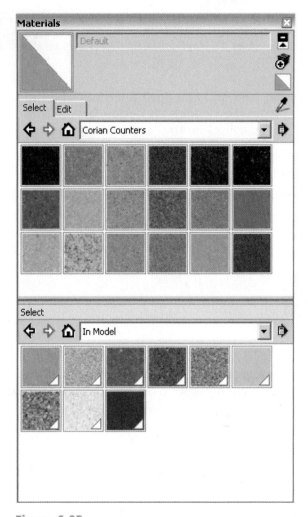

Figure 6-95

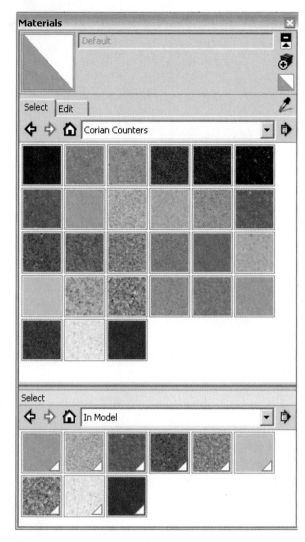

Figure 6-96

> **NOTE**
>
> Of course, you can use the same dual-pane method to add materials to existing collections. For example, perhaps you create a few new brick textures and don't want to create a new collection for them because SketchUp already has a "Brick" collection. In one pane, display the "Brick and Cladding" collection, and in the other pane, display the "In Model" collection. Then drag each brick from "In Model" into "Brick and Cladding."

8 Once a collection like this has grown large, it might be tough to tell one material from the next just by looking at its swatch. So click the **Details** arrow once more and choose **List View**, which displays the materials by name, in alphabetical order (Figure 6-97). List View is handy when you have a material name and too many similar-looking materials to pick it out visually.

9 To get back to thumbnail view, use the **Details** arrow again and choose one of the thumbnail options, which vary by size.

10 Now skip to Model It Yourself on page 251.

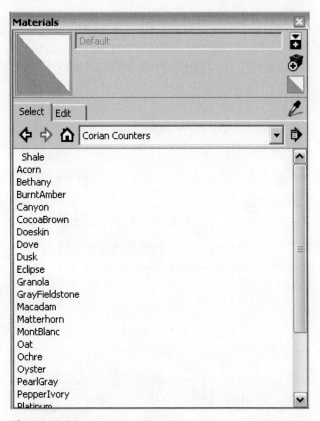

Figure 6-97

Material Collections: Instructions for Mac Users

1 These materials don't belong in any of SketchUp's existing collections; they need their own collection. So click the **List** drop-down menu and choose **Duplicate** (Figure 6-98).

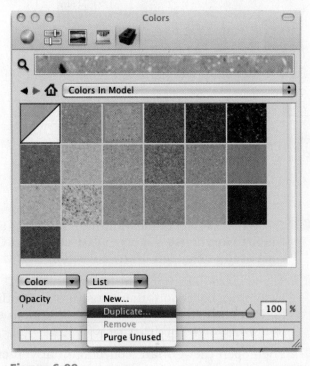

Figure 6-98

2 Assign a name to the new collection, such as "Corian Counters" (Figure 6-99). After clicking OK, the new name appears as the collection name (Figure 6-100), and this collection will be available from now on, and for future files, in the collections drop-down menu.

Figure 6-99

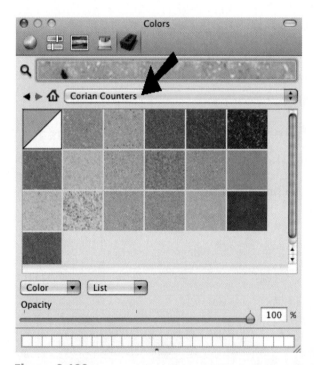

Figure 6-100

3 Close the SketchUp file, and find and open another Corian model from the 3D Warehouse. Figure 6-101 shows 08 Corian Grays. These materials are to be added to the collection that you just created.

4 These materials appear in "Colors in Model" collection. To place them in another collection, they must first go in the small color wells at the bottom of the **Colors** window. So drag each swatch, one by one, into its own color well (Figure 6-102).

5 Then open the "Corian" collection that you created, and drag the swatches up from the color wells (Figure 6-103).

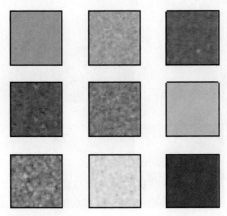

Figure 6-101

Figure 6-102

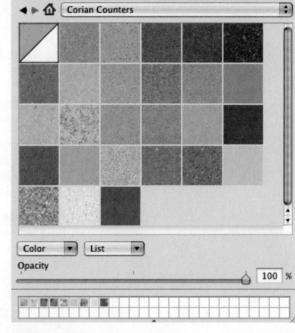

Figure 6-103

> **NOTE**
>
> The color wells are very handy. You can keep any often-used materials here, or erase them by dragging an empty well over an occupied one. You can click the small circle below the color wells if you want a new row of wells.

Model It Yourself

Create a collection of several floor tile materials based on images from a manufacturer's website. Figure 6-104 shows some cork tiles from Globus Cork, but you can look for parquet, hardwood, ceramic tiles, and so forth. PC users: Make sure that your collection will be available in future

Snow   Alabaster   Whitewashed

Golden Oak   Scotchwood   Lemon

Terra Cotta   Amber Pine   Cherry

Figure 6-104

SketchUp models. (Mac users: Any new collection that you create will automatically be available in future models.)

6.6 Painting Groups and Components

You're going to use 3D Warehouse models all the time as a designer, and you're certainly going to want to change the colors and materials of these models. 3D Warehouse models are imported as components, and you know that changes can be made to a component by editing it. But many 3D Warehouse models come unpainted, which makes painting them a bit easier.

1 Use **Get Models** to find the couch shown in Figure 6-105, which you can find by searching for "lounge couch author:google." Import this couch twice, or just make a copy of the first one.

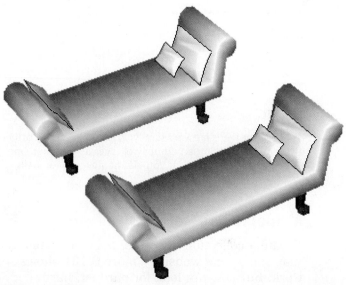

Figure 6-105

2 The legs of this couch have a brown material, but the other elements of the couch are unpainted. In other words, the couch was created using SketchUp's default colors, and only its legs were painted. If you use the Eyedropper to sample the material anywhere but the legs, you'll see that the material is the default. The default material can be used like any other material; painting with it essentially unpaints a face.

3 You can paint any unpainted faces of a component (or group) without editing it. Keeping the couches as-is (not open for editing), apply two different colors to the couches. Everything except the legs gets the new color (Figure 6-106).

Figure 6-106

4 If you paint any part of a component, the new color or material will replace the color that you just used to replace the default. Open either couch component for editing, then select one of the pillows (use a single click; don't open a pillow for editing). You can see that each pillow itself is a component (Figure 6-107).

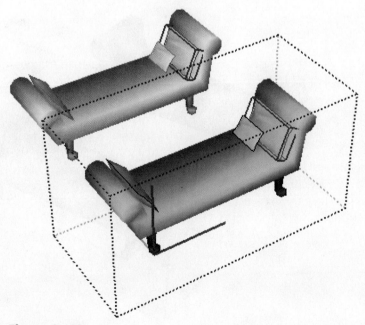

Figure 6-107

5 Don't open any pillow component for editing, but use three new colors to paint each pillow a different color. The colors are applied to the pillows of *both* couches because this change is made while editing the overall couch component: Identical components get identical changes (Figure 6-108).

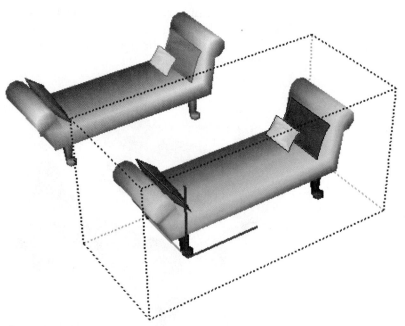

Figure 6-108

6 Now open one of the pillows for editing and paint it a color: Make sure that you click both the front and back faces of the pillow. Because all three pillows are identical components (with different sizes), painting the faces of the edited pillow changes the faces of all of the pillows (Figure 6-109).

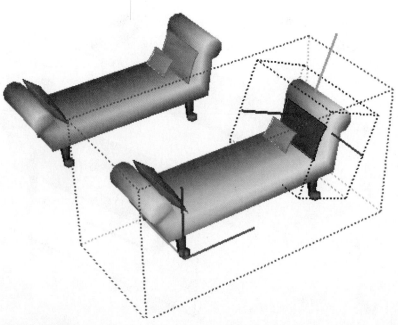

Figure 6-109

7 Close the pillow component, then close the couch component.

8 Look at the couch thumbnail in the "In Model" collection of the **Components** window (remember to click the House icon). Its main color is still the default, but its pillows are now painted, along with its legs (Figure 6-110).

9 Insert another couch from the "In Model" collection of the **Components** window, then choose a new color and paint it (without editing). As you'd expect, the couch body gets the new color, but the pillows and legs keep their assigned colors (Figure 6-111).

Figure 6-110

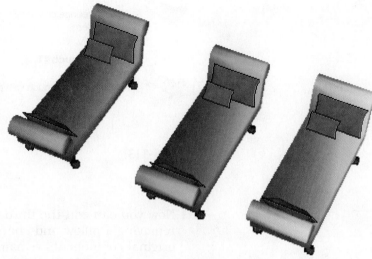

Figure 6-111

10 What if you want the third couch to have different pillows from the first two? Right-click on this couch and choose **Make Unique** (Figure 6-112). A new, copied component is now listed in the **Components** window (Figure 6-113). This new component gets a default name, which you can add via the **Entity Info** window.

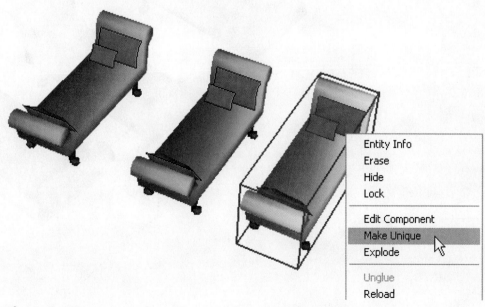

Figure 6-112

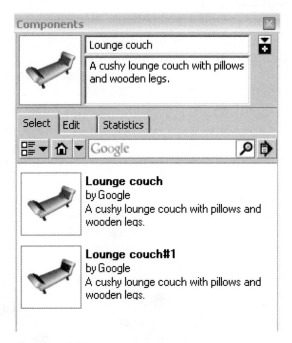

Figure 6-113

11 Now you can edit the third couch and make some changes, such as removing a pillow and changing pillow material (Figure 6-114). The original components remain unaffected by these changes because they are no longer identical to the third couch.

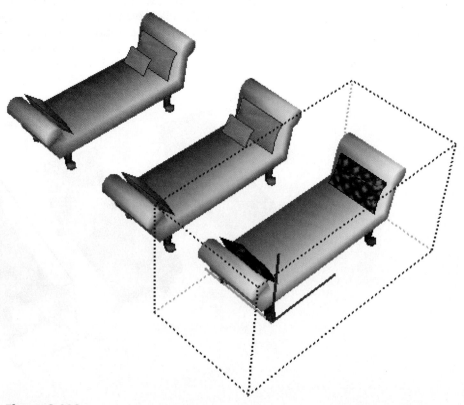

Figure 6-114

Model It Yourself

Create a room (two walls and a floor, as usual), and bring in two of the same model: Series A 9 Drawer Dresser by Google (Figure 6-115).

Figure 6-115

If you sample the material of any face on this model, you'll see that it's *not* unpainted, rather, each face is painted ivory.

Edit either component so that all faces, except the drawer fronts, are made of wood. And *unpaint* the drawer fronts so that when the component is closed, each dresser can be painted a different color (Figure 6-116).

Figure 6-116

6.7 Painting Textures on Organic Faces

Organic shapes are those that have a bumpy or more random look than most objects that we've created or seen so far. A blanket smoothed over a bed is not organic, but when it's rumpled around pillows, it has random-looking angles and bumps. Models of cars and animals also have organic surfaces. When painting such faces with tiling materials, as opposed to solid colors, the material is applied with a random look; however, there is a neat trick that we can use to fix this. The pillows from the couch in the previous section are the organic objects that we'll paint with stripes.

> **NOTE**
>
> SketchUp's Sandbox tools can be used to create organic surfaces. These tools are beyond the scope of this book because you won't use them when modeling rooms and designing furniture. But if you want to try them out, they are in the **Draw/Sandbox** and **Tools/Sandbox** menus, and you can find information about these tools online. They take a bit of artistic or geometric skill, but are quite useful!

1. Striped swatch images are easy to find online, so do an image search for one and create a new material from it (Figure 6-117). Or use the striped wallpaper that you found earlier in this chapter.

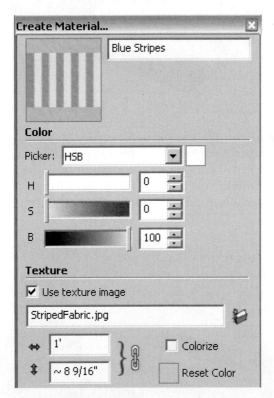

Figure 6-117

2. Download the same lounge couch that you used in the previous section, and use the striped material to paint the pillows. (You can edit the couch component once you import it, or right-click on it and choose **Explode** so that it will no longer be a component. The pillows will still be components; leave them as components so that each will turn out the same.) The pillows don't turn out evenly striped; the stripes go in random-looking directions (Figure 6-118).

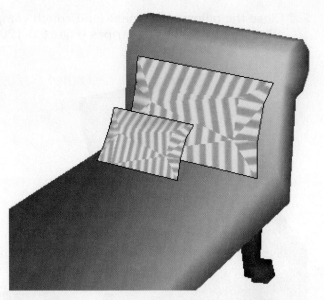

Figure 6-118

3 Draw a rectangle anywhere in blank space on the floor, and paint this rectangle with the same stripes.

4 Right-click on the striped rectangle and choose **Texture/Projected**. This projected material is what we need to apply to these pillows.

5 Open one of the pillow components for editing, then use the Eyedropper to sample the projected material from the rectangle on the ground (you can sample a face even when it's outside the component or group being edited). Click the pillow to paint it with the projected material. The results might look a little strange at first (Figure 6-119).

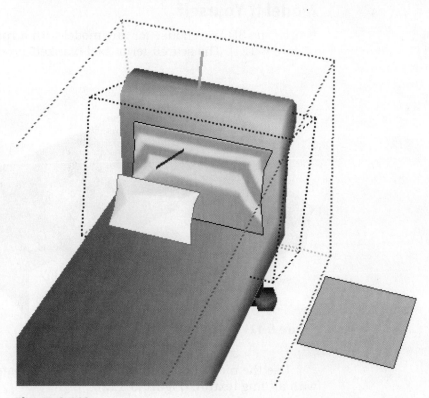

Figure 6-119

6 Close the pillow component (and couch component, if needed), and the pillows show their true stripes (Figure 6-120).

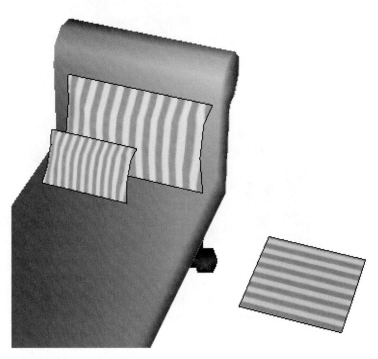

Figure 6-120

If you wanted the stripes to have a different size or angle, you would use fixed pins on the rectangle to set the material you want, then sample it again to paint with it.

Model It Yourself

Search the 3D Warehouse for any model with a rumpled-looking blanket (Figure 6-121). The search term "bed blanket" produces a few such models.

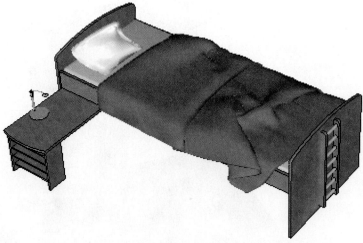

Figure 6-121

Use the method for sampling a projected material to paint the blanket with a tiling texture (Figure 6-122).

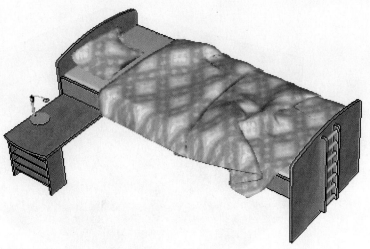

Figure 6-122

6.8 Translucent Materials

You've already seen how windows can be painted with translucent solid colors, but did you know that materials can also be translucent? This section takes a closer look at how translucency works in SketchUp.

1 Start with a room with two walls, and draw rectangles for two narrow, vertical windows at the ends of both walls (Figure 6-123). A curved shower will go in the corner, which is why the windows are pushed to the sides. Don't paint anything yet.

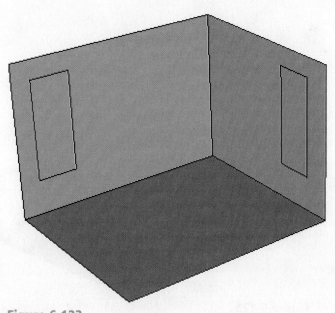

Figure 6-123

2 Paint the walls and floor with whatever materials or colors you like, and paint both windows with any solid-colored material from the "Translucent" collection (Figure 6-124).

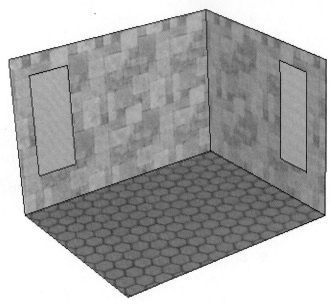

Figure 6-124

3 Orbit to the other side of one wall and peek in through a window. The opaque materials are applied only to the inside faces, but the window faces are translucent on both sides (Figure 6-125). This is logical; SketchUp assumes that windows should be glass on both sides. But this two-sided painting *only occurs when both sides of the face have the default colors.* If either side of this window had been painted with a color or material, then painting one side with a translucent material would only affect the side that you painted.

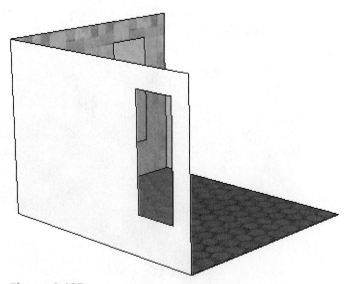

Figure 6-125

If you painted the back of the window with a different color or material, you could make it opaque from the back, but it still would be translucent from the front. This probably isn't something you'd want to do every day, unless you were designing one-way windows for police interrogation rooms.

4 As you should always do after you create an unfurnished room, make the entire room into a group.

5 In the corner of the room, draw the base of the shower using an arc and two lines as indicated in Figure 6-126.

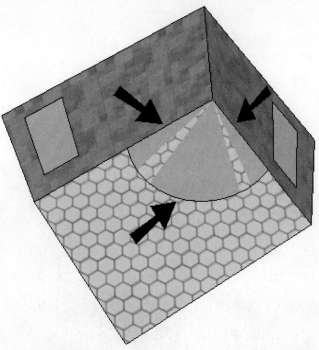

Figure 6-126

6 Use **Push/Pull** to pull up a small distance to form the shower base, then press the Ctrl/Option key and pull up again to complete the shower wall. Erase extra edges along the bathroom walls, and paint the shower wall a solid color (Figure 6-127).

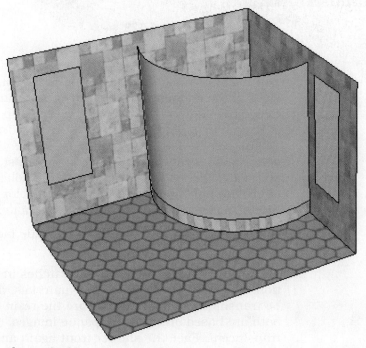

Figure 6-127

7 Find this "In Model" color, edit it, and move its **Opacity** slider down (Figure 6-128). While you're adjusting the slider, look at the shower door, which goes from opaque to translucent (Figure 6-129). Also note that the material swatch is split diagonally, with the base color on one side and its translucent version on the other side.

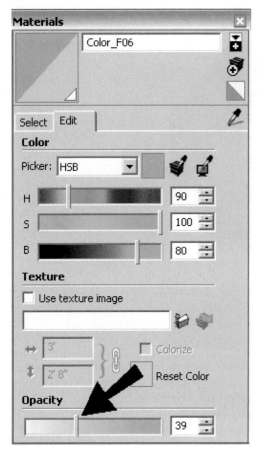

Figure 6-128

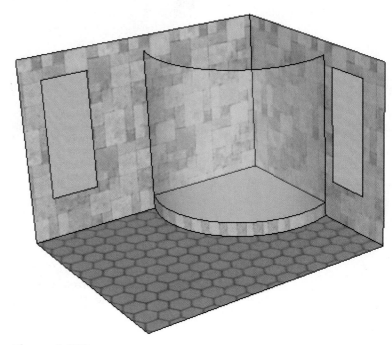

Figure 6-129

8 You might assume that this translucent color gets applied to both sides of the shower door, but you'd be wrong. Orbit to see that from inside the shower, the door still has the opaque default color (Figure 6-130). Why is that? It's true that both sides of this door had the default colors, and if you had painted the door with a material that was *already* defined as translucent, both sides would have been painted. What's different here is that a solid color was used first, applied to only one side, and then the color was *changed* to be translucent. So even when translucent, the material stays only on its side.

9 But it's an easy fix: Just paint the inside face with the same translucent color (Figure 6-131).

10 After taking a look at the other swatches in the "Translucent" collection, you may have noticed that materials, as well as solid colors, can be translucent. Two examples are the resin and glass block materials; both are based on regular, opaque images. Any material can be made translucent. Face the shower front again and paint the door with Tile_Navy from the "Tile" collection (Figure 6-132).

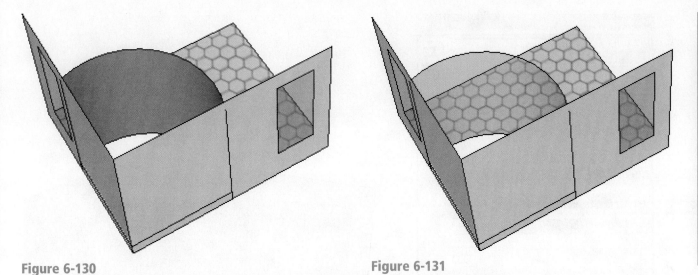

Figure 6-130　　　　　　　Figure 6-131

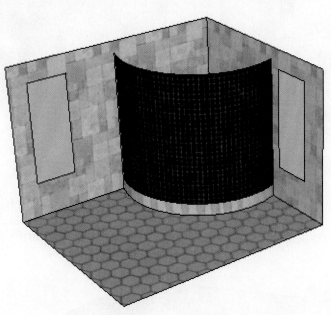

Figure 6-132

11 Edit this "In Model" material and reduce its **Opacity**. You can also change the base color and size like we've done before in this chapter (Figure 6-133). The result is a pretty good imitation of glass blocks (Figure 6-134). Of course, the inside face of the door still has the translucent solid color, which you could change.

We've got just one concept left to cover in this chapter. It isn't related to translucency but rather it has to do with positioning materials on curved surfaces (and we just happen to have a curved shower door). Perhaps you want to use diamond-shaped glass blocks in this door (an unconventional choice, but it's good to be prepared for eccentric clients). If you right-click on the door face, the texture positioning option won't be found. This is because positioning can only be done on *flat* faces.

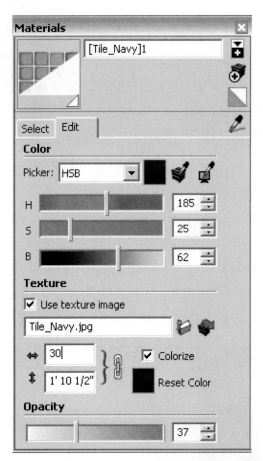

Figure 6-133

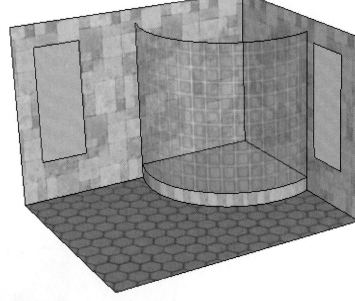

Figure 6-134

12 Remember that a curved surface in SketchUp is actually composed of several flat faces. To see where these flat faces are, choose **View/ Hidden Geometry** to see the dashed lines (Figure 6-135).

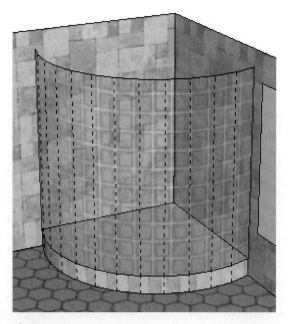

Figure 6-135

13 Right-click on one of these flat faces and enter positioning mode. Drag the green pin to rotate the blocks 45 degrees (the angle doesn't have to be exact), and make the blocks larger or smaller. Exit positioning mode; the change is applied only to the one flat face (Figure 6-136).

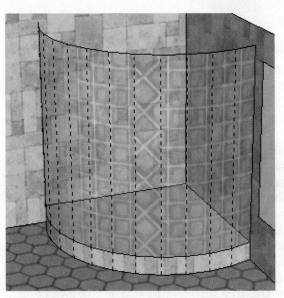

Figure 6-136

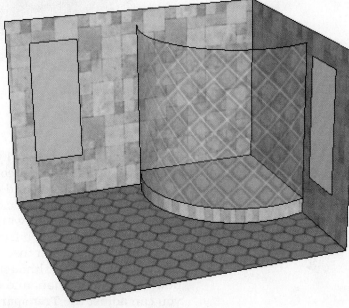

Figure 6-137

14 Applying the changed material to the rest of the door requires three steps: First, sample the new material. Then turn off hidden edges by choosing **View/Hidden Geometry** again. Finally, click anywhere on the door to paint the entire curved face with the new material (Figure 6-137). This is a very handy technique!

Model It Yourself

From the 3D Warehouse, find a model of a bowl and a couple pieces of fruit (Figure 6-138). Change the material of the bowl so that the entire bowl is translucent (Figure 6-139).

Figure 6-138

Figure 6-139

Depending on the bowl you find, if it's already painted, you may have to apply your translucent color or material a few times on the back and front of both the inside and outside faces. Remember that you can turn a face inside-out by right-clicking on it and choosing **Reverse Faces**.

You can experiment with changing the fruit models into glass objects as well, but SketchUp has a few bugs when handling translucent materials in front or behind other translucent materials. If you get unexpected results, here's a possible fix (although it is not always perfect): Open the **Styles** window, click the **Edit** tab, and display the **Face** settings (Figure 6-140). Here you can adjust the **Transparency Quality** settings: **Faster** is the lowest quality; **Nicest** is the highest quality, but it uses more of your computer's graphics resources.

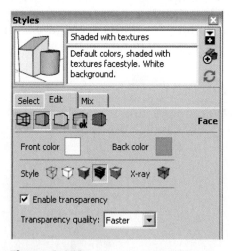

Figure 6-140

Review Questions

- How do you change the base color of a material?

- There are four fix pins used for texture positioning. What are the functions of the red, green, and blue pins?

- Once you've used texture positioning to change the size or orientation of a material, how do you apply the changed material to other faces?

- What tool is used to create a guide line at a specific angle?

- How can you import a digital image to be used as a texture?

- How do you create a new material collection?

- How can you place new materials in an existing material collection?

- When you paint a group or component (without opening it for editing), which of its faces get painted?

- Painting a material onto an organic surface can produce a random or jumbled look. How can you fix this?

- How do you make a color or material translucent?

- How can hidden edges help you position a material along a curved face?

7 chapterseven

Working with Digital Images

In the previous chapter, we used digital images for tiling textures such as brick or stone. This chapter will cover the various ways that you can use a digital image on its own, without repeating or tiling it.

You'll learn how to do the following:

- Create pictures and rugs using digital images.
- Create a framed painting.
- Create irregularly shaped objects based on images.
- Paint entire 3D objects using one or more images.
- Trace photos to create 3D objects.

NOTE

This chapter makes use of images of paintings, furniture, wall hangings, decorative windows, and so forth. Many images found on the web are copyright protected and cannot be used for commercial purposes without permission. However, there is a wealth of public domain images that are available online, and it's usually not difficult to obtain permission to use an image (as was done for many of the images in this and the previous chapter).

7.1 Decorating with Digital Images

In this section, you'll learn how to use digital images to create three decorating accessories: a framed poster, a painting, and a rug.

1 Start by downloading the 3D Warehouse model Image Import Living Room by Bonnie Roskes. If you import this model into another SketchUp file, leave it as a component. If you open this model from its own file, make the room into a group (Figure 7-1).

2 This model already contains the three images that you'll need. But in order to pretend that this model didn't come pre-loaded, we'll extract the images from the model and import them later, as though they were images that you found yourself. Go to your "In Model" material collection and find the three images: a Bechstein poster, a painting called *Getaway*, and a rug.

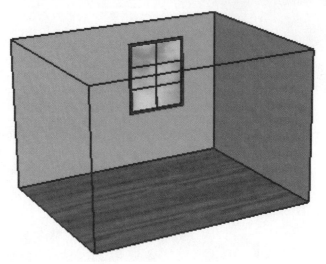

Figure 7-1

3 PC users: Right-click on each of these images and choose **Export Texture Image** (Figure 7-2). Save each image to your hard drive, noting the default image names so that you can easily find them later.

Figure 7-2

Mac users: Double-click on one of the images to edit it. In the **Texture** drop-down menu, choose **Edit** (Figure 7-3). This opens the image in your default graphics editor, where you can use **File/Save As** to save the image to your hard drive. Note the image's default file name so that you can easily find the image later. Repeat this step to save all three images.

We'll start with the Bechstein poster. This image is perfect for SketchUp use: no distortion, decent resolution, and no border.

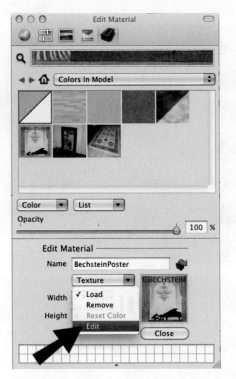

Figure 7-3

Figure 7-4

4 Choose **File/Import** from the main menu, and make sure that you're
   looking for image files (not SketchUp models). Browse to find the
   Bechstein poster. We only used the texture import in the previous chapter;
   this time, choose **Use as image** before importing the poster (Figure 7-4).

5 This poster will be placed on the wall with the window. Click anywhere
   to place its lower left corner (we can always move it later). Don't click a
   second point; move the cursor around while looking at the measurement
   field. If the cursor is anywhere along the right edge of the image, the
   field lists the poster's width (Figure 7-5). If the cursor is along the top
   edge, the field lists the poster's height (Figure 7-6).

Figure 7-5

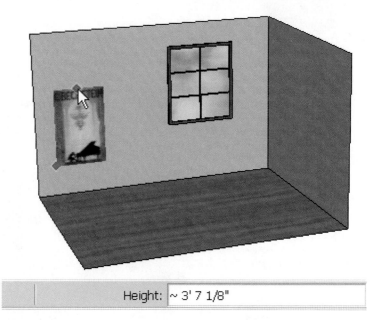

Height: | ~ 3' 7 1/8" |

Figure 7-6

6 Assume we know that this poster is 40″ tall. While the cursor is at the top of the poster, and the measurement field reads **Height**, type 40 and press Enter to size the poster correctly. After the image is placed, it is selected; leave it selected and use the **Move** tool to place it where you want it on the wall (Figure 7-7).

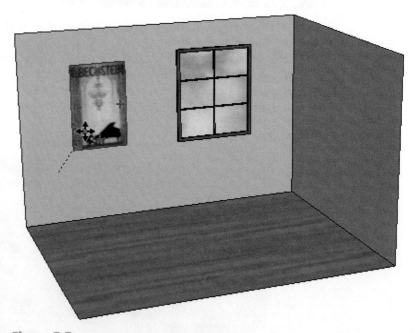

Figure 7-7

7 The poster looks nice, but there's not much you can do with an image except move, rotate, or scale it (later in this chapter, we'll also use images for tracing). In order to place a frame around an image, you first have to change the image into a regular SketchUp face. To do this, right-click on the image and choose **Explode** (Figure 7-8).

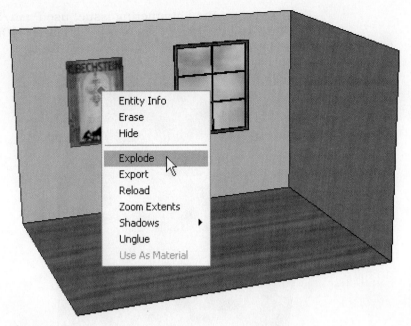

Figure 7-8

Once you explode an image, it becomes a SketchUp face and the image itself becomes a SketchUp material that can be found in your "In Model" material collection. But in this case, the material is already in this collection because the image was provided in the downloaded model.

◼ If you orbit, you'll recognize the shimmering effect (Figure 7-9); the poster and its wall occupy the same plane, and SketchUp can't tell which is supposed to be on top. (This shimmering effect doesn't occur with an unexploded image, which always appears above the face on which it is placed.)

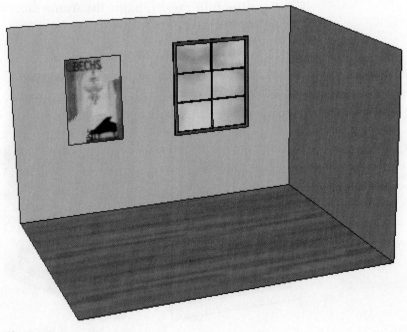

Figure 7-9

9 To resolve the shimmering issue, use **Push/Pull** to pull out the poster by a small amount, such as ¼″ (Figure 7-10).

Figure 7-10

10 To create the frame, it's easier to work from the back of the poster. So hide the room by right-clicking on any wall or floor face, and choose **Hide**.

11 Orbit to face the back of the poster (both sides of the face are painted when an image is exploded), and use **Offset** to make a larger rectangle around the back border (Figure 7-11).

12 Face the front again, paint the frame face, and pull it forward past the poster itself (Figure 7-12).

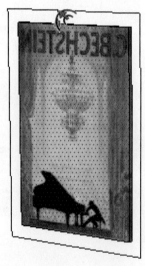 

Figure 7-11   Figure 7-12

13 Bring the room back by choosing **Edit/Unhide/All** (Figure 7-13).

Figure 7-13

14 The *Getaway* painting will go on the other wall. Use **File/Import** to bring it in as an image, at a reasonable size (Figure 7-14).

Figure 7-14

15 Explode the image and pull it out slightly (Figure 7-15). Obviously, we can't keep this painting as is because the image is distorted.

16 In the previous chapter, we used fixed-pin texture positioning (the four multicolored pins); now is the time to use free pins. Right-click on the front face of the painting and choose **Texture/Position**. To switch the fixed pins to free pins, right-click again and choose **Fixed Pins** to toggle it off. Now you should see four identical yellow pins (Figure 7-16).

Figure 7-15

Figure 7-16

17 For each pin, click to lift it and place it at a corner of the painting's frame (Figure 7-17).

Figure 7-17

18 Drag each pin to its closest corner of the SketchUp face (Figure 7-18).

Figure 7-18

19 If necessary, lift and adjust the pins so that the painting and the frame completely and evenly fill the face. This is the essence of free pins: You use them to distort an already distorted image so that it looks correct. Right-click and choose **Done**, then move the painting to where you want it on the wall. You can also paint the sides of the frame a solid color that approximates the color of the frame in the image (Figure 7-19).

Figure 7-19

The last item to add to the room is the rug, whose dimensions are 5′ × 8′. We could import it as an image, but the image is a distorted view of the rug, and entering a 5′ width might not correspond to an 8′ length. So it's better to start with a blank slate: a correctly sized empty object onto which the rug image can be painted.

20 Draw a 5′ × 8′ rectangle on the floor and paint it light gray (the base color of the rug). (Painting it now means that you won't have to paint the sides of the rug later.) Pull up the rectangle an inch or less, and center the entire rug in the room (Figure 7-20).

Figure 7-20

21 Use **File/Import** to find the rug image (it's called Living Room Rug). This time, choose **Use as texture** (Figure 7-21).

Figure 7-21

22 Click any two corners on the top face of the rug to paint it with the image (Figure 7-22). As you saw in the previous chapter, as soon as you click the second point, the image will tile to fill the face.

Figure 7-22

> **NOTE**
>
> Of course, this material already exists as a material in your model, so you could take the easy way out and just paint your rug face using that material, without importing anything.

23 Use free pins to mark the corners of one of the tiling rugs (Figure 7-23).

Figure 7-23

24 When dragging each pin to a corner, you'll also be turning the rug. So you might want to move each of the four pins just a bit in order to start turning the rug. When the orientation is approximately correct, drag the pins to the correct corners (Figure 7-24).

Figure 7-24

NOTE

Here's a helpful tip about free pins and fixed pins. Sometimes when using free pins, you might find that you also want to use the fixed pins, perhaps to change the overall image size, rotation angle, and so forth. You can make this switch *temporarily*: While the free pins are displayed, press the Ctrl and Shift keys at the same time (for both PC and Mac) to switch to the fixed pins. Keeping these keys pressed, make the switch to the fixed pins, then let go of the Shift and Ctrl keys and the free pins return. This works in reverse as well; you can temporarily switch from fixed pins to free pins.

25 Right-click and choose **Done**, and your room should look something like Figure 7-25.

Keep in mind that the file size of the images that you use can greatly affect the size of your SketchUp file. The entire image becomes part of the model, even if only a small part of the image appears in the model itself. So if you have a high-resolution image, it's a good idea to use a graphics editor to trim any parts of the picture that you don't need. Also, you may find that you don't need to import the image with the highest possible resolution: A large 2MB image that shows every fiber of a rug will look only marginally crisper in SketchUp than a 500KB image. The easiest way to reduce an image's resolution is simply to shrink it.

Figure 7-25

Model It Yourself

From the 3D Warehouse, download Image Import Utility Room by Bonnie Roskes (Figure 7-26). Explode the model if you imported it into another model. The two cabinets on the left are identical components, as are the three wider ones in the middle; the tall cabinet to the right is its own component. There is an empty frame for a poster and blank space for more wall art.

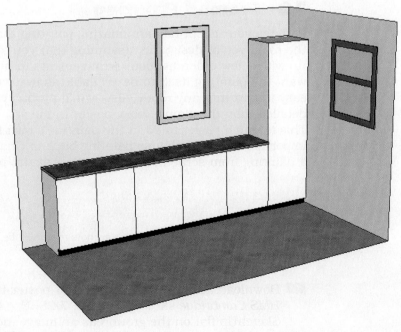

Figure 7-26

There are several images in the "In Model" collection: a balloon poster, a Mexican wall hanging, and three photos of cabinet doors. You can extract these images and import them, or you can just paint faces using the material swatches. Place the poster in the frame (adjusting the frame size as needed), place the wall hanging next to it (unframed), and paint the cabinet doors (Figure 7-27). For the cabinet sides and tops, use a wood color and adjust its base color. For the wall hanging, softening its edges will give it a more organic look.

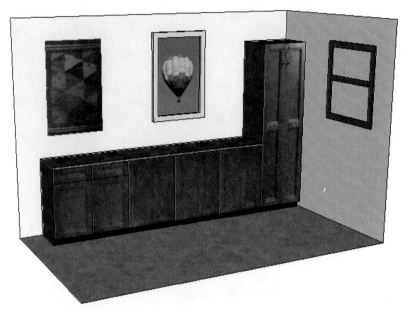

Figure 7-27

Bonus: Can you download this model again, and paint it with images that you find yourself?

7.2 Framed Painting

Perhaps your client has an amazing painting that is to be the focus of the room you're designing. Assuming that you're probably going to come up with a few different room arrangements to highlight this piece, you'll want the painting itself to be available as its own SketchUp model for easy import into any room. Also, you'll probably want a frame that's more detailed than the simple, boxy poster frame created in the previous section. This is much easier to do in the painting's own file. We looked briefly at importing a 3D Warehouse painting back in Chapter 2, and now we'll create a painting from scratch, starting with a digital photo.

> **NOTE**
> Exploring multiple design ideas for a single room will be covered in Chapter 9.

1 Download an image of a painting or poster that you like, such as the *HMS Cambridge* shown in Figure 7-28. Use **File/Import** to bring it into SketchUp flat on the ground as an image (not a texture), or just drag its filename into SketchUp. The size doesn't matter; we'll fix that later.

Figure 7-28

2 Explode the image, and draw a small rectangle for the frame cross section, touching one corner of the painting (Figure 7-29).

Figure 7-29

3 Draw some lines and arcs for the frame, and trim away the rest of the rectangle (Figure 7-30).

Figure 7-30

4 Select the face of the painting, activate **Follow Me**, and then click the frame face to drive it along the edges of the painting (Figure 7-31).

5 As you already know from previous chapters, the painting should be located at the origin so that when it's imported into another model, it will be dragged in correctly. Move the entire painting so that the lower left corner of the frame meets the origin (Figure 7-32).

6 The painting must also be a reasonable size. Use the **Tape Measure** (without creating a construction line) to measure one of the edges (Figure 7-33), and enter the desired dimension.

Figure 7-31

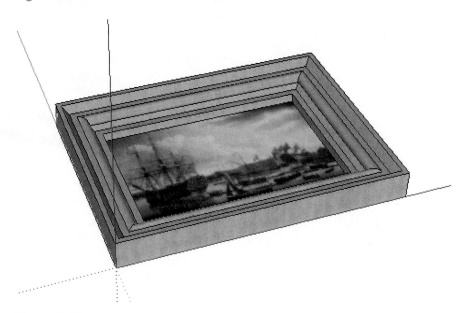

Figure 7-32

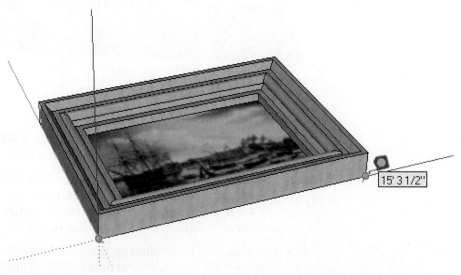

15' 3 1/2"

Figure 7-33

7 So that the face of the painting will sit in front of the wall, as opposed to occupying the same exact face as the wall, pull the painting itself forward a very small distance.

8 As the final step, we'll set this file's alignment properties. Choose **Window/Model Info** and open the **File** page. Under **Alignment**, set the gluing plane to **Any** plane (Figure 7-34), which means that the painting will align with whatever face the cursor touches.

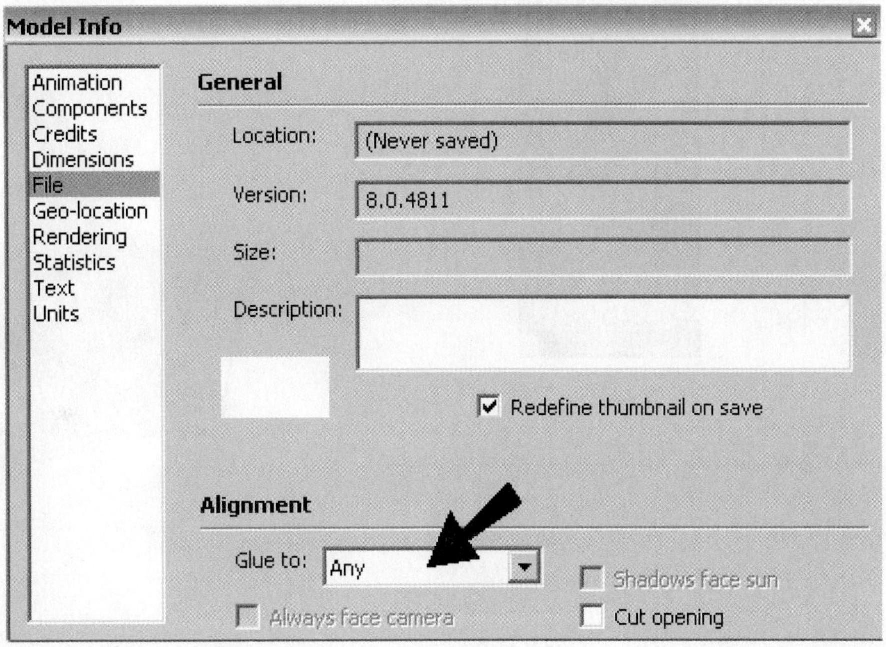

Figure 7-34

9 Close the **Model Info** window, save the file, and you're done!

10 In a new SketchUp file, create a room model such as the "man cave" shown in Figure 7-35. Use **File/Import** to place the painting on any wall (or floor) that you like.

Figure 7-35

Model It Yourself

From the 3D Warehouse, download ZNR4 Window Image by Bonnie Roskes. Explode the model if you import it into another model. The model contains only one object: a photo of a stained-glass window created by Degenhardt Glass Studios (Figure 7-36).

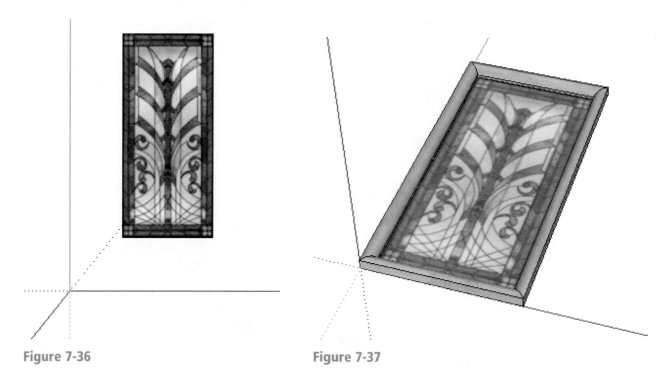

Figure 7-36   **Figure 7-37**

Make the window a reasonable size (about 18″ wide), add a frame around it, and place it at the origin. Edit the material to be translucent (Figure 7-37). In addition to setting the model to align to any face, set it to also cut faces (this is another option in the **Model Info** window).

Save the window model, then create a new model of a room with a door. Place the stained glass window inside the door itself (Figure 7-38). If

Figure 7-38

Figure 7-39

you set the proper level of translucence, you should be able to see through the window (Figure 7-39).

Bonus: Can you create a more elaborate door that has vertical stained glass panels next to the right and left sides of the door?

7.3 Objects Created from Irregularly Shaped Images

The images that we've seen so far in this chapter have all been used to produce rectangular objects such as paintings, rugs, and windows. But not all design elements are so straightforward; along the way, you'll encounter arches, ovals, and maybe even octagons. This section will show you how to create an arched patio door by using a photo and some simple tracing techniques to get the correct door shape.

1 From the 3D Warehouse, download Image Import Patio Door by Bonnie Roskes (Figure 7-40). Explode the model if you imported it into another model. The model is an empty room that leads out onto a patio.

2 Say we know that the rectangular part of this door is 6′ × 6′. (In other words, it is a square.) On the wall between the room and the patio, draw a square with the correct dimensions and center it in the wall (Figure 7-41).

3 The image for the patio door is in the "In Model" material collection; it comes from the website of Marvin Windows and Doors. Use this material to paint the door (Figure 7-42).

4 Use free pins to mark the corners of the door (Figure 7-43), and drag these pins to the corners. Adjust the pins if necessary so that the wood frame looks even on all sides, and exit texture positioning (Figure 7-44).

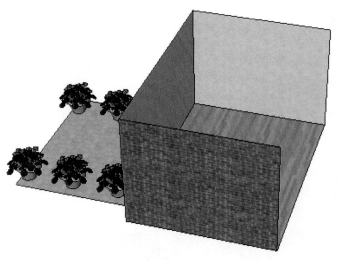

Figure 7-40

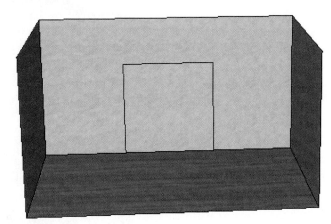

Figure 7-41

Figure 7-42

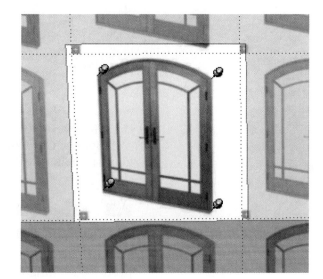

Figure 7-43

Figure 7-44

5 Adding the arch at the top is easy; just use the **Move** tool to raise the top edge of the door, continuing past where it needs to stop (Figure 7-45). Then use the **Arc** tool to trace the top of the arch, clicking Points 1, 2, and 3 as shown in Figure 7-46. Trim away the extra edges, and you've got your door (Figure 7-47).

Figure 7-45

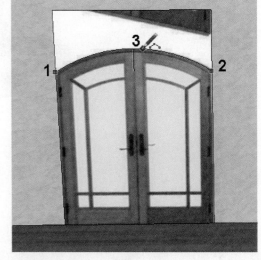

Figure 7-46

Figure 7-47

6 Orbit to face the patio door from the outside. Because you only painted the inside face of the door, the outside face is still bricked in. This is an easy fix: Just sample the door's material on its inside face and apply it to the outside face (Figure 7-48).

7 What if you want to give your client an idea of the patio views that this door will provide? The entire door is opaque, but adding the translucent parts will require some simple tracing. On half of the door, use the **Line, Rectangle**, and **Arc** tools as needed to trace the five panes of glass; paint them so that they are translucent (Figure 7-49).

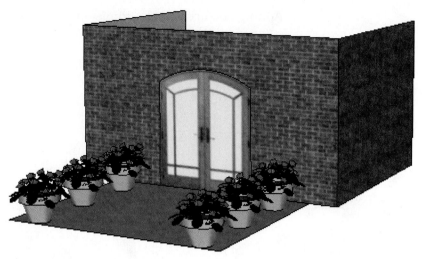

Figure 7-48

Figure 7-49

Figure 7-50

8 Select all five of these faces, copy them into blank space, and use the **Scale** tool to turn them inside-out in the red direction (to flip them over). Then move these copied faces into place on the other side of the door. You'll have to repaint these faces with the same translucent material (Figure 7-50), but if you leave them selected after moving them, you'll only have to click one of the selected faces to paint all of them at one time.

9 Orbit back to the other side of the door; there are no translucent faces here (Figure 7-51). As we saw in the previous chapter, double-sided translucence only works when *both* faces have the default color, and both sides of this door were already painted with the door image.

Figure 7-51

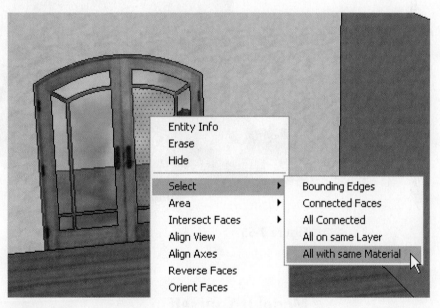

Figure 7-52

10 This is another easy fix: Inside the room, right-click on any translucent face and choose **Select/All with same Material** (Figure 7-52). This selects all 10 translucent faces at once. Then right-click on any of these selected faces and choose **Reverse Faces**, which switches the front and back faces. This makes a bit of a mess: The inside window faces now show what was previously painted on the outside (Figure 7-53). Leave all of these faces selected.

11 Paint the same translucent material on the selected faces (Figure 7-54), and now the windows are translucent both inside and outside (Figure 7-55).

Figure 7-53

Figure 7-54

Figure 7-55

Model It Yourself

This model also contains an image of a stained-glass octagonal window by Glass by Design Studio. You could use the **Polygon** to create an octagon for this window, but you can also use the easier **Rectangle**, too: Draw a small square next to the door and paint it with this image (Figure 7-56).

Use free pins to set the portion of the window that you know fits inside a square, using the midpoints of the square instead of the corner points (Figure 7-57). Make the image translucent, move and trim the edges as needed to complete the window, and then add a copy on the other side of the door (Figure 7-58). If you want to add a frame around the window, use this trick: Make a copy of the window and use **Offset** to place a frame around the copy. Then copy the frame to fit the original window, and erase the extra objects. This may "break" a wall, but that's easy to fix by just adding a line.

Figure 7-56

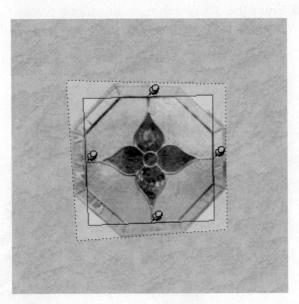

Figure 7-57

Figure 7-58

7.4 Using Images to Create 3D Objects

Perhaps your client has a unique piece of furniture that can't be found in the 3D Warehouse or anywhere online. As you've seen, it's pretty easy to model anything if you know its dimensions and have all of the photos that you need. Ideally, you'd have one photo for each face (e.g., for a chest, you'd have a photo of each of the four sides, plus one of the top). Then you'd use free pins to affix each photo to its face.

This section covers a similar scenario, showing you what to do when you *don't* have all of the ideal photos to work from. For instance, instead of one photo for each face, you may have one photo that needs to be used for two or three faces. Once the basic model is painted, you can use the photo as a guide for minor changes to the model.

Painted 3D Object: Wooden Chest

In this section, you'll model a basic painted chest, for which you only have one photo.

1 From the 3D Warehouse, download Sticks Chest Unpainted by Bonnie Roskes. Explode the model if you imported it into another model. The idea is to take the unpainted box, whose dimensions are shown in Figure 7-59, and use the photo included in the model to paint three of the sides.

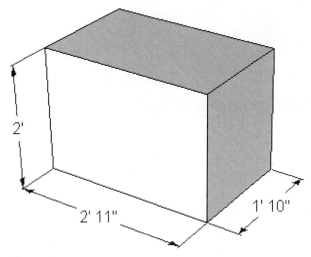

Figure 7-59

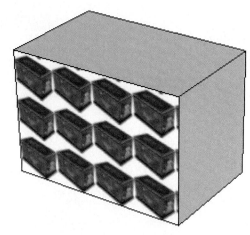

Figure 7-60

2 Find the photo of the painted chest and use it to paint the front of the box (Figure 7-60). This picture came from the Sticks Furniture website.

3 Use free pins to position the correct part of the image to this face. Adjust the pins so that the borders look even (Figure 7-61). Small portions of the photo on either side of the chest's base and the edge under the lid won't appear on this face, but you can fix that later.

4 The same photo can also be used to paint the top and right side of the box. So you *could* use the same photo to paint the right side (Figure 7-62), but there's a more efficient way. If you painted this face, click **Undo** or use the default material to unpaint this face.

Figure 7-61

Figure 7-62

5 Sample the positioned material on the front face, and apply this material to the side. The images line up perfectly along the vertical edge shared by the two faces (Figure 7-63).

6 Display the free pins for this face; the two pins along the common vertical edge are already in place. The other two pins, indicated in Figure 7-64, are the only ones that need to be moved.

Figure 7-63

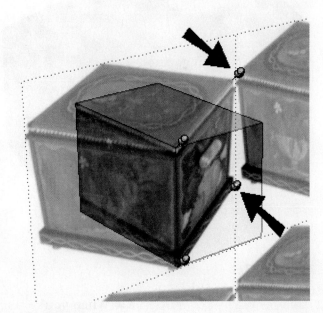

Figure 7-64

7 Adjust these pins to complete the side face (Figure 7-65).

8 You've probably figured out how to paint the top face: Sample the material from either the front or the side, and use it to paint the top (Figure 7-66). This leaves just one pin to adjust (in the far corner). After this quick positioning, all three sides of the box are painted (Figure 7-67).

Figure 7-65

Figure 7-66

Figure 7-67

Figure 7-68

9 When you're using one photo to paint multiple faces, it's likely that not all of the faces will look perfect. In this example, the top face looks a little dark because of the angle at which the photo was taken. But you can fix this without having to take a new photo. First, right-click on the top face and choose **Make Unique Texture** (Figure 7-68).

This creates a separate material that represents only what appears on the top face itself (Figure 7-69). What's great about this technique is that you can edit this material without affecting the original image that's being used for the other two faces.

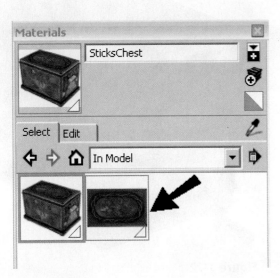

Figure 7-69

Figure 7-70

10 To lighten this face, edit the unique material, set the color picker to either HLS or HSB (as opposed to RGB), and gradually increase the lightness or brightness (Figure 7-70).

> **NOTE**
>
> For more sophisticated image editing, you can use an external graphics editor such as Photoshop. PC users: Right-click on the swatch and chose **Edit Texture Image**. Mac users: As you've already seen when extracting an image from a model, edit the material, and then choose the **Edit** option from the **Texture** drop-down menu. The image will open in your default graphics editor. Make the change, and then close the image and save the change. Your default graphics editor is set on the **Applications** page of the **Preferences** window (for PC users, it is **Window/Preferences**; for Mac users it is **SketchUp/Preferences**).
>
> You probably won't go to this length for a simple lightening procedure, but a graphics editor is great for image touch-ups, such as covering up scratches on wood or removing reflections from a window.

11 For a hand-painted piece like this, the left side of the actual box probably looks different from the right side. But because we don't have a photo of that face, we have to improvise. Sample the material from the right side, and apply it to the left side (Figure 7-71).

12 If you're a perfectionist, you'll be bothered by the fact that this model doesn't include a wider base for the bottom of the chest. So let's fix this: Start by tracing on one side of the edge, along the top of the base (Figure 7-72).

13 Tracing gets a little tricky when you're drawing on painted faces. In the next section, you'll see how to change the edge color to make tracing easier. Another solution is to temporarily remove the images altogether: From the main menu, choose **View/Face Style/Shaded**. This changes each painted face to its base color, making it easy to continue the base edges along the front face and the other side face (Figure 7-73). (The **Monochrome** face style would also work here.)

Chapter 7 | Working with Digital Images   **299**

Figure 7-71

Figure 7-72

Figure 7-73

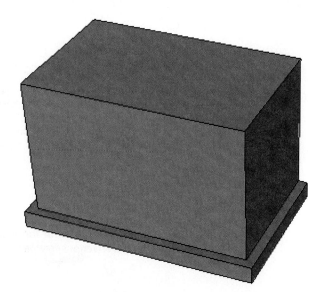

Figure 7-74

14 Pull out the base 1″ on all three sides. Erase any small edges that remain on the top of the base (Figure 7-74).

15 Bring back the painted faces by choosing **View/Face Style/Shaded with Textures**. Some paint repair is needed along the top and sides of the base (Figure 7-75).

16 Paint the top of the base a matching solid color. For the sides of the base, use free pins to adjust the images, making sure that the images meet correctly at the corners (Figure 7-76).

Figure 7-75

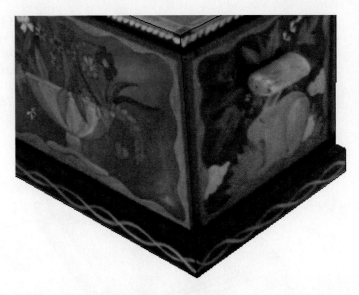

Figure 7-76

Painted 3D Object: Princess Chair

In this section, you'll model a painted princess chair, for which there are two photos. The chair has an unusually shaped back, which will be created by tracing on the photo itself.

1. From the 3D Warehouse, download Sticks Chair Unpainted by Bonnie Roskes. Explode the model if you imported it into another model. This model contains only the two images in Figure 7-77, which show the front and back of this chair.

2. Explode both images so that the materials appear in the In Model collection, and erase the faces that contain both images.

Figure 7-77

Figure 7-77

3 Imagine that you were handed these photos and were not told anything about the chair's dimensions. Start with a reasonable assumption: The seat is 18″ × 18″. Draw an 18″ × 18″ × 2″ yellow box (it doesn't hurt to apply the colors you know from the start). For the cushion, offset the top slightly inward, paint the offset square light blue, and pull it up another ¾″ (Figure 7-78).

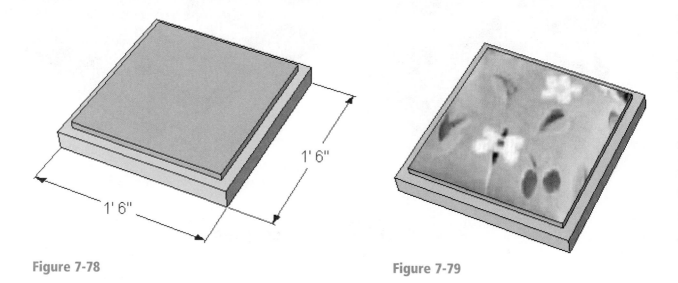

Figure 7-78

Figure 7-79

4 Paint the top of the cushion with the photo that shows the chair's seat, and position the photo so that the seat cushion fills in this face (Figure 7-79).

5 Apply the same photo to the front face of the seat (the yellow face, not the front of the cushion itself), and position the correct portion of the photo (Figure 7-80).

Figure 7-80

6 This image looks a little dark, so make the texture for this face unique and lighten it. The other sides of the seat are not very clear in either photo, so just sample the front face that you just painted and use its material for the other faces of the seat (Figure 7-81).

Figure 7-81

7 On the back of the seat (near where the little white flower appears on the cushion), draw the two small lines shown in Figure 7-82; this creates a new rectangle, which will be used to create the chair back.

8 With the Ctrl/Option key pressed, pull up this narrow rectangle higher than it needs to go, approximately 3 feet (Figure 7-83). Erase any extra lines on this face.

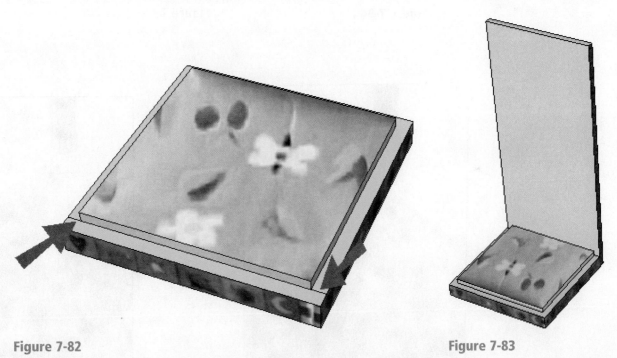

Figure 7-82   Figure 7-83

9 Paint the chair front picture onto this face, and position it so that it looks even and symmetrical (Figure 7-84).

10 Now the top of the chair can be traced. Start by activating the **Arc** tool and hovering over the midpoint shown in Figure 7-85.

11 Move the mouse straight down to start the arc at the very top of the chair; trace one side of the chair back with the arc and line shown in Figure 7-86.

12 Select the line and arc, copy both into blank space, and turn them inside-out. Then move them back into place so that the top points of both arcs meet at the center of the chair top (Figure 7-87).

Figure 7-84

Figure 7-85

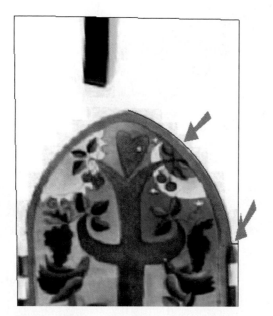

Figure 7-86

Figure 7-87

13 Use **Push/Pull** to shave off the extra faces above the top of the chair. If necessary, adjust the free pins to better fit the photo to the face. For the narrow sides of the back, you can paint the curved part a solid red to match the photo. For the side of the zebra-striped post, you can sample the front face and then paint the side with the material, adjusting the pins only slightly to get the stripes to appear correctly (Figure 7-88). Copy these narrow painted faces to the other side of the chair back.

Figure 7-88

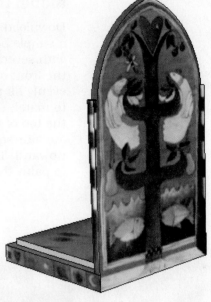

Figure 7-89

14 For the back of the chair, use the other photo provided, adjusting the pins as needed (Figure 7-89).

15 The legs are a solid color, and you can ignore the splayed front legs that appear in the photo. Just create identical vertical legs that are about 16″ high (Figure 7-90).

16 As the final step, soften the edges around the cushion, as well as the top and back of the chair, to make the chair appear more realistic (Figure 7-91).

Figure 7-90

Figure 7-91

Model It Yourself

Download the model Hand-Painted Server by Bonnie Roskes. The model is a simple box that includes the overall dimensions of the piece and comes with several photos from ECustomFinishes.com, which you can use to paint the front and sides. Start by painting the front face, adjusting the image to evenly fill the face (Figure 7-92). Use your tracing skills to modify the box to match the actual shape of the server: Push in the sides and front, curve the top of the server, and add legs at the bottom (for the legs, you can create four squares on the bottom of the box and push the rest of the face upward). Then use other images to paint the sides. You can use an image to paint the top and legs, or just use a light wood material (Figure 7-93).

Figure 7-92

Figure 7-93

7.5 Tracing Photos to Create 3D Objects

We've already done some tracing throughout this chapter, but it has always been on a face that's already painted. In this final section of the chapter, we'll create a model from scratch, just by tracing a photo of the finished piece.

1. From the 3D Warehouse, download Avalon Table Photo by Bonnie Roskes. The photo can be seen in **Front** view; it's a photo of Crate and Barrel's Avalon dining table (Figure 7-94). The tabletop diameter is 45″, and the table is 29½″ high. If you measure the image, you'll see that it's a good bit larger than the table itself, but importing a large image isn't a bad idea because it can be hard to trace over photos that are too small. The overall size of the model will be adjusted later.

2. Centering the table at the origin will make this model much easier to complete: Move the image so that the blue axis passes through the center of the pedestal, and the right-most leg sits atop the red axis (Figure 7-95).

   Before getting started with the tracing, it's helpful to change the way that edges and faces are displayed. For this particular image, black edges would be easy to see, but not every image you find will be so bright and crisp. Imagine a black table in a shadowy picture; only edges of a different color would stand out.

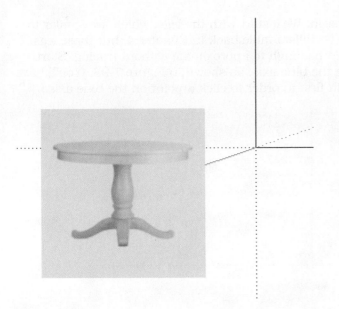

Figure 7-94

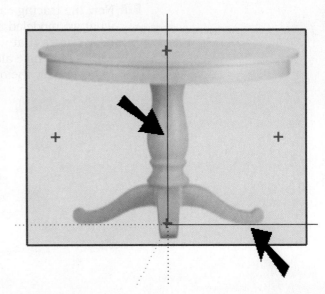

Figure 7-95

3 Open the **Styles** window to the **Edit** tab and **Edge** settings (the first icon at the top of the **Edit** tab). Check **Profiles** so that the edges will appear thick, and set the profile value to a thickness of 4. At the bottom of the window, click the edges color box to set a bright, easily seen color such as pink (Figure 7-96).

4 Continuing in the **Styles** window, click the icon next to the **Edge** icon to open the **Face** settings. Because we want to easily see when a face is created, change the **Front color** and **Back color** to something that will easily stand out against the white background of the photo (Figure 7-97).

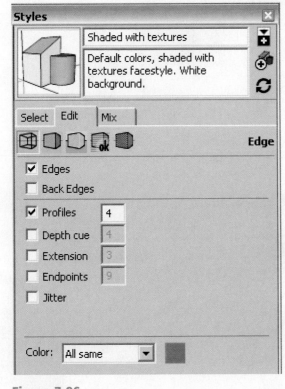

Figure 7-96

Figure 7-97

5 Now the tracing can begin. We'll start with the legs, which are similar to what we modeled for the Billsta table back in Chapter 4, but these legs have curves that would be tough to approximate without tracing. Start with a rectangle along the blue axis, as shown in Figure 7-98. (You'll have to hover over the origin first in order to click a point on the blue axis.)

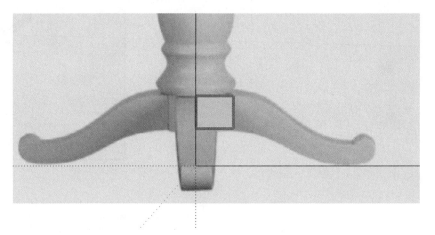

Figure 7-98

6 Use **Arc** to trace along the curves, starting at the corner of the rectangle that you just drew (Figure 7-99). When you make it all the way back to the rectangle, you should have the leg shape completely traced, and you can erase the vertical edge of the rectangle that divided the leg (Figure 7-100).

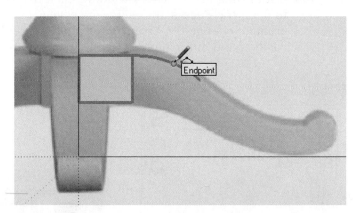

Figure 7-99

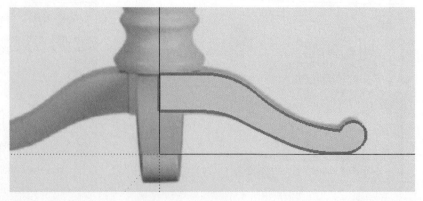

Figure 7-100

7 Hide the picture (right-click on it and choose **Hide**), and use **Push/Pull** on one side to give the leg a little thickness. Remember the distance that you use, such as the 2″ shown in Figure 7-101.

8 To keep the leg centered with respect to the blue axis, pull out the other side by the same distance (Figure 7-102).

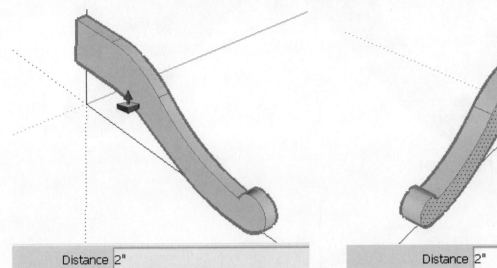

Distance 2″

Figure 7-101

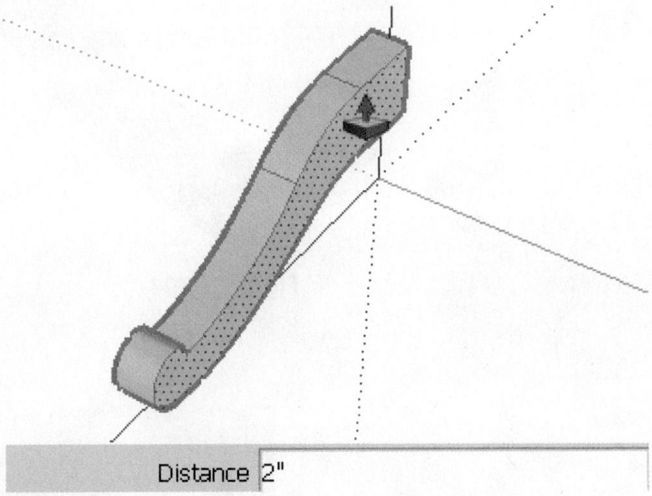

Distance 2″

Figure 7-102

9 Select the entire leg, and use the **Rotate** tool with the Ctrl/Option key pressed to make three 90-degree copies (Figure 7-103). The protractor can be placed directly on the origin.

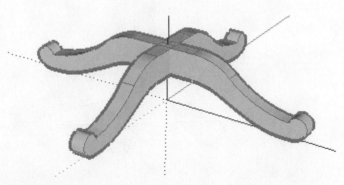

Figure 7-103

10 Make the set of four legs into a group.

11 The next step is to trace around half of the pedestal. The first edge will be along the blue axis, so activate **Line** and start the line at the top center point of the leg group (Figure 7-104).

12 Before clicking to complete the line, bring back the image (**Edit/Unhide/All**). Then click the point at the top center of the pedestal (Figure 7-105).

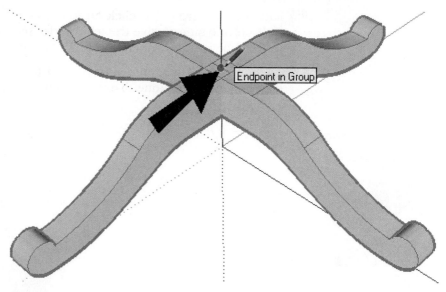

Figure 7-104

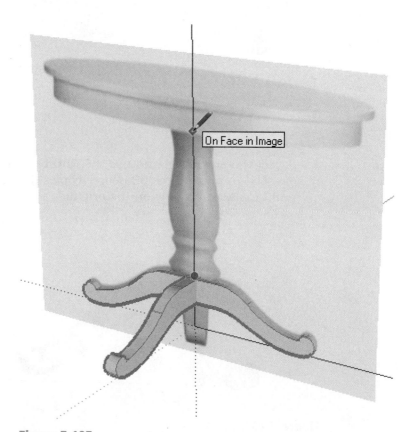

Figure 7-105

13 Draw another line across the top, then add some more arcs on the way down (Figure 7-106). Stop right *before* you draw the very last arc.

14 To complete this face, it's helpful to hide the image again. Then draw a line across the bottom of the face by clicking Points 1 and 2 as shown in Figure 7-107, and add one more arc to complete the face (Figure 7-108). If you *don't* get a completed face after creating this last arc, orbit to see whether any of your arcs or lines are going in the wrong direction.

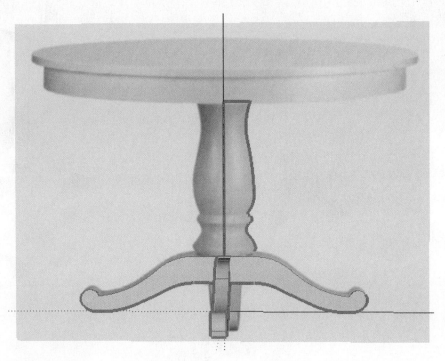

Figure 7-106

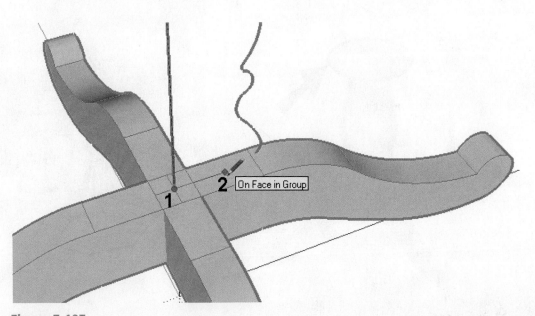

Figure 7-107

15 The steps for completing the pedestal should be familiar: Draw a flat **Follow Me** circle anywhere below the center of the table, and use it as the **Follow Me** path for the half-pedestal face. When finished, make the pedestal into its own group (Figure 7-109).

16 To complete the tabletop, move the circle straight up to meet the top of the pedestal (Figure 7-110).

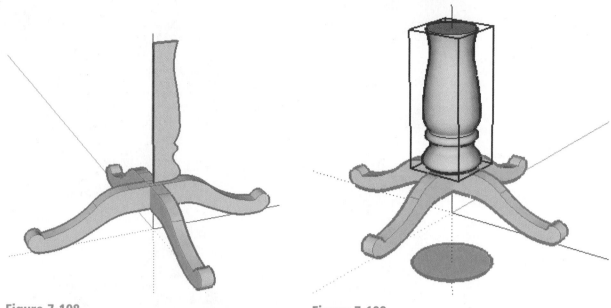

Figure 7-108

Figure 7-109

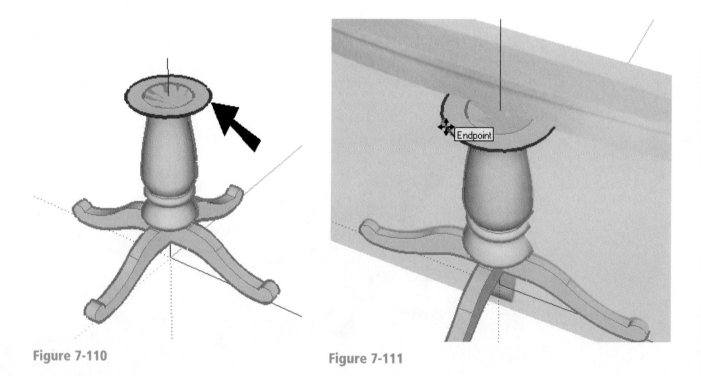

Figure 7-110

Figure 7-111

17 Bring back the image once again. To resize the tabletop circle, we could use the **Scale** tool or the **Entity Info** window, but this is a good place to demonstrate a handy feature of the **Move** tool. First, make sure that nothing in the model has been selected by right-clicking on blank space to unselect everything. Then activate **Move**, and move your cursor along this circle. Along most of the circle, you'll see that the entire edge is highlighted (Figure 7-111).

18 There are four points along any SketchUp circle (or polygon) that can be used for resizing. Assuming that you drew your circle in the red or green direction, these four points should be directly above the red and green axes. They will highlight on their own, without the rest of the edge, when your cursor passes over them (Figure 7-112).

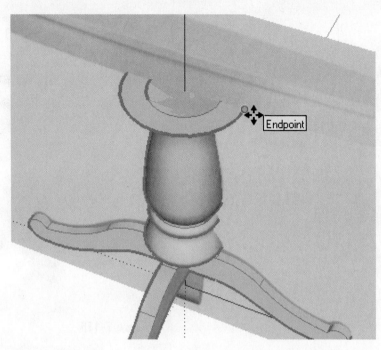

Figure 7-112

19 Click and drag one of these highlighted points so that the circle approximates the bottom of the tabletop in the photo (Figure 7-113).

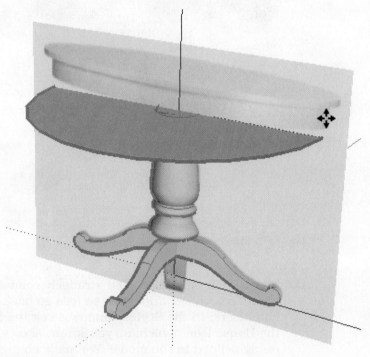

Figure 7-113

20 Pull up this circle to match the photo (Figure 7-114), then use **Offset** for the larger circle at the top. Pull up as needed to complete the tabletop (Figure 7-115); erase any extra edges; and, finally, hide or erase the image (Figure 7-116).

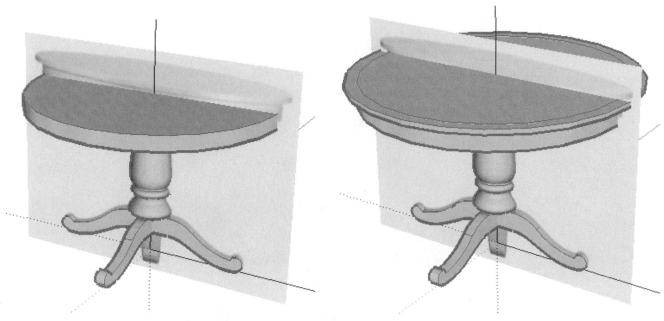

Figure 7-114   Figure 7-115

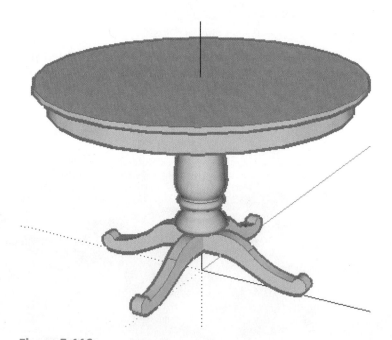

Figure 7-116

21 These thick pink edges and strangely colored faces are probably starting to look rather annoying, so let's go back to the default style that we had before. In the **Styles** window, click the **Select** tab and then click the House icon, which, as you know, shows any styles that are currently defined in the model. We made changes to our style but we never *saved* these changes, so the original style thumbnail still appears in

Figure 7-117

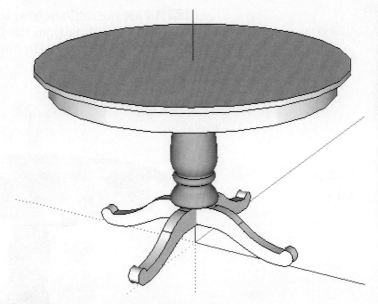

Figure 7-118

the In Model collection (Figure 7-117). Click this thumbnail (don't click the larger thumbnail at the top that shows the changed style!), and your table returns to the original style (Figure 7-118).

22 At this point, you can paint the table, which is obviously manufactured in white; however, a wood finish looks better in pictures (Figure 7-119). Use whatever color or material you desire.

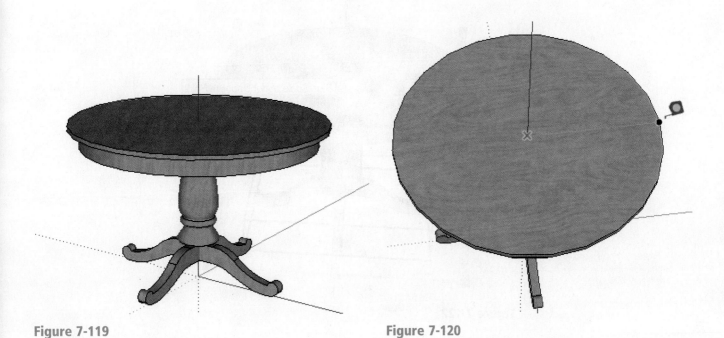

Figure 7-119

Figure 7-120

23 Now for the sizing: It's easiest to start with the diameter, which we know is supposed to be 45″. So use the **Tape Measure** to set the distance from the center of the tabletop to its edge (Figure 7-120), then enter 22.5″ to resize the entire table accordingly.

24 To set the table height, which is 29.5″, draw a dummy line in blank space, starting from the green or red axis and proceeding straight up 29.5″ (Figure 7-121).

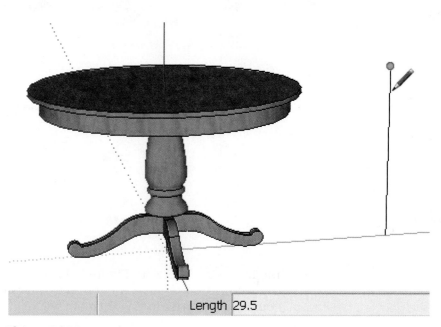

Length 29.5

Figure 7-121

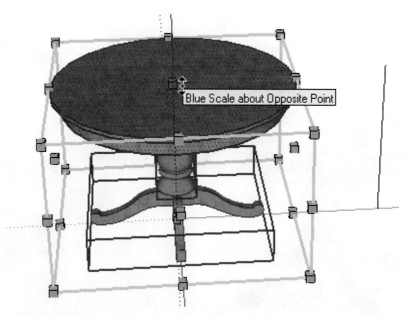

Blue Scale about Opposite Point

Figure 7-122

25 Select the entire table and activate **Scale**. Click the top Blue Scale handle shown in Figure 7-122, then click the top of the dummy line (Figure 7-123). You are done!

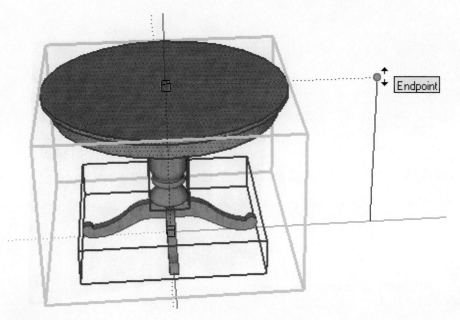

Figure 7-123

Model It Yourself

Download the model Turned Table Leg Photo, which contains only an image of a country-style dining table with turned legs (Figure 7-124).

Place the model so that one leg is centered at the origin, and trace over the turned part of the leg (Figure 7-125).

Figure 7-124

Figure 7-125

For the top part of the leg, which is not turned, use a square that is pulled into a box (Figure 7-126).

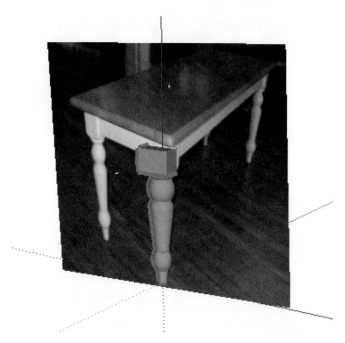

Figure 7-126

Make the leg a component, create copies of it, and create a rectangle that sits on top of the legs that you can offset to create the edge of the tabletop (Figure 7-127). The final model, with rounded tabletop corners, is shown in Figure 7-128. Make sure that the final table model has reasonable dimensions.

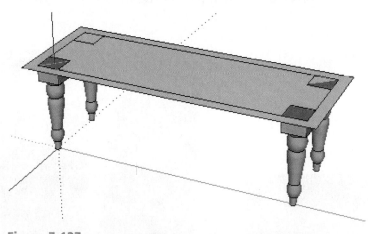

Figure 7-127

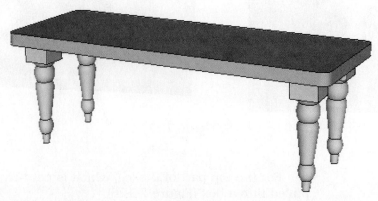

Figure 7-128

Review Questions

- How do you place an image onto a wall, specifying the image's exact width?

- In texture positioning, how do free pins differ from fixed pins?

- When saving a SketchUp model of a painting or other model that should align with walls when imported, what do you need to do to set its alignment properties?

- When using a single photo to paint two or more faces of a model, some of the faces may appear too dark or too light. How can this be fixed?

- While tracing, how can you change the color and thickness of edges?

- How can you resize a circle with the **Move** tool?

8 chaptereight

Kitchen Design

At some point, nearly every interior designer is asked to remodel a kitchen. You already know how to find or model cabinets, appliances, and accessories, and this chapter will introduce a few new concepts that you'll need to tie the entire kitchen together.

In this chapter, you'll learn how to do the following:

- Use and find dynamic cabinet components.
- Place base cabinets and appliances.
- Place wall cabinets.
- Add a countertop.
- Add a sink.

8.1 Dynamic Components

1 Use your Internet browser to download the model Kitchen Design Start by Bonnie Roskes. To save yourself the time and effort of hunting down 3D Warehouse cabinets and appliances, all of the objects that you need for this kitchen are found outside the kitchen, in blank space (Figure 8-1). Each cabinet and appliance is a component, and the room itself is a group (as it should be).

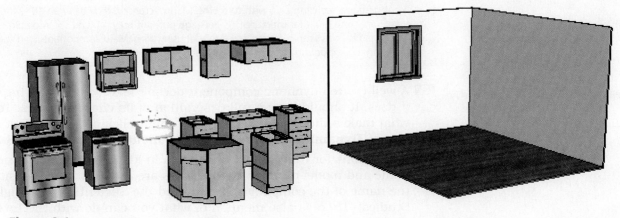

Figure 8-1

2 The cabinets in this example are from the "Malibu" collection by KraftMaid. The finish is natural maple. This information is available in the **Outliner** window (Figure 8-2), or by looking at the **Entity Info** window for an individual component.

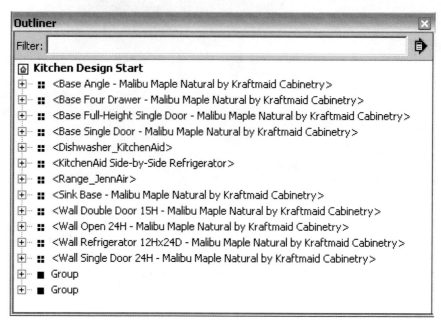

Figure 8-2

The reason that KraftMaid cabinets were chosen for this project is that KraftMaid has created models for just about all of its standard cabinet lines. These are not just regular 3D Warehouse models; each of these cabinets is what's called a dynamic component. In some cases, dynamic models can physically move or rotate; others have material or color options; some merely have descriptions or pricing information; and others, such as these cabinets, have sizing options. These cabinets can also be opened and closed.

> **NOTE**
>
> At the time of this writing, Quick Cabinets and General Casework are two other manufacturers that have created dynamic cabinet models. There are also a few generic ones by the SketchUp staff. The number of dynamic models (cabinets and other items) increases all of the time, so more brands are likely to be available in the future. If your client wants to use a cabinet line that isn't available in the 3D Warehouse, be aware that not all manufacturers offer *exactly* the same features in the same sizes. For example, KraftMaid makes an 18"-wide pull-out garbage/recycling unit with two bins. Manufacturer X may offer an 18"-wide pull-out with only one bin. Manufacturer Y's garbage pull-out may only be 15" wide. So designing a kitchen isn't as simple as creating a model using KraftMaid components and then exchanging a component for another manufacturer's product later.

3 A well-crafted dynamic component doesn't leave you wondering what it does. It should have a full description of its characteristics. To see what makes these cabinets dynamic, right-click on any cabinet and choose **Dynamic Components/Component Options** (Figure 8-3).

The options for this cabinet are shown in Figure 8-4. The cabinet name and model number are listed, as are the KraftMaid website and the name of the company that provided the SketchUp model (Igloo Studios). There is also mention of what you can do with the **Interact** tool (open doors or drawers). But the most useful feature of this cabinet

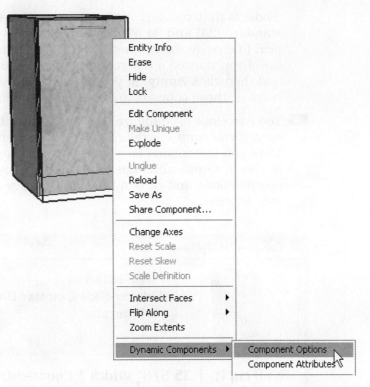

Figure 8-3

Figure 8-4

Chapter 8 | Kitchen Design **323**

model is that you can choose its size. The depth and height are standard (24″ and 34.5″, respectively), but you can click the **Model** field to change the cabinet's width. This particular cabinet is 18″ wide, but if you wanted a different width, you could choose a different model and then click **Apply**. (If you change any widths, change them back because these cabinets are sized to fit the kitchen space.)

4 You can close or minimize the **Component Options** window, or leave it open if you want to explore options for other cabinets. This window will show you the options for whatever model is selected. The refrigerator is also dynamic, although its options are just a list of the appliance's specifications and cannot be changed; they are for reference purposes only (Figure 8-5).

Component Options

KitchenAid
Side-by-Side Counter Depth Refrigerator

23.8 cu. ft. | 35 5/8″ Width | Counter-Depth | Side-by-Side Dispensing | Freestanding Refrigerator | Flat, Smooth Doors | Architect® Series II

KSCS25MVMK (monochromatic stainless cab.)
KSCS25MVMS (monochromatic stainless steel)

The uninterrupted, sleek exterior of this counter-depth side-by-side refrigerator features flat, smooth doors and a flush-to-cabinet look that reflects the style and integration of built-in models. The added floor space allows for kitchen traffic to flow easily through an evening of entertaining.

Product & MSRP Information

Use & Care Guide

Dimension Guide

Energy Guide

Energy Star Compliant	Yes
Energy Star Home Compliant	Yes
NAHB Green Guidelines EE 3.3.4	3.0 Pts.
NAHB Green Guidelines WE 4.1.3	N/A
LEED for Homes EAc9.1	0.5 Pts.
LEED for Homes EAc9.2	N/A

Figure 8-5

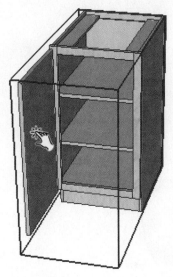

5 To see how the cabinets interact, choose **Tools/Interact** from the main menu. The cursor becomes a pointing hand. When the cursor finds something with which to interact, it looks like the one shown in (Figure 8-6). Click on a drawer or door to open it (Figure 8-6); to close it, just click it again.

> **NOTE**
>
> Dynamic components are available for anyone to download and use, but they can only be *created* in the Pro version of SketchUp. This is why the **Component Attributes** option is available in Pro only, but **Component Options** are available for everyone.
>
> How can you find models that are dynamic? One way is to append "is:dynamic" to your 3D Warehouse search term (e.g., "kraftmaid sink base is:dynamic"). This search isn't all-inclusive, unfortunately, because not all modelers specify that their model is dynamic when they upload it.

Figure 8-6

8.2 Placing Base Cabinets and Appliances

Now that we've seen what these cabinets can do, we can start moving them into place. For each cabinet, you'll start by moving it by a specific point, always on a corner or edge, and using the arrow keys to lock an axis direction. In order to click specific points, you'll be doing a lot of zooming and orbiting with your mouse.

1 The first base cabinet to place is the one in the corner. With nothing selected in advance, find the base angle cabinet, activate **Move**, and click the corner point shown in Figure 8-7.

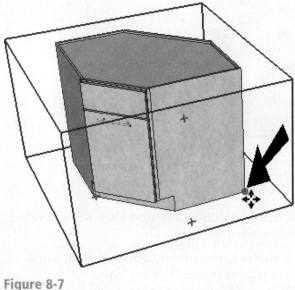

Figure 8-7

Figure 8-8

2 For the second move point, click anywhere on the right edge of the floor (Figure 8-8).

3 Keep **Move** active. To slide the cabinet into the corner, click anywhere along the left back edge (Figure 8-9).

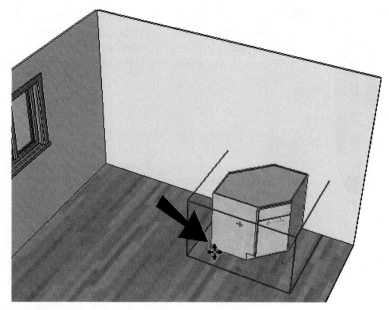

Figure 8-9

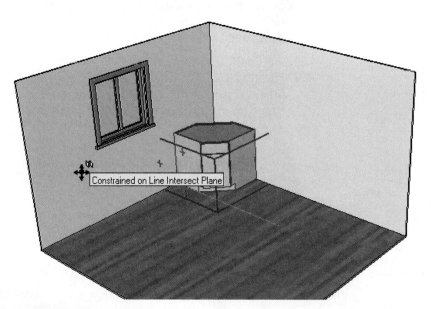

Constrained on Line Intersect Plane

Figure 8-10

4 Press the left arrow to lock the green direction, and click anywhere on the wall with the window (Figure 8-10).

5 Every time that you place a cabinet, you should check it from a few angles to make sure that it is placed correctly. Check the corner cabinet from above to make sure that its back edges meet both walls (Figure 8-11).

6 Now we'll continue with the row of cabinets that proceeds along the wall with the window. Find the four-drawer cabinet (remember that the **Entity Info** window can help you identify a cabinet) and click a point along its back edge (Figure 8-12). Move this cabinet to any point on the edge of the floor below the window (Figure 8-13).

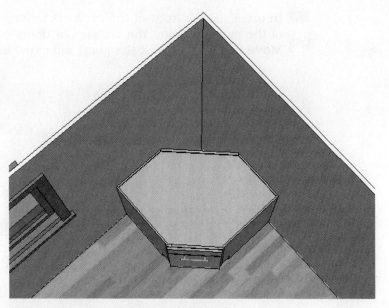

Figure 8-11

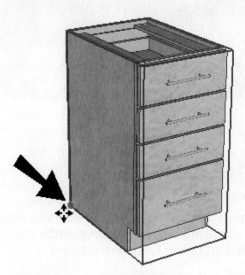

Figure 8-12

Figure 8-13

7 In order for the front of the cabinets to align correctly, the front faces of the panels behind the drawers or doors must meet exactly. So with **Move** still active, click the point indicated in Figure 8-14.

Figure 8-14

8 Press the right arrow to lock the red direction, and slide the drawers along the floor to the right so that they meet the corner cabinet. Because of the corner angle, these two cabinets should not actually touch; we need to leave a small gap (about 1½″) so that the doors and drawers can open (Figure 8-15). The easiest way to create this gap is to slide the drawers so that they touch the corner cabinet, then move the unit 1.5″ to the left.

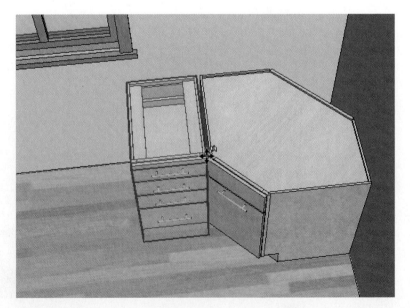

Figure 8-15

9 Next in the row is the two-door sink base. This requires just one move because the front panels of the sink base and the four-drawer cabinet should touch. Click the first move point as indicated in Figure 8-16, and move the sink base to the corresponding point of the four-drawer cabinet (Figure 8-17).

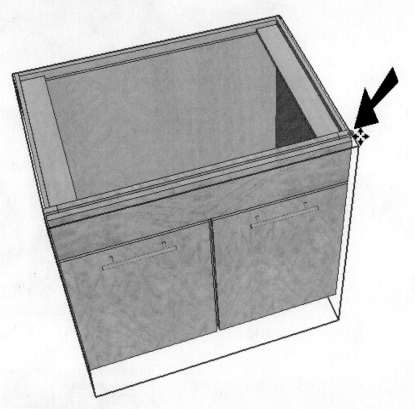

Figure 8-16

Figure 8-17

10 The dishwasher is next. Click the point indicated in Figure 8-18, at the top left corner of the dishwasher box, behind its door. Move this point to meet the front of the sink base (Figure 8-19).

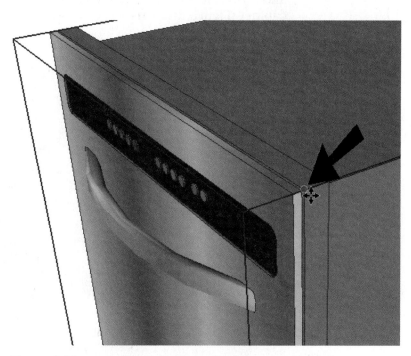

Figure 8-18

Figure 8-19

11 To complete this row, move the single door and drawer cabinet to the left of the dishwasher (Figure 8-20).

12 Now we can complete the row along the other wall. **Move** should still be active; so move the cursor to the top of the single-door cabinet and click one of the red plus (+) signs to rotate the cabinet 90 degrees so that it faces the correct way (Figure 8-21).

13 Move this cabinet to the edge of the floor (Figure 8-22), then use the green direction to slide it along the wall to meet the corner cabinet. Again, leave a 1.5″ gap so that the doors can open (Figure 8-23).

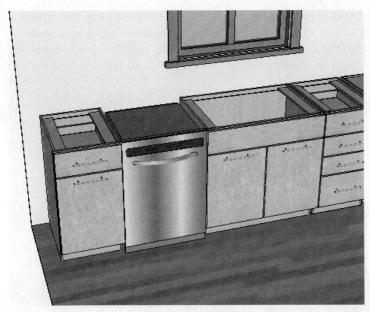

Figure 8-20

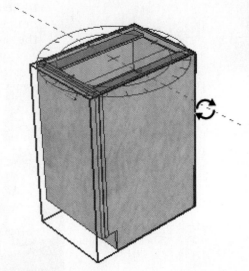

Figure 8-21

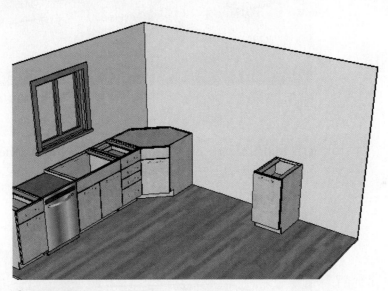

Figure 8-22

Figure 8-23

14 Next we will add the oven (Figure 8-24). Because the top of the range is *above* the top of the cabinets (it should be slightly above the soon-to-be-added countertop), move the oven like you did the previous cabinet: Move its bottom to the floor edge, and slide it to the left to meet the single-door cabinet.

Figure 8-24

15 Make a copy of the single-door cabinet to the left of the oven, placing it directly to the right of the oven (Figure 8-25).

Figure 8-25

16 Finally, add the refrigerator, again moving it to the floor first, then moving it to meet the cabinet to its left (Figure 8-26).

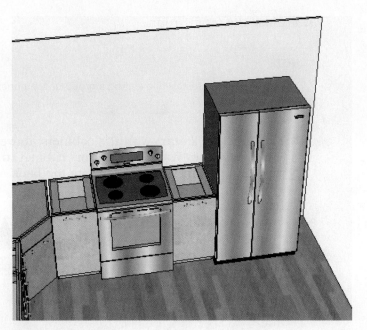

Figure 8-26

8.3 Placing Wall Cabinets

Wall cabinets will be aligned at their *tops*, unlike the base cabinets, which all sit on the floor. In some kitchen designs, wall cabinets extend all the way to the ceiling, but we're going to position these wall cabinets so that the tops are 7′ from the floor.

1. Open the room group for editing. The properties of this model are set to hide all objects except for what's being edited, so all cabinets and appliances temporarily disappear from view. Use the **Tape Measure** tool to create guide lines for both walls, offset 7′ from the floor (Figure 8-27).

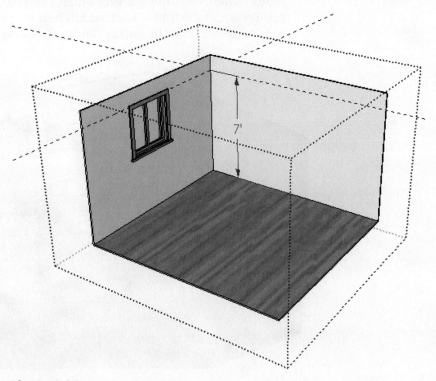

Figure 8-27

2 Close the room group.

3 This time, we'll start with the cabinets above the refrigerator. Activate **Move**, find the "Wall Refrigerator" cabinet, turn it to face the right way, and click any point along its top back edge (Figure 8-28).

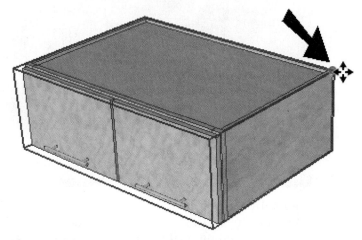

Figure 8-28

4 Move this cabinet anywhere along the guide line above the refrigerator (Figure 8-29). Then slide it to the right to align it with the side of the refrigerator (Figure 8-30). Make sure that you align the panel behind the cabinet doors, and not the doors themselves, to the side of the refrigerator! There should be a very small gap below the cabinet, above the refrigerator, which in an actual kitchen would probably be covered with a wood panel. But the gap is not at all noticeable in a SketchUp model.

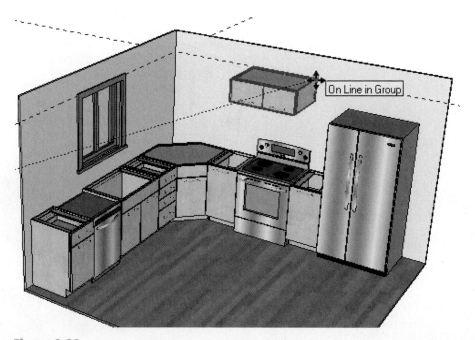

Figure 8-29

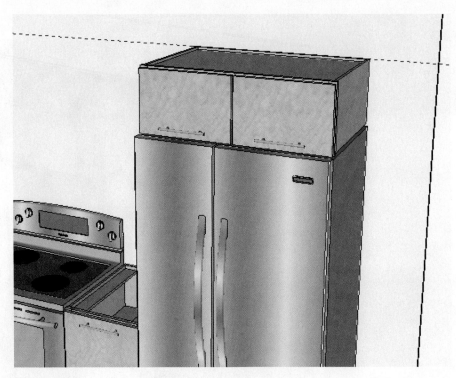

Figure 8-30

5️⃣ A single-door wall cabinet will go to the left of the refrigerator. This cabinet is not as deep as the one above the refrigerator, so you can't line up their front panels. As before, move this cabinet first by its top to the guide line (Figure 8-31), then slide it over to meet the refrigerator cabinet (Figure 8-32).

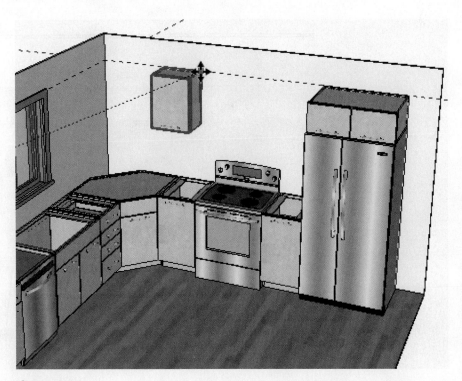

Figure 8-31

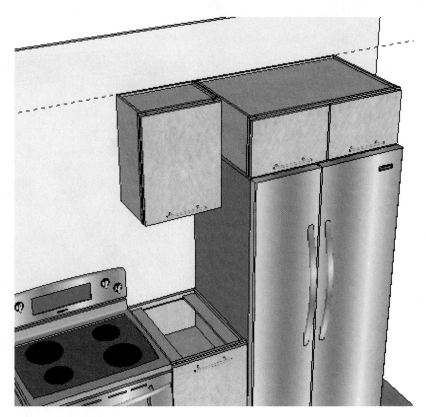

Figure 8-32

6 Next, the double-door wall cabinet goes above the oven. This can be done in one move by aligning the front of the door panels (Figure 8-33).

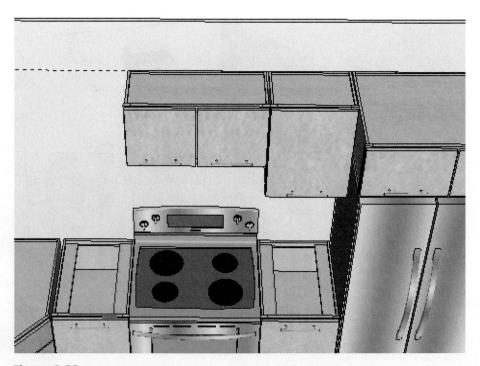

Figure 8-33

7 The next two cabinets are both copies of the single-door wall cabinet that you placed to the left of the refrigerator (Figure 8-34).

Figure 8-34

8 The last wall cabinets are the open shelves. Place one on either side of the window, aligning their tops to the 7′ guide line (Figure 8-35).

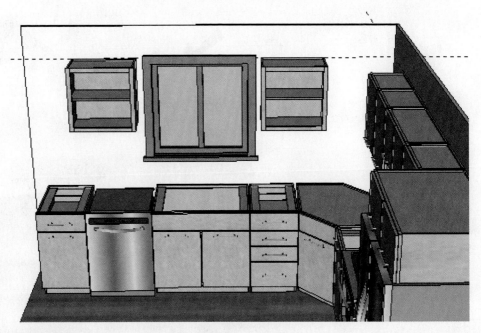

Figure 8-35

9 The cabinets are all in place, so open the room group again and erase the guide lines (Figure 8-36).

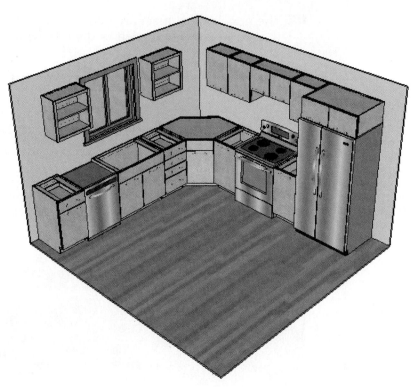

Figure 8-36

10 The last step in placing the cabinetry is to add a panel to cover the right side of the refrigerator. This requires a simple rectangle: Start the rectangle at the top corner of the refrigerator wall cabinet, as indicated in Figure 8-37. End the rectangle at the floor (Figure 8-38).

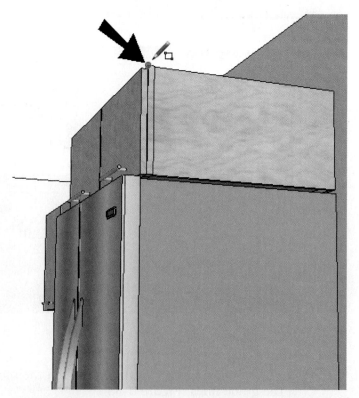

Figure 8-37

Figure 8-38

11 Pull this rectangle out about 1″, and paint its faces to match the other cabinets (Figure 8-39). To find the exact material to use, open the In Model materials collection; there aren't too many swatches to choose from. Remember to press the Ctrl/Option key while painting any face of this panel so that you'll paint the entire panel at one time.

Figure 8-39

8.4 Adding a Countertop

Just as an actual countertop is not added to a kitchen until all of the cabinets and appliances are in place, so it is in SketchUp as well. Once the kitchen infrastructure is laid out, some simple tracing is all that you need for the countertop. The counter for this kitchen will be added in two parts: the L-shaped counter that goes up to the oven, and another small section between the oven and the refrigerator.

1 To start the L-shaped counter, activate the **Line** tool and click the corner point shown in Figure 8-40.

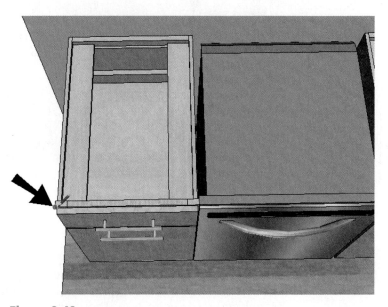

Figure 8-40

2 For the second point, lock the green direction with the left arrow and click anywhere along the wall with the window (Figure 8-41).

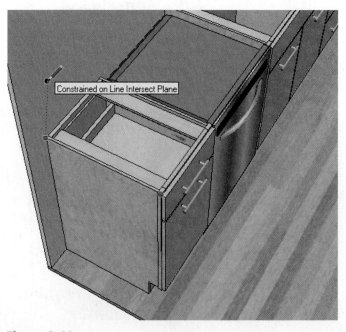

Figure 8-41

3 Continuing on, lock the red direction and click anywhere along the other wall (Figure 8-42).

Figure 8-42

4 Lock the green direction and click the point shown in Figure 8-43, which is the top right corner of the cabinet panel behind the door.

Figure 8-43

5 For the next line, which will proceed along the left edge of the oven, click the same point as before: the top right corner of the cabinet panel (Figure 8-44).

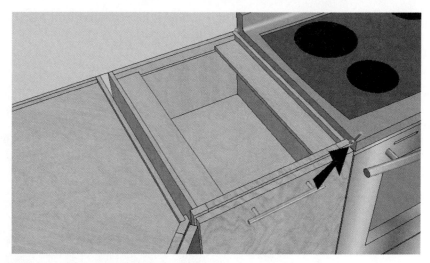

Figure 8-44

6 The angled corner cabinet requires an angled countertop, but we'll add that later. For now, continue in the green direction and click the point where you started drawing these lines, as indicated in Figure 8-45.

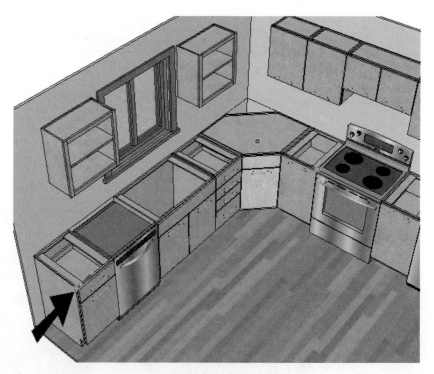

Figure 8-45

7 You just completed the second-to-last line; to complete the last line, click the same point again. You should now have a flat, L-shaped face that traces the tops of the cabinets (Figure 8-46).

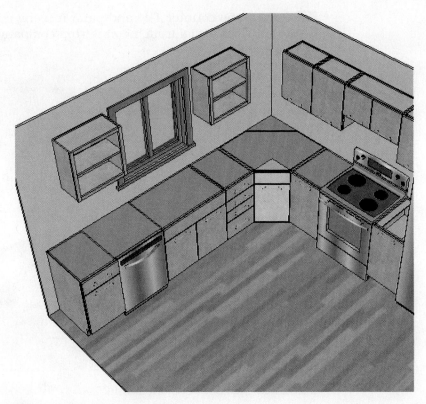

Figure 8-46

8 To add the angled portion in the corner, draw a line along the angled front of the corner cabinet, meeting the other front edges of the countertop. Then erase the extra lines (Figure 8-47).

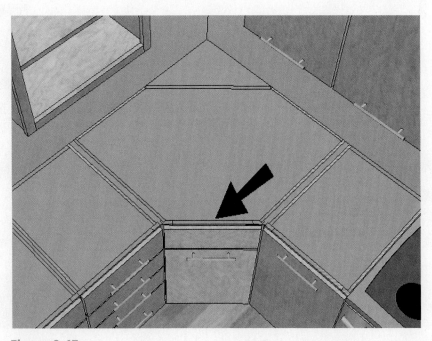

Figure 8-47

9 Pull up the counter 1½″ and paint it using a stone or granite material, or find a material from a countertop company website (Figure 8-48).

Figure 8-48

10 Now that you know how to do the tracing, use the same axis-locking method to trace above the cabinet to the right of the oven. Use the same counter height and material (Figure 8-49).

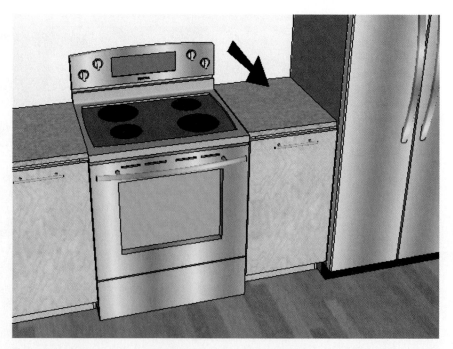

Figure 8-49

11 The last step is to add a backsplash. Select the two back edges of the L-shaped counter (Figure 8-50) and use **Offset** to create two new edges 1″ inward. Pull up this new narrow face 4″ (Figure 8-51).

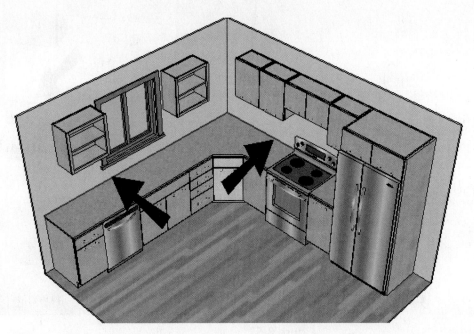

Figure 8-50

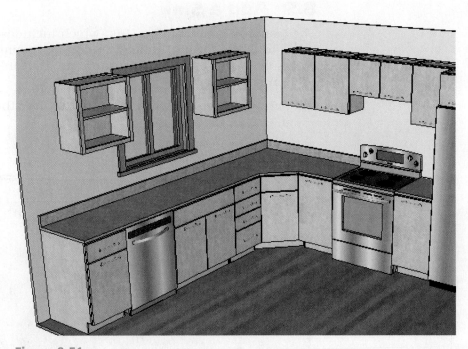

Figure 8-51

12 For the smaller counter section, copy the back edge 1″ inward, and pull up the back face 4″ (Figure 8-52).

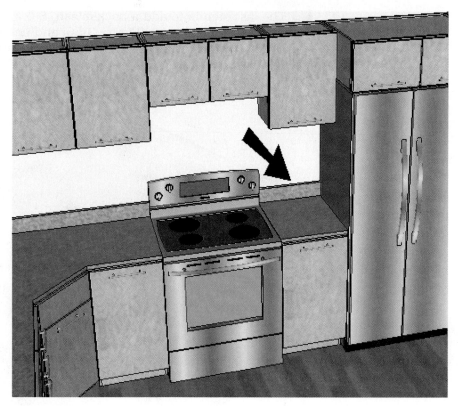

Figure 8-52

8.5 Add a Sink

The last step is to install a sink, which includes cutting the countertop to make a hole for it. Although undermount sinks are more common with solid-surface or stone countertops, the sink in this example is a drop-in sink.

1 Activate **Move** and click a point at or near the bottom of the sink rim (Figure 8-53).

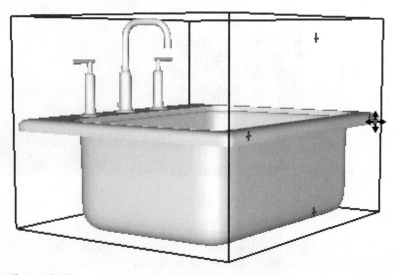

Figure 8-53

2 Move the sink onto the counter, below the window (exact placement will be done in the next step), and click when you see the "On Face" popup (Figure 8-54).

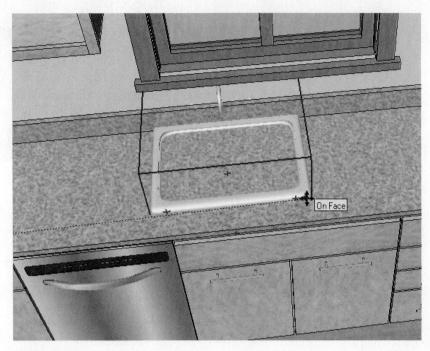

Figure 8-54

3 The sink is only approximately placed, so move it by small amounts in the red and green directions until it is where you want it to be (Figure 8-55). Of course, you can center it exactly above the sink base if you use midpoint constraints.

Figure 8-55

4 To cut the counter, we need to create the edges where the counter meets the sink. So select the entire countertop by triple-clicking any countertop face, then right-click on any counter face, and choose **Intersect Faces/With Model** (Figure 8-56).

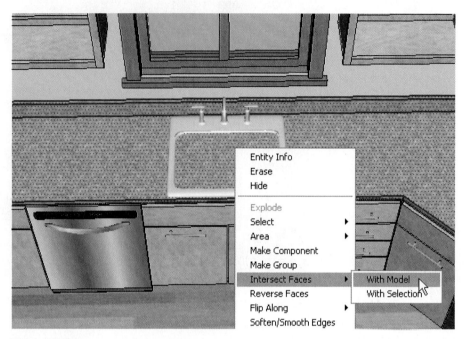

Figure 8-56

5 To see the intersections, hide the sink itself, as well as the cabinets and appliances below it (Figure 8-57). Because the **Intersect Faces** tool can sometimes be inconsistent in SketchUp, look closely at the intersection edges to make sure that they go all the way around where the sink was located. If the countertop *is not* divided into sink and non-sink faces, you have incomplete edges! But this is easily solved by tracing over any gaps.

Figure 8-57

6 Erase the sink face on the top and bottom of the counter, as well as any other edges in the sink area (Figure 8-58). An easy way to erase a loop of edges is to activate **Select** and triple-click any edge in the loop. Then press the Delete key.

Figure 8-58

7 Unhide the sink and cabinets (Figure 8-59), and the kitchen is complete! Your completed model should look like the one shown in Figure 8-60.

Figure 8-59

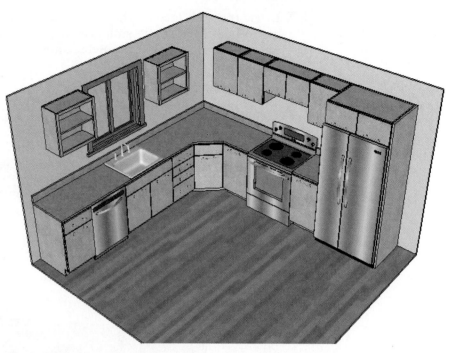

Figure 8-60

Model It Yourself

Use dynamic cabinets to build an 8′-long kitchen island like the one shown in Figure 8-61. The cabinets shown in this image are from the KraftMaid "Hayward" line, in the natural maple finish, but you can use any model

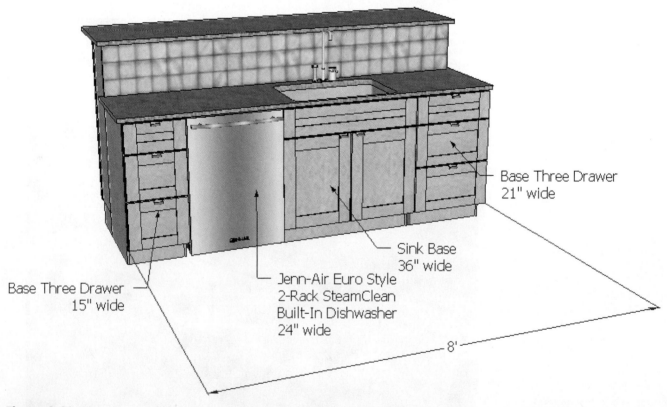

Base Three Drawer
21" wide

Sink Base
36" wide

Jenn-Air Euro Style
2-Rack SteamClean
Built-In Dishwasher
24" wide

Base Three Drawer
15" wide

8′

Figure 8-61

and finish that you like. One side of the island should feature two cabinets (with or without drawers), a sink base, and a dishwasher. Your cabinets can be configured like those in Figure 8-61 or differently, as long as the total island length is 8'. (Check your dishwasher width carefully. The Jenn-Air model used here is actually 1'-11 7/8" wide. So a 1/16" clearance is needed between the dishwasher and its neighboring cabinets. The easiest way to add this clearance is to first move the two objects together, then move the cabinets away 1/16".)

The other side of the island should feature four identical cabinets (42"-high wall cabinets are shown in Figure 8-62). So that this side of the island will have enough height for barstools, first create a 6"-high wood block for these wall cabinets to sit on. Don't forget to adjust the cabinets so that the door handles face each other.

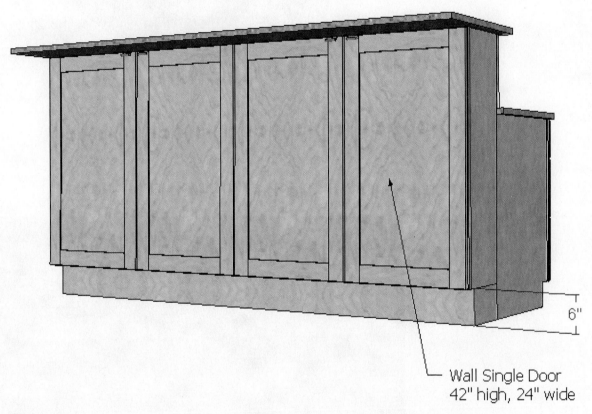

6"

Wall Single Door
42" high, 24" wide

Figure 8-62

The countertops should extend past the island sides by 1", for a total counter width of 8'-2". Both countertops should be 2' deep. For the taller part of the island, the countertop should extend past the wall cabinets below to allow for bar seating (Figure 8-63). Between the two countertops, add a decorative backsplash.

Don't forget to include a sink and faucet, and cut the counter to accommodate the sink (Figure 8-64). There are a few dynamic sinks in the 3D Warehouse that will cut the top of the counter automatically (search for "undermount sink is:dymamic"), or you can find a sink that you can intersect with the counter, then trim the counter manually.

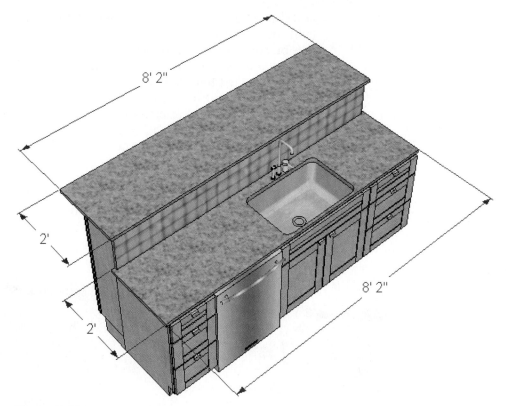

Figure 8-63

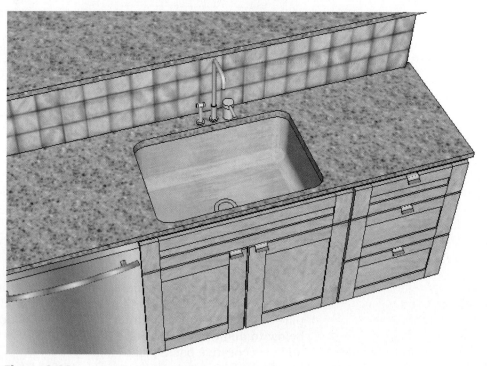

Figure 8-64

Review Questions

- How can you tell what a dynamic component can do?

- List two ways that you can identify a component by its name.

- What SketchUp tool do you need in order to create edges in a counter that you can use to cut a hole for the sink?

9 chapternine

Presenting Your Designs

It is a rare client who will agree to the first design that you present. It's far more likely that you'll be presenting clients with options that include different materials, colors, furniture, and room layouts. This chapter will introduce you to SketchUp layers and scenes, which, when combined, enable you to easily and quickly present an array of design options. You'll also learn how to create specific views of a space.

In this chapter, you'll learn how to do the following:

• Use layers to hide and display objects.

• Present furniture options.

• Present different room arrangements.

• Present options for finishes (floor and counter materials).

• Create and present specific room views.

9.1 Using Layers to Hide and Display Objects

This section is an introduction to SketchUp layers, which are used to control object visibility. To quickly and temporarily hide one or more objects, the **Edit** option on the right-click menu works well. But when you want to quickly turn sets of objects on and off, layers are a better bet.

1 From your Internet browser (not via the **Get Models** tool), download and open the 3D Warehouse model Sunshine Living by Surya Murali. (You should not use **Get Models** to import this model because you may lose some of the model's display settings.) What appears when you first open the model is shown in Figure 9-1, which is actually a rendered image, not the SketchUp model itself.

> **NOTE**
>
> Murali, an engineer by profession and an interior designer by hobby, has become well known in the SketchUp world for the room and furniture models that she's uploaded to the 3D Warehouse. She always creates a rendered image of her room models, and stores that rendering as part of the model, somewhere off to the side in blank space. Murali uses an application called SU Podium, which will be described, along with other similar applications, at the end of this book.

Figure 9-1

2 Zoom out to see the entire model. The rendered image is off to one side, and the model itself is a room with two walls (Figure 9-2).

Figure 9-2

3 To prepare this model for this exercise, first erase the rendered image. Then turn off the shadows by choosing **View/Shadows** from the main menu (the shadow display can cause slow model performance). Erase the five hanging light fixtures above the dining table. Finally, turn on the edge display by choosing **View/Edge Style/Edges**. You can leave the rest of the room as is, although Figure 9-3 shows all black objects in white because black doesn't present as well in pictures. (Optional: If you want to change the background, open the **Edit** tab of the **Styles** window. Open the **Background Settings** and uncheck **Sky**, then change the background color to white.)

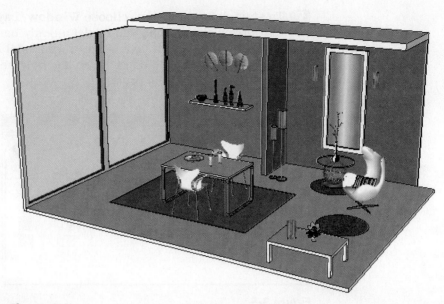

Figure 9-3

4 Take a moment to explore the furniture and accessories in this room. Each object is a component or group, which is exactly how such models should be set up. As you've seen from earlier chapters, components and groups are much easier to select and manipulate than a set of objects that must be selected as a group. However, the room itself is not a group, and neither is the shelf along the left side of the wall. (We'll fix both of these problems later.)

5 There's one other interesting thing to note about this model that you might encounter in models by Murali and others: Zoom in closely around any of the light fixtures, such as the floor lamps shown in Figure 9-4. You'll see small, hovering circles attached to each light. This circle doesn't represent an actual object in the SketchUp model, but it will be defined as a light source when exported into a rendering application. Defining lights while rendering enables you to create the realistic lighting effects and shadows that were visible in this model's rendered image. These circles are not needed for this project, so if you like, you can erase the circles from each light (each light is a component that will need to be edited).

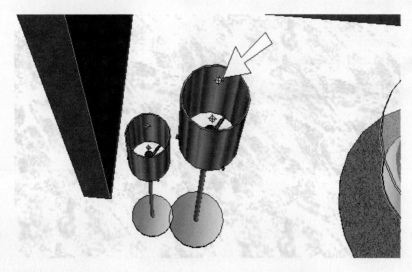

Figure 9-4

6 To start defining layers, choose **Window/Layers**. The **Layers** window that opens shows that this model already has four layers (Figure 9-5). Layer0 is the default layer that every model has; this layer should never be erased. The other three layers were created by Murali and aren't needed for this project.

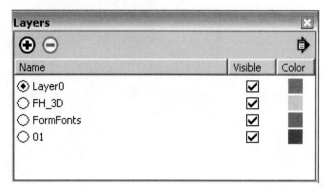

Figure 9-5

NOTE

If you've used other CAD or modeling applications, you may be familiar with the concept of layers. However, layers in SketchUp work differently from those in AutoCAD and other modelers. SketchUp layers are only used for controlling visibility, and a SketchUp object can be housed on only one layer.

7 To erase each of these three layers one by one, highlight the layer and click the Minus icon indicated in Figure 9-6. (You could also use the Shift key to select multiple layers at one time.) These layers all contain objects, so move the objects into the default layer (Layer0, in this case). Laycr0 should be the only remaining layer.

8 Now we'll set up layers that contain the various design elements in this room: rugs, furniture, and so forth. To create the first layer, click the Plus (+) icon at the top of the **Layers** window, and rename the new layer "Rugs" (Figure 9-7).

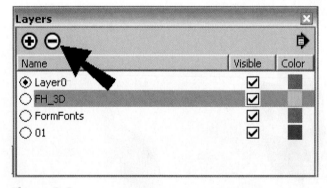

Figure 9-6

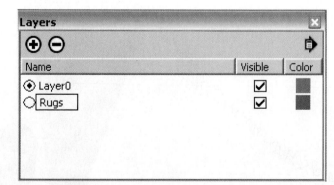

Figure 9-7

NOTE

When you create a layer, you're not creating or selecting any actual objects. You're essentially creating a category to which objects can later be assigned.

9 Create two more layers the same way, one for furniture and one for accessories (Figure 9-8).

10 For each of these three new layers, uncheck the **Visible** box (Figure 9-9). This means that any object that gets placed on any of these layers will be hidden from view.

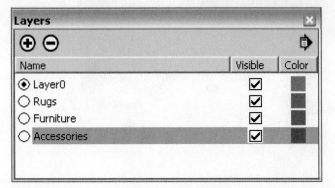

Figure 9-8

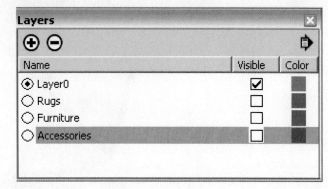

Figure 9-9

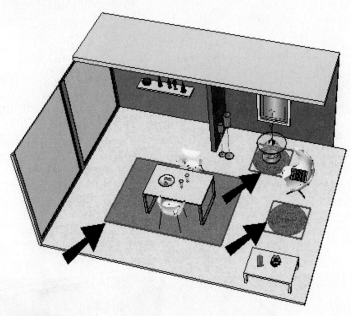

Figure 9-10

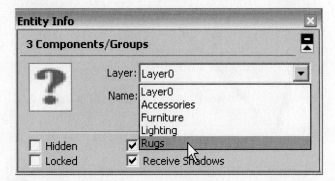

Figure 9-11

11 Layer placement is done via the **Entity Info** window. We'll start with the three rugs: Select all three of the rugs (Figure 9-10) and open **Entity Info**. Set the layer to Rugs (Figure 9-11). The rugs are hidden (Figure 9-12).

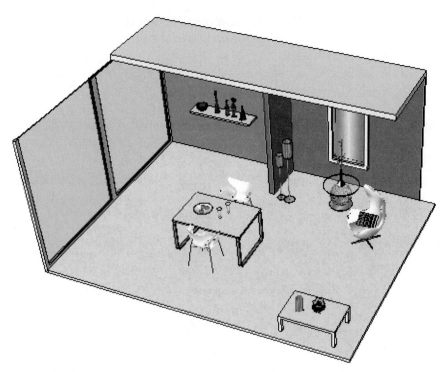

Figure 9-12

12 Next, select the six pieces of furniture: dining table, two dining chairs, egg chair, coffee table, and accent table (Figure 9-13). Use the **Entity Info** window to place these pieces on the Furniture layer; all six pieces are now hidden (Figure 9-14). All that remains are lights, accessories, and objects on the walls.

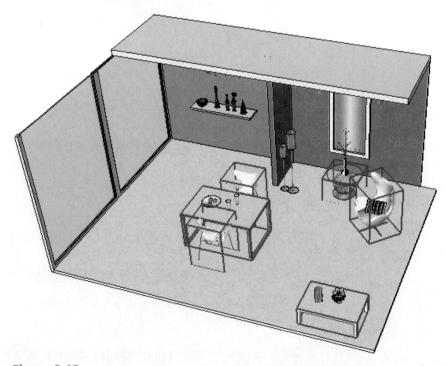

Figure 9-13

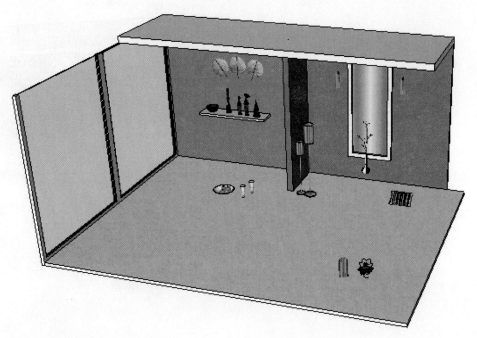

Figure 9-14

13 Select all other objects (but not the room itself) and place them on the Accessories layer. Now the room is empty (Figure 9-15). This shows how handy layers are; you can easily show your client an empty room before filling it up with objects.

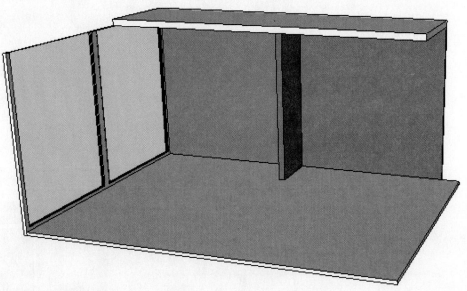

Figure 9-15

14 Now you can turn on layers to fill the room in stages. First check the **Visible** box for the Rugs layer (Figure 9-16), then add the furniture (Figure 9-17), and finally add the accessories (Figure 9-18).

15 Keep this model open, or save it, because it will be used in the next section.

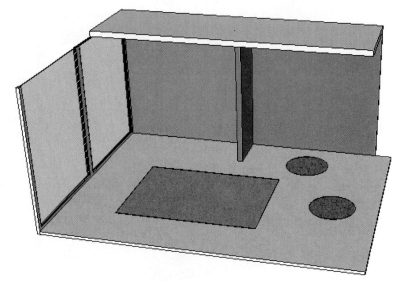

Figure 9-16

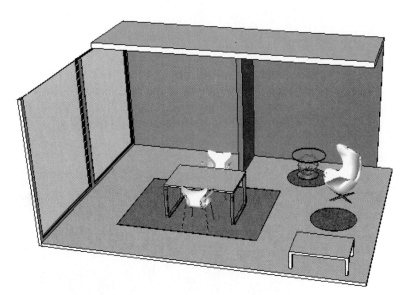

Figure 9-17

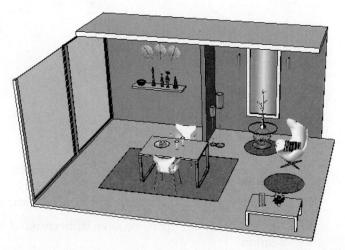

Figure 9-18

In the next few sections, you'll see how to combine layers with scenes in order to switch between two or more design options.

Model It Yourself

Download and open a bedroom model by Surya Murali, such as her Mediterranean Bedroom. (You can search for her other bedrooms by using the search term "surya bedroom.") Create layers so that you can show the empty room (Figure 9-19); the basic pieces of furniture (Figure 9-20); accessories such as plants and lamps (Figure 9-21); and, finally, the entire design complete with artwork (Figure 9-22).

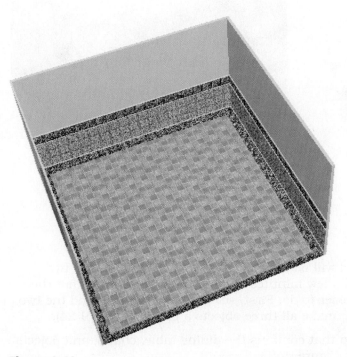

Figure 9-19

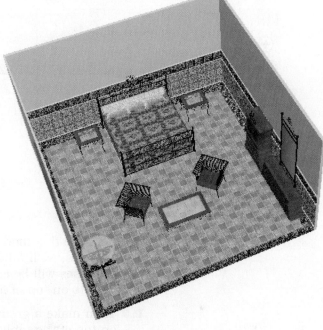

Figure 9-20

Figure 9-21

Figure 9-22

9.2 Comparing Design Options for the Walls

As a designer, you'll want to present more than one design option to your clients. You've already seen how layers can be used to hide and show objects, and when you add SketchUp scenes, you can easily switch between two or more options.

In this section, we'll create another arrangement for the wall décor, and create two scenes (one for each arrangement).

1 Continue with the Sunshine Living model from the previous section. Erase all layers, placing everything back on Layer0 (Figure 9-23).

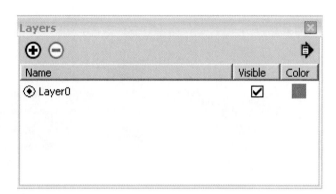

Figure 9-23

Figure 9-24

2 Because this model will be used for this section and the next two sections, we'll take a few minutes to create some groups so that the exercises will be easier to do. First, select the coffee table and the two objects on top of it; make all three objects a group (Figure 9-24).

3 Then make a group that contains the dining table, chairs, and objects on top of the table (Figure 9-25).

Figure 9-25

4 Make a group for the accent table, vase, and flower (Figure 9-26), and another group for the shelf and all of the objects on top of it (Figure 9-27).

Figure 9-26

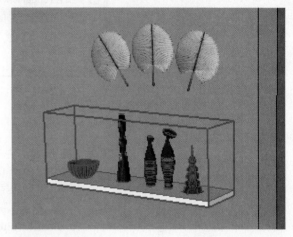

Figure 9-27

5 Finally, make the entire room a group (as you know, a room should always be a group) (Figure 9-28). The easiest way to select all of the walls and the floor of the room is to activate **Select** and triple-click on any wall or floor. Because all of the objects in the room are already part of a group or component, nothing but the bare bones of the room will be selected this way.

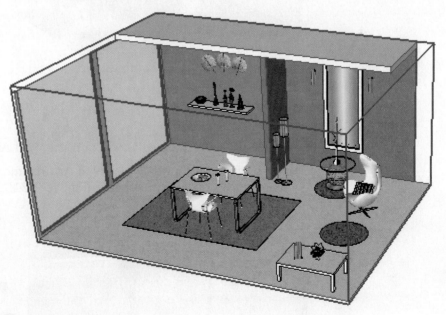

Figure 9-28

6 Save this file because it will also be used as the starter model for the next two sections.

7 Create two new layers for the two wall arrangements (Figure 9-29). Leave both layers visible for now.

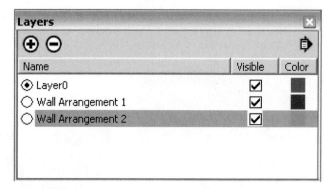

Figure 9-29

8 Select the five objects along the wall (the leaves, shelf, mirror, and two lights), and use the **Entity Info** window to place these objects on the Wall Arrangement 1 layer. Leave all objects selected.

9 Activate **Move**, press the Ctrl or Option key, and copy these five objects to blank space (Figure 9-30). Again, leave these copied objects selected.

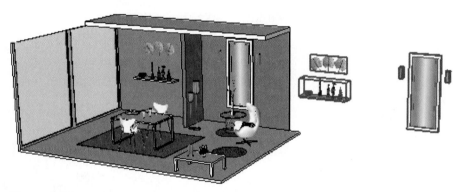

Figure 9-30

10 Place these five copied objects on the Wall Arrangement 2 layer.

11 Turn off the visibility of the Wall Arrangement 1 layer. Now only the copied wall objects are visible (Figure 9-31).

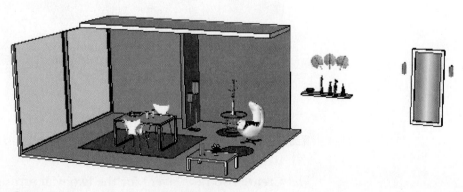

Figure 9-31

12 Move each of these objects back onto the wall, using a different arrangement from that in the original model. Figure 9-32 shows the lights and mirror (with one extra light and one extra mirror) on the left side, with the leaves and shelf on the right.

Figure 9-32

13 From the main menu, choose **Window/Scenes** to open the **Scenes** window. A SketchUp scene is basically a saved view, and the items on the lower part of this window are the various features of the current view that can be saved. The important step here is to *uncheck* **Camera Location** (Figure 9-33). This means that the only feature of this view that won't be saved is the orientation of the model. In other words, this scene will allow you to switch to any orientation of the room; the advantage of this will become clear once the scenes are created.

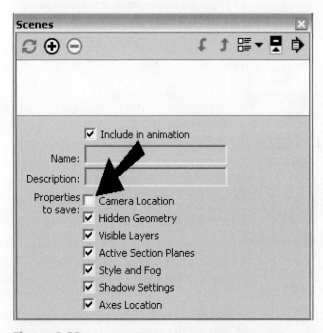

Figure 9-33

14 To create the scene, click the Plus icon at the top of the **Scenes** window. The scene is given a default name; replace this name with "Wall Arrangement 2" (Figure 9-34).

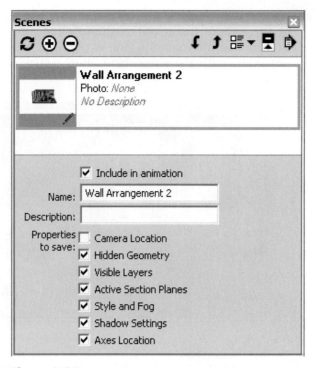

Figure 9-34

15 In the **Layers** window, reverse the visible layers: Turn off the visibility of Wall Arrangement 2 and turn on Wall Arrangement 1.

16 Use the **Scenes** window to create a new scene: Wall Arrangement 1 (Figure 9-35). The **Camera Location** option should still be unchecked.

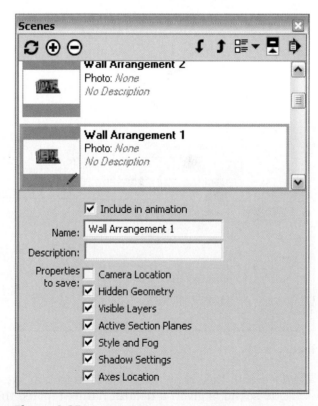

Figure 9-35

17 The two scenes can be accessed by tabs at the top of the SketchUp window. Click each tab to go back and forth between the two arrangements (Figure 9-36 and Figure 9-37, respectively). In this example, the information about which layers are displayed and which are hidden has been saved in these scenes. Of course, you could also display each arrangement by hiding and displaying layers in the **Layers** window, but that would require more clicks. Switching scenes is an easy, one-click operation. Also, because the camera location for each scene is not saved, you can orbit to any view you like, and investigate the wall designs.

Figure 9-36

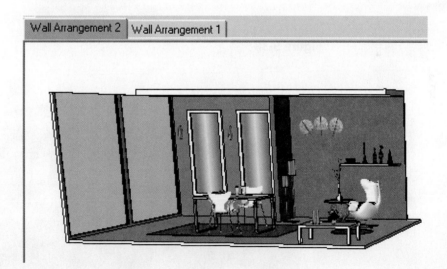

Figure 9-37

NOTE

You can right-click on a scene tab for more options. You can adjust the order of the scenes (**Move Right** and **Move Left**), add a new scene, delete a scene, or update a scene.

18 If you want to save this file, use a different name so that you don't overwrite the starter model, which you will need for the next two sections.

Model It Yourself

Download another room model, such as Murali's Cantania Lounge (Figure 9-38). Make a copy of all furniture and create a second furniture arrangement for the room (Figure 9-39). Use layers and scenes so that you can switch between the two arrangements. When creating scenes, don't forget to uncheck **Camera Location**; this item is always checked by default!

Figure 9-38

Figure 9-39

9.3 Comparing Furniture Options

So far in this chapter, we've rearranged objects that are already in the model. In this section, we'll compare a chair with another one from the 3D Warehouse.

1 Continue with the starter model that you saved during the previous section.

2 Next to the egg chair, import another chair from the 3D Warehouse. You can find the new chair shown in Figure 9-40 by searching for "coconut chair," or bring in something that you like better.

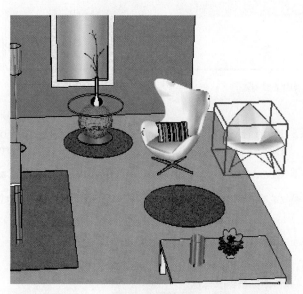

Figure 9-40

3 The striped pillow on the egg chair should also appear on the coconut chair, so make a copy of the pillow and place it on the new chair (Figure 9-41).

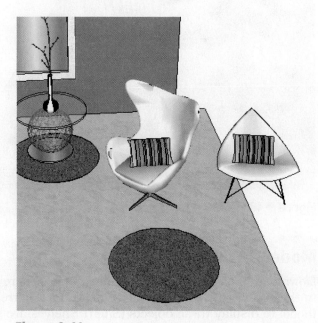

Figure 9-41

4 Create two layers, one for each chair (Figure 9-42). Place the egg chair and its pillow on the Egg Chair layer, and the coconut chair and its pillow on the Coconut Chair layer.

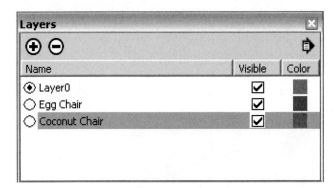

Figure 9-42

5 Hide the Egg Chair layer, and move the coconut chair and its pillow to the same spot the egg chair occupied (Figure 9-43).

6 Create two scenes, one for each chair, with **Camera Location** unchecked.

7 Again, if you save this model, do not overwrite the starter model.

Figure 9-43

Model It Yourself

Download Murali's Cantania Lounge model. There is a set of display stands in the corner with a few accessories on top (Figure 9-44). Find a replacement model to display these objects (Smart Shelves are shown in Figure 9-45), and use layers and scenes to show both options.

Figure 9-44

Figure 9-45

9.4 Comparing Room Arrangements

We already know how to display different arrangements of furniture and accessories in a room. This section puts a slightly different twist on what we've already done; it allows you to set up rooms differently so that you can see all of the design options at one time, making sure that you are not repeating elements from another design. This is a useful technique for a client who has existing pieces and wants a few ideas on how to arrange them in a specific space.

1. Go back to the starter model from the last section. Create two layers, one for each arrangement (Figure 9-46).

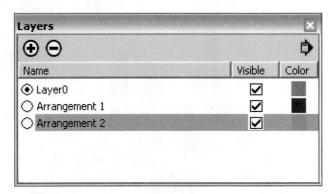

Figure 9-46

2. Make a copy of the entire room (Figure 9-47). Place all of one room's contents (not including the room itself) on one layer, and place the other room's contents on the other layer. Keep in mind that the original room, not the copy, will be the space used for all of the scenes that we'll create. The copied room will only be used to temporarily house a second room arrangement.

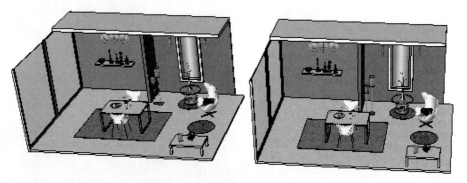

Figure 9-47

3. In one of the rooms, rearrange the furniture and accessories (Figure 9-48). Because both rooms are displayed, you can make sure that the two arrangements look completely different from one another.

> **NOTE**
>
> Showing your client two or more arrangements at one time, without separating objects into layers and scenes, can also be a great way to show your designs. The advantage of using scenes and layers is that all designs can be shown in the same space, from any perspective.

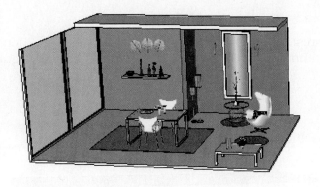

Figure 9-48

4 Hide the layer for the contents of one of the rooms (Figure 9-49).

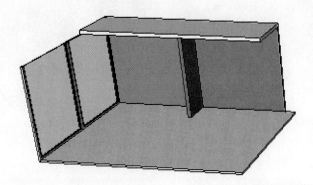
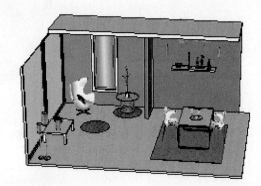

Figure 9-49

5 Select all of the contents of the other room (an easy way to do this is to drag a window to select the entire room, then press Shift and click the room itself to unselect it). Move these objects into the empty room, and for the two move points, make sure that you click identical points of the two rooms, such as Points 1 and 2 in Figure 9-50. The reason for moving this furniture is so the scenes that you're about to create will allow you to compare both sets of furniture *in a single space*, rather than in two separate rooms.

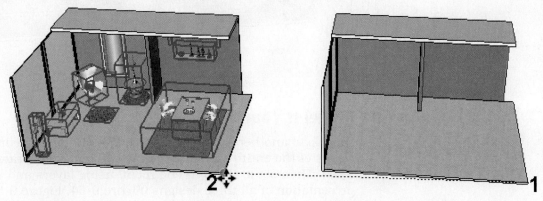

Figure 9-50

6 The empty room is no longer needed, so erase it.

7 You know the rest: Display one layer and create its scene, then switch layer visibility and create a second scene (Figure 9-51 and Figure 9-52, respectively).

Figure 9-51

Figure 9-52

Model It Yourself

Download another Murali model, such as Bamboo Bedroom. Make *two* copies of the entire room and create two different arrangements (Figure 9-53). Then set it all up in one room, using layers and scenes for an easy presentation of all three designs (Figure 9-54, Figure 9-55, and Figure 9-56, respectively).

NOTE

The images shown for the Bamboo Bedroom model don't include textures and materials; for the purposes of this book, the images look crisper when faces are painted with a single color. Working without textures displayed can also help your model perform faster if you're working with a slower computer. These display options can be found on the **View/Face Style** menu.

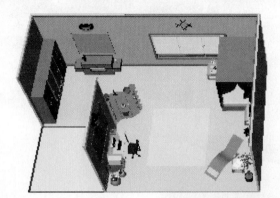
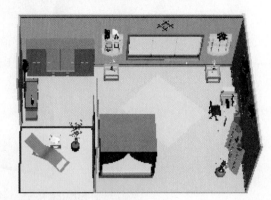
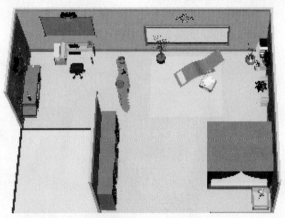

Figure 9-53

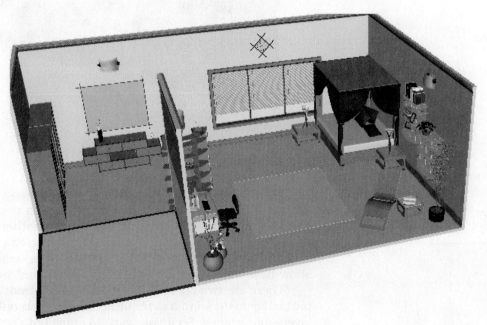

Figure 9-54

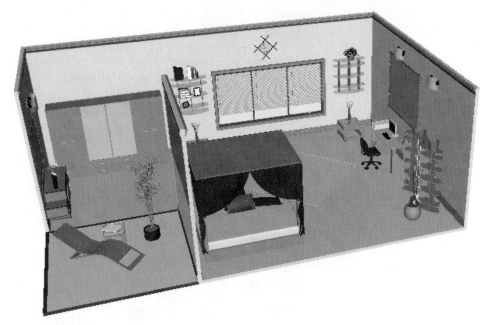

Figure 9-55

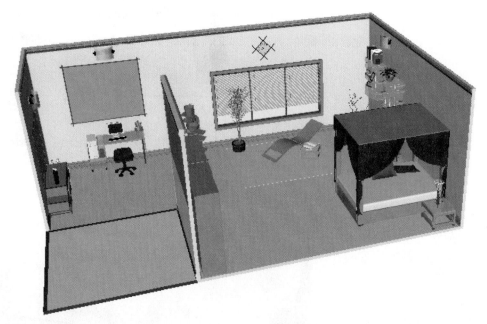

Figure 9-56

9.5 Comparing Materials

So far in this chapter, we've copied objects to new locations and placed them on layers for display purposes. But another important component of design presentation is showing what a space can look like with different materials for specific objects. In this section, we'll take a kitchen model and show how it looks with two different floors and two different counters.

There are two crucial things to keep in mind: First, you can't assign a particular *material* to a layer or scene; you can only assign painted *objects* to layers and scenes. So if you want to show both a wood floor and a tile floor, you need to create two separate floors, each painted with a different material.

Second, two separate faces can't occupy the same physical space in SketchUp, even if one is on a hidden layer. So you can't have both a wood floor and a tile floor in the same place. However, you can get around this restriction if both floors are part of separate groups because groups (and components) *can* occupy the same space in SketchUp.

1 From the 3D Warehouse, download the model Kitchen Material Options by Bonnie Roskes (Figure 9-57). This model should look familiar because it's the same kitchen that we modeled in Chapter 8.

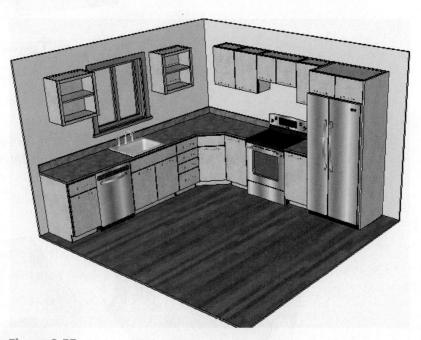

Figure 9-57

2 We'll create the floor options first. Start by creating two layers: one for the current wood floor and one for a tile floor (Figure 9-58).

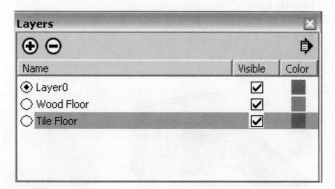

Figure 9-58

3 The entire room is already a group, and we can create a copy of the entire group even though only the floor needs to be changed. Make a copy of the room in the green direction, and set the move distance to a specific length, such as 20′ (Figure 9-59). This will make it much easier to move the copied room back into place at another time.

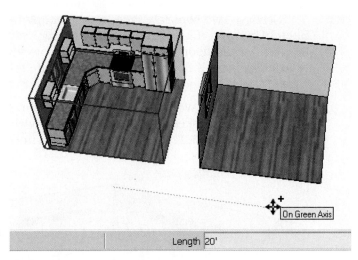

Length 20'

Figure 9-59

4 Edit the copied room group, and paint its floor with a tile material. Figure 9-60 shows a gray tile pattern rotated 45 degrees using fixed-pin positioning.

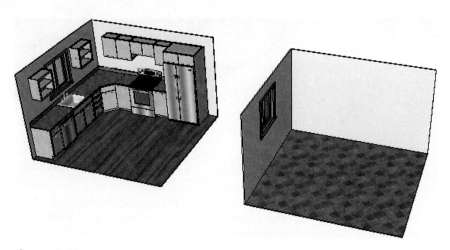

Figure 9-60

5 Place each room group on its own layer, and hide the layer containing the wood floor (Figure 9-61).

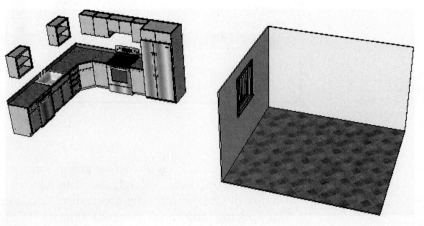

Figure 9-61

6 Now move the copied room to replace the room that you just hid using the same move distance from before, in the reverse direction along the green axis (Figure 9-62).

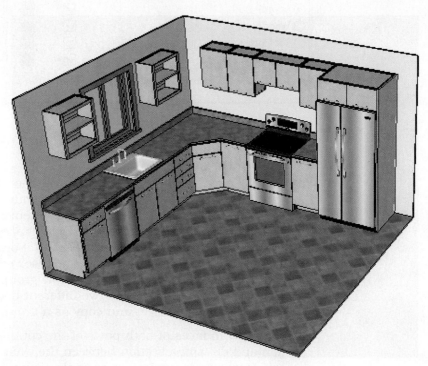

Figure 9-62

7 Create one scene that shows the tile floor (Figure 9-63) and another that shows the wood floor (Figure 9-64).

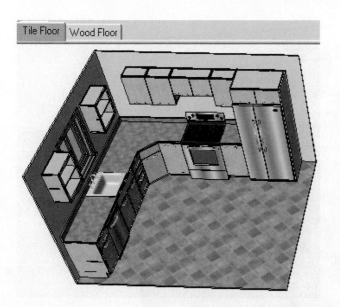

Figure 9-63

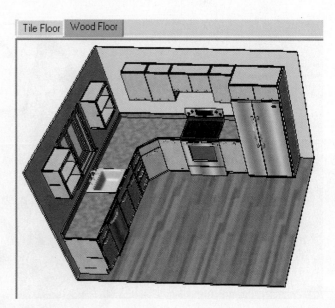

Figure 9-64

8 Now we'll set up the model to show two different counters. First create two more layers, one for the current gray counter, and another for a red counter (Figure 9-65).

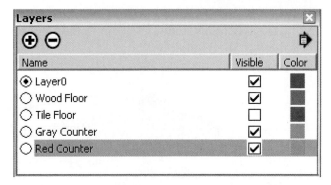

Figure 9-65

Now we need to copy the gray counter and change the copied counter's material. But there's a hitch: The counter is not a group; it is a set of many separate faces and edges. Remember that SketchUp does not allow two faces to occupy the same space, so you can't have two counters in the same exact space, even if one of those counters is on a hidden layer. This problem can be resolved by making the entire counter into a group because multiple groups *can* occupy the same space; we saw that with the two different floors. (Besides, the counter is much easier to select and copy as a group.)

9 To select all faces of both parts of the counter (the large L-shaped section and the small section between the oven and the refrigerator), you could use window selection or triple-click selection. But for a quicker selection, right-click on any counter face and choose **Select/All with Same Material**. Once all gray counter faces have been selected, make them into a group (Figure 9-66).

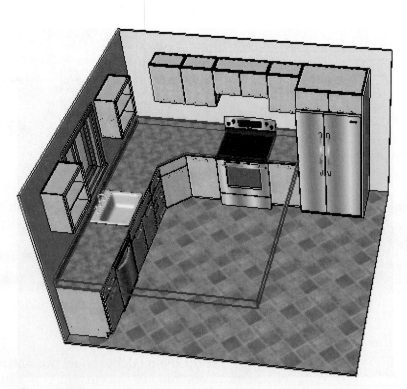

Figure 9-66

10 Make a copy of the counter, again using a specific move distance. Then edit the copied counter and paint it with a red material, as shown in Figure 9-67).

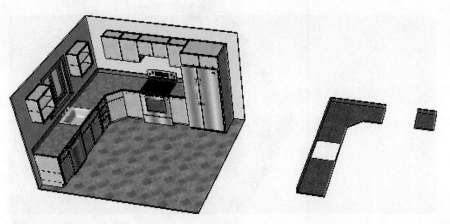

Figure 9-67

11 Place each counter on its own layer, and hide the layer for the gray counter. The tops of the cabinets are now visible (Figure 9-68). Then move the red counter into place (Figure 9-69).

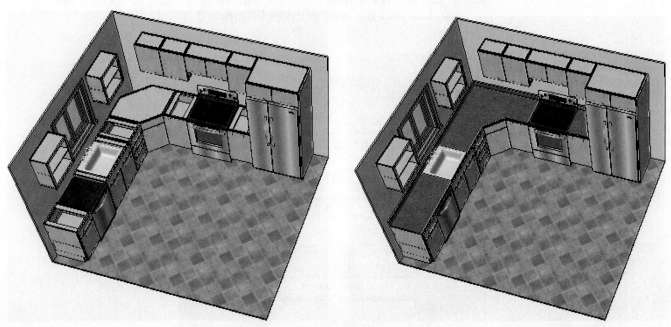

Figure 9-68   Figure 9-69

So far, we have two scenes, one for each floor. But now that there are two counters thrown into the mix, the total number of scenes is *four*: one for each floor/counter combination.

12 First, we need to rename the two scenes that we have already created. Click the Scene tab that shows the tile floor, and adjust the layers so that the gray counter is displayed. The layers for the wood floor and the red counter should be hidden (Figure 9-70).

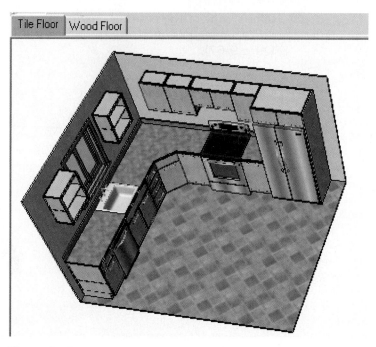

Figure 9-70

13 In the **Scenes** window, change this scene's name to include both the tile floor and the gray counter (Figure 9-71).

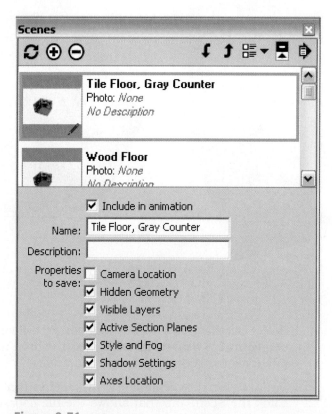

Figure 9-71

14 Click the Scene tab that shows the wood floor, and again make sure that only the gray counter is visible (the tile floor and red counter are hidden). Then rename that scene accordingly (Figure 9-72).

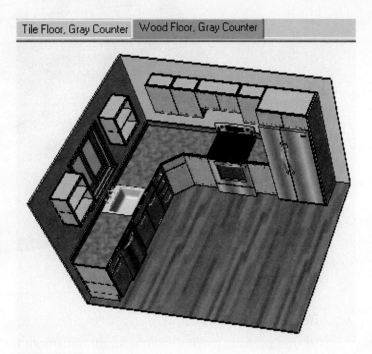

Figure 9-72

15 Now adjust the layers so that only the tile floor and the red counter appear, and create a new scene (Figure 9-73).

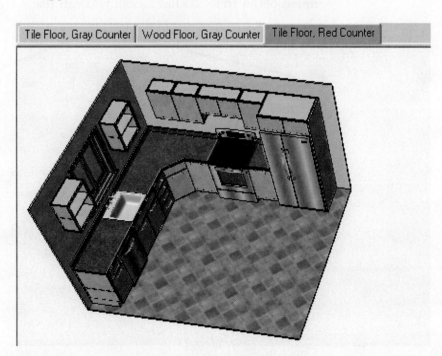

Figure 9-73

16 Finally, create the fourth scene that shows the wood floor and the red counter (Figure 9-74).

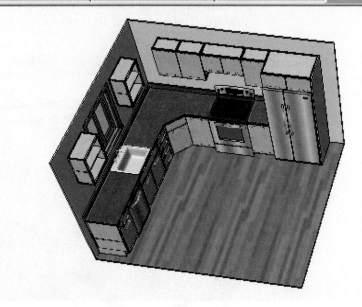

| Tile Floor, Gray Counter | Wood Floor, Gray Counter | Tile Floor, Red Counter | Wood Floor, Red Counter |

Figure 9-74

Model It Yourself

In this project, you'll design a small bathroom for which you'll show a choice of two wall materials and two floor materials. As with the kitchen project, this will require four scenes.

The bathroom should measure 11′ × 8′ wall to wall, with a ceiling height of 8′ (Figure 9-75). The walls and floor should be thick (this looks much better than 2D flat faces); you can use a thickness of 2″.

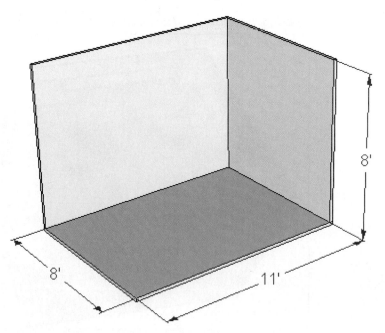

Figure 9-75

An efficient way to model this room is as follows:

• Start with a rectangle measuring 11′-2″ × 8′-2″ and pull it up 2″.

• Select two adjacent edges of this rectangle and offset them 2″ inward.

This creates a narrow, L-shaped face for the 2″-thick walls.

- Use **Push/Pull** with the Ctrl/Option key to pull the walls up 8′.
- Because the material options will be presented for the floor and walls, make one group that includes only the walls, and another group for just the floor.

Bring in two or three 3D Warehouse models to fill the space, such as the vanity and tub shown in Figure 9-76.

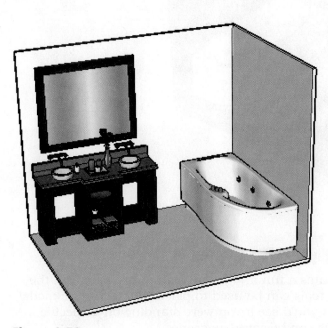

Figure 9-76

Figure 9-77

Use copied groups, layers, and scenes to present the four design options. For example, you could show tile or wallpaper for the walls, and wood or tile for the floor (Figure 9-77, Figure 9-78, Figure 9-79, and Figure 9-80).

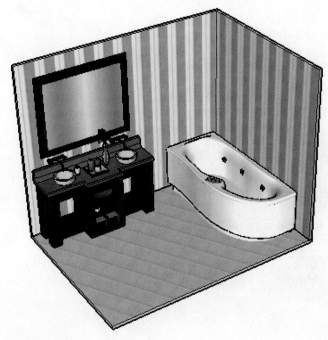

Figure 9-78

Figure 9-79

Figure 9-80

9.6 Presenting Specific Room Views

This last section demonstrates a fun and useful feature of SketchUp: the **Walkthrough** tools. These tools can be used to place yourself in the model and show you exactly what you'd see if you were standing on a specific spot in a room. These views can be saved as scenes.

1 Download Murali's Bamboo Bedroom model, shown with full textures in Figure 9-81. This bedroom is a good model to use for this section because it is effectively divided into two separate spaces, and a client would be interested in knowing what he or she will see from either space.

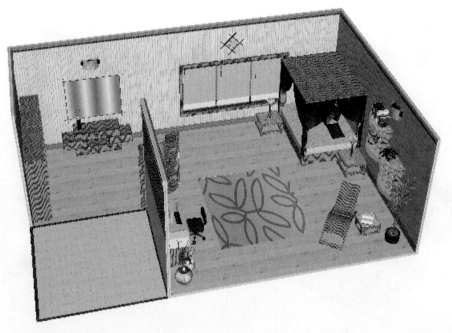

Figure 9-81

Figure 9-82

■2 The **Walkthrough** tools can be found in the **Camera** menu, and also as icons at the bottom of the **Large Tool Set**. Activate **Position Camera**, indicated in Figure 9-82.

■3 Look at the **Height Offset** field at the bottom of the SketchUp window. The default value is 5′-6″ (or about 1.7 m if you're working in metric units); enter 5′-6″ if you see a different number here (Figure 9-83). Height offset refers to the height of the camera, or how high your eyes are off the ground. So 5′-6″ is a reasonable height for someone about 5′-10″. (If you were designing a child's room, you might want to enter a lower height offset value.)

```
Height Offset  5' 6"
```

Figure 9-83

NOTE

The **Height Offset** is the distance between your eyes and the *ground*. If you're stand-ing in a room in a one-story house, the height offset is basically equal to the distance between your eyes and the room's floor. But say that you want to check a view while standing in a second-story room; the height offset will be your eye height from the floor, *plus* the 10′ or so between the ground and the second-story floor. SketchUp will usually make this height adjustment automatically, but you should always check that the **Height Offset** value makes sense.

■4 There are two ways to use **Position Camera**: Click to place the camera, or drag the cursor toward a certain point. We'll use the first method now: Click to place the camera approximately where indicated in Figure 9-84.

Figure 9-84

5 The view adjusts to show how the room looks from this perspective. Figure 9-85 shows the view facing the mirror. (Your view might look different; it depends on how the model was oriented when you placed the camera.) Immediately after the view changes, check the **Height Offset** field again; this number can be inadvertently changed if you use the scroll wheel on your mouse (and sometimes SketchUp seems to change it for no apparent reason!). If you see anything other than 5′6″, enter the correct value.

Figure 9-85

6 The cursor is now a pair of eyes, which means that the **Look Around** tool is active. Image that your feet are planted on the floor and you can move your head by dragging the mouse. Dragging the mouse left and right turns your head from side to side, and dragging the mouse up or down simulates looking up or down. Drag the mouse left or right so that you can see the bed (Figure 9-86).

Figure 9-86

7 Open the **Scenes** window and, this time, make sure that **Camera Location** *is* checked because we want to preserve this specific view. Save this scene, giving it an appropriate name (Figure 9-87).

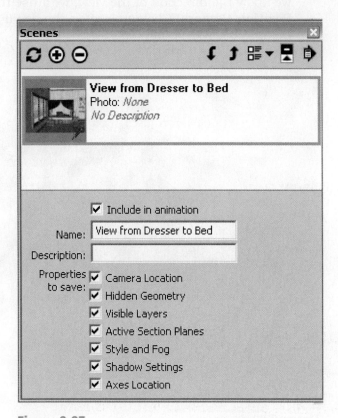

Figure 9-87

8 Stay in this position and drag the mouse a bit to the right so that you can see the curvy shelves. Save this as a new scene (Figure 9-88).

Figure 9-88

9 The next view will simulate sitting on the bed, looking toward the desk. Activate **Position Camera** again, and specify 3′-6″ for the **Height Offset** because your eye height is lower when seated. Because we know the direction of the view, we'll use the dragging feature of **Position Camera**. Click a point on the bed (Figure 9-89) and keep the mouse button pressed.

Height Offset 3′ 6″

Figure 9-89

10 Drag the cursor to a point on the desk (Figure 9-90) and then release the mouse button.

Figure 9-90

11 You're now looking from the bed at the desk (Figure 9-91). Again, make sure that the **Height Offset** is still 3′-6″. Save this as a third scene.

Figure 9-91

You now have three scenes to show a client, and you can easily create more if the client requests them.

If you want to adjust the camera view of a scene, get the view that you want, right-click on that scene, and choose **Update**. Another option on a scene's popup menu is **Play Animation**, which will show each scene in order, in a continuous loop. The **Animation** page on the **Model Info** window has options for controlling the speed of these animations. The **File/Export** menu enables you to save the animations.

> **NOTE**
>
> There are three **Walkthrough** tools: **Position Camera** and **Look Around**, which we've already used, and **Walk**. The icon for the **Walk** tool is a pair of feet. This tool takes a bit of practice, but briefly, you enter your eye height, click to place your feet on the ground, and drag the mouse up to walk forward. The **Walk** tool is well suited to large design projects, such as a city block or a shopping mall, but is less useful for small spaces like a single room. However, it can be fun to use: If you walk into a staircase, SketchUp will take you up the stairs, and if you walk into a wall, you can press the Alt key to break through the wall!

Model It Yourself

Download Murali's model Modern Living for Two (Figure 9-92). Create three scenes: standing near the bookshelves looking toward the dining space (Figure 9-93), standing near the coffee table looking toward the book-shelves (Figure 9-94), and sitting on the couch looking toward the dining space (Figure 9-95).

Figure 9-92

Figure 9-93

Figure 9-94

Figure 9-95

Review Questions

- How can you use layers to control which objects are visible in your model?

- How do you place an object on a specific layer?

- How can layers and scenes be combined to show different designs for the same room?

- When saving a view as a scene, when should you check **Camera Location**, and when should you *not* use this option?

- When creating different room arrangements using the same pieces, why is it helpful to create copies of the room before creating the scenes?

- When comparing different materials for the same object (such as for a counter or a floor), why is it necessary to create two (or more) separate groups or components for the objects to be painted?

- How can you select all faces that have the same material at one time?

- When using the **Position Camera** tool, how can you control the camera's point of view?

- Oncc the camera view is set using **Position Camera**, how can you simulate looking around the room from that point?

10 chapterten
Labels, Dimensions, and Plans

You've now worked through all of the preceding chapters in this book, so you're an expert on creating and presenting beautiful SketchUp models of any furnished room! It's time for the last step of the design process: the production of detailed drawings and plans for the client, contractors, and/ or tradespeople who are going to turn your concept into reality.

In this chapter, you'll learn how to do the following:
- Create labels and dimensions.
- Produce a floor plan.
- Create a cabinetry plan for a kitchen.
- Print your plans.

10.1 Labels and Dimensions

Throughout this book, you've seen images that feature dimensions and callouts. These images are SketchUp screen captures; the dimensions and callouts (known in SketchUp as labels) were created in SketchUp (they were not added by a graphics editor). This section will introduce the two tools used to create these objects: **Text** and **Dimension**.

1 Use your Internet browser (not the **Get Models** tool) to download Sunshine Living by Surya Murali, which is the same model that was featured so prominently in Chapter 9 (Figure 10-1). For simplicity, erase the rendered image, and remove all lights and objects on the walls. Display the edges (**View/Edge Style/Edges**), and turn off shadows (**View/Shadows**). Figure 10-2 also shows the furniture as white, but you can leave yours black. And if you want a white back-ground, you can use the **Edit** tab of the **Styles** window and adjust the **Background** settings.

2 Save the current version of this model, because it will also be used in the next section.

3 We'll be adding labels with leader arrows to identify some of the pieces of furniture in the room. But before diving in with the **Text** tool, we'll

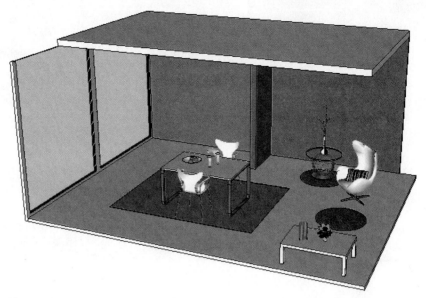

Figure 10-1

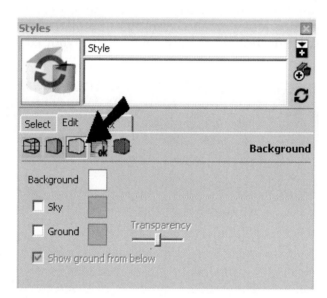

Figure 10-2

set the appearance of the labels and their leader lines. Open the **Model Info** window to the **Text** page (Figure 10-3). This page has options for three types of objects:

- Screen text: text that's "glued" to the screen and not attached to a particular object
- Leader text: text that is attached to a particular object, either with or without a leader line
- Leader lines: lines that link text to a particular object, usually with an arrow at the end

The **Leader Text** and **Leader Lines** options are relevant to the labels that we're about to create. Here you can set the font and color for the text itself (this example will use 12 pt, black Tahoma font), as well as the look of the leader line (the pointer will be a closed arrow). Leave the leader itself as a **Pushpin**.

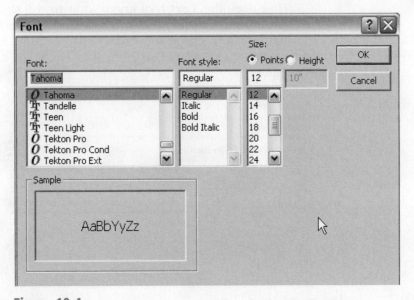

Figure 10-3

NOTE

The leader types are **Pushpin**, **View-Based**, and **Hidden**. **Pushpin** means that the leader and text will always be visible, regardless of the viewing angle. **View-Based** means that if the object to which the leader is pointing is not visible in the current view, its leader and text will not be displayed. **Hidden** means that only the text, not the leader, will be displayed. We'll see later how to make appearance changes to all text objects at once.

All of these options are also available in a text object's **Entity Info** window.

4 Click the **Fonts** button for **Leader Text**. This opens the **Font** window, where an important option to note is **Size**. If you choose **Points**, the text will always be the same size, regardless of the model view. In other words, if you zoom in and out, the text will remain the same size. Choosing **Height** means that the text size will always be a specific size; if you zoom out, the text will appear to shrink. **Points** is used here, but you can use either option (Figure 10-4).

Figure 10-4

Figure 10-5

5 Choose your font and size (or accept the defaults), and close the **Font** window. Back in the **Model Info** window, adjust the text color and leaders if you like, and close this window as well.

6 Activate the **Text** tool, available as an icon in the **Large Tool Set** (Figure 10-5), or choose **Tools/Text** from the main menu.

7 The first click for a leader text label is directly on the object to which the text will refer. The end of the leader arrow will touch the point that you click. Click somewhere on the egg chair (Figure 10-6).

8 The second click determines where the text will go. Move your cursor into blank space where you want the text to appear, then click. The default text is "egg chair" (Figure 10-7); to accept this text, just click anywhere outside the text.

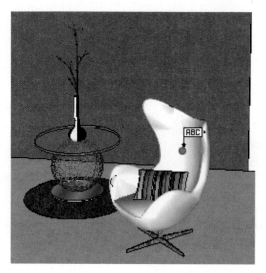

Figure 10-6

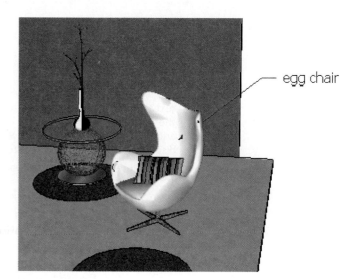

Figure 10-7

How does the **Text** tool know what to call this chair? When clicking on a group or component, the default text is the group or component's name. If you check the **Entity Info** window for this chair (Figure 10-8), or look it up in the **Outliner**, you'll see "egg chair" as the component name.

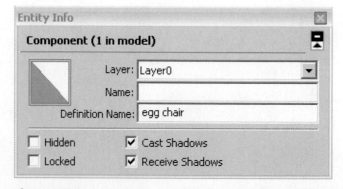

Figure 10-8

9 Of course, you can change the default text for a label. With the **Text** tool still active, double-click on the "egg chair" text. It has been selected and it is ready to be overwritten (Figure 10-9). For a client presentation, you would want this label to be more informative, perhaps including a manufacturer's name or model number, so enter "Arne Jacobsen Egg Chair" with no line breaks. To accept this new text, either click outside the text, or press Enter twice (Figure 10-10).

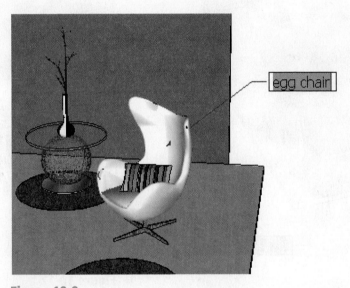

Figure 10-9

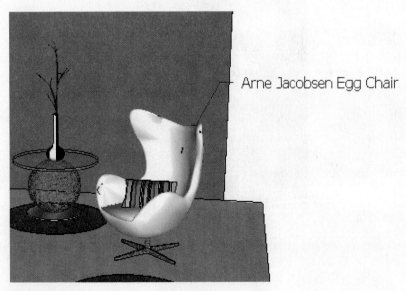

Figure 10-10

10 You can also specify the correct text before completing the label. Create a label for the coffee table, and leave the default text, "Table_Coffee_Simple," highlighted (Figure 10-11). Overwrite this string with "Parsons Coffee Table," pressing Enter to create the line break after the word "Coffee," as shown in Figure 10-12). As before, press Enter twice or click outside the text to complete the label (Figure 10-13).

Table_Coffee_Simple

Figure 10-11

Parsons Coffee imple
Table

Figure 10-12

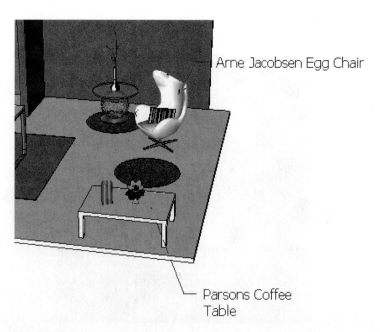

Arne Jacobsen Egg Chair

Parsons Coffee
Table

Figure 10-13

11 Continue creating labels for the dining table, one dining chair, and the accent table (Figure 10-14). If you need to move the labels around, move your cursor over the label text while the **Text** tool is active, and you can drag the text to a new spot. You can also add or remove line breaks by editing the text.

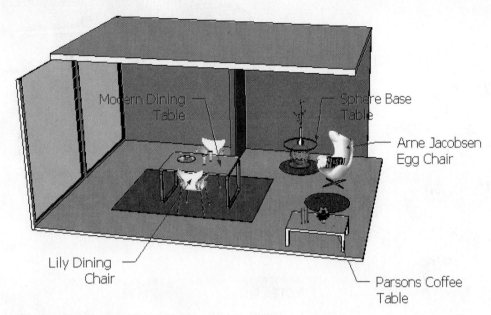

Figure 10-14

12 You can change the look of all of your labels at one time. Return to the **Text** page of the **Model Info** window and change the font and color, perhaps to green, 18 pt bold font, as shown in Figure 10-15. Then click **Select all leader text**. This selects all of the labels that you've created.

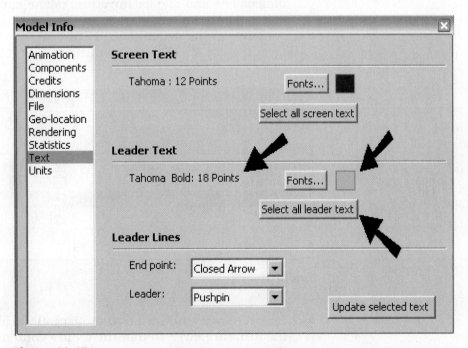

Figure 10-15

13 At the bottom of the **Text** page, click **Update selected text**. All labels take on the new font, size, and color (Figure 10-16). You can keep the changes, or change the labels back to the way that they were before.

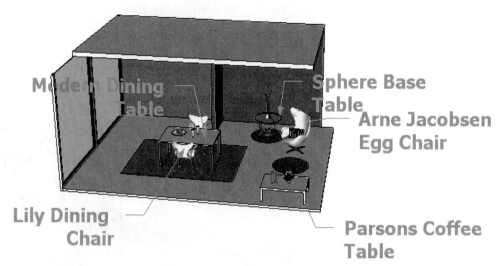

Figure 10-16

> **NOTE**
>
> If you wanted to change only *some* of the labels, you could select only those that you want to change and use **Update selected text**. If you have leader lines that aren't entirely visible, switching the leader to **View-Based** will fix this.

14 We're going to add dimensions to this room, but having all of the labels and dimensions visible simultaneously can crowd the model. Using techniques from Chapter 9, we can use scenes and layers to create a clean, annotated presentation. Start by creating two new layers, one for dimensions and one for furniture. (Make sure that you erase all of the layers that are already in the model except for Layer0, placing all layer contents on the default layer.) Turn off the visibility of the furniture layer (Figure 10-17).

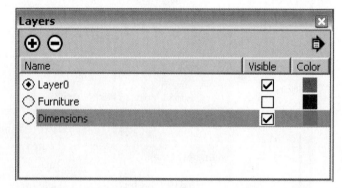

Figure 10-17

15 Use the **Entity Info** window to place all furniture and their labels on the furniture layer so that the room's contents temporarily disappear (Figure 10-18).

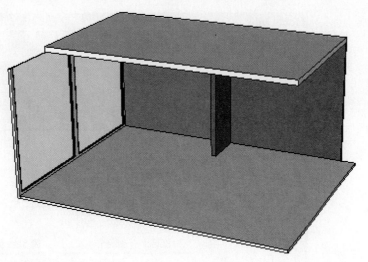

Figure 10-18

16 Before creating the dimensions, open the **Model Info** window again, this time to the **Units** page (Figure 10-19). The units for this model are architectural, but you could use this page to switch to metric or decimal units. Another field to note is **Precision**; the smaller the value here, the more exact your dimensions will be.

All dimensions will appear in the units set on this page. If you switch units after the dimensions have already been created, they will update to the new units. Also, if you move objects around, any dimensions linked to those objects will update accordingly.

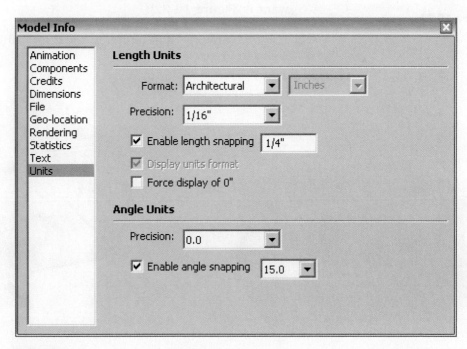

Figure 10-19

17 Now switch to the **Dimensions** page of the **Model Info** window. Here you can control dimension text (font, size, and color) and how the dimension lines appear (closed arrows have been set in Figure 10-20). Keep the default settings for now.

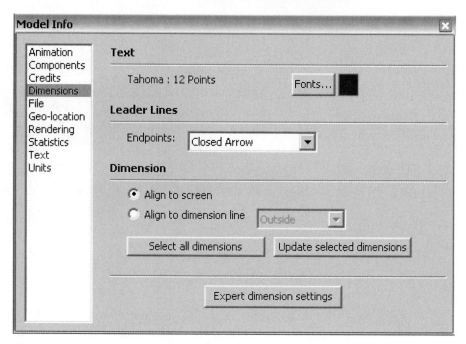

Figure 10-20

Figure 10-21

18 Activate the **Dimension** tool (Figure 10-21).

19 The easiest way to create a dimension is simply to click the edge whose length you want to show. Click the right edge of the floor, move the cursor to the right, and click again when the dimension is where you want it (Figure 10-22).

20 Use the same method to create the 26′-6″ and 12′-3″ dimensions indicated in Figure 10-23.

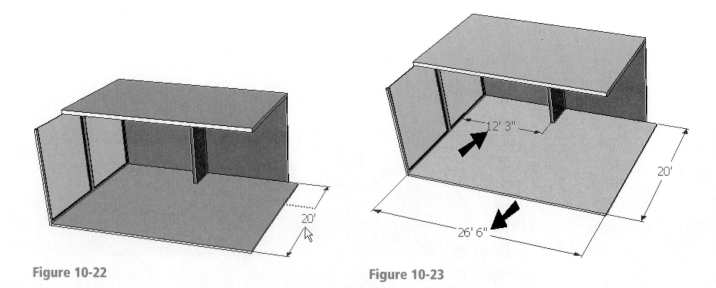

Figure 10-22

Figure 10-23

21 In cases where there is no single edge to click, you can click two points instead. Click Points 1 and 2, as indicated in Figure 10-24, and move the cursor so that the 13′-9″ dimension is aligned with the 12′-3″ dimension to the left (Figure 10-25).

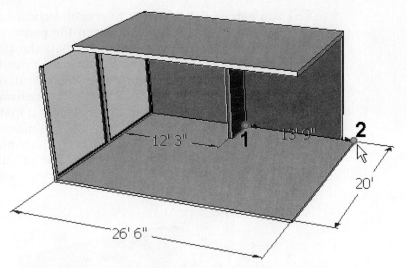

Figure 10-24

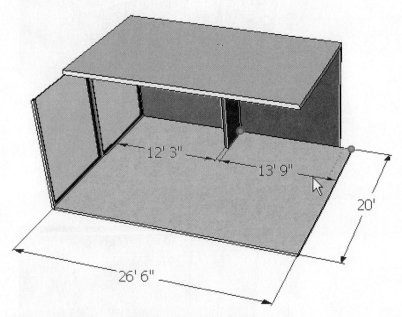

Figure 10-25

22 Now create the 12′ ceiling height dimension (Figure 10-26).

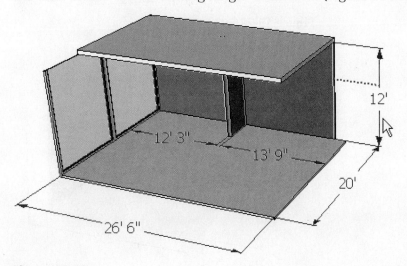

Figure 10-26

23 You can click two points to create vertical or horizontal dimensions, even when the distance between the points is not precisely vertical or horizontal. As an example, we'll create the 12′ ceiling height dimension another way. Click Points 1 and 2, as indicated in Figure 10-27. Before clicking to place the dimension, orbit so that you're facing directly into the room. In this view, the 12′ dimension appears to the left of the room (Figure 10-28). Don't click yet; instead, orbit to face into the room toward the window. Now the 12′ dimension appears in the same plane as the window (Figure 10-29). Your point of view matters when placing dimensions! Click to align the 12′ dimension with the 26′-6″ horizontal dimension.

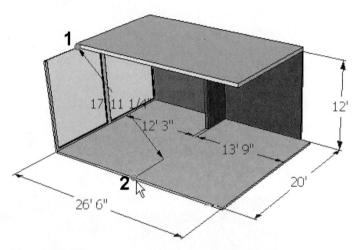

Figure 10-27

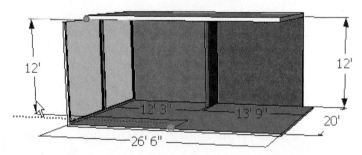

Figure 10-28

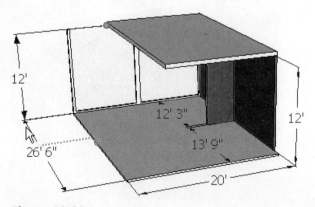

Figure 10-29

24 Place all dimensions on the layer that you created for them. Then create a scene for this dimensioned view (Figure 10-30), keeping **Camera Location** unchecked so that the scene can be viewed at any angle.

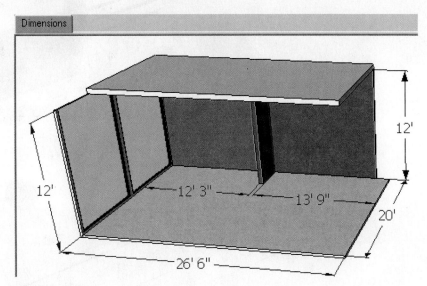

Figure 10-30

25 Hide the dimensions layer, display the furniture layer, and create another scene that shows this view (Figure 10-31).

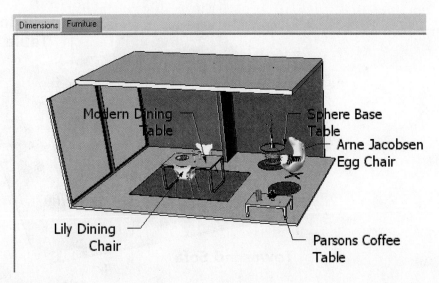

Figure 10-31

26 If you save this model, use a different file name because the version that you saved at the start of this section will be used in the next section.

Model It Yourself

Download Modern Living for Two by Surya Murali. Remove the ceiling and the hanging lights. Create one scene that shows the empty room with its dimensions (Figure 10-32) and another scene that shows the furniture, including the labels for the sofa, chairs, and tables (Figure 10-33).

Chapter 10 | Labels, Dimensions, and Plans   **409**

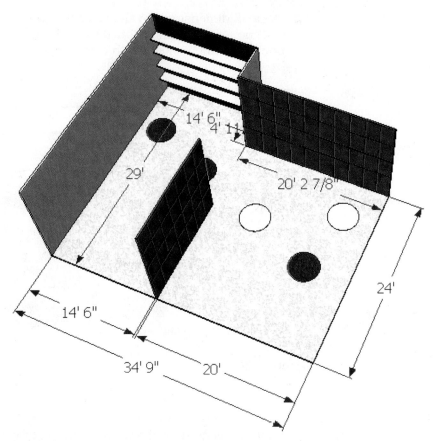

Figure 10-32

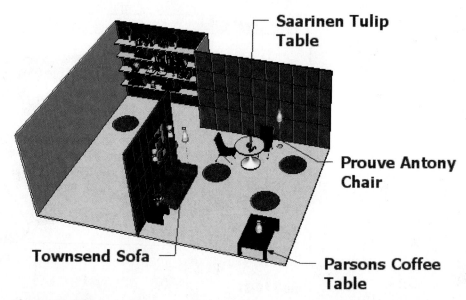

Saarinen Tulip Table

Prouve Antony Chair

Townsend Sofa

Parsons Coffee Table

Figure 10-33

10.2   Floor Plans

The dimensioned views created in the previous section are appropriate for an informal model that you can present to a client. This section describes how to create a more formal floor plan for a contractor, installer, or tradesperson.

1 Open the version of Sunshine Living that you saved at the start of the previous section (Figure 10-34).

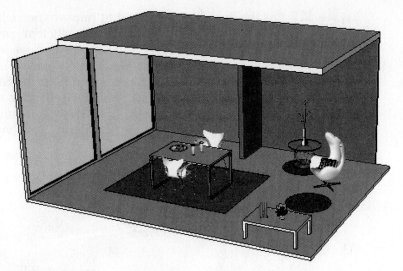

Figure 10-34

2 As before, create a layer for the dimensions and a layer for the furniture. These layers and Layer0 should be the model's only layers (Figure 10-35). Place all furniture on the furniture layer and leave that layer displayed.

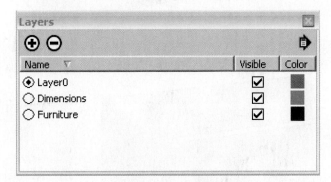

Figure 10-35

3 Create a General View scene that shows a view into the room with its furniture (Figure 10-36). This time, do check the **Camera Location** option so that this particular view will be saved.

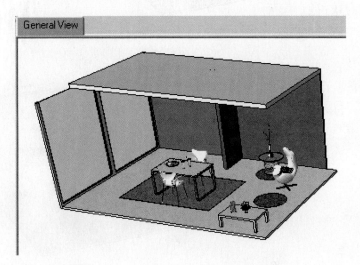

Figure 10-36

4 For the floor plan, we need to remove the ceiling. We could hide the ceiling's edges and faces, but a more efficient way is to simply slice through the ceiling. Activate the **Section Plane** tool, and move the cursor to the top of the ceiling so that the section plane lies along it (Figure 10-37). Don't click yet; instead, press and hold the Shift key to lock the section plane's orientation. With Shift pressed, click a point along any wall just below the ceiling (Figure 10-38). Now you can see into the room from above, without the ceiling obstructing your view (Figure 10-39).

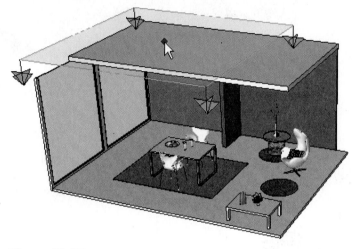

Figure 10-37

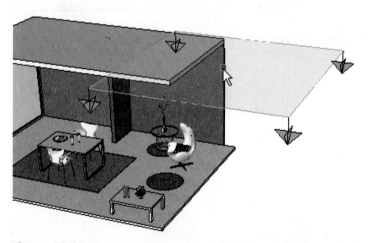

Figure 10-38

Figure 10-39

5 To hide the section plane itself, uncheck **View/Section Plane** on the main menu (Figure 10-40).

Figure 10-40

6 To look straight down into the room, choose **Camera/Standard Views/Top**. This is not a true plan view because the top of the room appears to be larger than the bottom (Figure 10-41). This is a perspective view: objects that are closer appear to be larger, reflecting how our eyes actually see objects.

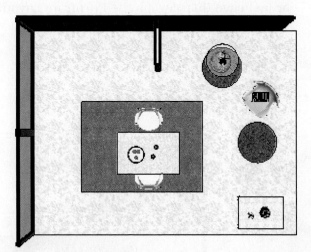

Figure 10-41

> **NOTE**
>
> SketchUp has a toolbar that enables you to switch easily among the standard views: Top, Front, Back, and so forth. PC users: Choose **View/Toolbars/Views**. Mac users: Choose **View/Customize Toolbar** and drag the **Standard Views** toolbar onto the main toolbar.

7 To switch to a true plan view, choose **Camera/Parallel Projection**. Now the room appears to be a uniform size from top to bottom (Figure 10-42).

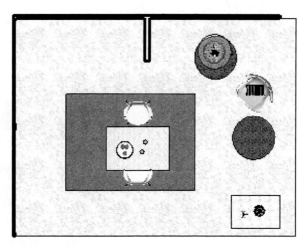

Figure 10-42

8. The edges along the walls appear thick; these are the edges where the walls meet the now-hidden section plane. For this model, you may decide that you can live with thick edges, but when we get to cabinetry layouts, you'll need to know how to make them thinner. So we might as well learn this now! Open the **Styles** window to the **Edit** tab, and click the last icon along the top row, which opens the **Modeling** settings. Change the **Section cut width** to 1 (Figure 10-43). Now all edges of this view are thin (Figure 10-44).

9. You could add some labels to identify the various pieces of furniture, or just save this view as the Furniture Layout scene.

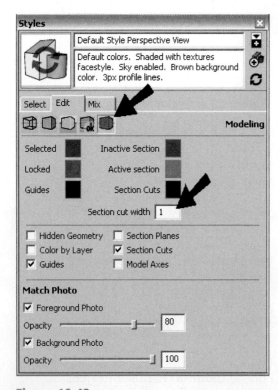

Figure 10-43

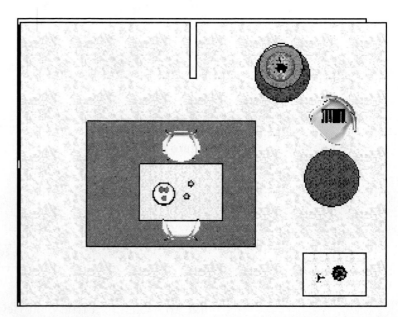

Figure 10-44

10 Hide the furniture layer, leaving just a plan view of the empty room. Use the **Dimension** tool to create the dimensions shown in Figure 10-45.

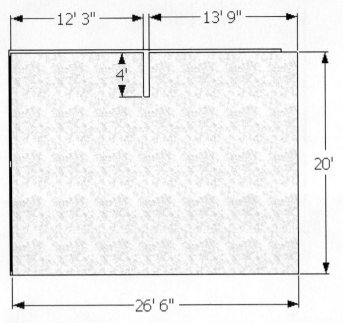

Figure 10-45

11 For this plan, we'll switch to a cleaner type of dimension leader line. On the **Dimensions** page of the **Model Info** window, switch to **Slash** endpoints (Figure 10-46), then use **Select all dimensions** and **Update selected dimensions** to change them all (Figure 10-47).

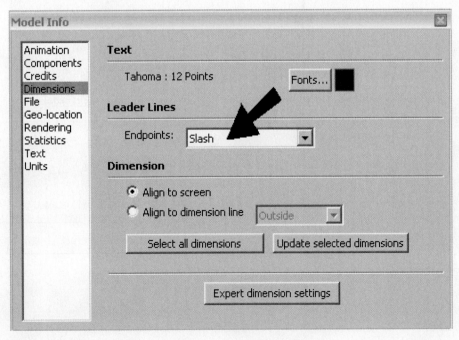

Figure 10-46

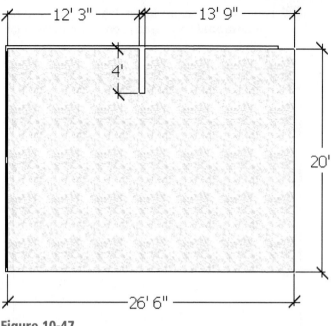

Figure 10-47

12 To create labels for the rooms on the plan, activate the **Text** tool again. Move your cursor to the right side of the floor, and you should see the "On Face" popup (Figure 10-48).

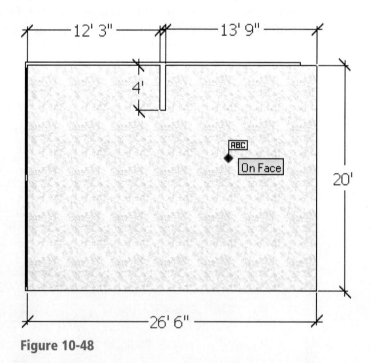

Figure 10-48

13 This label doesn't need a leader arrow, so *double-click* on the face. The default text is the area of the face (Figure 10-49). Replace this text with

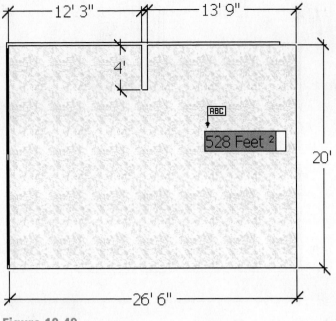

Figure 10-49

"Living Room," using a line break between the two words (Figure 10-50). Create another label without a leader for the other side of the floor, identifying it as "Dining Room" (Figure 10-51).

NOTE

You can also use the **Text** tool to create screen text, which is text that's fixed in place on the screen. This type of text is created when you click anywhere in blank space. Screen text is useful for labeling an entire view; for example, you could create screen text in blank space that reads "Floor Plan."

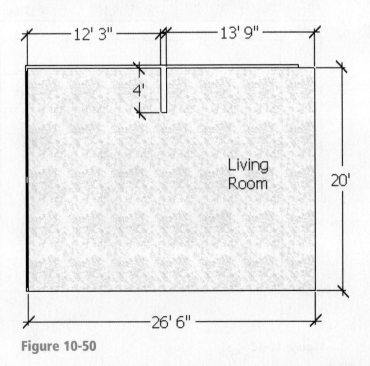

Figure 10-50

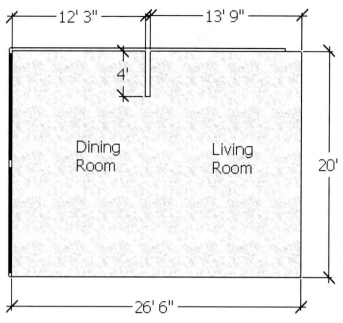

Figure 10-51

14 Place all labels and dimensions on their appropriate layers, and create another scene, which you will save as the Floor Plan scene.

15 Now we have a bit of cleanup to do. Because the dimensions layer was not hidden when the first two scenes were created, all objects on this layer will now appear in those scenes. Click the scene tab for Furniture Layout; it's cluttered with furniture, labels, and dimensions (Figure 10-52).

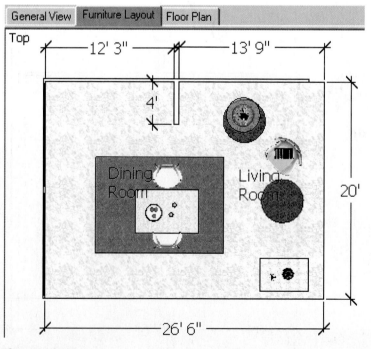

Figure 10-52

16 It's easy to fix this clutter: Just hide the dimensions layer (Figure 10-53). In order to save this modified view, right-click on the Furniture Layout tab and choose **Update** (Figure 10-54).

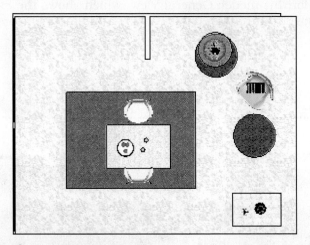

Figure 10-53

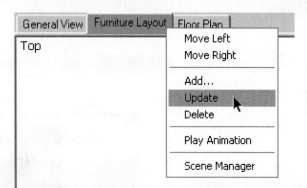

Figure 10-54

17 The first scene, General View, will have the same problem. So use the same solution: Hide the dimensions layer and update the scene (Figure 10-55).

Once you have scenes showing various views of the model, you'll want to hand these plans to your client, contractor, or installer. The last section in this chapter discusses how you can create a printed or digital plan from a SketchUp model.

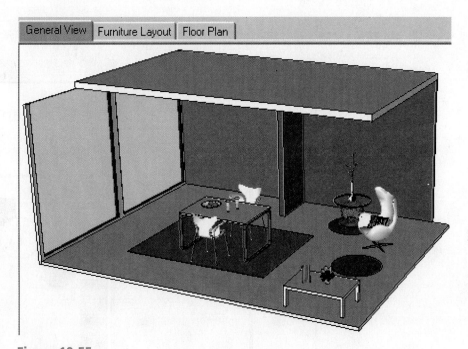

Figure 10-55

> **NOTE**
>
> If you had hidden the dimensions layer *before* creating the first two scenes, these scene updates wouldn't be necessary. Of course, that requires a bit of planning!

Model It Yourself

Download the same Modern Living for Two model that you used at the end of the previous section. Along the lines of the scenes created in this section, create three scenes for this model: General View, which shows the furnished room (Figure 10-56); Furniture Plan (Figure 10-57); and a dimensioned Floor Plan (Figure 10-58).

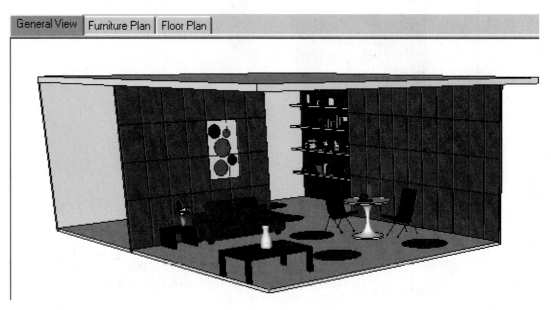

Figure 10-56

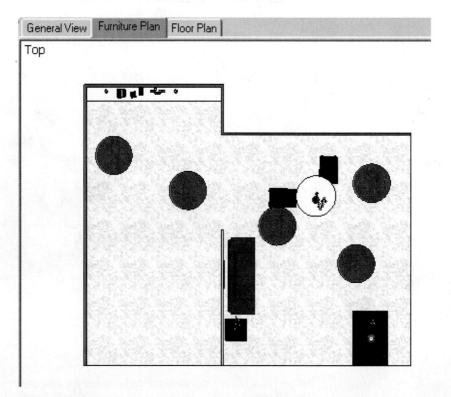

Figure 10-57

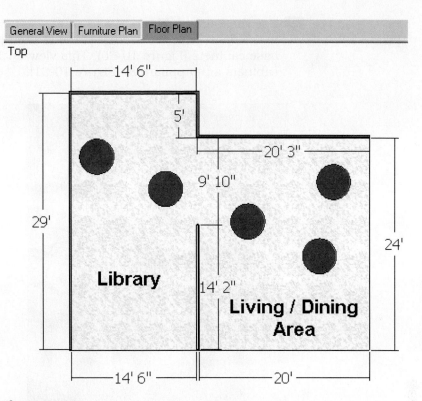

General View | Furniture Plan | Floor Plan

Top

Figure 10-58

10.3 Cabinetry Layouts

It's *always* important to produce accurate drawings, but never more so than when you design kitchens and baths. This section will show you how to produce a precise, easy-to-read cabinetry layout.

1 Download the model Kitchen Material Options by Bonnie Roskes, which is the same model that was used in Chapter 8 (Figure 10-59).

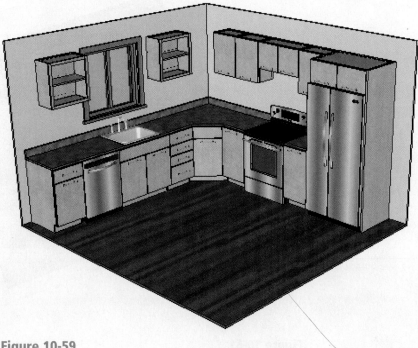

Figure 10-59

2 Use the **Section Plane** tool to create a sectioned view that is parallel to the floor, with the section plane located just below the tops of the base cabinets (Figure 10-60). This view enables you to see into the cabinets and appliances (Figure 10-61).

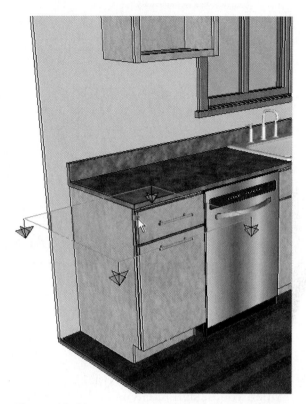

Figure 10-60

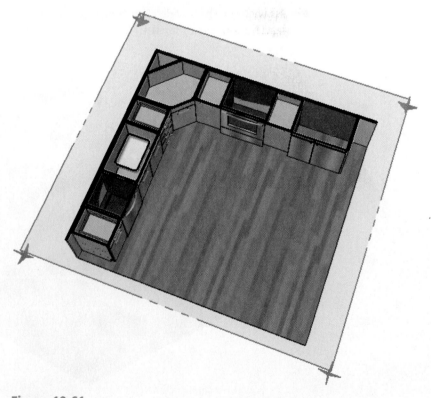

Figure 10-61

3 Switch to **Top** view and **Parallel Projection** (Figure 10-62).

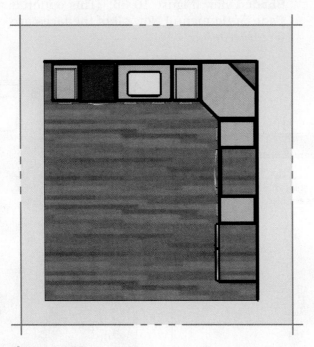

Figure 10-62

4 Open the **Modeling** settings of the **Styles** window and reduce the section cut lines. You can also use this window to hide the section plane (Figure 10-63). The plan is starting to look more like a plan (Figure 10-64), but the texture of the hardwood floor is distracting.

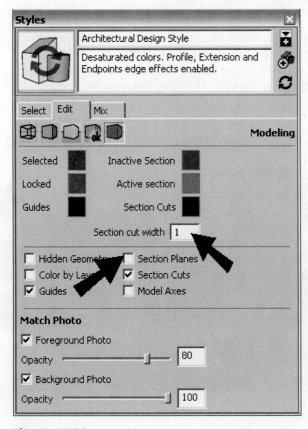

Figure 10-63

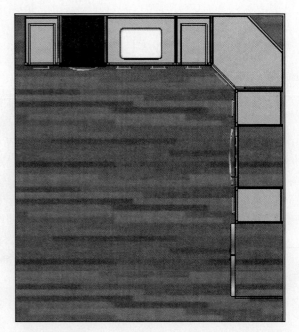

Figure 10-64

5 In the **Styles** window, switch to the **Face** settings and switch to **Shaded** view (Figure 10-65). (This option is also available in the **View/Face Style** menu.) Now all of the faces are rendered in solid colors (Figure 10-66).

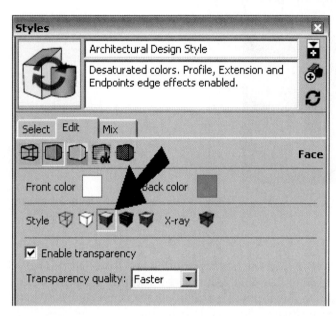

Figure 10-65

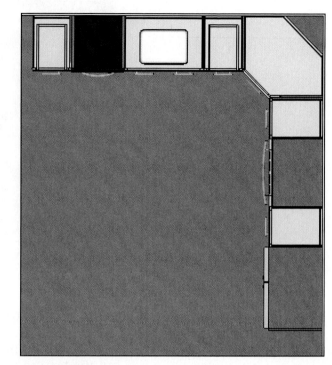

Figure 10-66

6 The floor material is visible through the bottom of the refrigerator and oven. So select both of these appliances (Figure 10-67) and move them up by a small amount, perhaps ¼". Note that you're still in parallel project view, which is making the kitchen look distorted.

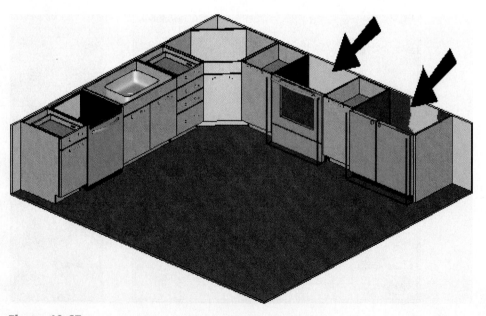

Figure 10-67

7 Return to **Top** view; now the bottoms of these appliances are visible (Figure 10-68).

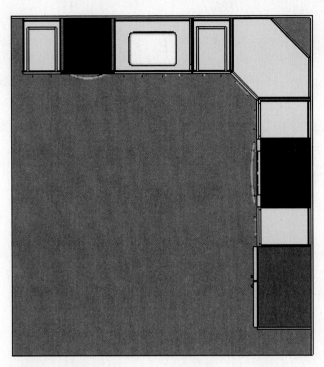

Figure 10-68

8 The colors are still rather dark, which will make dimensions and labels hard to read. So use the **Materials** or **Colors** window to lighten all of the colors (Figure 10-69). You could also make these colors translucent; the effect in **Top** view is the same as lightening the colors.

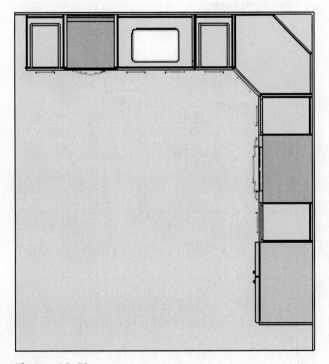

Figure 10-69

9 Now we can add dimensions. Start with the cabinet at the top left, using two points at either end of the panel behind the cabinet doors. This dimension should be 1'-6" (Figure 10-70).

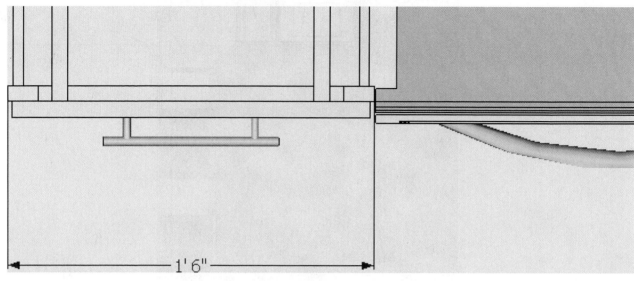

Figure 10-70

10 Continue adding dimensions along this row, proceeding to the right. For the dishwasher, instead of measuring the appliance itself, measure the distance between its two neighboring cabinets, which should be 2' (Figure 10-71). Don't add the dimensions for the corner cabinet just yet.

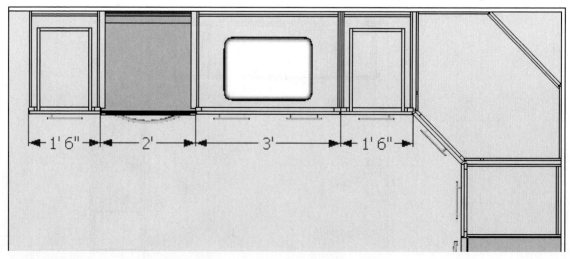

Figure 10-71

11 Add a similar row of dimensions along the other row; do not include the corner cabinet (Figure 10-72).

12 Add the dimensions for the corner cabinets along their backs, starting from the corner where the walls meet (Figure 10-73).

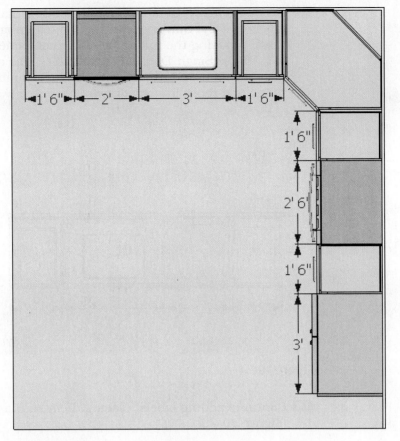

Figure 10-72

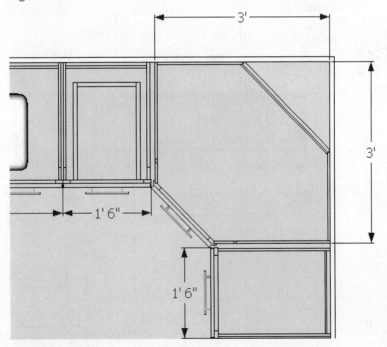

Figure 10-73

NOTE

If you measure, you'll find a 1" gap between both backs of the corner cabinet and its neighboring cabinets to accommodate the doors and drawers on the front. This dimension doesn't need to be shown on this plan; the cabinet installer will know to leave space here.

Chapter 10 | Labels, Dimensions, and Plans   **427**

13 Because each cabinet and appliance is a named component, creating labels is easy. Starting with the top left cabinet, create a leader text label, reducing the full name of the component to a simpler description (e.g., "Base Single Door") (Figure 10-74). The cabinetry manufacturer will generate its own drawings with product numbers, so it's not necessary to include those in your drawing.

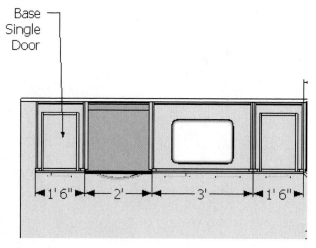

Figure 10-74

14 Continue adding labels, placing them so that there are no overlaps (Figure 10-75).

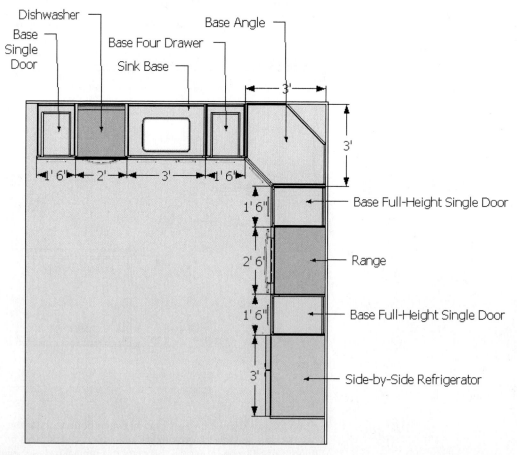

Figure 10-75

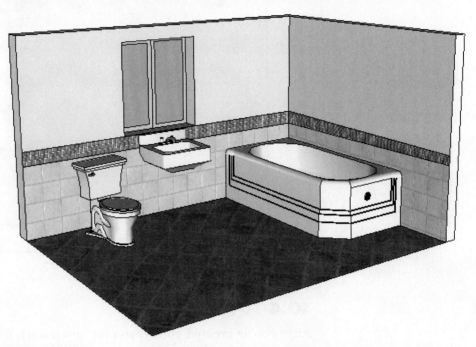

Figure 10-76

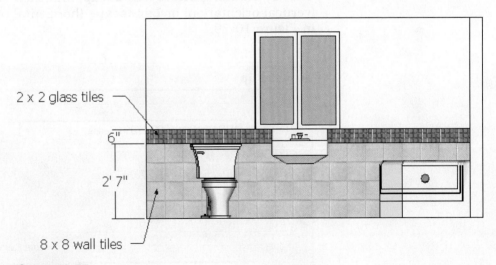

2 x 2 glass tiles

6"

2' 7"

8 x 8 wall tiles

Figure 10-77

Model It Yourself

Using the same kitchen model, create a similar plan for the wall cabinets. A section plane isn't necessary because these cabinets are entirely visible from the top of the room, but you will have to hide the base cabinets below (Figure 10-78).

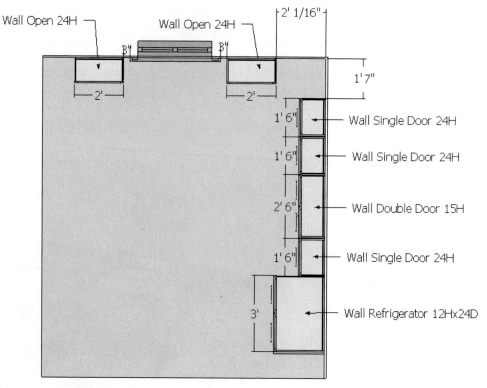

Wall Open 24H

Wall Open 24H

2' 1/16"

8"

8"

2'

2'

1' 7"

1' 6" — Wall Single Door 24H

1' 6" — Wall Single Door 24H

2' 6" — Wall Double Door 15H

1' 6" — Wall Single Door 24H

3'

Wall Refrigerator 12Hx24D

Figure 10-78

10.4 Printing

After you've created your plans (or any model, for that matter!), the next step is to print them.

First choose how you want the paper itself to be oriented. This is done by choosing **File/Print Setup**, and then selecting either **Portrait** (vertical orientation) or **Landscape** (horizontal orientation) as indicated in Figure 10-79.

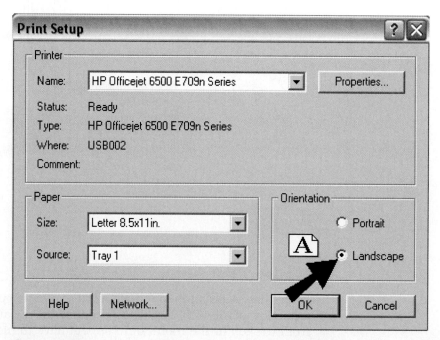

Figure 10-79

Close the **Print Setup** window. To view more print options, choose **File/Print Preview**. Here you can choose whether you want to print to scale, or print so that the entire model will fit on one page. Note that if you do want to print to scale, such as the ½″ = 1′ scale listed in Figure 10-80, you must be in a *parallel project view*, not a perspective view. Depending on the scale that you choose, the **Print Preview** window will also tell you how many pages will be needed to accommodate the entire view.

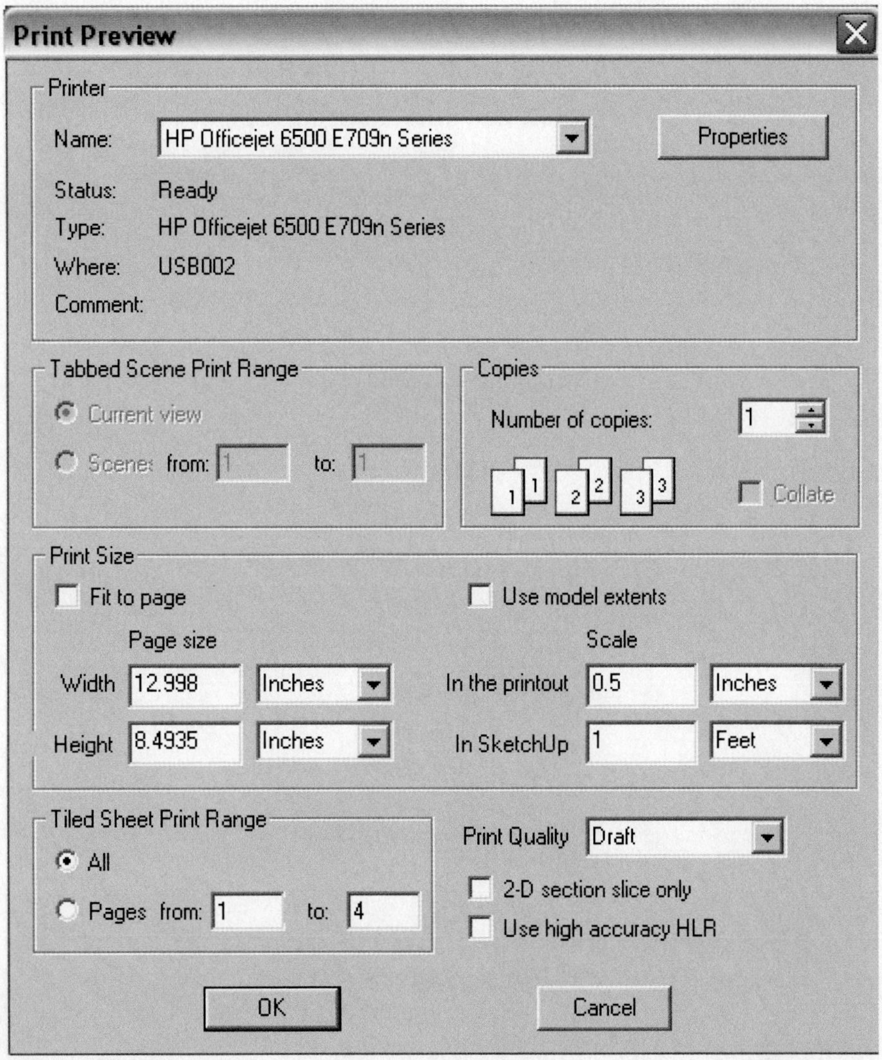

Figure 10-80

Click OK to view the preview, and if everything looks good, click the **Print** button.

For clients who prefer digital files instead of printed plans, you can save SketchUp models as graphics. The **File/Export/2D Graphic** option enables you to save your model in a variety of graphic formats or as a PDF. For any graphic format that you select, click the **Options** button to see the available settings and adjust as desired.

Review Questions

- When creating labels using the **Text** tool, how do you control whether the label will have an arrow?

- How can you change a label's text?

- How can you move a label to a new spot?

- How can you change the font and size of all labels in your model? Of only *some* of the labels?

- How can the **Section Plane** tool be used to create a floor plan?

- How can you change the leader lines of your model's dimensions?

appendix

Additional Resources

This book focuses exclusively on interior design, but SketchUp can be used for a wide variety of other types of projects For example, SketchUp integrates seamlessly with Google Earth, enabling you to assign a specific location to a building model. Still other features and tools that weren't covered in these pages are used primarily by industries such as set design, woodworking, and landscape architecture.

SketchUp Tutorials

If you want to learn more about SketchUp, here are several resources:

- **SketchUp Online Help:** From the main SketchUp menu, choose **Help/Help Center**. This takes you to an online help page where you can search for whatever issue is presenting a challenging for you.

- **SketchUp Video Tutorials:** The videos at http://sketchup.com/intl/en/training/videos.html can help you see for yourself how certain tasks can be accomplished. At the time of this writing, there are five categories that contain more than 50 videos.

- **YouTube Tutorials:** Finding a useful tutorial on YouTube might take some time, and you might have to sift through some less-than-helpful material, but there are many wonderful videos uploaded by SketchUp enthusiasts. At the time of this writing, entering the generic term "sketchup tutorial" into YouTube's search field produces almost 4,000 results. So you should be more specific in your search, such as using the term "sketchup kitchen tutorial."

- **3D Warehouse Tutorials:** People don't often think of the 3D Warehouse as being a place to look for tutorials, but it's actually a great resource. These tutorials are generally SketchUp models that contain multiple scenes in which each tutorial step is placed on its own scene, sometimes with accompanying text. If you use the Get Models tool to find a tutorial model that has scenes, make sure you open the model in a new SketchUp file, because scenes do not appear when imported into another model! Google has placed a few self-paced tutorials in the 3D Warehouse (mostly on the topic of dynamic components), which you can access from the Training link on the SketchUp website.

SketchUp Models

If you can't find the model that you need in the 3D Warehouse or you're finding only subpar models, and you'd rather not tackle the job of creating the model from scratch, here are some other places to which you can turn for help:

- **Generic SketchUp Models:** The SketchUp team has placed a small collection of generic models in the 3D Warehouse. On the main 3D Warehouse page, the "SketchUp Components" collection is always listed under Featured Collections, but you may have to use the scroll arrows to find it. This collection is divided into subcollections, of which "Architecture" is the collection that is most relevant to interior design. The advantage of using SketchUp-produced models is that they are well made, have the correct size alignment and insertion points, and have small file sizes. At this time, you can also find a SketchUp-produced model by using a search term such as "sofa author:google." (These models were uploaded when Google owned SketchUp.)

- **Product Connect:** Igloo Studios offers a nice service for designers; their free Product Connect plug-in gives you access to catalogs of professionally modeled SketchUp objects such as cabinets and fixtures. You can also add or edit properties of these models and compile reports for contractors to use. Find more information at http://www.igloostudios.com/productconnect.

- **Form Fonts:** For a yearly subscription fee, you can find all sorts of high-quality models at http://www.formfonts.com. The collections here include models not available in the 3D Warehouse, including pieces from manufacturers such as Crate and Barrel, Delta, Herman Miller, Habitat, and many more. In addition, you can get access to images that you can use for textures and materials. Form Fonts can save you hours of searching in the 3D Warehouse, fixing models, and modeling from scratch. Plus, if they don't have exactly what you need, you can request that one of their modelers create it for you.

- **Other 3D Model Sites:** Check these sites for free or inexpensive 3D models that you can download: Cadyou (http://www.cadyou.com), Archive 3D (http://archive3d.net), and TurboSquid (http://www.turbosquid.com). These sites provide models that use SketchUp and other formats, so make sure that you download the correct version!

Rendering Applications

You've seen Surya Murali's sleek, photo-realistic images of her models, such as the image on the cover of this book. There are a number of applications that can produce photo-realistic renderings; they take a SketchUp model and apply lighting and material properties to it. Some renderers work with just one 2D view at a time, others work dynamically within SketchUp (i.e., they orbit your model and the rendered view also orbits). Still others work outside of SketchUp altogether; thus, you would need to export the view from SketchUp and import it into the rendering application. Many of these applications require that you create a dummy SketchUp object to define as a light, as you saw in some of Surya's models. These dummy objects are then assigned lighting properties within the rendering application.

Getting into the detailed inner workings of each of these applications would require a book unto itself, so this section will include just a few of the easier-to-use renderers. Check out the website of each of these applications for gallery images. You'll be impressed!

- **Photoshop** (http://www.photoshop.com): While not specifically an engine for rendering 2D views of 3D models, Photoshop remains the top choice for enhancing the look of SketchUp models. Perhaps this is because so many designers already know Photoshop, and learning a new application takes time and sometimes money. If you're a Photoshop user, you can do a Google search for "sketchup photoshop" for some nice examples and tutorials. You might also want to download one of the applications mentioned below to see how a true 3D rendering can be accomplished.

- **Shaderlight** (http://www.artvps.com, free, Pro, and Educational versions available): Shaderlight works dynamically within SketchUp, which means that if you orbit your view or move objects around, the rendered view also updates the object. The Pro version includes lighting features that are not available in the free version.

- **Kerkythea** (http://www.kerkythea.net/joomla, free but no longer actively supported): This is a stand-alone program that takes an exported SketchUp view and renders it. Although it is no longer supported, Kerkythea's website has tutorials and an active blog, and you can find other resources via a web search.

- **IDX Renditioner** (http://www.idx-design.com, free Express version or Full version): This application works directly within SketchUp, rendering the current 2D view. The Express version has limited export image size and sometimes works more slowly, but otherwise has the same features as the for-purchase version: materials, lighting, and backgrounds.

- **Twilight Render** (http://twilightrender.com): Built using an engine that is similar to the above-mentioned Kerkythea, Twilight Render works within SketchUp as a plug-in, and includes the ability to export animations. You will also have access to models with predefined materials that can be used as entourage (e.g., people, plants) in your renderings.

- **SU Podium** (http://www.suplugins.com, Pro and Educational versions available): One of the original and most popular SketchUp renderers, SU Podium works within SketchUp as a plug-in, and renders the current 2D SketchUp view.

- **Render[in]** (http://renderin.com): This is an integrated application, updating dynamically within SketchUp. You can add many types of lights, enhanced materials, and backgrounds.

> **NOTE**
> There are also a number of high-end rendering applications. They cost more money, have more sophisticated production options, and often have a steeper learning curve. However, they produce stunning images. Some of these high-end applications include Indigo Renderer, Artlantis, 3D Studio Max, Maya, V-Ray, Vue, and Maxwell Render.

Index

2D Graphic option, 431
3D objects
  creation
    from images, 296–306
    tracing photos and, 306–317
  painted princess chair, 301–305
  painted wooden chest, 296–301
3D Warehouse
  disadvantage of, 43
  downloading models, 43, 167, 188, 321
  importing models, 42, 43–44, 52–53, 167
  models, 167–203
    composition of, 169
    location of, 167–168
    size of, 168–169
  overview, 37
  searching
    for furniture/accessories, 40–65
    materials, 243–244
  sharing models in, 40

A

accent chair
  insertion in room, 54–57
accent table
  creation, steps for, 176–181
Add collection to favorites option, 246
Advanced Search window, 52
Alignment, File page, 287
alignment, objects, 61–65
Angle field, 44, 131–132, 228, 232
angle of rotation, 131
Animation page, Model Info window, 393
Any plane option, 287
Applications page, Preferences window, 299
aprons, 82
  extension, 85
  face, Move tool on, 126
  pulling, with Push/Pull tool, 83
Arc tool, 117–118, 124, 137–138, 291
  and photo tracing, 308
arrow keys, 169
Axes option, 9, 73, 167

B

Background settings, 356, 397–398
base cabinets, placement of, 325–333
baseboard, 2
  insertion of, 31–33
Basque Honey Dining Table
  creation, steps for, 76–86
Billsta table (Ikea)
  creation, steps for, 129–141
Billy Bookcase System (Ikea)
  creation, steps for, 87–95
blue pin (fixed pins), 218–220

bookcase
  creation, steps for, 87–95
Brick and Cladding collection, 211, 212
Bulge field, 118, 138

C

cabinetry layout, 421–429
cabinets
  base, placement of, 325–333
  creation, steps for, 96–108
  interaction, 325
  kitchen, 322–325
  wall, placement of, 333–339
Camera Location option, 367, 368, 372, 391, 409, 411
Camera/Parallel Projection option, 413–414
Camera/Standard Views/Front option, 144
Camera/Standard Views/Top option, 137, 413
Chaise
  conversion to sofa, 188–190
Change Axes option, 62
china cabinet, editing, 192–200
circle
  creation of, 112, 130, 134
  insertion of, 144–146
Circle tool, 99, 112, 113, 134, 153, 176
Close Component option, 31
coffee table
  insertion in room, 47–49
collection, materials
  creation of, 243–251
    Mac users, instructions for, 249–251
    PC users, instructions for, 245–249
  naming, 250
  removing, 247
Colorize, 213
colors
  base, changing, 216, 238
  components, 252–257
  editing of, 46, 425
  faces, 211, 212
  groups, 252–257
  material, changing, 205–217
  naming, 210, 239
  room, 6–8
  text, 398
  walls, 8
  window moulding, 16
Colors in Model collection, 206, 211, 250
Colors window, 7–8, 206–207, 239, 250, 251
Component Attributes option, 325
Component Options window, 323, 324
components
  Definition Name, 172
  editing, 93
  grouping, 32–33, 92, 170–171
  kitchen, 321–325
  naming, 169

components (Continued)
    painting, 252–257
    scaling, 81
components, SketchUp feature, 15
Components window, 47–48, 54, 63–64, 212, 255, 256
composition, 3D Warehouse model, 169
console table
    insertion in room, 57–61
construction line, 10
Copy option, 105
copying
    doors, 107
    objects, 57, 80
    with Move tool, 57, 87, 90, 120
    with Rotate tool, 147
Corian collection, Materials window, 247–248
corners, rounded
    creation of, 137–139
couch, painting of, 252–257
countertop, placement of, 340–346
Create Component window, 19
Create Group from Slice option, 197
Create Material icon, 238
Create Material window, 258
cushioned ottoman
    creation, steps for, 158–163

D

Definition Name, component, 172, 173
Delete Guides option, 30
design template
    room, 3–8
Details arrow, 245, 246, 248, 249
digital images, 271–317
    and 3D objects creation, 296–306 (*See also* 3D objects)
    editing, 272
    exploding, 285
    file size of, 282
    for decorating accessories, 271–283
    frames for, 276, 284–287
    importing, 273
    irregularly shaped, object creation from, 289–294
    placement, 274
    saving, 272
Dimension tool, 405–409
Dimensions field, 4, 16
Dimensions page, Model Info window, 405–406, 415
dining table, editing, 174–176
dishwasher, placement of, 330
Distance field, 102
Divide option
    on edges, 89, 97
Done option, 220, 223, 279, 282
doors
    copying, 107
    insertion of, 8–14
drawers
    creation, steps for, 98–101

drawing
    circle, 112, 130, 134
    dimensions in, inserting, 405–409
    floors, 4–5
    labels in, inserting, 397–404
    saving, 33, 73, 74
drop-leaf table
    oval, steps for creation, 117–128
Duplicate option, Color drop-down menu, 239
Duplicate option, List drop-down menu, 249
dynamic components, kitchen, 321–325
    characteristics, 322
Dynamic Components/Component Options, 322, 323

E

edges
    creation, with Offset tool, 345
    display, 38, 84, 397
    erasing, 84, 97, 132, 139, 157, 185, 197, 210, 349
    Explode option on, 197
    hiding, 83, 84, 140, 199
    intersection, 132
    moving, 88, 130, 291
    rounding, 160
    segments, 28, 97, 148
    smoothing, 140
    softening, 148, 150, 305
    Tape Measure tool on, 285
    tracing, with Line tool, 132, 134, 148
    trimming, 144, 291
    windows, 223
Edit Group option, 32
Edit Material window, 206–207, 208–210, 213, 214–215
Edit option, Texture drop-down menu, 272, 273
Edit tab
    Materials window, 46–47, 64, 206, 208
    Styles window, 210–211, 307, 356, 397–398, 414
Edit Texture Image option, 299
Edit/Copy option, 105
Edit/Delete Guides option, 30
Edit/Paste option, 106
Edit/Unhide/All option, 277
editing
    china cabinet, 192–200
    colors, 46–47, 425
    components, 93
    digital images, 272
    dining table, 174–176
    group, 32
    images, 299
    material, color and size, 205–217
    round table, 167–181
    sofa, 182–187
    windows, 26–31
elevation view, 429
Entity Info window, 58–59, 154, 172, 173, 400, 404
    for layer placement, 359–363
    for objects placement, 366

Erase tool
   on faces, 197, 221
Eraser tool, 12, 49, 199
   on edges, 84, 97, 132, 139, 150, 157, 185,
      210, 349
   on section planes, 197
Explode option, 197, 258, 274, 275
Export Texture Image option, 272
Eyedropper icon, 46

F

Face settings, Styles window, 210–211, 307, 424
faces
   apron, Move tool on, 126
   arc, 148, 150
   cabinet, division of, 197
   colors, 211, 212
   cutout, 160, 162
   erasing, 197, 221
   frame, 276, 285
   inner frame on, 101
   intersection, 348
   moving, 122
   Offset tool and, 105
   organic, painting textures on, 258–260
   painting, 297–298
   pulling, 119
   pushing, 125
field measurements, 1–3
File page, Model Info window, 287
File/Export/2D Graphic option, 431
File/Print Setup option, 430
fixed pins, 218–220, 277–278, 282
   placement, zooming and, 222
   positioning, 227
Flip Along/Component's Red option, 107
floor lamp, insertion in room, 49–53
floors
   drawing, 4–5
   plan, creation of, 410–419
Follow Me tool, 86, 143–144, 146–147, 148,
     150, 152, 154, 161–162, 285
   for arc dragging, 158
Font window, 399
font, text, 399
frames
   for digital images, 276
   for paintings, 284–287
free pins, 282, 297
Front option, 144, 152
furniture
   accent table
     creation, steps for, 176–181
   cushioned ottoman
     creation, steps for, 158–163
   dining table, editing, 174–176
   insertion, in room, 40–49, 54–61
   options, comparing, 371–372
   oval drop-leaf table
     creation, steps for, 117–128
   rectangular table

     creation, steps for, 68–74
     with tapered legs, creation of, 76–86
   round table
     creation, steps for, 111–116
     editing, 167–181
Furniture Layout tab, 418–419

G

General View scene, 411
General View tab, 419
Get Models tool, 42, 47–48, 50, 167, 252
Glue to option, 63–64, 65
green pin (fixed pins), 218
groups/grouping
   components, 92, 170–171
   naming, 172
   Outliner and, 170–171
   painting, 252–257
   room components, 32–33, 365
guide line, 10
   creation, 155–156
   erasing, 30, 229
   offset, 28, 29

H

Hans J. Wegner Drop-Leaf Dining Table
   creation, steps for, 117–128
Height Offset field, 389, 390, 392
Height option, Font window, 399
Hidden, 399
Hidden Geometry option, 148, 185, 186,
     266, 267
Hide Similar Components option, 199
Hide tool, 50, 83, 84, 157, 309
hiding
   dimensions layer, 420
   edges, 83, 84, 140, 199
   walls, 50
HLS (hue, lightness, saturation), 208
horizontal dimensions, creation of, 408
HSB (hue, saturation, brightness), 208
HSV (hue, saturation, value), 208

I

IDX Renditioner, 433
images
   digital (*See* digital images)
   dimensions, setting of, 237
   editing, 299
   importing, 236–237
   saving, 236
   searching/using, 235–242
imperial units, 1
Import tool, 54, 73, 114, 116, 236–237,
     277, 284
Interact option, 325
Interact tool, 322
Intersect Faces tool, 348
Intersect Faces/With Model option, 132, 133, 348
intersection edges, 132

K

Kerkythea, 433
kitchen, design of, 321–352
    cabinets, 322–325
        base, placement of, 325–333
        wall, placement of, 333–339
    countertop, placement of, 340–346
    dishwasher, placement of, 330
    dynamic components, 321–325
    layout, 421–429
    oven, placement of, 332
    refrigerator, placement of, 332–333
    sink, installation of, 346–350
KraftMaid cabinets, 322–325

L

labels
    adding to drawings, 397–404
    creation, 401, 416–417
    default text for, 401
lamps
    floor, insertion in room, 49–53
Landscape, paper orientation, 430
Large Tool Set icon, 194
Large Tool Set toolbar, 146–147
layers
    and design options for walls, 364–369
    and materials, 378–386
    and object visibility, 355–363
    and room arrangements, 373–376
    creation of, 404, 411
    defining, 358
    dimension, 418, 419
    hiding, 415
    placement of dimensions on, 409
    placement, with Entity Info window,
        359–363
    visibility of, 404
Layers window, 358–359, 368
Leader Lines options, 398, 399
Leader Text option, 398, 399
left-to-right selection box, 19
Length field, 59, 168
Line tool, 10, 30, 91, 97, 168, 309
    for adding countertop, 340–346
    for drawers modeling, 98
    on edges, 132, 134, 148
lines
    curvy, 111–163
    preview color, 11
List View option, 248–249
location, 3D Warehouse model, 167–168
locking, move direction, 21
Look Around tool, 390

M

Make Component option, 188
Make Group option, 32, 71
Make Unique option, 92–93, 255
Make Unique Texture option, 298

Malibu cabinets (KraftMaid), 322–325
Match Photo, 76
materials
    collection, creation of, 243–251
        Mac users, instructions for, 249–251
        PC users, instructions for, 245–249
    color, changing, 205–217
    creation of, 258
    images as, searching/using, 235–242
    layers and, 378–386
    positioning, 217–225
        using exact dimensions, 226–234
    size, changing, 205–217
    stone, positioning of, 221–225
    translucent, 261–267
Materials window, 7, 46–47, 239
    Corian collection, 247–248
    Edit tab of, 46, 64, 206, 208
    folder creation in, 246
    Select tab of, 210, 211
mirroring, 107
    Scale tool for, 80
Model field, 324
Model Info window, 88, 212, 404
    Animation page, 393
    Dimensions page, 405–406, 415
    File page, 287
    Text page, 398, 399, 403
    Units page, 405
Modeling settings, 414
models
    bookcase, 87–95
    cabinet, 96–108
    downloading, 321
    drawers, 98–101
    importing, 244
    rectangular table, 67–74
        with tapered legs, 76–86
    wooden chest, painted, 296–301
mouldings
    color, 17
    windows, 15
Move tool, 19, 20–21, 24–25, 38, 44, 53,
        72, 93, 114, 128, 134–135, 168, 183, 195
    for base cabinet/appliances placement,
        325–333
    for copying objects, 57, 87, 90, 120
    for sink installation, 346–350
    for wall cabinets placement, 333–339
    on apron face, 126
    on edges, 88, 130, 223, 291
    on faces, 122
    on images, 274
muntins, 30
Murali, Surya, 355
Murphy's Law, 192

N

Name field, Entity Info window, 172
New Texture option, Color drop-down
    menu, 240

O

objects
accessing, 83
alignment, 61–65
copying, 57, 80, 87, 90, 120, 147
creation, from irregularly shaped images,
    289–294
mirroring, 107
resizing, 60, 180
scaling, 81
visibility, layers and, 355–363
Offset tool, 12, 16, 31, 69, 88, 98, 119, 314
and faces, 105
for edges creation, 345
for inner frame on face, 101
for inward path creation, 144
for rectangle creation, 229, 276
offsets
guide line, 28, 29
On Face popup, 416
On Section popup, 195
Opacity, 264, 265
Open or create a collection option, 246
Orbit tool, 5
origin
defined, 4
finding, 114
Orion Walnut Round Table (Crate and Barrel)
creation, steps for, 111–116
Outliner, 169–174, 188, 192, 322
and grouping, 170–171
and sofa editing, 183
naming in, 172
nested format in, 171
oval table
drop-leaf
    creation, steps for, 117–128
glass, with tulip pedestal
    creation, steps for, 152–157
oven, placement of, 332

P

Paint Bucket icon, 7
Paint tool, 46
painting
frame for, 284–287
importing, 277, 287
insertion in room, 61–65
Parallel Projection option, 413–414, 423
Parsons Counter
creation, steps for, 68–74
Paste option, 106
photos
background of, 307
tracing, and 3D objects creation, 306–317
Photoshop, 433
plans
floor, creation of, 410–419
printing, 430–431
Play Animation popup menu, 393
Points option, Font window, 399

Portrait, paper orientation, 430
Position Camera tool, 389–390
dragging feature of, 392
Precision, value in, 405
Preferences window, 299
princess chair, painted, 300–305
Print Preview window, 431
Print Setup window, 430
printing, of plans, 430–431
Projected option, 259
protractor, 131
Protractor option, 228
Pushpin, 398, 399
**Push/Pull tool, 6, 13–14, 39, 70, 78, 98,
    102–103, 112, 210, 263, 276**
and cutout faces, 162
apron pulling with, 83
on faces, 125, 304
on walls, 221
round corners pulling with, 158
usage, with Ctrl/Option key, 96

R

Radius feature, Entity Info window, 154–155
Rectangle tool, 4, 10, 30, 38, 89
rectangular table
creation, steps for, 68–74
with tapered legs
    creation, steps for, 76–86
Redo, 113
refrigerator, placement of, 332–333
Remove collection from favorites option, 247
Render[in], 433
rendering applications, 432–433
Reset option, 227
resizing, objects, 60
Scale tool for, 312
Reverse Faces option, 119, 211, 293
RGB (red, green, blue), 207
values, 209
RGB sliders, 208, 209
right-to-left selection box, 19
room
accessories, insertion of, 49–54, 61–65
arrangements, layers and, 373–376
as group, 32–33, 365
baseboard, insertion of, 31–33
colors, 6–8
design template, 3–8
doors, insertion of, 8–14
furnishing, 37–65
furniture, insertion of, 40–49, 54–61
rug in, 37–40, 280–282
table placement inside, 85
views, 388–393
windows, insertion of, 15–25
Rotate tool, 116, 129, 131, 136, 141, 158, 232
for copying objects, 147, 309
round table
creation, 111–116
editing, 167–181

rounded corners
creation of, 137–139
pulling, 158
rug
creation of, 37–40
insertion of, 280–282

S

Sandbox tools, 258
Satellite Oval Glass Top Table (Nuevo Living)
creation, steps for, 152–157
Save collection as option, 245
saving
digital images, 272
drawing, 33, 73, 74
images, 236
Scale tool, 54, 55–56, 76, 114, 122, 156, 175, 179, 180, 189, 292
for component placement, 198
for mirroring, 80
for objects resizing, 60
for resizing, 312
for tapering, 78
scaling
components, 81, 122–124, 175–176
Scenes window, 367–368, 384, 391
Screen Text option, 398, 399
Search 3D Warehouse, 51
Section cut width, 414
Section Plane tool, 192, 193–194, 412, 422
Select all dimensions, 415
Select all leader text, 403
Select tab
Materials window, 210, 211
Styles window, 314–315
Select tool, 12, 18, 106, 161
Select/All with same Material option, 293, 382
Shaded view, 424
Shaderlight, 433
Share Model tool, 40, 67
shimmering effect, 275–276
Sides field, 112
sink, installation of, 346–350
size
3D Warehouse model, 168–169
material, changing, 205–217
SketchUp
components feature of, 15
memory buffer, 99
models, 432
rendering applications, 432–433
tutorials, 431
welcome screen, 3
Slash endpoints, 415
Sliders icon, 208
sofa
changing chaise to, 188–190
editing, 182–187
insertion in room, 40–47
Soften coplanar option, 162
Soften Edges window, 151, 162, 163

Soften/Smooth Edges option, 150
softening, edge display option, 84
Standard Views toolbar, 413
Styles window
Edit tab, 210–211, 307, 356, 397–398, 414
Face settings, 210–211, 307, 424
Modeling settings, 414, 423
Select tab of, 314–315
SU Podium, 355, 433

T

tables
dining, editing, 174–176
oval
drop-leaf, steps for creation, 117–128
rectangular
creation, steps for, 68–74
with tapered legs, steps for creation, 76–86
round
creation, 111–116
editing, 167–181
with chrome tubular base
creation, steps for, 143–151
with cross pedestal base
creation, steps for, 129–141
Tape Measure tool, 10, 19, 22, 54, 59, 72, 76, 77, 176, 179, 182, 315
and diameter measurement, 180
and guide lines, 29, 155–156, 333
for objects resizing, 60, 180
on edges, 285
text
colors, 398
font, 399
Text page, Model Info window, 398, 399, 403
Text tool, 400–404, 416–417
for screen text, 417
texture
painting, on organic faces, 258–260
positioning, 218
Texture drop-down menu, 272, 273
Texture/Position option, 218, 221
Texture/Projected option, 259
Tools/Interact option, 325
Tools/Text option, 400
Top view, 423, 425
translucent materials, 22, 261–267
painting, 293
Transparency Quality settings, 268
Troy Ottoman (Crate and Barrel)
creation, steps for, 158–163
Tucker Buffet (Pottery Barn)
creation, steps for, 96–108
Twilight Render, 433

U

Undo, 113, 176, 296
Uniform Scale popup, 55
Units page, Model Info window, 405
Update option, 419

Update selected dimensions, 415
Update selected text, 403, 404
Use as image option, 273
Use as texture option, 280

V

vertical dimensions, creation of, 408
View-Based, 399, 404
View/Axes option, 9, 73, 167
View/Component Edit/Hide Similar Components
    option, 199
View/Customize Toolbar option, 413
View/Edge Style/Edges option, 356, 397
View/Face Style/Shaded option, 299
View/Face Style/Shaded with Textures option, 300
View/Face Style/X-ray option, 140–141
View/Hidden Geometry option, 148, 185, 186, 266,
    267
View/Shadows option, 356
View/Toolbars/Views option, 413
Visible box, Layers window, 359, 361

W

Walk tool, 393
Walkthrough tools, 388–393. *See also* Look Around
    tool; Position Camera tool

wall cabinets, placement of, 333–339
wall refrigerator cabinet, placement of, 334–335
walls
    color, 8
    design options for, layers and, 364–369
    hiding, 50
    measurement, 2
    Push/Pull tool on, 221
Welcome to SketchUp window, 3
windows
    edges, moving, 223
    insertion of, 15–25
    modification, 26–31
    mouldings, 15
wooden chest, painted, 296–301

X

X-ray option, 140–141

Y

yellow pin (fixed pins), 220

Z

Zoom Extents tool, 5, 45, 64
Zoom tool, 5